We Believe In The Communion Of The Saints

Jonathan Speegle, PhD

We Believe In The Communion Of The Saints
ISBN: Softcover 978-1-955581-16-5
Copyright © 2021 by Jonathan Speegle

All rights reserved. No part of this book may be reproduced or transmitted in any form or by any means, electronic or mechanical, including photocopying, recording, or by any information storage and retrieval system, without permission in writing from the publisher.

Parson's Porch Books is an imprint of Parson's Porch & Company (PP&C) in Cleveland, Tennessee. PP&C is an innovative organization which raises money by publishing books of noted authors, representing all genres. Its face and voice is **David Russell Tullock** (dtullock@parsonsporch.com).

Parson's Porch & Company *turns books into bread & milk* by sharing its profits with the poor.

www.parsonsporch.com

We Believe In The Communion Of The Saints

Contents

Preface xi
    Thesis Statement xiii
Dedication xv

Part One: Envisioning A Communion Lost

Chapter One: 5
    Introduction 5
        Augustine Inters his Mother and Plants the Seeds of the Reformation 5
        The Goal of both Earthly and Heavenly Life 9
        The Sacramental Life 10
        Baptism 14
        The Lord's Supper 15
        Penance 17
        Contrition 21
        Confession 22
        Satisfaction 23
        Satisfaction as a Regimen for Spiritual Health 24
        Satisfaction as a Remedy for Guilt 25
        Temporal Punishn 27
        Indulgences 28
        The Mathematizing of Penance 29
        Indulgences Extended to Those in Purgatory 32
        The Abuses of Indulgences 34
        Luther's Theological Critique of Indulgences 38
Chapter Two 41
    The Protestant Rejection of the Catholic/Orthodox Understanding of the Communion of Saints and its Results 41
        The Phrase and Its Meaning 41
        A Description of the Church 41

A Participation in Holy Things 42
A Communion with the Saints in Heaven..42
The Creedal Phrase in the Theology of the Reformers........................43
The Reformers Dismember the Body..45
The Historic Reasons for the Reformer's Rejections 46
Attempts to Reform Purgatory 51
The Impetus to Curb Abuses Results in the...54
Rejection of Related Doctrines and Practices...54

Part Two: Envisioning A Creedal Eschatology

Chapter Three 60
   What Happens When We Die?

Chapter Four..63
   We Believe in . . . the Life Everlasting
   The Reality of Death..63

   The Triumph of Life..66

   The Witness of the Resurrection in the Lord's Supper........................66

   What and Where is Heaven?..68

   What is Between Death and Eternal Life? 71

   Soul Sleep...72

   Immediate Reward of either Bliss or Torment..............................75

   Purgatory..77

   History of the Concept of Purgatory 79

   Orthodox Toll Houses 81

   Purgatory as Hospital not Prison...83

   Soul Building...88

   Purgatory for Protestants 90

   Death Itself as Purgatory...95

   Purgatory as the Fire of Christ's Holy Spirit..................................96

   Summary 98

Chapter Five..99

    We Believe in . . . the Resurrection of the Body
- Dualism 100
- Monism 103
- Holistic Dualism 104
- Summary 107
- The Created Soul and the Resurrected Body 107
- The Moral Significance of the Body 110
- Summary 111

Chapter Six 112
    We Believe in . . . the Forgiveness of Sins
- "He Shall Come to Judge the Living and the Dead" 114
- The Three-fold Coming of Christ 114
- The Final Coming of Christ 115
- What Kind of Judge? 116
- Judgment as Revelation 117
- The Pilgrims' Progress 120
- What is Hell? 123
- Jesus . . . "descended into hell." 129
- Making Captivity a Captive 131
- The Eternal Fire of Hell 134
- As Purgatory Is the Porch of Heaven, Sin Is the Porch of Hell 136
- Summary 138

Part Three: Envisioning A Saintly Communion

Chapter Seven 142
    We Believe . . . in the Church
- Is There Any Biblical Basis For This Idea? 143
- The One Body of Christ 145
- The One Priesthood of Christ and the Priesthood of All Believers 147
- Replacing Traditional Terminology 148
- The Church Above 149
- The Two Dimensions of the One Church 151

Chapter Eight 153
    The Communion of Faith: Fellowship in Redemption
    Faithfulness as the Historical bond of the Church 153

    Our Common Identity: Called to Be Saints 153

    Commemoration 155

    We Grasp the Living Christ by Means of the Living Church. 156

    The Holy Scriptures 157

    The One Faith 158

    The Fellowship of Faith Defines and Continually Reforms 159
    the Teaching of the Church 159

    The Great Cloud of Witnesses 161

    Veneration 162

    The Common Martyrdom of All Christians and the Role of
    Hagiography 166

    Partners in Faith and Hope 168

    Paradigmatic Figures 169

    The Blessed Virgin Mary 171

    Canonization 174

    The Rise of the Patronage System 176

    Is the Veneration of the Saints a Pagan Influence on Christianity?. 179

    Relics of Saints 179

    Images of the Saints 181

    How to Read the Lives of the Saints 183

    Hymn Singing 184

    All Saints Day 188

    Summary 190

Chapter Nine 192
    The Communion of Hope: Fellowship in Prayer
    Prayer Is the Spiritual Bond of the Church 193

    Our Father and Our Common Priesthood 193

    We Should Pray for Each Other 194

    The Living and the Dead Inhabit the Same Kingdom 196

- We Should Pray for the Dead 197
- The Problem of Prayer 199
- Guidelines for Praying for the Dead 200
- Praying for the Faithfully Departed and the Lost 201
- The Church Benefits When She Prays for the Dead 203
- The Dead Pray for Us 203
- The Church Below May Request the Prayers of the Church Above 204
- Spiritual Communion Not Spiritual Communication 205
- Unspoken Requests 206
- Spoken Requests 206
- Criticisms in Opposition to the Practice 209
- The Mistakes of the Patronage Model 210
- The Corrections of the Reformation 214
- Answering Common Objections 215
- Three Ways the Church May Invoke the Saints 219
- Thanksgiving 220
- Lament 221
- The Litany of the Saints 222
- Hymn Singing 225
- The Church Prays with All the Heavenly Host 228
- For What do the Saints Above and the Heavenly Hosts Pray 229
- Recapitulation, Quantum Interconnectedness, and the Seamless Whole 230

Chapter Ten 235
The Communion of Love: Fellowship at the Table

- The Eucharist is the Physical Bond of the Church: 235
- The Life Blood of the Mystical Body 235
- The Celestial Eucharist 237
- The Eucharist is a Transtemporal Expression of the Trinitarian Life 238
- The Eucharist is Eternally Present in the Memory of the Father 239

The Eucharist is the Completion of the Incarnation	240
and the Sign of the Resurrection	240
The Communion of Holy Things	241
The Holy Communion	242
Holy Communion is Thanksgiving	243
Holy Communion is Remembrance	244
Holy Communion is Sacrifice	246
Holy Communion is Grace	247
Holy Communion is Fellowship	248
Chapter Eleven	**254**
Good and Useful	
Public Liturgical Remembrance	254
Private Devotion	255
The Succession of the Saints	257
Summary	258
Chapter Twelve	**262**
Conclusion	

Preface

Disagreements about the role of the saints, and especially about their prayers and the prayers of the living for and to the Christian dead, have been a source of hostility between Christian groups for hundreds of years. It remains a notable difference in the opinions and convictions of ordinary Christian people today. While many Protestant Christians still liturgically affirm their belief in "the one . . . Church," "the Communion of Saints," and "the life everlasting," doctrinal uncertainty still abounds for traditional doctrines in terms of Purgatory, paradise, hell, and heaven are not preached with much conviction, if at all. All the while, concern to know about the life of those whom they have known who are now dead, and concern to know what will happen to them, compel Christians to explore the world beyond.

Far from being simply a matter of traditional rivalries, the Communion of Saints is one of the issues of Christian belief that believers are least able to ignore or dismiss as speculative theology. For death will come to every person and nearly all persons have been or will be profoundly affected by the death of their beloved. The questions that arise from such experiences and fears are urgent and important, calling upon theologians for an answer. In short, what we say about the great saints of history is, at heart, also what we say about all the departed and, at last, what we say about ourselves.

This book, then, will ultimately serve as an attempted corrective to historic Protestant theology and modern Protestant popular piety in at least three ways. First, it will assure Christians that no member of the Church, whatever his or her condition, stands alone: "If one member suffers, all suffer together with it; if one member is honored, all rejoice together with it. Now you are the body of Christ and individually members of it."[1] The Church is not a collection of individuals having their own personal relationships with Christ to the exclusion of all others. To commune with Christ requires a communion with his Body, for one cannot claim to possess the Head to the exclusion of the Body. "For [God] has put all things under his feet and has made him the head over all things, for the church, which is his body, is the fullness of him who fills all in all."[2]

Second, it will seek to assure Christians that, as they are united with Christ their Head, so are they united with his members triumphantly reigning with him. Death in no way impedes our union with the Church in glory any more than it impedes our union with Christ himself. Together, the Church on earth and the Church in glory unceasingly bless and praise God. Further,

---

[1] 1 Corinthians 12, 26-27
[2] Ephesians 1, 22

as the saints below request with confidence the prayers of their sisters and brothers on earth, so they can be assured that the saints above pray to God on their behalf, hoping to be finally united with them on the last day.

Third, it will show that the doctrine of the Communion of Saints can be separated from the overemphasized, erroneous, and almost financial notion of "the spiritual treasury of the saints" in such a way that it recognizes Christ's work as the ultimate and only meritorious act upon which all salvation rests, and Christ's body as the mystical but real unity of persons both living and dead, the focal point of which is the praise of God in an atmosphere of full disclosure and mutual prayer, that does not issue into super-meritorious salvific works. The purpose of the book is not debunk to theologically the theology of merit, as indeed reformers have been doing for 500 years, but to provide a genuinely Protestant paradigm and eschatological framework which allows for the Communion of Saints without necessarily attaching to it the false idea of the "treasury of the merits." The book will include recommendations on reintegrating the doctrine of the Communion of Saints into the worship and devotional life of Protestant churches.

The reclamation of the doctrine of the Communion of Saints living and dead for Protestant Christianity will be accomplished in this book in three parts. Part one will survey the historical development of the doctrine and outline the reasons for its ultimate rejection. Part two will construct a biblically grounded eschatological context through which we can understand, in part, the life beyond. Part three will explore the Church's understanding of the various interactions between believers on earth and those in heaven.

The story of Monica's internment, chapter one of part one, will introduce the Communion of Saints as a spiritual bond which knits together the faithful in this world and the saints beyond in a mystical organic unity within which there exists a mutuality of love and prayer that is best and most fully expressed in the Eucharistic feast. An explication of incarnational sacramentalism will follow showing how institutionalized penance was derived from the sacraments of Baptism and the Lord's Supper, so central to the Church of Augustine. The scholastic trisection of penance into contrition, confession, and satisfaction will then be examined and the eventual evolution of the practice of indulgences will be sympathetically understood. Chapter two will lay out the Protestant rejections of the Roman Catholic theology of the Communion of Saints and its results. It will begin by identifying the great reformer's definitions of the creedal phrase and then lay out the historic reasons for their elimination of the traditional sense of the doctrine. Chief among these rejections will be their attempts to reform the theology of Purgatory which finally ended in its wholesale denunciation along with the many abuses attached to it.

Part two will consist of envisioning a creedal eschatology through which we are to understand the Communion of Saints. Chapter one of part two will verify that the Creed clearly establishes belief in life after death. In that life, heaven will be envisioned as the divine moment of success in God's self-communication to his creation. The existence of an intermediate state connecting the present moment and that great moment beyond will be biblically and philosophically grounded. The doctrine of Purgatory will then be revisited. Elucidated by both ancient Eastern Orthodox and modern theologies, a Purgatory for Protestants will be proposed. Chapter two will maintain the resurrection of the body and its significance for the life beyond. Chapter three will clarify the forgiveness of sins illuminated by the judgment of the Christ who descended into hell.

In the eschatological light provided by the previous chapters, part three will define the creedal phrase "we believe in the Church." The Communion of Saints will thus be understood as the product of the one organic mystical body of Christ which exists in two aspects or modes: one earthy and one heavenly. These two aspects of the one Church inform two supernal streams of faith, hope, and love. The first of these streams is horizontal within the Church on earth, the second vertical between the Church on earth and that in heaven. Within these two streams, faith corresponds respectively to the gospel preached and handed down; hope, to prayer; and love, to Holy Communion. This book will conclude that death does not destroy human relationships but raises them to a higher sphere whose focal point is the praise of God in a community of full disclosure and mutual prayer; and that the communion that the saints have with Christ and with each other, both living and dead, is most fully and beautifully expressed at the Lord's Table. This was the faith Augustine expressed at his mother's funeral.

Thesis Statement

The Communion of Saints is the spiritual bond which knits together the faithful in this world and the saints beyond in a mystical organic unity within which there exists a mutuality of love and prayer, the greatest symbol of which is the Holy Eucharist. Death therefore does not destroy human relationships but raises them to a higher sphere whose focal point is the praise of God, and wherein Christians both living and dead have communion with each other in Christ.

Dedication

For all the saints;
for Lynn, Tiffany, and Buffy,
and all sisters and brothers in Christ, and those in their care;
for the United Methodist Chruch,
and its congregations at Perry, Mooreville, Dresden, and Blooming Grove,
and all the friends of God;
for Bob, Ralph, Fisher, and Bill,
and all mentors, teachers, preachers, and colleagues;
for Kallistos, Hans, Clive, and Karl,
and all theologians and doctors of the Chruch;
for Martin, Issac, Augustine, and Monica,
and all reformers, fathers, and mothers;
for Polycarp, Perpetua, Paul, and John,
and all martyrs, prophets, apostles, and evangelists;
for Mary, the Mother of God;
for Jesus Christ the Son, by him, with him, and in him,
in the unity of the Holy Spirit,
giving all honor and glory to the Father,
now and forever.

Very truly, I tell you, the hour is coming and now is, when the dead will here the voice of the Son of God, and those who hear will live.

Part One: Envisioning A Communion Lost

Chapter One

Introduction

Augustine Inters his Mother and Plants the Seeds of the Reformation

In his fourth century *Confessions* Augustine of Hippo recounts the words of his mother to her son as she lay dying of a fever: "Put this body away anywhere. Don't let care about it disturb you. I ask only this of you, that you remember me at the altar of the Lord, wherever you may be."[1] With these words she fell silent. Augustine himself closed her eyes as his own "overflowed into tears."[2] He soon dried his weeping as he "did not think it fitting to solemnize that funeral with tearful cries and groans . . . [for] she did not die in misery nor did she meet with total death."[3] After chanting Psalm 100 the body was prepared for burial. Augustine and the others gathered around his mother's tomb, and "with the corpse already placed beside the grave before being lowered into it," as "prayers poured forth to God," "the sacrifice of our redemption was offered up on her behalf."[4]

Ten years later, in the writing of his *Confessions*, Augustine not only divulges the true depths of his grief at that time but also notes that "now with a heart healed of that wound . . . I pour out to you, O God, on behalf of her who was your handmaid, a far different kind of tears."[5] Augustine concluded that though his mother "had been made alive in Christ"[6] and lived a virtuous life, she was not free from all sin: I dare not say that from the time you regenerated her by Baptism no word had issued from her mouth contrary to your commandment."[7] He is thus moved to pray for his mother's sins: "if she contracted any in so many years after receiving the water of salvation, forgive her, Lord, forgive her, I beseech you."[8] Though he believed that his petition was already accomplished, still he prayed that she "rest in peace,"[9]

---

[1] Augustine, *Confessions*, 9.12, trans. John Ryan (New York: Doubleday, 1960) 223.
[2] Ibid., 9.12, 224.
[3] Ibid., 9.12, 224.
[4] Ibid., 9.12, 225.
[5] Augustine, *Confessions*, 9.13, 227.
[6] Ibid., 9, 13, 227.
[7] Ibid., 9, 13, 227.
[8] Ibid., 9, 13, 227.
[9] Ibid., 9, 13, 228.

her sins be forgiven by him who was hung upon the tree but now sits at the right hand of God to make intercession for us.

The offering of the Eucharist on her behalf takes on a similar tone as the "offerings of [his] mouth."[10] That which began as thanksgiving to God for her good deeds becomes a plea for the removal of her post-Baptismal and perhaps unconfessed sin. Augustine brings to a close the story of his life with the hope that "his mother's last request may be granted through the prayers of many occasioned by [his] confessions."[11]

In this short reminiscence we have in a nutshell everything we mean by the Communion of Saints. First, that the saints are our forbearers in the faith, in whose footsteps we follow and for whose faith and faithfulness we are to continually give thanks to God. Second, that the Church, following the example of Christ the great intercessor, prays for all its members, even those who have passed beyond the veil into the next life. Third, that Eucharistic fellowship is the deepest expression of remembering and praying with the saints.

Augustine affirmed the Communion of Saints as the spiritual bond which knits together the faithful in this world with the saints beyond in an organic unity that is the mystical body of Christ its head, and within which there exists a mutuality of love and prayer that continues even beyond the barriers of death.[12] Augustine, too, watered the seeds that would eventually flower into the Reformation when he seemingly affirmed the doctrine of Purgatory[13] by declaring that his prayers for his mother Monica could improve her status in the next world, a status that was not determinably fixed until the judgment on the Last Day.[14] His seemingly inordinate, by today's

---

[10] Ibid., 9, 13, 227.

[11] Ibid., 9, 13, 228.

[12] As early as the martyrdom of Polycarp in AD 156 and that of Perpetua and Felicity in 203 a theological eschatology had emerged in primitive Christianity that emphasized all the faithful, living and departed, in a unity in which mutual prayer had its place. For an excellent history of the evidence of the doctrine of the Communion of Saints in the early Church see J.P. Kirsch, *The Doctrine of the Communion of Saints in the Ancient Church* (Willits, CA: Eastern Orthodox Books, nd).

[13] An excellent summary of Augustine's thought concerning the nature of purgatorial fire in be found in Joseph Ntedika's work *L'Evolution de la Doctrine du Purgatoiure chez Saint Augustine* (Paris, Nauwelearts, 1966). See also Eugene Portalie, *A Guide to the Thought of Saint Augustine* (Chicago: Regnery, 1960).

[14] Augustine further speculated that some souls although not altogether good could by means of a purging fire arrive in paradise before the resurrection of the dead. See Augustine's *City of God* 21: 24 where he writes: "Temporal punishments are suffered by some in this life only, by some after death, by some both here and hereafter, but all of them before that last and strictest judgment. But not all who suffer temporal

standards, concern with her post-Baptismal sin was a situation that would be remedied in a few hundred years by the institution of the Indulgence.

A thousand years later, the developed doctrine of the Communion of Saints as it was practiced in the popular Roman piety of the time, paired with an overdeveloped doctrine of the treasury of merits, prompted Tetzel, a famous trafficker in indulgences, to preach "once a coin in the coffer clings,

---

punishments after death will come to eternal punishments, which are to follow after that judgment" and "That there should be some fire even after this life is not incredible, and it can be inquired into and either be discovered or left hidden whether some of the faithful may be saved, some more slowly and some more quickly in the greater or lesser degree in which they loved the good things that perish, through a certain purgatorial fire" (*Handbook on Faith, Hope, and Charity* 18:69 [A.D. 421] trans. Albert Outler (Grand Rapids, MI: Christian Classics Ethereal Library, 2004). And still further "The time which interposes between the death of a man and the final resurrection holds souls in hidden retreats, accordingly as each is deserving of rest or of hardship, in view of what it merited when it was living in the flesh. Nor can it be denied that the souls of the dead find relief through the piety of their friends and relatives who are still alive, when the Sacrifice of the Mediator [Mass] is offered for them, or when alms are given in the Church. But these things are of profit to those who, when they were alive, merited that they might afterward be able to be helped by these things. There is a certain manner of living, neither so good that there is no need of these helps after death, nor yet so wicked that these helps are of no avail after death" (*Sermons*, 3 vols. edited by John E. Rotelle, O.S.A. [New York: New City Press] 1992. 29:109).
See also "There is an ecclesiastical discipline, as the faithful know, when the names of the martyrs are read aloud in that place at the altar of God, where prayer is not offered for them. Prayer, however, is offered for other dead who are remembered. It is wrong to pray for a martyr, to whose prayers we ought ourselves be commended" (*Sermons* 159:1 [A.D. 411]).
"But by the prayers of the holy Church, and by the salvific sacrifice, and by the alms which are given for their spirits, there is no doubt that the dead are aided, that the Lord might deal more mercifully with them than their sins would deserve. The whole Church observes this practice which was handed down by the Fathers: that it prays for those who have died in the communion of the Body and Blood of Christ, when they are commemorated in their own place in the sacrifice itself; and the sacrifice is offered also in memory of them, on their behalf. If, then, works of mercy are celebrated for the sake of those who are being remembered, who would hesitate to recommend them, on whose behalf prayers to God are not offered in vain? It is not at all to be doubted that such prayers are of profit to the dead; but for such of them as lived before their death in a way that makes it possible for these things to be useful to them after death" (*Sermons*, 172:2).

a soul from Purgatory springs."[15] A bold and critical response from a local German monk and confessor would spark a fire of purification throughout the Church. But as the pendulum of the Reformation drastically swung, Protestant Churches often over-purged and in doing so infected their progeny with spiritual anorexia. Afraid they might over-emphasize the saints, and preferring to err on the side of caution, many chose not to deal with the saints at all, or at least as little as possible.

Beginning with Martin Luther, the churches of the Reformation, although adopting the Apostles' Creed, either began to pass over in silence the Communion of Saints or to explain it as the Church's "union with Jesus Christ in the one true faith."[16] John Calvin insisted that such a fellowship enabled the benefits that God bestowed upon the believers to be mutually communicated to one another—but to the living only, not the dead.[17] His view was followed in the Heidelberg Catechism wherein communion is made to mean the efforts of believers to strengthen mutually themselves in the fear of God. The Anglican Thirty-nine Articles are unambiguously Lutheran, rejecting as they do "the Romish Doctrine concerning Purgatory, Pardons, Worshipping and Adoration as well of Images as of Relics, and also Invocation of Saints," because they see in it "a fond thing, vainly invented, and grounded upon no warranty of Scripture, but rather repugnant to the Word of God".[18] The Methodist Articles of Religion, used in 1784, as well as the Reformed Episcopal Articles of Religion, 1875,[19] followed the Thirty-nine Articles, as does its daughter the Westminster Confession, and it was adopted in the Second London Confession of Faith, 1688,[20] the Philadelphia Baptist Confession, 1742, and in the Confession of the Cumberland Presbyterian Church, 1829.[21]

This understandable overreaction to the Roman Catholic overemphasis on meritorious works performed by both the blessed dead and

---

[15] This couplet attributed to Tetzel's preaching can be traced to and substantially acknowledged in his *Frankfort Theses* in Gröne von Valentin, *Tetzel und Luther* (Soest: Nasse, 1860) 365ff. See also Thesis 27 of Luther's "Ninety five Theses" in Henry Bettenson, *Documents of the Early Christian Church* (London: Oxford, 1963) 187.

[16] *Luther's Small Catechism,* which can be found in *Martin Luther's Basic Theological Writings*, edited by Timothy F. Lull (Minneapolis, Minn: Fortress, 2005).

[17] John Calvin, *Institutes* IV, 1, 3, trans. Ford Lewis Battles, ed. John T. McNeill (Philadelphia: The Westminster Press, 1960) 1014.

[18] See Philip Schaff, *The Creeds of Christendom* Vol. III (Grand Rapids, Michigan: Baker Book House, 1931) 501.

[19] See Schaff, *The Creeds of Christendom* Vol. III, 814.

[20] Ibid., Vol. III, 738.

[21] Ibid., Vol. III, 771.

those who make intercession for them, combined with the relatively late dispositional doctrines of soul sleep[22] and other explanations of the so-called intermediate state, have left modern Protestantism bereft of a satisfying doctrine of the Communion of Saints.[23] In its place has fallen the shallow substitute imbibed mainly in popular hymnody[24] of what might be called the "reunion of the saints," that is, a looking forward to some time in the distant future when the faithful will finally be joined in true fellowship but denying or at least ignoring any common unity that we now share with those who have gone on before us into glory.

The Goal of both Earthly and Heavenly Life

Augustine believed that whatever knowledge, trust, or love of God that one had at the time of death would be eventually fully developed (although not without cost to oneself.) This, he said, was the purpose of the spiritual life: to become fit to see God, contemplate God's love, and participate in the triune divinity. This is the essential goodness in the last resort, the supreme finale of the human person.[25] All human activity, then, is to be directed to this end when at last all human understanding and love will be perpetually renewed and deepened by grace. Augustine stressed that this knowledge of God was not an achievement but the free gift of God;[26] a gift that was both the gift of God's unmerited forgiveness and the gift of God's healing love; the gift of God that both justifies and sanctifies. This can be clearly seen, Augustine preached, in the healing stories of Jesus, where

---

[22] See Jean Calvin, *Psychopannychia* (Leipzig: Deichert, 1932); and Oscar Cullmann, *Immortality of the Soul or Resurrection of the Dead?* (New York: Macmillan, 1958).

[23] This theological shortfall has come to a head recently in the world's largest congregation, The Full Gospel Central Church of Seoul, South Korea. Associated with the Assemblies of God Church of Springfield, Missouri the 200,000 member Korean congregation is under investigation and its Pastor has cut official ties with the denomination over the issue of honoring the dead, which Pastor Cho has asserted is allowed by scripture and even implied in the commandment to honor our parents. While the "rites controversy" cannot be aligned exactly with "the Communion of Saints" it serves to highlight that "the veneration-of-the-dead issue cannot be forever swept under the rug." Harry Genet, "Big Trouble at the World's Largest Church" in *Christianity Today* (Jan. 22, 1982) 30.

[24] See, James M. Black, "When the Roll is Called Up Yonder" in *The Baptist Hymnal* (Nashville, Tennessee: Conventional Press, 1977) 516; among others.

[25] Augustine, *The Trinity* 1:31, trans. Edmund Hill (New York: New City Press, 1991) 89.

[26] See Augustine, *The City of God*, 10, 29. See also Confessions 13.9 "By your gift we are enkindled and carried upwards."

with the same word persons were both forgiven and healed.[27] For Augustine this gift is received at Baptism. As one participates in the dying and rising of Christ, the love that gives freedom to the will is enkindled within them and they embark on a Christian pilgrimage,[28] imitating Christ, sharing in his sufferings, and caught up in his love. Augustine envisioned this process "necessarily extending beyond death as it seeks ultimate fulfillment in the perfection of love and in the contemplation of God."[29] Even on the Last Day, Augustine speculated, when we see God face to face, there will be no end to love's increase, "and the ultimate realization of the contemplation of God will itself yield an infinite perspective for growth"[30] While upon the earth initiation into and growth within the life of God occurs as believers are united with Christ in his body called the Church, this happens in and through the Church's sacramental life.

The Sacramental Life

Grace alone was the first phrase in the tripartite slogan[31] of the Reformation. Grace refers to the specific and effective action of God upon a person's life and being, whereby that person is enabled to approach the oneness with God for which we were all created and to which we are all called. The reformers emphatically remind us that only by God's grace is this possible—we cannot make it on our own. The sacraments are the channels of grace by which this restoration of communion (made possible in the

---

[27] See Augustine, *Sermons*, 88. 5. See also Matthew 2:9 "Which is easier, to say to the paralytic 'Your sins are forgiven' or to say 'Stand up and take your mat and walk.'"

[28] This is a soul cleansing journey that involves the removal of sin, the only barrier that separates the creature from the creator. Sin can only be purged by an act of God, its only remedy is the blood of God, and so both forgiveness and holiness are the gift of God. See Augustine, *The Trinity* 4.2.4. But to make this journey "we should have been wholly incapable, had not Wisdom condescended to adapt Himself to our weakness, and to show us a pattern of holy life in the form of our own humanity." Augustine, *On Christian Doctrine* 1.11, trans R. P. H. Green (New York: Oxford University Press, 1997) 123.

[29] Robert Attwell, "Aspects of St. Augustine of Hippo's Thought and Spirituality Concerning the State of the Faithfull Departed" in *The End of Strife* ed. D M Loades (Edinburgh: T. & T. Clark, 1984). Dr. Attwell's article contributed much to shaping the Augustinian argument of this work.

[30] Ibid., referencing Augustine, *The Expositions on the Psalms* 104, 3, trans. J. H. Parker (Oxford: Oxford Press, 1847-1857).

[31] Grace alone, faith alone, scripture alone. *Sola gratia, sola fides, sola scriptura*. For an excellent explication of the theological formation of this Reformation slogan see Timothy George, *Theology of the Reformers* (Nashville, TN: Broadman Press, 1988).

incarnation) is made effective and present in the lives of Christians. In the continuing sacramental life of the Body of Christ, all persons within the Church are brought into communion with God and each other. In its fulfillment, this restoration to divine communion is life eternal. Through the sacraments we approach that restoration. They provide a means by which we even now, to some degree, experience upon the earth the abundant life of God.

Because God has created and is creating all that is, physical objects of creation can become the bearers of divine presence, power, and meaning. As such a sacrament is a means of God's grace and indeed the effective means of God's presence mediated through the created world. God becoming incarnate in Jesus Christ is the supreme instance of this kind of divine action. In the coming of Jesus of Nazareth, God's nature and purpose were revealed and active through a human body. In Jesus God became a human being. "The Word was made flesh, and dwelt among us"[32] as God and creation were united "once and for all."[33] Through the incarnation the material world is redeemed and as promised, God is with us "always, even unto the end of the world."[34]

Fundamentally, then, the whole of creation is in some degree a sacrament, for God is everywhere present and fills all things. But while God is ubiquitously present in all things, this enduring presence of Christ in creation, made possible through the incarnation, is not some vague or diluted divine pantheism but a particular and intense presence in particular and reliable ways that Christ himself established. The Church traditionally calls these particular forms of Christ's enduring presence "sacraments." Through the sacraments God's life is infused into the present age and mingled with it, without change or confusion. The sacraments are the manifestations of our Lord's saving power, and the means by which Christ is present and works in his Church.[35] The Church itself is a sacrament—a means of grace. It is a

---

[32] John 1:14.
[33] Hebrews 7:27; 9:12.
[34] Matthew 28:20.
[35] Huldrych Zwingli, the great Swiss reformer was "single-mindedly concerned to uphold the sovereignty of God and rout out every practice which encouraged the placing of one's trust in the creature" rather than the creator. (Timothy George, *Theology of the Reformers* [Nashville: Broadman Press, 1988] 160) He therefore emphasized the immediacy of God's grace, available through Christ alone, and imparted directly by the Holy Spirit. In his rejection of incarnational sacramentalism he wrote: "So completely did he [Christ] obtain all things from the Father by his death that whatever we ask in his name is granted. Hence no created thing [water or bread and wine] ought to be worshipped or held in such esteem as if it had any power

grace-filled and grace-sharing community of faithful people,[36] "the fullness of him who fills all and all,"[37] his body—the visible, material instrument through which Christ continues to be made known and the divine plan fulfilled. Moreover, the proclamation of the Word through preaching, teaching, and the life of the Church is also a primary means of God's grace.[38]

Beyond the universal presence of the Lord in the Church and in the scripture, Christ has provided in and through the Church certain specific and regular forms of his presence. These channels of grace are what we specifically refer to as the sacraments. "A sacrament is an outward sign of inward grace, and a means whereby we receive the same."[39] Combining words, actions, and physical elements, sacraments are sign-acts which both express and convey God's grace and love. The ritual action of a sacrament does not merely point to God's presence in the world, but also participates in it and becomes a vehicle for conveying that reality. God's presence in the sacraments is real. This embodiment of spiritual realities in material form is rooted in the mystery of the Incarnation and the ultimate redemption of

---

for the cleansing of our consciousness or the salvation of our souls." (*The Latin Works of Huldrych Zwingli* 2, ed. Samuel M. Jackson [Durham, N.C.: Labyrinth Press, 1983] 27.) For Zwingli Baptism with the Spirit rather than Baptism in water was the means by which individuals were drawn into divine salvation. Water Baptism was primarily a human response to God's prior act and word; the public initiatory ceremony by which one pledged to live faithfully in the covenant community; and an indispensable symbol of ecclesial unity. Likewise, the Lord's Supper was "to inform the whole Church rather than yourself of your faith." (*Hudreich Zwinglis Samtliche Werke*, 8 vols. ed. Schuler and Schulthess [Zurich: NP, 1828-1842] 3, 761.) The Supper, too, was a human response of praise and thanksgiving for the work of grace already received by faith quite apart from the consecrated elements, for, Zwingli quoted, "it is the Spirit that gives life the flesh is of no avail." (John 6:63) To this end the Church in Zurich observed the meal only four times a year to proclaim the Lord's death and bear witness to the fact that they were members of one body. (See *Hudreich Zwinglis Samtliche Werke*, 8 vols. ed. Schuler and Schulthess [Zurich: NP, 1828-1842] 3, 807.) While Luther declared Zwingli's new doctrine "seven times more dangerous than when he was a papist," Zwingli's theology was adopted and further radicalized by the Swiss (Anabaptist) Brethren and the radical Puritans of England. (*Luther's Works* 37, trans. ed. Theodore G. Tapert, [Saint Louis, Concordia Publishing. House, 1955-1958] 231).

[36] Where two or three are gathered together in my name, there am I in the midst of them. Matthew 18:20.
[37] Ephesians 1:22.
[38] 2 Timothy 3:16, "All scripture is given by inspiration of God."
[39] John Wesley, "Means of Grace," *Sermons* Vol. 1, *Wesley's Works*, Vol. 5 (Peabody, Massachusetts Hendrickson Publishers, 1991) 187.

matter. It is consistent with the very nature of the Church as the divine-human institution and the continuing mystery of Christ's presence in history. It also affirms the basic "goodness" of nature and recognizes the psychosomatic nature of humankind.

While the sacraments do not convey grace either magically or irrevocably, they are powerful channels through which God has chosen to make grace available to us.[40] These outward signs-acts convey grace tangibly not of themselves but by the very presence of the Holy Spirit in them. The grace given is not at all ambiguous or symbolic but real and actual, in order to truly recreate and perfect each person in the image and likeness of God.

So the Church continues to practice and cherish the various means through which divine grace is made present to us. Baptism and the Lord's Supper are sacraments that were instituted or commanded by Christ in the Gospels. Baptism is the initiatory sacrament by which persons enter into the covenant[41] with God and are admitted as members of Christ's Church. This sacrament is properly identified with justification and is therefore unrepeatable.[42] The Lord's Supper nourishes and empowers the lives of Christians and as such is properly identified with sanctification and therefore repeatable and necessarily so.

---

[40] The effect of the sacraments is not based upon the personal faith and moral character of the administrator nor in the faith and good will of the recipient, but in the power of the Holy Spirit, for the sacraments derive their power from God and not from human beings.

[41] In both the Old and New Testament, God enters into covenant relationship with his people. A covenant involves promises and responsibilities of both parties; it is instituted through a special ceremony and expressed by a distinguishing sign. By covenant God constituted a servant community of the people of Israel, promising to be their God and giving them the Law to make clear how they were to live. The circumcision of male infants is the sign of this covenant (Genesis 17:1-14, Exodus 24:1-12). In the death and resurrection of Jesus Christ, God fulfilled the prophecy of a new covenant and called forth the Church as a servant community (Jeremiah 31:31-34, 1 Corinthians 11:23-26). The Baptism of infants and adults, both male and female, is the sign of this covenant.

[42] Since Baptism is primarily an act of God in the Church, the sacrament is to be received by an individual only once. Baptism rests on the steadfast faithfulness of God and is therefore unrepeatable. It is God's initiative that establishes the covenant of grace into which we are incorporated in Baptism. While we may misuse our God-given freedom and live in neglect or defiance of that covenant, we cannot destroy God's love for us. When we repent and return to God, the covenant need not be remade, because God has always remained faithful to it.

Baptism

Jesus was baptized by John[43] and he commanded his disciples to teach and baptize[44] in the name of the Father, Son, and Holy Spirit[45]. Baptism then is grounded in the life, death, and resurrection of Jesus Christ. The grace which Baptism makes available is that of the atonement of Christ which reconciles us with God. Baptism involves dying to sin,[46] newness of life,[47] union with Christ,[48] receiving the Holy Spirit,[49] and incorporation into Christ's Church.[50]

In Baptism God manifests and we recognize the forgiveness of our sin.[51] With the remission of sin, which has alienated us from God, we are justified—freed from the guilt and penalty of sin—and restored to right relationship with God. This reconciliation is made possible in, by, and through the atoning life, death, and resurrection of Christ and made real in our lives by the work of the Holy Spirit. We respond to God's mighty acts of salvation by confessing and repenting of our sin, and affirming our faith that Jesus Christ has accomplished everything that is necessary for our salvation. God's forgiveness makes possible the renewal of our lives and our transformation into new beings in Christ.

Through the work of the Holy Spirit the Church is born as the community of the new covenant.[52] Within this community, Baptism is by water and the Spirit.[53] Because the mystery of Christ's death and resurrection

---

[43] Matthew 3:13-17.

[44] In Baptism water is administered in the name of the triune God: Father, Son, and Holy Spirit by an authorized person and the Holy Spirit is invoked with the laying on of hands, in the presence of the congregation. The power of the Spirit in Baptism does not depend upon the mode by which water is administered, the age or psychological disposition of the baptized person, or the character of the minister. It is God's grace that makes the sacrament whole.

[45] Matthew 28:19.

[46] Colossians 2:12.

[47] Romans 6:4.

[48] Romans 6:3.

[49] Acts 2:38.

[50] John 3:5.

[51] Acts 2:38.

[52] The Baptismal font becomes at once a tomb and a womb: "at the self-same moment you die and are born; the water of salvation is at once your grave and your mother." Cyril of Jerusalem, *Lecture XX*, "On the Mysteries II: of Baptism," Romans VI. 3-14, in *Nicene and Post-Nicene Fathers*, Series II, Vol. VII (Grand Rapids, Mich.; Eerdmans, 1978-1979).

[53] John 3:5, Acts 2:38.

is inseparably linked with the gift of the Holy Spirit given on the day of Pentecost,[54] likewise, participation in Christ's death and resurrection is inseparably linked with receiving the Spirit at Baptism.[55] Working in the lives of persons before, during, and after their Baptism, the Spirit is the effectual agent of salvation. God bestows upon baptized persons the presence of the Holy Spirit, marks them with an identifying seal as God's own,[56] makes them into new spiritual creatures,[57] and implants in their hearts the first installment of their inheritance as sons and daughters of God.[58] It is through the Spirit that the life of faith is nourished until the final deliverance of the Last Day when they will enter into the fullness of salvation.[59]

Baptism is the beginning of that process of growth in grace and holiness through which God brings us into participation in the divine life of the Trinity. Sanctification is both the goal and result of this participation in the divine life of love; which encompasses the gift of the gracious presence of the Holy Spirit, a yielding to the Spirit's power, and a deepening of our love for God and neighbor.

The Lord's Supper

As Holy Baptism is the doorway[60] to the sanctified life Holy Communion is the divine food[61] which sustains and nourishes us in our journey of salvation. Holy Communion is Eucharist. It is an act of thanksgiving in which Christians "brake bread . . . and eat together with glad and sincere hearts, praising God and enjoying the favor of all the people"[62] This sharing at the table exemplifies the nature of the church and models the

---

[54] Acts 2.
[55] Romans 6:1-11, 8:9-14.
[56] Ephesians 4:30.
[57] 2 Corinthians 5:17.
[58] 2 Corinthians 1:21-22.
[59] Ephesians 1:13-14.
[60] John 3:5; Titus 3:5.
[61] "This is the food of our souls: this gives strength to perform our duty and leads us on to perfection." John Wesley, 'Duty of Constant Communion," *Sermons* Vol. 3, *Wesley's Works*, Vol. 7 (Peabody, Massachusetts Hendrickson Publishers, 1991), 148. God makes spiritual sustenance available through the sacrament of the Eucharist. In John 6:35, Jesus tells the crowd: "I am the bread of life. Whoever comes to me will never be hungry, and whoever believes in me will never be thirsty." In our return to the table again and again, we are continually and repeatedly strengthened and empowered to live as disciples, reconcilers, and witnesses to the world.
[62] Acts 2:46-47.

world as God would have it be. The Lord's Supper is also a remembrance, commemoration, and memorial, but this remembrance[63] is much more than simply intellectual recalling; it is a dynamic re-presentation of past gracious acts of God in the present, so powerfully as to make them truly present now. This same action makes Holy Communion a type of sacrifice wherein the sacrificial actions of Christ are re-presented.[64]

Finally, Holy Communion is eschatological, meaning that it has to do with the end of history and the outcome of God's purpose for the world. In it we commune not only with the faithful who are physically present but with the saints of the past who join us in the sacrament anticipating the heavenly banquet celebrating God's victory over sin, evil, and death[65] even in the midst of the personal and systemic brokenness in which we live. Nourished by sacramental grace, the Church strives to be formed into the image of Christ and to be made instruments for transformation in the world.

From early in the Church's history participation in the Lord's Supper was not permitted without preparation. Traditional practice allows participation only by those who are baptized;[66] are in unity with the faith as expressed in the scripture, tradition, and the Creed; and are not restrained from participation on account of some grave sin or other impediment. The Church is concerned that her children not fall into receiving the Body and Blood of the Lord unworthily.[67] To prevent persons from "eat[ing] and

---

[63] "Do this in remembrance of me" (Luke 22:19; 1 Corinthians 11:24-25) is *anamnsis*. "an action whereby the object is re-presented in memory." Kittel, G. and Friedrich, G., ed. *Theological Dictionary of the New Testament*, 10 vols, (Grand Rapids: Eerdmans, 1964-76) 1, 348-349.

[64] This is not a repetition as Hebrews 9:26 makes clear that "he has appeared once for all at the end of the age to remove sin by the sacrifice of himself."

[65] Jesus' self-presentation as the bread of life in John's Eucharistic account (6:25-58) makes clear the connection: "Those who eat my flesh and drink my blood have eternal life, and I will raise them up on the last day" (6:54). Ignatius of Antioch (circa 50-117 AD), described the Eucharist as "the medicine of immortality which is the antidote which wards off death but yields continuous life in union with Jesus Christ" (*Letter to the Ephesians*, 20.2 See Henry Bettenson, *Documents of the Early Christian Church*, [London: Oxford, 1963] 74). This union with Christ is eternal life. It is a dynamic loving relationship with Christ in the here and now; which extends beyond physical death and indeed never ends because it is grounded in the everlasting love of God who comes to us in the sacraments.

[66] See The *Didache* IX in Henry Bettenson, *Documents of the Early Christian Church* 63.

[67] 1 Corinthians 11:27.

drink[ing] judgment against themselves"[68] the Church turns to another sacramental act[69]—penance.

Penance

The desire to be free from guilt and anxiety is one of the oldest human spiritual yearnings on record. While struggling against the weight of public gestures the psalmist intoned of God: "you have no desire for sacrifice, if I were to give a burnt offering you would not be pleased. The sacrifice acceptable to God is a broken spirit, a broken and contrite heart."[70] So the long history of penance has been the history of the struggle between the need of the inner self to be unburdened and the requirement of the institutional Church to have its members within its embrace. The evolution of its name within Roman Catholicism—from penance to confession, and more recently to reconciliation—bespeaks this tension.

In the early church, penance was thought of primarily as public reconciliation, necessary to the very survival of the congregation. For if, after the drenching purification of Baptism, people continued to sin, as Paul's letters clearly indicated they did, there needed to be some method of re-conversion and restoration. There were those who believed that after Baptism no sin was possible. It is to these that John replies in his first letter

---

[68] 1 Corinthians 11:29.

[69] It could be said that the whole of Christianity is a single Mystery or Sacrament – The Triune God redeeming the world through Christ. In the tradition of the Church, however, a large number of acts have been called Mysteries or Sacraments. In the 12th century, the Italian theologian Peter Lombard summarized the growing consensus that these were seven: Baptism, confirmation, Eucharist, penance, extreme unction, anointing of the sick, Holy Orders, and marriage. These sacraments the Church found necessary for the regular and adequate liturgical celebration of the Christian Mystery. The number of sacraments was finally fixed at seven during the medieval period (at the councils of Lyons 1274, Florence 1439, and Trent 1547). In addition Roman Catholicism has innumerable sacramentals, for example, holy water, holy oil, blessed ashes, candles, palms, crucifixes, and statues. Sacramentals are said to cause grace not *ex opere operanto* (through the deed itself) like the sacraments, but *ex opere operantis*, through the faith and devotion of those using them. Orthodox churches also recognize the seven sacraments, but no official decision enjoins that number. The 16th-century Protestant reformers generally declared that there are but two sacraments, Baptism and Eucharist – these having been instituted by Christ – but further claimed that God's grace is accessible through the more personal channels of prayer, the Scripture, and preaching. The Anglican (Episcopal) church, however, accepted the other five as *sacramental rites* that evolved in the church.

[70] Psalm 51:16-17.

that such thoughts are self-deception.[71] There were others who claimed that that sin was indeed possible but that if it occurred, all was lost and damnation was certain. The Church recognized the deficiencies in both claims and confronted the problem with the sacrament[72] of ritual penance. Penance affirms that Christians can and do sin after Baptism and that this failure is serious and that if the backslidden are to be reclaimed by the Church the community needs first to see sure signs of repentance in the clear symbols of public weeping, prayer, fasting, and almsgiving.

Returning penitent sinners were treated roughly parallel to catechumens. Though usually barred from Holy Communion during the penitential process they were supported and encouraged by the community.[73] Finally, in a public liturgy which praised God's mercy for their return, their status as faithful Christians was reinstated.

In this way penitence was seen essentially as a healing ministry, and sin was viewed primarily as a disease that needs to be healed, rather than a crime to be punished. John Chrysostom preached, "Did you commit sin? Enter the Church and repent for your sin; for here is the physician, not the judge; here one is not investigated, but receives remission of sins"[74] As a

---

[71] "If we say that we have no sin, we deceive ourselves" 1 John 1:8.

[72] Pope Pius X in his Decree "Lamentabili sane" (3 July, 1907) condemned the following position: "In the primitive Church there was no concept of the reconciliation of the Christian sinner by the authority of the Church, but the Church by very slow degrees only grew accustomed to this concept. Moreover, even after penance came to be recognized as an institution of the Church, it was not called by the name of sacrament, because it was regarded as an odious sacrament." *On the Doctrine of the Modernists: Pascendi Dominici: Syllabus Condemning the Errors of the Modernists: Lamentabili Sane* (Boston: Pauline Books & Media, 1973) 46.

[73] "There is a harder and more grievous penance, the doers of which are properly called in the Church *penitents*; they are excluded from participation in the sacraments of the altar, lest by unworthily receiving they eat and drink judgment unto themselves "(Augustine, "De utilitate agendae poenit." Sermon 332, c. iii, in *Sermons, (306-340A) on the Saints,* Vol. III/9, trans. Edmund Hill, O.P, series ed. John E. Rotelle, O.S.A, (Hyde Park, New York: New City Press, 1994.)

[74] And also, "Be not ashamed to approach (the priest) because you have sinned, nay rather, for this very reason approach. No one says: Because I have an ulcer, I will not go near a physician or take medicine; on the contrary, it is just this that makes it needful to call in physicians and apply remedies. We (priests) know well how to pardon, because we ourselves are liable to sin. This is why God did not give us angels to be our doctors, nor send down Gabriel to rule the flock, but from the fold itself he chooses the shepherds, from among the sheep He appoints the leader, in order that he may be inclined to pardon his followers and, keeping in mind his own fault, may not set himself in hardness against the members of the flock" (John Chrysostom,

perceptive physician seeks to heal wounds, so a confessor healed sins. He or she offered counsel, and prescribed remedies, called penances. These looked to the preservation of the spiritual health of the penitent. Such penances were not seen as punitive in nature but remedial. They included such things as spiritual reading, fasting, increased prayer, and charitable works.

By the sixth century, however, the sacrament of penance, like Baptism, was allowed only once in a lifetime. Moreover the process by which penitents were restored had callused into a canonical procedure whose legalisms undermined the impulse among many Christians to pursue reconciliation at all.[75] Penance had degenerated into a harsh penalty rather than a reasonable rehabilitation. For publicly known and serious sins such as apostasy, murder, and adultery the penitential process could last three and sometimes fifteen years, with the added requirement that those restored remain celibate for the remainder of their lives; a severity that caused the breakup of many marriages. These harsh and rigorous requirements led the majority of Christians to postpone intentionally penance as long as possible. By the year 700, penance had been transformed into a sacrament of the dying.

During the Middle Ages Celtic monks and nuns led the return of the medieval church to the earlier model of private confession by grafting an indigenous pagan idea—the Druid soul-friend—onto the sacrament of penance.[76] The monks redeveloped the idea of a confessor and began to discuss frequently their sinfulness and need to reform with their abbess, abbot, or other spiritual director who would hear a private recitation of offenses and assign a penitential act. This method for unloading the burden of sin and its corresponding guilt involved no social stigma, no public exposure, and in place of one chance on earth to wipe the slate clean before final judgment, it offered a repeatable pattern of forgiveness. As Celtic missionaries traveled to continental Europe their form of private and frequent confession became popular and was eventually considered the

---

Homilies, "On Frequent Assembly" in *Patrologiae Cursus Completus Series Graeca*, Vols. 1-161, by Jacques Paul Migne (Paris: Migne, 1886) hereafter abbreviated PG, LXIII, 463).

[75] For more on the development of Penance see J. Dallen, *The Reconciling Community: The Sacrament of Penance* (New York, Pueblo, 1986) and L. Orsy, *The Evolving Church and the Sacrament of Penance* (Danville, New Jersey, Dimension Books, 1978).

[76] See Oliver Davies, ed. *Celtic Spirituality* (Mahwah, New Jersey; Paulist Press, 2000) 230-258.

normal sacramental rite of penance.[77] The more sever public form virtually disappeared from the local Church.

The publicity of penance did not disappear entirely, however, but was maintained through the pilgrimage. Confessors assigned different satisfactions to different sins, trying to achieve a balance according to their seriousness. Local standards were listed in books called Penitentials. Pilgrimage was a form of public penitence. One's friends, neighbors, and fellow Christians could see the shriven hearts of sinners as they dawned the pilgrims scallop shell and joined a band of fellow penitents on a journey of faith.[78] The journey itself was a remedial one in which the pilgrims shared with one another the stories of their sin. This is demonstrated by Chaucer who has his characters retell their sins as stories on a pilgrimage to Canterbury, and in doing so, finding the liberation that is at the heart of the sacrament.

In the twelfth and thirteenth centuries the Schoolmen provided the theological base for private confession utilizing as the model; contrition, confession, absolution, and satisfaction.[79] This four-fold process assumed at the very start a previous conversion through Baptism when the wash of regeneration and the invocation of the Father, Son, and Holy Spirit claimed the sinner for Christ, for membership in His body, and called believers to live in the world as a sign of promise, a priestly and prophetic people, proclaiming

---

[77] In 1215, at the Fourth Lantern Council, the Church officially adopted the Celtic form of Penance in its requirement that every baptized Christian was to confess their sins and receive the Eucharist at least once a year.

[78] The pilgrimage was not only a penitential act but many times taken on voluntarily as a sort of spiritual tourism wherein "the tedium of rustic existence was undoubtedly relieved by the stimulation that travel brings." Carl Volz, *The Medieval Church* (Nashville: Abington Press, 1997) 160. See also R.A. Markus "How on Earth Could Places Become Holy? Origins of the Christian Idea of Holy Places," *Journal of Early Christian Studies* 2:3 (1993) 270; and John Shinners, *Medieval Popular Religion* (Ontario: Broadview Press, 1999) 149-210, in which the author includes a sketch of a thirteenth century lead ampule containing water infused with the blood of Thomas a Becket or dust from his tomb, meant to be "part curative, part souvenir."

[79] This model was first developed by Peter on Pointers (d. 1197) and popularized by Alexander of Hales (d. 1245). Albert Magnus (d. 1280), Thomas Aquinas (d. 1274), Bonaventure (d. 1274), and John Dun Scotus (d. 1308) while formulating the theology of penance in different ways all follow the four-fold path. See John T. McNeill and Helena M. Gamer, *The Medieval Handbooks of Penance: A Translation of the Principal Libri Poenitentiales and Selections from Related Documents* (New York: Columbia University Press, 1990) as well as Frank P. Cassidy, *Molders of the Medieval Mind* (St. Louis, Missouri: London, B. Herder Book Co., 1944) and Yves M. J. Congar, *A History of Theology*, trans. Hunter Guthrie (Garden City, N.Y., Doubleday, 1968).

the kingdom of God. It is Christ's call to a continuous and ongoing conversion which echoes in each Christian heart which draws them again to God's mercy and forgiveness and invites them back into right relationship with God and their brothers and sisters.

Contrition

The most important act of the penitent is contrition: that is, one must be genuinely sorry for one's sins, and have an understanding that they have offended God and the Church as the Body of Christ.[80] True contrition includes the intention of sinning no more. This purpose of amendment does not mean swearing never to sin again, but rather intending not to sin and taking reasonable steps to change the circumstances leading up to a particular sin. Of course, the confessor has no way of knowing with absolute certainty whether or not the contrition and confession of a penitent is sincere. As is proved by the prayer of David, "Cleanse me from hidden faults,"[81] we see that not even the penitent is completely conscious of the full extent of his or

---

[80] There are two kinds of contrition—perfect and imperfect. The difference between them is found in the motive. Perfect contrition is motivated by the goodness and love of God above all things. That is one is sorry for ones sins because they are acts against the love and goodness of God. Imperfect contrition called attrition is defined as sorrow for sin for a motive less than the love of God, such as the ugliness of sin or the fear of hell or other punishment. While Aquinas made the distinction between the two in his *Commentary on the Sentences* 4.17.2.2 (trans. Simon Tugwell in *Albert & Thomas: Selected Writings*, 363-418, The Classics of Western Spirituality [New York: Paulist Press, 1988] he expounded no way of telling whether a penitents sorrow was one or the other. The question arose in the fifteenth century: Is a confession valid if it has been made by someone who is not contrite, who does not sorrow sufficiently for his [or her] sins or does not intend to refrain from them in the future?" (Antoninus Pierozzi, *Confessional* [Rome, 1490] on this work see Thomas N. Tentler, *Sin and Confession on the Eve of the Reformation* [Princeton, N.J., Princeton University Press] 39-42). Martin Luther rightly responded that "no one is sure of the truth of [their] own confession. (*Ninety-Five Thesis*, 30 See Bettenson, *Documents of the Christian Church*, 187) Consequently assurance of forgiveness could not be based on the quality or quantity of ones contrition which could never be worthy or sufficient (See Luther's *Defense and Explanation of All the Articles, Luther's Works, 55 Volumes of Lectures, Commentaries and Sermons* (Concordia Publishing House and Fortress Press, 1957; released on CD-ROM, 2001) 7:385-387) but through the objective work of Christ. Luther went on to define authentic repentance as the awareness of divine judgment through the revelation of the law of God. (See Luther, *Commentary on Galatians* 3:19 (Grand Rapids: Fleming H. Revell, 1988) 206-208).
[81] Psalm 19:12.

her sin. So before God to whom all hearts are open and all desires known, and from whom no secrets can be hid, the sinner made confession and did penance, "not that [God] would change his judgment in response to our prayer, but so by our prayer we might acquire the proper disposition and be made capable of obtaining what we request."[82]

Confession

With a contrite heart the penitent must honestly and specifically confess all serious sins.[83] One cannot be faulted however, for deficient arithmetic, anxious forgetting, or sparing the confessor abominable details. It is important to note that this is the point of the process in which the penitent receives absolution,[84] that is, forgiveness, and is fully restored to the

---

[82] Gabriel Biel, *Exposition of the Canon of the Mass*, 31.C (Oberman-Courtenay) 1:315.

[83] Tracing its origin to scripture Church tradition has distinguished two kinds of sin: mortal and venial. Mortal, also called grave or serious, sin is any act wherein a person freely and consciously rejects God, God's law, or God's covenant of love, preferring to turn in on his or herself or to some created and finite reality, that is, something contrary to the divine will. This can occur directly and formally in the sins of apostasy, idolatry, and atheism; or in an equivalent way in every act of disobedience to God's commandments. For a sin to be mortal, three conditions must be together met: a sin whose object is a grave matter, is committed with full knowledge and deliberate consent. *Grave matter* is specified by the Ten Commandments. *Full knowledge* presupposes knowledge of the sinful character of the act. It also implies a *consent* sufficiently deliberate to be a personal choice (*Catechism of the Catholic Church* (New York: Doubleday, 1995) 1857-1859). "Mortal sin, by attacking the vital principle within us—that is, charity—necessitates a new initiative of God's mercy and a conversion of heart which is normally accomplished within the setting of the sacrament of reconciliation" (*Catechism 1856*).

A person commits venial sin when, in a less serious matter, he or she does not observe moral law or when he or she disobeys moral law in a grave manner, but without full knowledge or without complete consent. Venial sin weakens charity; it manifests a disordered affection for created goods; it impedes the soul's progress in the exercise of the virtues and the practice of the moral good. While deliberate and even un-repented venial may disposes persons little by little to commit mortal sin, it does not set us in direct opposition to the will and friendship of God nor does it break covenant with God. The Church teaches that the sacrament of penance is not strictly necessary for the forgiveness of venial sin—these sins are forgiven through reception of the Eucharist (*Catechism 1394*), acts of sorrow, works of charity, prayer, and penitential rites; however the Church strongly recommends confession of venial sins (*Catechism 1458*).

[84] The Council of Trent affirmed the Church's power to absolve sins committed after Baptism when it declared: "But the Lord then principally instituted the Sacrament of

state of grace. When the penitent has completed his or her confession, the confessor by a laying on of hands and/or a special formula prays the prayer of absolution, within which the forgiveness of God is pronounced and bestowed. It is God who is the forgiver and the healer of the penitent, not the human confessor.[85] The confessor is not a vindicating agent of God, nor merely a recipient of secrets, but primarily a witness of repentance. Through absolution the penitent is forgiven of sin and freed from guilt and all eternal penalties.

Satisfaction

Satisfaction is the last part and also the fruit of penance. It is an act usually assigned by the confessor and preformed by the penitent to prove true contrition, assist in healing the disorders caused by sin, and above all to express ones gratitude to God for the forgiveness of sins received in, by, and through Christ Jesus. At first sight, to speak of some sort of punishment after forgiveness might seem inconsistent, but the Old Testament shows us how normal it is to undergo reparative punishment after forgiveness. God, after describing himself as "a God merciful and gracious . . . forgiving iniquity and transgression and sin", adds: "yet not without punishing."[86] God's fatherly love, then, does not rule out punishment, even if the latter must always be understood as part of a merciful justice that re-establishes the violated order for the sake of man's own good.[87] In this context, temporal punishment expresses the condition of suffering of those who, although reconciled with God, are still marked by those remains of sin which do not leave them totally open to grace. Precisely for the sake of complete healing,

---

Penance, when, being raised from the dead, he breathed upon his disciples saying, 'Receive ye the Holy Ghost. Whose sins you shall forgive, they are forgiven them, and whose sins you shall retain, they are retained.' By which action so signal, and words so clear the consent of all the Fathers has ever understood that the power of forgiving and retaining sins was communicated to the Apostles, and to their lawful successors for the reconciling of the faithful who have fallen after Baptism" (Sess. XIV, i)." Biblical scholars of the time also referenced Matthew 16:19; 18:18; and John 20:21-23 to support absolution, defined as the legislative and judicial power to forgive sins and free persons from sin's penalties.

[85] A point recognized by Duns Scotus in his *Oxford Commentary on the Sentences*, 4.16.1.7 (Wadding) 18: 421)

[86] Exodus 34:6-7. See also 2 Samuel 12:13, wherein King David's humble confession after his grave sin obtains God's forgiveness but not the prevention of the foretold chastisement.

[87] See Hebrews 12:4-11.

the sinner is called to undertake a journey of conversion towards the fullness of love. In this process God's mercy comes to his aid in special ways. The temporal punishment itself serves as medicine to the extent that persons allow it to challenge them to undertake their own profound conversion.

Satisfaction as a Regimen for Spiritual Health

After forgiveness is declared[88] actual penance or satisfaction is assigned. This can be either prayer or action, and is both a sign of genuine repentance, and an act of reparation and healing of the harm one's sins have caused to oneself and others. Because many sins wrong one's neighbor, true repentance requires that one do what is possible in order to repair the harm such as return stolen goods, restore the reputation of someone slandered, or pay compensation for injuries. Sin also injures and weakens the sinner, as well as their relationships with God and neighbor. While absolution takes away sin, it does not remedy all the disorders that the sin has caused. Raised up from sin, the sinner must still recover his or her full spiritual health by doing something to make amends for the sin. This satisfaction which the confessor imposes takes into account the penitent's personal situation and seeks the penitents spiritual good. As far as possible, it should correspond with the gravity and nature of the sins committed. It can consist of prayer, an offering, works of mercy, service of neighbor, voluntary self-denial, sacrifices, and above all the patient acceptance of the cross we must bear. Such penances help configure the baptized to Christ, who alone expiated sins once for all. Doing satisfaction is the purposeful and deliberate working out of that salvation. In careful self-examination and reflective dialogue with the Church, the forgiven penitent takes on sanctifying tasks that through the power of the Holy Spirit "strip off the old self with its practices, and clothe[s] oneself with the new self which is being renewed in knowledge according to the image of its creator."[89]

The effective agent in penance, as in all the sacraments, is not the penitent nor the confessor but God the Holy Spirit heals the infirmities and wounds of the sinner. Forgiveness here is seen not as just a clearance of a debt owed but the healing of the penitent. As such it is a gift from God which one learns to receive: "Let us apply to ourselves the saving medicine

---

[88] In the Middle Ages theologians debated whether absolution caused the forgiveness of sins or simply declared sins forgiven. The Council of Trent promulgated that absolution was not merely an announcement of the gospel but an effective part of God's forgiving grace. (Council of Trent, Sess. XIV, c. 3)

[89] Colossians 3:9.

of repentance; let us accept from God the repentance that heals us; for it is not we who offer it to him, but he who bestows it upon us."[90]

This line of thought is at the very core of the Church's vocabulary. The root meaning of the English term "salvation" which derives from the Latin *salus* is health or wholeness. The episodes recorded in the Gospels wherein the forgiveness of sins is accompanied by the restoration of physical health[91] further highlights this model where through the forgiveness of sins the past is no longer an intolerable burden but rather an encouragement for what lies ahead. Seen in this way confession and penance become the way out of the impasse caused by sin and life in return acquires an attitude of expectation, not of despondency. In this respect, repentance is an eschatological act, realizing in the here and now, the promises of the age to come.

Satisfaction as a Remedy for Guilt

The cloud of guilt darkens the lives of sinners and sometimes serves the good use of moving them to confession. Guilt is a part of the tragedy experienced by people in their personal lives as well as in the face of the appalling sufferings and misery of the world for which we all share some responsibility. In their feelings of guilt, human beings judge themselves and see themselves as unworthy of the gifts of God. In contrast God is seen to declare His love for human persons at their most unacceptable. It is this identification with humanity and God's loving acceptance of the worst that human beings can do that makes repentance and confession a way of rediscovering God and one-self, and thereby the path to a full and loving relationship with God and with one another.

An overwhelming sense of guilt, however, is the negative aspect of being self centered and seeking in and through oneself some means to propitiate God's judgment or wrath. The failure to recognize one's overwhelming sense of guilt as the negative expression of undue confidence in one's own achievement, works, and merit many times results in a too individualistic and self-regarding view of sin and salvation, which unchecked may give rise to an attendant legalistically oriented penitential system.[92] This

---

[90] John Chrysostom, *De Poenitentia* 7, 3 in PG 49:327.
[91] See Mark 2:1-12.
[92] For an intriguing explication of how guilt, in the specific context of repentance and confession, is a highly misleading concept, largely fostered by Western thinking, see: Timothy Ware, *Eustratios Argenti: A Study of the Greek Church under Turkish Rule* (Oxford, 1964) 20 ff; also Bishop Kallistos Ware, 'The Orthodox Experience of Repentance,' in *Sobornost/Eastern Churches Review* 2:1 (1980), 24-25.

was the case during the Middle Ages as the Church's concept of sin became increasingly defined within the theology of Anselm of Canterbury who in his treatise *Why God Became Human* maintained that crimes are evaluated according to the nature of the offense and with reference to those against whom they have been committed. Because human sin was ultimately against God, Anselm reasoned that it would require a human being to compensate for sins committed by humans, and that such a human being must also be divine in order to atone for the offense of having committed such sins against God. Christ was therefore necessarily human and divine. As the God-man, Christ was uniquely able to satisfy injustice suffered by God and to creation due to sin. Through his life and in his death Christ more than compensated for the injury to God's honor and gained forgiveness for all human beings.

Anselm's theology provided fodder for the Reformation in more ways than one. Not only did it lay the foundation for various theories of the atonement having representative suffering as their centerpiece (not the least of which is the penal substitutionary model) but he gave preeminence to the expression of forgiveness in the legal terms of his day and sin as a punishable crime.[93]

The schoolmen who followed further develop Anselm's paradigm of sin and forgiveness. In this legal configuration of penance, the performance of satisfaction is required not for remission of guilt or eternal penalties "but for the temporal penalty which, as the scriptures teach, is not always forgiven entirely as it is in Baptism."[94] Thomas defined satisfaction as "the payment of the temporal punishment due on account of the offence committed against God by sin."[95] Satisfaction came to be seen not only as a preventive remedy meant to hinder further falls but reparation to the honor of God, as well, as far as one is able to make such in this life or beyond in Purgatory. Because the remission of guilt and eternal punishment was (and is) already obtained without satisfaction, it was not (and is not) considered an essential part of the sacrament. It became however an integral part because through satisfaction one obtains the secondary effect; the remission of this temporal punishment.[96] The schoolmen often quoted Augustine who wrote

---

[93] The reduction of sin to a punishable legal crime, an act of law breaking inviting a penalty, is almost wholly absent in patristic literature, see J. Meyendorff, *Byzantine Theology: Historical and Doctrinal Themes* (London 1974) 195ff.

[94] The Council of Trent (Sess. VI, c. 14).

[95] Suppl. to *Summa*, Q. xii, a. 3.

[96] The Church claimed scriptural evidences for this theology in the judgment pronounced upon David by the prophet Nathan who said: "Now the Lord has put away your sin, you shall not die. But nevertheless because by this deed you have scorned the Lord, the child that is born to you shall die." (2 Samuel 13-14) See also

"Man is forced to suffer even after his sins are forgiven, though it was sin that brought down on him this penalty. For the punishment outlasts the guilt, lest the guilt should be thought slight if with its forgiveness the punishment also came to an end."[97]

Temporal Punishment

Augustine recognized that sin has both temporal and eternal consequences, and that it affects the sinner, in relation to God and his fellow human beings. While God forgives a person, the consequences of their sin may remain. A murderer, for example may be forgiven and yet the victim remains dead. A repentant drunkard may be forgiven but the damage to liver and brain may well be permanent. The suffering of the consequences of sin in this life, however, should not be seen as a vindicatory punishment but the loving discipline of a parent for the benefit of his children. The purpose of temporal punishment is to bring about repentance of evil ways,[98] and growth in righteousness and holiness;[99] to teach persons that they should not repeat the same failures;[100] to promote humility;[101] and to strengthen faith.[102] The schoolmen deduced that sinners who fail to do penance in this life may well be punished in another world, in a state between death and the Last Day,[103] and so not be cast off eternally from God. In this way Purgatory became an integral part of the good news of the medieval gospel.

Purgatory evolved into a place between earth and heaven, between death and eternal bliss, wherein the baptized, through the power of the Holy Spirit, "would throw off all remaining personal obstacles to the full

---

Genesis 3:17; and Numbers 20:11. Paul seemingly taught a similar truth in 1 Corinthians 11:32 when he wrote: "But when we are judged by the Lord we are disciplined so that we may not be condemned along with the world."

[97] Tract. cxxiv, "In Joann.", n. 5, in *Patrologiae Cursus Completus Series Latina*, Vols. 1-221, by Jacques Paul Migne (Paris: Migne, 1878) hereafter abbreviated PL, XXXV, 1972.

[98] Psalm 32.

[99] Hebrews 12:5-11.

[100] 1 Corinthians 10:6.

[101] 2 Corinthians 12:17.

[102] 2 Corinthians 1:9.

[103] Paul wrote to the Corinthians (1 Corinthians 6:9) "Do you not know that the unrighteous will not inherit the kingdom of God? Do not be deceived. Neither fornicators, nor idolaters, nor adulterers, nor homosexuals, nor sodomites, nor thieves, nor covetous, nor drunkards, nor revilers, nor extortionists will inherit the kingdom of God." Purgatory allows the baptized who dies in the state of sin a time and place to be made ready to enter the Kingdom of God.

enjoyment of eternal union with God."[104] This after-death purification is a continuation and completion of the sanctification process in which justified and reconciled persons are fully and finally prepared for and participate in the divine life of the Triune God.

Indulgences

The abundance of God's forgiving love in Christ Jesus and the unity of all Christians in the Communion of Saints combined in the Roman Church to form the foundation of the theology of Indulgences.[105] The starting-point for understanding Indulgences then, is the abundance of God's mercy revealed in the Cross of Christ. The crucified Jesus is the great Indulgence that the Father has offered humanity through the forgiveness of sins and the possibility of living as children[106] in the Holy Spirit.[107] In this economy of salvation God forgives and then obliges satisfaction. His gift of grace requires and elicits acceptance and response. In the light of this principle, it is not difficult to understand how the Church came to teach that reconciliation with God, although based on a free and abundant offer of mercy, at the same time implies an arduous process which involves an individual's personal effort and the Church's sacramental work.

So an Indulgence is not permission to commit sin, nor a pardon in advance for a future sin. Moreover, it is not the eternal forgiveness of sin for indeed it presumes that the sin has already been forgiven. And finally, it is not the release of all the obligations that result from sin, such as restitution to a neighbor wronged. An Indulgence is the remission of temporal punishment due to sin (that has been forgiven) in response to certain prayers or good works. It is an act of God through the Church. Its essential element is the application to one person of the satisfaction performed by another. This transfer of satisfaction or merit is based on the Communion of Saints, the principle of vicarious satisfaction, and the Treasury of the Church.

---

[104] Richard M. McBrien, "Purgatory" in *The Encyclopedia of Catholicism* (San Francisco, Harper Collins Publishers, 1989) 1070.
[105] On 29th November 1998 Pope John Paul II issued a papal bull entitled *Incarnationis Mysterium*, or "The Mystery of the Incarnation," bearing the subtitle *Bull of Indiction of the Great Jubilee of the Year 2000*. The document outlined the key aspects of Catholic millennium celebrations and the Indulgences connected with the Jubilee year and generally reaffirmed the Church's teaching on Indulgences.
[106] See John 1:12-13.
[107] See Romans 5:5; 8:15-16.

The Communion of Saints affirms that "we who are many, are one body in Christ, and individually we are members one of another."[108] Each member of the body shares in the life of the whole body and in so doing each Christian benefits from and by the prayers and good works of the others. Because good is much stronger than evil, "in this wonderful exchange the holiness of one profits well beyond the harm that the sin of one could cause others."[109] The Principle of Vicarious Satisfaction is seen most manifestly in the death of Christ who, as Anselm taught, vicariously satisfied our debt to God.[110] Each Christian, then, in imitation of Christ, suffers for one another to "complete what is lacking in Christ's afflictions for the sake of his body, that is, the Church."[111] These good works add as a secondary deposit (not independent of, but rather acquired through, the merits of Christ) to the Treasury of the Church, an infinite and inexhaustible fund of satisfaction, established through the life and death of Christ, which is more than sufficient to cover the indebtedness of the sin of the whole world.[112] Thought of in this way, forgiveness and salvation are communal and social instead of isolated and individual. As we "bear one another's burden and so fulfill the law of Christ"[113] we reflect the image and likeness of the God who created us, who himself exists in a triune society of mutual love.

The Mathematizing of Penance

As private penance became established within the Church toward the end of the ninth century various satisfactions that a penitent may find difficult to fulfill, such as a pilgrimage to Jerusalem, were commuted to a set number of prayers, fast days, or an amount of alms; with this the mathematizing of penance had begun. With the beginning of the Crusades under Urban II (1088-99) Indulgences became increasingly popular and monetary. In 1095 the Pope in partial response to the Byzantine Emperor's pleas for defense against the Turks, called upon the nobles of the west to put aside their differences and join together in order to liberate Jerusalem and the

---

[108] Romans 12:5.
[109] *Catechism of the Catholic Church*, 1475 (New York: Doubleday, 1995) 412.
[110] See the excellent introduction to Anselm's work by Joseph Colleran in *Why God Became Man and The Virgin Conception and Original Sin by Anselm of Canterbury* (New York: Magi Books, 1969) 21-30.
[111] Colossians 1:24.
[112] For the development of this doctrine in explicit form see Alexander of Hales (Summa, IV, Q. xxiii, m. 3, n. 6), Albertus Magnus (In IV Sent., dist. xx, art. 16), and Thomas (In IV Sent., dist. xx, q. i, art. 3, sol. 1).
[113] Galatians 6:2.

Holy Land from Muslim rule. In an effort to attract crusaders Indulgences were offered.

The Muslims taught that when a soldier died in battle, his soul immediately went to heaven. However, this was not the case with the Christian; unless Christian fighters had performed sufficient penance for their sins, they might still belong to the suffering in Purgatory after death. The crusade Indulgence granted that those who carried the cross into battle merited the remission of all temporal punishment of their sin.[114] But not all persons were physically fit to participate in the holy war, and a means was sought to allow this group to also make a contribution. The idea developed whereby the individual who contributed an amount equal to that of sending a soldier on a crusade might regard the payment of that sum as the equivalent to actual participation in the crusade itself and thereby share in the merits of the sponsored soldier. This being the case, it was but a small step to assume that a person contributing any monetary amount to the furthering of a crusade would in turn receive an Indulgence proportionate to that amount. So that by the time of Innocent III (1198-1216), the mere payment of money was sufficient to gain the advantages of a crusading Indulgence.[115]

Sanctification by good works was the proof that the confession of forgiven sins had been sincere. It had traditionally taken the form of one actually performing some good deed; such as erecting a church, building a bridge, engaging in poor relief, making a pilgrimage, or saying a prayer. Now these requirements could be satisfied with the purchase of an Indulgence.[116]

The Treasury of the Church

The Bull of Clement VI (1343) mentions the Church's Treasury of Merits[117] in connection to the granting of Indulgences. This heavenly

---

[114] Wilhelm Moeller, *History of the Christian Church*. (Durham, NO; Labryinth Press, 1910) 18-19.

[115] Heinrich Boehmer, *Luther in the Light of Recent Research* (New York; Castle Press Philadelphia, 1916) 160.

[116] In his *Reply to the Articles of Luther*, Johannes Cochlaeus concluded that the use of Indulgences grew out of expediency so that persons who may not have otherwise made confession or done penance might be moved so to do in a world in which love and devotion for acts of penance and self-denial had grown increasingly cold. See Adolf Herte, *Das Katholische Lutherbild im Bann der Lutherkommentare des Cochlaeus* 3 vols. (Fakultäts-Schrift:Münster, 1943). See also Gotthelf Wiedermann, "Cochlaeus as Polemicist," in Peter Newman Brooks ed., *Seven-Headed Luther* (Oxford: Clarendon Press, 1983).

[117] In the sixty-second of his *Ninety-five Thesis* Luther wrote "The true treasure of the Church is the sacrosanct Gospel of the glory and grace of God." (See Bettenson,

treasury was said to be filled with the merits of Christ and all the saints. Since one drop of Christ's blood was sufficient for the salvation of the whole world, and yet Christ, a man who was without stain, shed all his blood, a vast surplus of merit was accumulated.[118] From this depository the church had the right to draw, in granting remission to sinners from the temporal penalties resulting from the commission of sins. The very term "keys," it was said, implied a treasury which was locked away and to which the keys gave access.[119] Because the treasury was funded with the merits of Christ Himself, it is by its very nature, endless.[120]

The saints are first and foremost persons justified through the gift of Christ and sanctified through the gift of his Holy Spirit. As such, "during their mortal life, [they] amass beyond the measure of their duty a store of wealth and of sacrificial values made precious by the blood of Christ."[121] The superabundance of their love and penance grows into a rich deposit that is combined with the merits of Christ, from which they are derived, and added to the treasury of the Church. This sharing of the saint's spiritual wealth with their struggling counterparts on earth is the continuation and ultimate fulfillment of the sharing began there when "awe came upon everyone" and "all who believed had all things in common" distributing to all, "as any had need."[122]

Though it may be a crass comparison one can think of the Treasury of the Church as a sort of celestial bank, where the infinite merit of Christ is deposited on humanity's account. The local Church becomes the branch office, where priestly tellers dispense the sacraments, the means by which one

---

Documents of the Christian Church, 189). The target of this statement was the claim that there was a "treasury of the Church" containing the merits of Christ and the saints from which the Church was authorized too draw for the remission of temporal punishments.

[118] H. C. Lea, *A History of Auricular Confession and Indulgences* (London; Ire and Spottiewood, 1963) 345.

[119] Ibid.

[120] In his Bull *Unigenitus*, Clement VI (on January 27th 1343) stated: "Upon the altar of the cross Christ shed of his blood not merely a drop, though this would have sufficed, by reason of the union with the Word, to redeem the whole human race, but a copious torrent. . . thereby laying up an infinite treasure for mankind. This treasure he neither wrapped up in a napkin nor hid in a field, but entrusted to Blessed Peter, the key-bearer, and his successors, that they might, for just and reasonable causes, distribute it to the faithful in full or in partial remission of the temporal punishment due to sin."

[121] Karl Adam, *The Spirit of Catholicism* (New York: The Crossroad Publishing Company, 1997) 121.

[122] See Acts 2:43-45.

benefits from the divine deposit. In Holy Baptism ones name is added to the family account and all debts are cleared; this is justification and adoption. In Holy Communion one makes regular withdrawals on Christ's account for the forgiveness of post-Baptismal sin and to empower ones continued sanctification. All of this is a gift from God in, by, and through the life, death, and resurrection of Christ Jesus. As a forgiven and reconciled child of God, one's acts of mercy, service, and self-sacrifice now gain merit which is added to the family account. This merit is still and also the merit of Christ because it is gained through his grace and by the living presence of Christ's Holy Spirit within the Christian.[123]

So in this sense, through the Indulgence, the members of the Body of Christ most fully participate in the redeeming ministry of Christ by uniting their meritorious sacrifices, however small they may have been, to Christ's, and thereby co-operated in some way in the loving expiation of others. Within this system, the Church was thought to be growing into "the measure of the full stature of Christ."[124] Here the body was "growing up in every way into him who is the Head, into Christ, from whom the whole body, joined and knit together by every ligament with which it is equipped, as each part is working properly, promotes the body's growth in building itself up in love."[125] Through the Treasury of the Church the solemnity and joy, the humility and contrition, the love and faithfulness of all the members of the body are especially combined and joined to Christ their head and manifested in his redemptive work. For this reason the Council of Trent concluded "the use of Indulgences is very salutary for the people of Christ."[126]

Indulgences Extended to Those in Purgatory

By the end of the 13th century the crusades had lost most of their glamour, and with their decline the Roman Curia began to feel the loss of a lucrative source of income. Consequently, Boniface VIII (1294-1303) sought new sources of raising money through Indulgences. After searching through the Old Testament, the idea was conceived of instituting a Jubilee Indulgence which would be celebrated every one hundred years. Originally, the plan was to have Christians from all over the world make a pilgrimage to Rome to leave their gifts on Peter's tomb. The first Jubilee Indulgence in 1300 proved to be a huge success, which wet the appetite for more. The period of time

---

[123] See Galatians 2:20; Colossians 1:27-29; and Philippians 2:12-13.
[124] Ephesians 4:3.
[125] Ephesians 4:15-16.
[126] Sess. 25 *De Indulg*.

was variously reduced from 100, to 50, to 33, to 25 years, each decrease with accompanying rationalizations to explain why the change had been made.[127]

In 1393 Pope Boniface IX made the purchase of Indulgences much easier and more systematic, as another feature was added which greatly facilitated their sale. An impressive document was drawn up, The Indulgence Letter, elaborately ornamented with both papal signatures and seals. The purchaser now had tangible evidence of heavenly forgiveness, and sales of the "sacred commodity" increased greatly.[128] The final step in the evolution of Indulgences was taken by Pope Sixtus IV, who in 1476 established Indulgences for the dead in Purgatory.[129] Thomas Aquinas had taught that such souls belonged to the jurisdiction of the church on earth. So if Indulgences could be granted to the living, certainly the benefit could be extended to the intermediate realm, over which the church also had control.[130] This meant that Indulgences could be purchased not only for ones own spiritual benefit but also for those departed loved one's enduring the fires of Purgatory.[131] Soon thereafter, an Indulgence known as plenary,

---

[127] Mandell Creighton, *A History of the Papacy* (New York; Logman's and Green, 1925) 113.

[128] Frederick William Bussell, *Religious Thought and Heresy in the Middle Ages* (London; Robert Scott Roxburghe House, 1918) 747.

[129] See Mandell Creighton, *A History of the Papacy*. (New York; Logman's and Green, 1925) 260.

[130] See Phillip Schaff, *History of the Christian Church, VI The Middle Ages*. (Grand Rapids, MI; Erdman's Publishing Co., 1910) 758.

[131] In medieval society the dead were present to the living not only spiritually but also physically. The Christian community was one of both the living and the dead. This fact is seen most clearly in that the burial of the dead in the midst of the living. (See Ejnar Dyggve, "The Origin of the Urban Churchyard," *Classica et Mediaevalia* 8, 2 (1952) 147-158; and Peter Brown, *The Cult of the Saints* (Chicago, University Of Chicago Press, 1981) 1-22.) The Christian dead were laid to rest in consecrated churchyard usually in the center of the village of town. This peculiar Christian practice reversed the longstanding practice of ancient Jewish and Roman culture as well as that of the Germanic tribes, in which the deceased, if not cremated, were buried outside the bounds of the city or settlement. This was the practice of early Christianity until the mid fifth century. As the saints themselves, that is, their relics came to reside among the living the ordinary Christian dead followed. This slow reversal occurred as persons desired to be buried beside the shrines of the martyrs. The shrines became basilica, which were eventually taken into and/or increasingly built within the city walls. Urban churchyard burial in due course became the established norm with the holy or privileged eventually being entombed within the church itself. (See Craig M. Koslofsky, *The Reformation of the Dead: Death and Ritual in Early Modern Germany, 1450—1700* (New York: St. Martin's Press Inc., 2000) 40-77.)

meaning complete coverage of every possible requirement became available. Papal power would now remove souls from Purgatory and transmit them to the realm of heavenly bliss if their relatives had the required funds.

The Abuses of Indulgences

It is easy to see how abuses crept in to the Indulgence system.[132] Among the good works encouraged as a condition for obtaining an Indulgence, alms giving naturally held a prominent place. Persons were encouraged to give to pious causes such as the building of a church, the endowment of a hospital, or the organization of a crusade. In this there was nothing intrinsically evil as giving money to God or to the poor is a praiseworthy act, when done from right motives. As such, almsgiving seemed a suitable condition for gaining the spiritual benefit of an Indulgence. However, this practice was fraught with grave danger, and soon became a source of evil. As in so many other matters, the love of money was the chief root of the evil as Indulgences were employed by unscrupulous clerics as a means of financial gain. The good work of almsgiving that accompanied the

---

Contemporaries of the Reformation, however, often complained of overcrowded, overfilled, and overextended churchyards which because of the stench associated with them were increasingly considered a public health hazard. Population growth within the walls of a city served to fuel opinion that a progressively larger churchyard was a misuse of valuable land. The establishment of new non-Church related cemetery sites "that separated the bodies of the dead form the world of the living was an essential cultural precondition of the German Reformation as well as one of its most profound consequences." (See Craig M. Koslofsky, *The Reformation of the Dead: Death and Ritual in Early Modern Germany, 1450—1700* (New York: St. Martin's Press Inc., 2000) 41.) This separation of the living and dead meshed effortlessly with their theological separation in the reformers growing rejection of Purgatory, as well as prayers, suffrages, and Masses for the dead. Moreover, the political reformists vigorously promoted this separation seeing rightly that it would weaken traditional clerical intercession for the dead and with it the financial basis of much of the Church.

[132] On September 29th 1999 in a reflection on the merciful Father's forgiveness of sins Pope John Paul II recognized that the *gift of Indulgences* is a sensitive subject, which has suffered historical misunderstandings that have had a negative impact on communion between Christians. He expressed the Church's desire that this practice be properly understood and accepted as a significant expression of God's mercy. He further admitted that experience shows Indulgences are sometimes received with superficial attitudes that ultimately frustrate God's gift and cast a shadow on the very truths and values taught by the Church. (*L'Osservatore Romano* Weekly Edition in English (6 October 1999) 15.

Indulgence began to be regarded as the price of the Indulgence, and those who granted Indulgences were tempted to make them a means of raising money.[133] Even if this was not the official doctrine and law of the Church the corrupt ideas of popular piety and popular preachers,[134] a caricature of which has been preserved in Geoffrey Chaucer's "Pardoner", with his bogus relics and Indulgences, prevailed. It was the destiny of the reformers to expose an immoral Roman Curia and condemn it for what they regarded as

---

[133] For an exposition on Indulgences as a corrupt money making venture leading up to the Reformation see William Edward Lunt, *Papal Revenues in the Middle Ages* (New York; Octagon Books, 1965) in which the author reports that to finance the renovation of the Vatican and the build of the Sistine Chapel a simonial scheme was hatched by Hohenzollern Elector Joachim of Brandenburg, his brother Albert, Pope Leo X, and the Fugger banking family. (117) These Indulgences offered the greatest possible advantages – sins no matter how "grave or enormous", were to be fully remitted upon confession. Sinners also had their choice of confessor. Those guilty of simony, un-canonical marriage, the acquisition of property through usury, or of perjury were offered full remission of their past sins. (See Great Britain, *Diplomatic Documents and Papal Bulls* [New York; Kraus, 1963] 1758). In addition, they were applicable to both the living and the dead, including those already in Purgatory and came with an Indulgence ticket permitting the dead to participate in the prayers, alms, fasts, pilgrimages, and masses of the church here on earth. Finnally, the Indulgence included the remission of all good works required of the souls in Purgatory. (See Henry Bettenson, *Documents of the Christian Church* (Oxford; Oxford University Press, 1967) 184.

[134] John Tetzel, an unscrupulous Dominican sub commissionaire, regarded himself as an extremely successful salesman, boasting that he had saved more souls through Indulgences than St Peter himself, through the Gospel. Tetzel's usual campaign started as he sent his advanced agents into town several weeks before his scheduled arrival. These agents would prepare the town and its people for the festive occasion. Tetzel was met at the city gate by a parade that proceeded to the town square, where the first service was held. So a record crowd might be attracted, Tetzel preached on hell as his agents built a roaring bonfire. For the second service the parade proceeded to the largest church or cathedral where Tetzel preached on Purgatory. He asked the audience if they could hear the anguishing cries of their poor parents there, while their children were calmly enjoying their inheritance on earth. Tetzel's third sermon was on Heaven in which he contrasted the saved and the eternally damned. "How sweet were the souls in heaven in contrast to the suffering of the poor souls in hell! Now the audience was fully conditioned for the sale of the sacred wares." (See Myconious, *History of the Reformation*. [Liepsburg; Liepsburg Press, 1718] 17-20.) On January 22, 1517, Tetzel began selling Indulgences in Martin Luther's territory. According to Luther's statement, people flocked to him from Wittenberg as though they were "insane" and "possessed." (Erwin Iserloh, *History of the Church* [New York; Crossroads, 1986] 46.)

replacing God's grace with good works, saving faith with letters of Indulgence, and Holy Scripture with the papal bull.[135] The Indulgence, they preached, reduced the value of the cross, negated Jesus, and cheapened redemption into a works salvation, and even worse, if one you did not want to work, it was for sale.[136] It was against this background that the slogan was

---

[135] On October 31, 1517, Luther nailed his *95 Theses* to the Church door confident he would have papal support as he exposed the problems of Indulgence trafficking. He summarized his position is his first thesis: Our Lord Jesus Christ in saying 'Repent ye,' meant the whole life of the faithful to be an act of repentance." (See H. Bettenson, "The Ninety-Five Theses" in *Documents of the Christian Church*, 185.) It was therefore impossible to harmonize the current teachings and practices of Indulgences with the scriptures. As the real counterpart to penance was not a letter of Indulgence but forgiveness, which rests solely with God every Christian who feels this inner contrition of heart already has God's forgiveness, and with it the perfect remission of guilt and pain, without the purchase of any Indulgence. The real danger of the whole Indulgence trade, Luther continued, lay in the tendency of the gullible masses to put their complete trust in the saving merit of an Indulgence letter, instead of the "sacrosanct gospel of the glory and grace of God;" "the true treasure of the church." (See Henry Bettenson, "The Ninety-Five Theses" in *Documents of the Christian Church* 189.) "Before a fortnight has passed, these theses had spread throughout Germany and in four weeks throughout all Christendom. It was as though the angels themselves were the messengers carrying the news to all peoples." (Myconious, *History of the Reformation,* 17-20.) Rome countered Luther's writings with open denunciations that called on to Arise and purge his vineyard of this "rude German wild boar." (Great Britain, *Diplomatic Documents and Papal Bulls* (New York; Kraus, 1963) 1758.) The papal bull *Exsurge Domini*, condemned forty-one of Luther's ninety-five theses as "heretical, scandalous, false, offensive to pious ears, misleading to simple folk, and contrary to Catholic doctrine." (Ibid.) Luther was given sixty days to recant and burn his heretical writings; if he did not, on the sixty-first day he would be automatically excommunicated. Luther responded to the bull by disposing of it in a bonfire built by his students outside the Wittenberg city gate on December 10, 1520, where he not only burned the bull, but a copy of the Canon Law as well.

[136] The counter-Reformation Council of Trent in its decree *On Indulgences* (Sess. XXV) declared: "In granting Indulgences the Council desires that moderation be observed in accordance with the ancient approved custom of the Church, lest through excessive ease ecclesiastical discipline be weakened; and further, seeking to correct the abuses that have crept in . . . it decrees that all criminal gain therewith connected shall be entirely done away with as a source of grievous abuse among the Christian people; and as to other disorders arising from superstition, ignorance, irreverence, or any cause whatsoever – since these, on account of the widespread corruption, cannot be removed by special prohibitions – the Council lays upon each bishop the duty of finding out such abuses as exist in his own diocese, of bringing them before the next provincial synod, and of reporting them, with the assent of the other bishops, to the Roman Pontiff, by whose authority and prudence measures will be taken for the

preached; grace alone. In their vehement rejection of the corrupt sale of Indulgences Martin Luther and his fellow reformers[137] rejected with it the sacrament of penance and eventually Purgatory[138] and later all fellowship with the dead as well.

---

welfare of the Church at large, so that the benefit of Indulgences may be bestowed on all the faithful by means at once pious, holy, and free from corruption." In 1567 Pius V canceled all grants of Indulgences involving any fees or other financial transactions. The Vatican II document entitled *Sacramentum Paenitentiae* (Pope Paul VI) reiterated the teaching of the Council of Trent concerning the precept of individual confession, but changed the name of the sacrament to Reconciliation and the rite from its old form of 1) sorrow for sins, 2) confession, 3) absolution, and 4) amendment or satisfaction; to a new form which includes the sign of the cross, a welcome by the priest, scripture reading, confession, act(s) of penance, prayer of sorrow, absolution, and praise of God.

[137] Calvin understood Roman penance as an attempt to "plug the leak so no more grace runs out" or grabbing hold of the "second plank after shipwreck," (John Calvin, *The Institutes of the Christian Religion* ed. John T. McNeill, trans. Ford Lewis Battles (Philadelphia: The Westminster Press, 1960) 1464-5) and as such he believed it to undermine Baptism, and therefore the gospel itself. He claims: the Romanists have severed the exercise of the keys from Baptism, and "this error has provided us with the fictitious sacrament of penance."(*Institutes*, 1306) Calvin claims that the power of the keys (in this context, the power to declare forgiveness) depends upon Baptism: "We see therefore that absolution has reference to Baptism." (*Institutes* 1306) Hence, absolution is not a stand-alone sacrament; it is a renewal of one's Baptism and the proper exercise of the keys – absolution rather than penance – looses us from our sins. It regularly reminds us of and reapplies to us the Baptismal promise of forgiveness. "Therefore, there is no doubt that all pious folk throughout life, whenever they are troubled by a consciousness of their faults, may venture to remind themselves of their Baptism, that from it they may be confirmed in assurance of that sole and perpetual cleansing which we have in Christ's blood." (See *Institutes* 1306-7) Baptism, not penance, is the believer's refuge after sin; and Baptism is best remembered by the pastor's declaration of absolution. So, weekly confession of sin and absolution are to be understood within the framework of Baptismal justification, in which absolution, "Your sins are forgiven, take heart" (*Institutes*, 639) harkens back to Baptism. It recalls, reapplies, and renews one's Baptism, providing "continual and unceasing forgiveness of sins even unto death." (See "True Relation of Baptism to Repentance" in *Institutes*, 1306.) Whereas the schoolmen taught that justification *begins* in Baptism and *continues* in penance, Calvin taught that the *once and for all* justification received in Baptism is *freshly enjoyed* through absolution.

[138] Luther concluded that the account of the sin offering by which Judas Maccabees made atonement for the sins of his kinsmen (2 Maccabees 12:43-45) lacked authority because the book in which it appeared did not properly belong to the canon of Scripture. He further concluded that Paul's statement that some will be saved but only through fire (1 Corinthians 3:15) referred not to Purgatory but to the fires of

Luther's Theological Critique of Indulgences

The Indulgence controversy was the springboard that projected Luther into the scholastic debate over the nature of justification and the extent of the human person's natural knowledge of God.[139] Medieval religious life was organized around the premise, popularized by Thomas Aquinas that persons cooperated in the attainment of their salvation when they freely preformed good works in a state of grace.[140] Thus understood, salvation became the just due to persons who did their moral best within the state of grace. Entrance into the state of grace however, remained "God's exclusive and special gift, not man's achievement, and it was the indispensable foundation for man's moral cooperation."[141] Yet moral cooperation was a necessity for salvation, that is, doing the best one can with the aid of grace. Eternal life was the reward for those who did their part morally cooperating with the grace with which they were preveniently infused.

Into this milieu came the late medieval Ockhamists or nominalists who questioned whether persons who loved God because he moved them to do so by a special infusion of his grace really love God freely? Added to that, biblical injunctions such as the words of Jesus in Luke 11:9 "So I say to you, ask, and it will be given you, seek and you will find, knock and the door will be opened for you"[142] indicated to them that persons had both the capability and responsibility to take the initiative for their salvation. These insights and

---

violent resistance through which the preaching of the gospel must pass. See Luther, *Disavowal of Purgatory* in Weimar, *The Works of Martin Luther* (1883) 30—II, 369.

[139] See Luther's *Disputation Against Scholastic Theology* of September 4, 1517. For an excellent overview of the mental world of Martin Luther and in particular his critique of the late scholastics as the "new Pelagians" see Steven E. Ozment, *The Age of Reform (1250-1550): An Intellectual and Religious History of Late Medieval and Reformation Europe* (New Haven: Yale University Press, 1980) 233-235.

[140] The reconciliation of the sinner with God has as a further consequence, the revival of those merits which he had obtained before committing grievous sin. Good works performed in the state of grace deserve a reward from God, but this is forfeited by mortal sin, so that if the sinner should die unforgiven his good deeds avail him nothing. So long as he remains in sin, he is incapable of meriting: even works which are good in themselves are, in his case, worthless: they cannot revive, because they never were alive. But once his sin is cancelled by penance, he regains not only the state of grace but also the entire store of merit which had, before his sin, been placed to his credit.

[141] Steve Ozment, *The Age of Reform*, 233.

[142] See also "Return to me and I will return to you" (Zechariah 1:3) and "Draw near to God and he will draw near to you" (James 4:8).

the desire to protect free will led the Ockhamists to modify the traditional scheme. Now the initial state of grace was not a free gift of God but an appropriate reward to those who did their best (loving others above themselves) in a state of nature. So, human persons find themselves in a state of nature with reason and free will; doing one's best according to one's natural moral ability; one then gains a fitting reward form God, an infusion of grace; morally cooperating with it, one does the best one can with the aid of grace to win as one's just due, the reward of eternal life. In essence Ockhamists theologians taught "that God meant for people to acquire grace as semi-merit within the state of nature and to earn salvation as full merit within a state of grace by doing their moral best."[143] This translated down to the populace that individuals could at least initiate their own salvation and at most earn it completely.

Based on his personal experience and his study of the Bible and Augustine, Luther argued that human beings by nature lack the freedom of will to do any sort of a moral best that would win them a reward from God. Luther soon realized that his battle was against the perennial heresy of Pelagius, who Augustine, to whose rule Luther was sworn, had fought 1200 years earlier. Luther traced the "new-Pelagian"[144] theology of Ockham, Scotus, and Biel to their infatuation with Aristotle who had taught that moral virtues are gained by practice and effort, that is, by habit. One becomes virtuous by performing virtuous acts.[145] This led Luther to condemn "the whole of Aristotle's Ethics [as] an enemy of grace"[146] and even more resolutely to denounce Indulgences, the papal powers of binding and loosing, and Purgatory, as well as severely criticize the then current practices of the sacrament of confession-absolution.

In the end the reformers unanimously rejected the Roman doctrine of Purgatory, with its accompanying prayers for the departed and the whole system of temporal satisfaction for sin. This was partially based on the ancient theological understanding of Christ's sacrifice upon the cross, and

---

[143] Steve E. Ozment, *The Age of Reform*, 234. Within this design, however, it was not technically human activity that secured one's salvation but God's willingness to value human effort so highly.

[144] See Luther, *Disputation Against Scholastic Theology*, thesis 5-8, 27-20, 28-30 in *Luther's Works* 1, 224-226.

[145] See Aristotle, *Nichomachean Ethics* 1103a-1103b, trans, David Ross (New York: Oxford, 1998) 28-29.

[146] Luther, *Disputation Against Scholastic Theology*, thesis 41.

the Christians Baptism into that event "for the remission of sins."[147] This remission of sins is a larger concept than that of mere forgiveness. Suppose, for example, a person steals from you ten dollars. You forgive him, but you still ask for your ten dollars back. Indeed, repentance demands the person comply and if able return the money. However, this is not so with the remission of the sin, the reformers concluded. Christ's remission was full and complete. No work that any person can achieve or offer will please God so much as Christ's sacrifice. His death was purposely intended not only to forgive sin, but to pay the price for sin as well. Christ Jesus remitted the full payment due for sin, so that we would not have to.

With the full remission of sin excised in Christ's sacrifice on the cross punitive satisfaction on earth and beyond in Purgatory was also expunged. In their thoroughly Christocentric theology what now would the reformers say of the Communion of Saints? Indeed, the question for the reformers now becomes what need is there at all for the saints, what role, if any, do they play in the kingdom of God, and what spiritual profit is there in their prayers? Finally, with the temptation of monetary profits so prevalent and oft and easily abused, can the reformers allow any teaching of Purgatory to stand, and without Purgatory what happens in that intermediate period between death and resurrection?

---

[147] See Acts 2:38 and Hebrews 10:18 as well as the affirmation of the Nicene Creed (357) "We acknowledge one Baptism for the remission of sins." See Schaff, *The Creeds of Christendom*, 1:28.

Chapter Two

The Protestant Rejection of the Catholic/Orthodox Understanding of the Communion of Saints and its Results

The Phrase and Its Meaning

Although the doctrine of the Communion of Saints was not inserted into the Apostle's Creed until about the middle of the fifth century, it is substantially contained in the teaching of Jesus (particulary his synonomous use of the terms "Kingdom of Heaven" and "Kingdom of God" in the synoptic gospels) and the letters of Paul. In effect the doctrine sets forth the meaning of Christian fellowship as it represents the Church's chief practice which is prayer. This explains why the apostolic affirmation "we believe in . . . the Communion of Saints" follows and is not before "we believe in . . . the Church." The order of the Creed is significant in that it shows us the Communion of Saints is a consequence of the Church or perhaps more correctly, the negative converse, the Church is not an outgrowth the Communion of Saints. So the doctrine of the Communion of Saints serves to expound and elucidate the doctrine of the Church.

A Description of the Church

In this explanatory function the Communion of Saints has traditionally been understood in three ways. First in its most basic meaning "Communion of Saints" is another way of describing the Church on earth. Herein the saints are not the ideal and exalted figures of whom we regularly think but what might be described as saints without halos. That is, they are believers who struggle with sin and failure but who—through the call of Christ—have turned their backs on the sinful world as they endeavor in everyday life to follow the way of Christ. As members in the Church of God they are "called to be saints"[1] "in Christ Jesus"[2] "God's chosen ones, holy and beloved."[3]

A Participation in Holy Things

A second meaning of the creedal phrase Communion of Saints refers to participation in holy things[4] within the earthly Church. These holy things are the sacraments, especially the Eucharist as it is the center and heart of liturgical life. The congregation is the place where the Word is rightly proclaimed and the Sacraments rightly administered, "and the fellowship of prayer takes place, not to mention the inward gifts and works, which are the meaning of these outward ones."[5] So the holy things and the holy people belong together and vice-versa.

A Communion with the Saints in Heaven

A third meaning of the creedal phrase Communion of Saints refers to the earthy Church's communion with the heavenly Church, that is, the saints in heaven. These are the martyrs, who gave their life for the faith, and confessors, who lived their life for the faith, whom the Church believes to be in God's consummation. These saints stand as guarantors of the future consummation of all Christians for which they pray and anxiously await.[6] This connotation is actually the most ancient explanation of the creedal phrase. The oldest commentators understood the Communion of Saints to be "communion with the saints in heaven but afterwards it assumed a wider meaning: the fellowship of all true believers living and departed."[7]

---

[1] 1 Corinthians 1:2.
[2] Philippians 1:1.
[3] Colossians 3:12.
[4] In this conception the Latin phrase *communio sanctorum* is understood as neuter and rendered *holy thing*, see page 298 of this work. Barth writes: "Is there not intended here a remarkable ambiguity in a deeper sense? For only when both interpretations are retained side by side, does the matter receive its full, good meaning." (Karl Barth, *Dogmatics in Outline*, [New York: Harper & Row Publishers, 1959] 144.)
[5] Ibid.
[6] Revelation 6:10.
[7] Phillip Schaff, *The Creeds of Christendom*, 22.

The Creedal Phrase in the Theology of the Reformers

Stemming from the centrality of their message of forgiveness of sins, eschatology plays an insignificant role in the theology of the reformers. The reformers stressed so much the affirmation of the forgiveness of sins that anything that could be said concerning resurrection and/or eternal life was simply understood as already stated within that creedal statement.[8]

The greatest and most influential of the reformers, Luther, Calvin, and Zwingli kept the Apostle's Creed without excising from it belief in the Communion of Saints. Each with his own nuance interpreted the affirmation as an explanatory extension expounding the previous affirmation "We believe in . . . the holy catholic Church." This was the primary position of Luther, who brought "the community of saints out of heaven and down to earth."[9] The Lutheran Churches explained the Communion of Saints as the Church's "union with Jesus Christ in the one true faith,"[10] or as "the congregation of saints and true believers."[11] The Communion of Saints was the creedal mode of speaking about the priesthood of all believers, a major emphasis in Luther's theology. After affirming belief in the tangible, historic reality of the true Church manifested in the Word rightly preached and the Sacraments rightly administered, the Creed goes on to affirm, within that holy Church, the priesthood of all believers as it describes an earthly community of intercessors, helpers, sharers, and burden-bearers. "The fact that we are all priests and kings means that each of us as Christians may go before God and intercede for one another."[12] In due course, however, Luther excluded from Church practice prayers to the saints because, he said, the scripture "propoundeth unto us one Christ, the Mediator, Propitiatory, High-Priest, and Intercessor"[13] "Turn your attention away from the dead toward the living. The living saints are your neighbors. . . . Direct your help toward them."[14]

---

[8] See Barth, *Credo*, trans. Robert McAfee Brown (New York: Charles Scribner's Sons, 1962) 161.
[9] Paul Althaus, *The Theology of Martin Luther*, trans. Robert C. Shultz (Philadelphia, Fortress Press 1966) 298.
[10] Luther's Short Catechism (which superseded the longer Catechism of 1528 becoming the standard instruction for Protestant Christians in Germany) in Martin Luther, *Luther's Primary Works*, ed., Henry Wace and C. A. Buchheim (Lonon, J. Murray, 1883).
[11] *Augsburg Confession*, III, 12.
[12] Martin Luther, WA 10/3, 308.
[13] *Augsburg Confession*, III, 26.
[14] Martin Luther, WA 10/3, 407.

John Calvin agreed with Luther that the creedal phrase was "added to express more clearly the unity which exists among the members of the Church"[15] but went further in insisting that the "Communion of Saints" was more than a definition of the Church, but that it implied a "society of Christ on the principle that whatever benefits God conferred upon them [possessions and graces] they should in turn share with one another."[16] Moreover, these "benefits ... are for the good and salvation of every Church, because they all have communion together."[17] So for Calvin, not only did the Communion of Saints exhort believers to "have all things in common"[18] but it affirms as well that the Church although seemingly divided, especially so at the time of the Reformation, was in fact still the one true Church. Calvin's view is followed in the Heidelberg Catechism and in the Gallican Confession where communion is made to mean the efforts of believers to mutually strengthen themselves in the reverence and love of God. Not to be included in these efforts, however, were Purgatory, Masses for the dead, or the invocation of the saints which were touted by Calvin as "a deadly fiction of Satan, which nullifies the cross of Christ, inflicts unbearable contempt on God's mercy, and overturns and destroys faith."[19]

Hesitating to condemn prayers for the dead, Zwingli proclaimed he did "not despise the saints and sacraments"[20] but rejected prayers "to saints or through them"[21] as injurious to Christ the sole mediator. He did however recognize the saints as "members of Christ and friends of God, who have gloriously overcome the flesh and the world; we love them as brethren, and

---

[15] *A Reformulated Catechism taken from the Geneva Catechism circa 1560* A Dialogue between the Minister and the child, by John Calvin *Calvin's Geneva Catechism of 1542/1545.*

[16] John Calvin, *Institutes of The Christian Religion*, IV, 1, 3, ed. John T. McNeill, trans. Ford L. Battles (Philadelphia: The Westminster Press, 1960) 1014.

[17] In his Analysis of the Westminster Confession Phillip Schaff concludes "Presbyterians therefore act in perfect consistency with their Confession if they take a leading part in all Bible Societies, Tract Societies, the Evangelical Alliance, and other catholic societies. They are among the most liberal of orthodox denominations in the support of these societies." Phillip Schaff, *The Creeds of Christendom*, Three Volumes (Grand Rapids, MI: Baker Books, 1931) 775.

[18] Acts 2:44.

[19] John Calvin, *Institutes of The Christian Religion*, III, 5, 6, 676.

[20] Huldreich Zwingli, *The Exposition of the Christian Faith to King Francis I* in Phillip Schaff, *The Creeds of Christendom*, 369.

[21] Henry Bullinger, The Second Helvetic Confession, A.D. 1566, in Phillip Schaff, *The Creeds of Christendom*, 398.

hold them up as examples of faith and virtue, desiring to dwell with them eternally in heaven, and to rejoice with them in Christ."[22]

The Anglican Confessions are often a conflicting compromise of Lutheran, Calvin, and Catholic theology. The Thirty-nine Articles reject "the Romish Doctrine concerning Purgatory, Pardons, Worshipping and Adoration as well of Images as of Relics, and also Invocation of Saints", because they see in it "a fond thing, vainly invented, and grounded upon no warranty of Scripture, but rather repugnant to the Word of God".[23] The Methodist Articles of Religion (1784) as well as the Reformed Episcopal Articles of Religion (1875) follow suit as do the Philadelphia Baptist Confession (1688) and in the Confession of the Cumberland Presbyterian Church (1829).

The Reformers Dismember the Body

In their explanation of the Communion of Saints the Reformers dismembered the body of Christ. Not only or necessarily in their division from Rome but essentially and certainly in their separation of earthy pilgrims from the saints in heaven. The same reformers who constantly called upon the living tradition of Augustine refused to acknowledge in many cases his true life in glory. And while they claimed to be his true inheritors they acknowledged only a historic interaction between themselves and the great saint. As they received theses reforming gifts from the saints of the past they recognized only their own particular part in that grace filled transaction. As they evermore emphasized their conception of justification as an individualistic act of faith instead of an actual rebirth from a common Father, the second Adam, and a corresponding incorporation into Christ, the head of the mystical body, they found little or no room for the reciprocal sharing of spiritual blessings between the saints of heaven and the saints of earth. Moreover, they reformed the definition of the Communion of Saints to bring it in line with the Protestant concept of the Church as a community of like-minded persons bound together by a common faith and pursuit and by the ties of Christian sympathy, but in no way organized and interdependent members of the same body.

---

[22] Henry Bullinger, "The Second Helvetic Confession," A.D. 1566, in Phillip Schaff, *The Creeds of Christendom*, 398.
[23] See Philip Schaff, *The Creeds of Christendom* Vol. III (Grand Rapids, Michigan: Baker Book House, 1931) 501.

The Historic Reasons for the Reformer's Rejections

The Reformation separated the living and the dead both spiritually and physically. First, the defining doctrines of the Reformation separated the souls of the dead from the living; and second the Reformation propagated the ongoing removal of the bodies of the dead from the spaces of the living. These two separations are parallel and fundamental to the Reformation.

Although varying greatly according to local customs, in general, the intercessions of the living were a key component of the rituals of dying. So much so that it could be said that medieval death rituals did not separate the dead from the living but drew them closer together marking death itself a transition within the community of saints. By the sixteenth century the rituals practiced by Augustine at his mother's passing had evolved into an elaborate and systematized Christian rite. When someone was about to die their family and close friends prayed the Our Father, the Ave Maria, and especially the Creed, and called on God, the Blessed Virgin Mary, and all the saints to intercede for the sick person and their soul. Dying Christians received from the priest "the last rites," confession, communion, and extreme unction (anointing with oil). Immediately following death the body was washed with Holy Water, blessed with a consecrated light, and commended to God. The body was then carried in procession to the Church or church yard where it would benefit from at least one funeral Mass, most often preformed in the presence of the body before burial, when it was laid in the ground facing the rising sun. The close proximity of the grave to the altar served as a visible reminder that would continue to solicit the prayers of the living. Masses for the dead were often sung on the seventh and thirtieth days following, on All Souls' Day, and on the anniversary of the funeral.[24] The excommunicated, heretics, suicides, and criminals were most often denied Christian burial in the Church yard, "the exclusion of their bodies reflecting the separation of their souls from salvation and the Christian community."[25]

---

[24] The Orthodox Church's practice grew into a forty-day memorial, that is, a daily commemoration at the Liturgy for the course of forty days. If the funeral was at a church where there were no daily services, the relatives themselves took care to order the forty-day memorial where there were daily services. As there is constant prayer in Jerusalem and other holy sites, families often sent contributions to their monasteries for commemorations. The forty-day memorial remains common practice today and should be begun immediately after death, when the soul is especially in need of help in prayer. See Orthodox Toll Houses on page 95 of this work.

[25] Craig M. Koslofsky, *The Reformation of the Dead: Death and Ritual in Early Modern Germany, 1450—1700* (New York: St. Martin's Press Inc., 2000) 24.

This peculiar Christian practice of laying the dead to rest in consecrated churchyard, usually in the center of the village or town, reversed the longstanding practice of ancient Jewish and Roman culture as well as that of the Germanic tribes, in which the deceased, if not cremated, were buried outside the bounds of the city or settlement. This was the practice of early Christianity until the mid-fifth century. As the saints themselves, that is, their relics came to reside among the living the ordinary Christian dead followed. This slow reversal occurred as persons desired to be buried beside the shrines of the martyrs. The shrines became basilica, which were eventually taken into and/or increasingly built within the city walls. Urban churchyard burial in due course became the established norm with the holy or privileged eventually being entombed within the church itself.[26] So, in medieval society the dead were present to the living not only spiritually but also physically. The Christian community was one of both the living and the dead. This fact is seen most clearly in that the burial of the dead in the midst of the living.[27]

Contemporaries of the Reformation, however, often complained of overcrowded, overfilled, and overextended churchyards which because of the stench associated with them were increasingly considered a public health hazard. Population growth within the walls of a city served to fuel opinion that a progressively larger churchyard was a misuse of valuable land. The establishment of new non-Church related cemetery sites "that separated the bodies of the dead from the world of the living was an essential cultural precondition of the German Reformation as well as one of its most profound consequences."[28] This separation of the living and dead meshed effortlessly with their theological separation in the reformers growing rejection of Purgatory, as well as prayers, suffrages, and Masses for the dead. Moreover, the political reformists vigorously promoted this separation seeing rightly that it would weaken traditional clerical intercession for the dead and with it the financial basis of much of the Church.

Purgatory, as earlier stated, emerged at the intersection of three distinct ideas of the Christian tradition: first was prayer for the dead; second was the idea of postmortem purification as a part of the process of salvation; and third, the localization of this postmortem purification in a unique

---

[26] See Craig M. Koslofsky, *The Reformation of the Dead: Death and Ritual in Early Modern Germany, 1450—1700* (New York: St. Martin's Press Inc., 2000) 40-77.
[27] See Ejnar Dyggve, "The Origin of the Urban Churchyard," *Classica et Mediaevalia* 8, 2 (1952) 147-158; and Peter Brown, *The Cult of the Saints* (Chicago, 1981) 1-22.
[28] See Craig M. Koslofsky, *The Reformation of the Dead: Death and Ritual in Early Modern Germany, 1450—1700*, 41.

eschatological time and place.[29] The doctrine of Purgatory had systematized Christian intercession for the dead. Hell was the abode of apostates and unrepentant sinners; heaven the home of martyrs and saints; and Purgatory the porch of heaven, where those who had been baptized into the Christian community and were therefore absolved of their sin but who had not sufficiently cast off their sin in this life and therefore still owed penance would work through fire.[30] Officially promulgated by the Church at the Council of Lyons in 1274 and of Florence in 1439, Purgatory was the state of or location where appropriate satisfaction integral to the penitential cycle could be carried out after death.

Intercessory Masses[31] offered for the dead were the most common way to shorten the sentences of those in Purgatory. It was a logical

---

[29] Jacques Le Goff, *The Birth of Purgatory*, trans. Author Goldhammer (Chicago, 1984) 52-95, 154-176. Herein Le Goff attempts to define the birth of Purgatory as a specific linguistic development in which the noun *purgatorium* is used to denote a fixed place. This distinct usage, he argues, occurs in the late twelfth century and represents a marked shift in mental, ideological and religious structures from binary (heaven and hell) to ternary (heaven, Purgatory, hell) systems. While this thesis is disputed (see Graham Robert Edwards, "Purgatory: 'Birth' or Evolution?" *Journal of Ecclesiastical History* 36, 4 (1985) 173—186) the value of his argument lies in its identification of the various elements that combined and as the doctrine of Purgatory evolved into place during the twelfth century. Le Goff further notes the social and moral reasons behinds the rise of Purgatory. A post plague city dwelling middle class stood between the peasants and the Lords demanding a more rational treatment in this life and the next. The move from "trial by ordeal" to proof of guilt or innocence substantiated by witnesses and confession marked the growing concern in both secular and canon law for more equitable ways of determining guilt or innocence. In this same manner, Purgatory provided a more equitable conception of the hereafter. For more on the evolution of Purgatory see also Barbra Newman, "Hildegard of Bingen and the 'Birth of Purgatory'" *Mystics Quarterly* 19 (1993) 90-97.

[30] The development of Purgatory also gave the Church more influence in and control of the political arena. The radical Millenarians had used the doctrine of the two realms, heaven and hell, to their political advantage. They incited the common people to demand reform with their claim that God would damn to hell kings and lords who crushed their subjects, but that the martyred subjects would be instantly translated to paradise. The introduction of Purgatory, however, put ones post worldly state in the hands of the Church. See Norman Cohn, *The Pursuit of the Millennium: Revolutionary Millenarians and Mystical Anarchists of the Middle Ages*, rev. and enl. ed., Temple Smith, 1970.

[31] The commercialization of the Mass relied on the belief of many medieval Christians that special favors could be secured from God by having the Eucharist offered on one's behalf. Usually celebrated in private, and many times by the priest alone, these votive masses (form the Latin word for promised or devoted) came to

progression to assume that if one mass said at the burial of the deceased is effective, and if the deceased are helped by the mass of All Souls and indeed all masses said on the holy ground in which they are interred, then successive masses offered especially for them would be especially effective in reducing ones time in Purgatory. This practice of successive masses for the dead led the German princes to submit grievances to the papal representatives at the Diet of Worms (1521). Among them was the charge that "the common people are burdened with intercessory masses and suffrages."[32] These created what amounted to perpetual rent on church graves to pay for clerical intercession for dead loved ones.[33]

Medieval families understandably wanted to do what they could to help their suffering members move from the fires of Purgatory to the bliss of heaven. The flames of their desires were fanned by zealous pastors longing to spur their people on to a higher spiritual life who devised stories that explained and expounded upon the purifying punishments souls there underwent.[34] These in turn gave rise to popular literature recounting visions of, and voyages to, the next world; including both sermons, which described its fire as "so hot, that if an anvil were thrown in, it would melt in a blink of an eye,"[35] and popular vernacular poetry, the most sublime of which is the Florentine Dante's *Divine Comedy: Purgatory*.[36]

---

be celebrated not only at funerals, but at weddings, and throughout the year for protection against disease and bad weather, for abundant crop yields, and even for the safe delivery of calves. As the practice increased in popularity priests began to charge a fee for such services and masses were sold to people willing to pay for the benefits they believed would result from services rendered. Luther raged against votive masses saying: "I regard the preaching and selling of the mass as a sacrifice or good work as the greatest of all abominations." *Luther's Works*, 55 volumes, ed. Jaroslav Pelikan (St. Louis: Concordia / Philadelphia: Fortress Press, 1955-1975) hereafter abbreviated LW, 37: 370-371.

[32] See Article 62 of the Diet of Worms, in B. J. Kidd, *Documents illustrative of the Continental Reformation* (Oxford, The Clarendon Press, 1911) Vol. 8, No. 42.

[33] See Lawrence P. Buck, "The Reformation, Purgatory, and Perpetual Rents in the Revolt of 1525 at Frankfort am Main" in *Pietas et Societas: New Trends in Reformation Social History. Essays in Memory of Harold J. Grimm*, ed. Phillip N. Bebb and Kyle C. Sessions (Kirksville, MO: Truman State University Press, 1985) 23-34.

[34] See Gregory the Great, *Dialogues*, trans. Odo Zimmerman, Fathers of the Church 39 (Washington: Catholic University of America Press, 1959).

[35] Johannes Pauli, *Schimpf und Ernst. Die alteste Ausgabe von 1522*, ed Johannes Bolte (Berlin 1924) 1: 276. See also Arlene Epp Pearsall, *Johannes Pauli (1450—1520) on the Church and the Clergy* (New York: Lewiston, 1994).

[36] Although the most magnificent, Dante's was not the first to recount a spiritual escapade through the underworld. Pope Gregory the Great (590-604) first

By the late 15th century the Church had developed another means to free souls from Purgatory: Indulgences for the dead. In 1475 Pope Sixtus IV issued an Indulgence for the living and the dead to benefit the Cathedral of Saintes, in France. This was the first instance of a papal Indulgence for the dead.[37] Now the bodies of the deceased need not be congruent to the altar or even in consecrated ground to benefit from rituals done in their name. A document would suffice as the tangible evidence that souls in Purgatory were helped, relieved, or their times shortened through the transfer of satisfaction from the living members to the dead members of the community.[38]

The introduction of the Indulgence for the dead swung wide open the doors to abuse. The alleviation of canonical penances through an Indulgence was easily verifiable upon the earth. If one's sin was gluttony, then an appropriate satisfaction would be a period of fasting. An Indulgence could lessen the prescribed duration of the fast from twelve weeks to three; the mitigation being offset by personal and/or community obligations as a substitute for the punishment's medicinal purpose. This, however, was not

---

popularized the stories and sermons that envisioned the purifying fires to come; the English Bede (672-735) related supernatural visions in his *Ecclesiastical History of England* ed. A. M. Sellar (New York: Kessinger Publishing, 2004); by 1180 the legend of Henry of Saltrey, a soldier who slipped into Purgatory through a cave in Lough Derg, Ireland, known as St Patrick's Purgatory, was a medieval best seller, translated into French by Jocelyn Furness in 1180,and disused by the likes of Bonaventure and Aquinas who in his discussions of ghosts and apparitions concludes that they are probably messengers from Purgatory (see *Supplement to the Third Part: Summa Theologica* 69. 3). This claim, no doubt, gave rise to the "ghost-stories" refuted by Luther in his preaching as well as his *Open Letter to the Christian Nobility* (See Bruce Gordon and Peter Marshall, eds. *The Place of the Dead: Death and Remembrance in Late Medieval and Early Modern Europe* (New York: Cambridge University Press, 2000). For more on Dante's literary forbearers see John C. Barnes and Jennifer Petrie, ed. *Dante and his Literary Precursors* (Dublin, Ireland: Four Courts Press, 2004).

[37] Indulgences had been known in practice since the mid fourteenth century, but it was not until the mid fifteenth century that theologians and cannon lawyers began to debate whether the Pope could free a soul from Purgatory through an Indulgence.

[38] This distribution should not be understood as a sort of automatic transfer, as if we were speaking of things. It is instead the expression of the Church's full confidence of being heard by the Father when—in view of Christ's merits and, by his gift, those of Our Lady and the saints—she asks him to mitigate or cancel the painful aspect of punishment by fostering its medicinal aspect through other channels of grace. In the unfathomable mystery of divine wisdom, this gift of intercession can also benefit the faithful departed, who receive its fruits in a way appropriate to their condition. (John Paul II, *Enchiridion Indulgentiarum, Normae de Indulgentiis*, (Libreria Editrice Vaticana, 1999) 24.)

so easily verifiable for the souls in Purgatory. While one might absolutely trust the effectiveness of the Indulgence to lessen a soul's stay, one could not, with any assurance, discern how long a soul was sentenced to suffer or, apart from canonization, identify when a soul had left Purgatory and entered heaven and therefore no longer needed sacrifices made on their behalf. This meant that as long as the memory of the dead endured and even beyond their living counterparts could pay for Masses or purchase Indulgences on their behalf. It also meant that those who had reason to expect an especially long sentence in Purgatory could endow Masses to be said on their behalf and Indulgences to be purchased after their death. So that although it may not have been the official teaching of the Church popular practice often saw the impious rich use a significant portion of their ill-gotten gains to provide for postmortem satisfaction. And even the poor often sought to substitute an easily purchased Indulgence for the harder work of sanctity. Financially strapped Church officials too often looked the other way or even promoted such misuse and misunderstandings in order to fund the construction and furnishing of great Church buildings or for other less virtuous and many times simonial acts.

Attempts to Reform Purgatory

While it may seem a misnomer, according to its most basic definition, the doctrine of Purgatory does not purge or purify but simply provides a place where satisfaction incomplete upon death can be completed. However in the mid fifteenth century Wessel Gansfort[39] offered a theology that attempted to reshape the Church's thinking about Purgatory. In his work entitled *Farrago* Gansfort speculates that the fire of Purgatory "does not torment, but rather cleanses the inward [person] of the impurity which accompanies him [or her] even when released from the flesh."[40] Purgatorial fire he suggests is the "zeal of burning love of the soul for God."[41] He bases his argument on 1 Corinthians 3:11-16 where Paul writes "Now if anyone builds on the foundation with gold, silver, precious stones, wood, hay, straw—the work of each builder will become visible, for the Day will disclose it, because it will be revealed with fire, and the fire will test what sort of work each has done. If what has been built on the foundation survives, the builder

---

[39] Also called John Wessel.
[40] Wessel Ganfort, *Opera* (829) *in Wessel Ganfort, Life and Writings, Principal Works*, ed. Edward W. Miller, trans. Jarred W. Scudder, 2 Vols. (New York: G. P. Putnam's sons, 1917) 2:281.
[41] Ganfort, *Opera* (833) Miller and Scudder, *Principal Works*, 2:281.

will receive a reward. If the work is burned up the builder will suffer loss; the builder will be saved but only through fire."

In opposition to an infernal Purgatory of fire and suffering Gansfort proposed that it is only the spiritual fire of reason that can really purify; materially fire, he asserted, can only torment. He goes on to point out that Church Tradition no where teaches that suffering in itself purifies, reminding his readers that "the most blessed and holy Lord Jesus endured a thousand torments and yet was in no way purified."[42] "To be made like God and to be united with him in love is to be purified."[43] This celestialization of Purgatory can best be understood through the eschatological metaphor of darkness, dawn, and daylight.[44] In our life upon the earth "everything is done by lamplight". After death "the saints are freed from all their infirmities . . . and as happy wayfarers they pass into the dawn of the approaching day, until the sun shall rise clearly before them."[45] Herein the dawn is a spiritual Purgatory in which the faithful are gradually enlightened until they reach the full light of God's presence. This being the case, intercession aimed at the release of souls from Purgatory would be undesirable as it would mean the end of their enlightenment. Thinking about Purgatory in this way sharply decreases opportunities for clerical abuses of the penitential system without ending all prayers for the dead as the Church could continue to pray that their members beyond the veil be "illumined by the sun of righteousness."[46]

This seems to have been Luther's initial take on Purgatory. He first criticized the Roman Catholic doctrine in the context of the Indulgence controversy, but he did not deny its existence. In the *Resolutiones Disputationem de Indulgentiarum Virtute* (1518) to his ninety-five theses he stated "It is certain to me that Purgatory exists."[47] What Luther did deny was that souls in

---

[42] Ganfort, *Opera* (830) Miller and Scudder, *Principal Works*, 2:283.

[43] Miller and Scudder, *Principal Works*, 2:292.

[44] The careful reader of Dante's *Divine Comedy* will notice that Dante enters hell in darkness, Purgatory at Dawn, and paradise in the full light of day.

[45] Ganfort, *Opera* (855-856) Miller and Scudder, *Principal Works*, 2:294.

[46] According to his student, Master John of Amsterdam, Gansfort "did not wish prayer to be offered for him, except in order that he be illumined by the sun of righteousness." Miller and Scudder, *Principal Works*, 1:265.

[47] *D. Martin Luthers Werke: Kritische Gesamtausgabe*, ed. J.K.F. Knaake, et al. (Weimar: Akademische Druck, 1883) hereafter abbreviated WA, 1: 555-58, 586. In a 1519 Leipzig debate, with Johann Eck Luther continued in his belief that Purgatory did indeed exist but conceded that there was no scriptural basis for it. (See Martin Luther, *Works*, 1:586.) In sermons given in 1522-23 Luther stated that he could neither deny nor affirm the existence of Purgatory, but that it was "within God's power" to purify souls after death.

Purgatory made satisfaction for unfulfilled earthly penance. He argued instead, like Gansfort, that they were purified through suffering and despair. So, sympathetic to the idea of postmortem purification, Luther sought to remove Purgatory from the jurisdiction of the Church, whom he claimed in his theses had no power to affect the state of souls there suffering. This he hoped would deny the doctrine of Indulgences which was at the root of curial financial abuses that branched all the way to Peter's Basilica.

After he broke with the Roman Church, Luther's view of Purgatory gradually shifted until he finally ruled out any intermediate state between death and the Last Judgment in favor of the doctrine of soul-sleeping.[48] He wrote "Death is called sleep in the scriptures. Just as one who falls asleep and wakes up unexpectedly the next morning not knowing what has happened, so we will suddenly rise up on the Last Day without knowing that we were in death and have passed through death."[49] Luther then began to describe Purgatory as a torment of the soul rather than a distinct location.[50] He wrote in his *Confession Concerning Christ's Supper* "I know of a Purgatory, however, in another way, but it would not be proper to teach anything about it in the church, nor on the other hand, to deal with it by means of endowments or vigils."[51] True Purgatory is being "oppressed by the sorrows of sin and God's wrath."[52] This reformed view of Purgatory as state of inner sorrow and separation from God seems more akin to Augustine's view of purgation both before and after death.[53]

Calvin too rejected Purgatory citing that the scriptures used to support it failed due to scriptural twisting and poor exegesis of the given texts.[54] He dismisses thirteen hundred years of Church tradition with the

---

[48] See his *Refutation of Purgatory*, which established his position on the soul after death. Also note that when his earlier sermons were reprinted in the 1530s, Luther removed from them every reference to Purgatory or a purgatorial state. (Julius Köstlin, *Luthers Theologie*, (Leipzig, LPS: 1901) 1: 376.

[49] WA 17, 2: 235.

[50] Martin Luther, *D. Martin Luther's Werke; kritische Gesamtausgabe* (Weimar, H. Böhlau, 1883-19), 2: 422-28.

[51] Heiko Obermann, "Luther and Mysticism," in *The Reformation in Medieval Perspective*, ed. Steven Ozment (Chicago, 1971), pp. 219-51. See also *Luther's Works*, 55 volumes, ed. Jaroslav Pelikan (St. Louis: Concordia / Philadelphia: Fortress Press, 1955-1975) hereafter abbreviated LW, 37: 369.

[52] See Luther's 1532 lectures on Psalm 51 where he refers to David's purgatorial experience in WA 40: 436; and LW, 12: 387.

[53] See RR Atwell, "From Augustine to Gregory the Great: An Evaluation of the Emergence of Purgatory," *Journal of Ecclesiastical History* 38 (1987), 173-86.

[54] Matthew 5:25-26; 12:32; Mark 3:28; 1 Corinthians 3; Revelation 5:13 and Luke 12:10. See John Calvin, *The Institutes of the Christian Religion* 3, 5, 7; 676 ff.

argument that the Church Fathers can equally be quoted against prayers for the dead, including Augustine, who was taken in by "an old woman's request, which [he] did not test by the norm of scripture; [because] he wished to be approved by others."[55] Zwingli, as well, in his *Sixty-seven Theses* declares: "The Holy Scripture knows nothing of a Purgatory after this life."[56] And further, "God alone knows the condition of the departed, and the less he has made known to us, the less we should pretend to know."[57]

The Impetus to Curb Abuses Results in the Rejection of Related Doctrines and Practices

Since the Reformation the traditional catholic concept of the Communion of Saints has been either dismissed or ignored by the Protestant Churches. If they address their rejection at all, each Reformation theologian may put forward a nuanced reason for their disregard but they generally fall into one or more of three categories which naturally follow one from the other. First, the reformers were attempting above all to reform the then current malpractices of the Church, especially the clerical abuses surrounding curial financing and the corrupt sale of Indulgences. Stopping the Church's "fishing for men's riches"[58] instead of their souls was the chief aim of the reformers. To debunk these shady transactions the reformers not only debated among themselves but preached to their parishioners[59] the faulty premises under girding what they considered a spiritually fraudulent activity.

---

[55] John Calvin, *The Institutes of the Christian Religion* 3, 5, 10; 682-683.
[56] Thesis 57: On the Sixty-seven Conclusions and the Three Disputations see Zwingli: *Werke*, I. A. 105; 153–157; in modern German and Latin, in Schaff, *Creeds of Christendom*, III, 197–207; I, 364.
[57] Theses 58-59, Ibid.
[58] Martin Luther, *Ninety-five Theses*, 66.
[59] In his *Ninety-five Theses*, numbers 42 through 51 begin either with the words "Christians must be taught" or "Christians are to be taught." Correcting the theology of the common Christian was paramount to Luther's project. The problem at hand was not just that some crooked Churchmen were knowingly allowing Indulgences to be gained under false and misguided circumstances, that is, without true contrition (see theses 35-40) but that the state of the Church was such that it was failing to properly indoctrinate its members and therefore creating a climate of ignorance where such abuses could easily occur. This causes Luther, in thesis 11, to jab at those charged with defending the faith "that the tares concerning the changing of canonical penance into penance in Purgatory seem surely to have been sown when the bishops were asleep."

A key component of this effort was their attack on the powers of the pope and especially his jurisdiction over the beyond, that is, the souls in Purgatory.

Second, growing out of their crusade against Indulgences the reformers began to question not only the validity of Purgatory, but prayer for and to the dead, as well as many other commonly held beliefs about the saints on the grounds that they lacked scriptural support. With their slogan "scripture alone"[60] the reformers did not cast off everything the Church had previously taught but insisted that all things necessary for salvation and concerning faith and life be taught in the scriptures clearly enough for the ordinary believer to find and understand. The scriptural support for Indulgences and Purgatory was vague and imprecise and passages in support of the invocation of the saints were scant. It was this plain teaching of the scriptures, the reformers claimed, that had been obscured by the additions of the Church. Now that the scriptures were more widely available and in their original languages the reformers returned to a close study of them. In their view all teachings, traditions, and practices of the Church were to be brought to the bar of the scriptures to determine if they were correct. In this way the study of the scripture itself becomes a continually reforming activity that maintains the true doctrine of the Church.[61]

Third and foremost the reformers protested that the veneration of saints bordered on idolatry and that the alleged intercessory prayers of the saints detracted from Christ's mediatorship.[62] The reformers protested that "Even if the saints do pray fervently for the church it does not follow that they should be invoked."[63] They based their opposition to such invocation on three main flaws. First that such prayer is not scripturally sound. Unlike prayer to Christ, there is no teaching in scripture which commands prayers to the saints, nor is there any promise in scripture that God will hear such

---

[60] In his 1520 treatise *On the Babylonian Captivity of the Church* Luther stated "What is asserted without the scriptures or proven revelation may be held as an opinion but need not be believed." LW, 36, 29.

[61] In this spirit Barth asserts "Dogmatics is the science in which the Church, in accordance with the state of its knowledge at different times, takes account of the content of its proclamation critically, by the standard of the Holy Scripture and under the guidance of its Confessions," (Karl Barth, *Dogmatics in Outline* (New York: Harper and Row, 1959) 9.

[62] This despite the instance of Thomas in Suppl., 72:2, ad 1 that the ministerial mediatorship of the saints does not detract from, but only enhances, the magisterial mediatorship of Christ.

[63] Phillip Melanchthon makes this argument in his *Apology of the Augsburg Confession*, article 21, 10 "The Invocation of the Saints," in *The Book of Concord*, Theodore Tappert, ed. (Philadelphia: Fortress, 1959).

prayers. Second, prayers to the saints have no epistemological basis, that is, there is no way to know that the saints hear our individual prayers. Third, but most important, they claimed that such prayer is not Christological; Jesus Christ alone is the one mediator between God and sinful humanity. As the Scriptures make plain, "there is one God, and there is one mediator between God and human beings, the human being Christ Jesus, who gave himself as a ransom for all."[64] So invoking the saints would seem to remove Christ from his unique mediating role, making him stand over against us as the judge with whom we need to be reconciled, and the saints as mediators needed to bridge the gulf. Within this framework the saints are seen as more understanding of human weakness and more approachable than the judging Jesus, who reigns in severe majesty.[65] This, in turn, gives rise to the idea that the merits of the saints can be transferred or applied to those who petition them, thus giving the saints a mediating role in redemption itself. This, the reformers objected "is completely intolerable, for it transfers to the saints honor belonging to Christ alone."[66] Moreover, and even more dangerous, the invocation of the saints causes a transfer of trust from Christ to the saints, and thus causes a distortion in the structure of faith itself. In their rejection of the invocation of the saints the reformers popularized yet another slogan: *sola Christo*—Christ alone.[67]

As their recognition that "the true treasury of the Church is the most holy gospel of the glory and grace of God,"[68] fueled their zeal to topple the Church's jurisdiction over Purgatory and thereby stop the abuses of curial financing the reformers eventually renounced not only the abuses but with them all intercessions[69] and suffrages for the dead. These included the more

---

[64] 1 Tim 2:5-6.

[65] The rise of medieval devotion to the Blessed Virgin Mary was in some ways a response to the medieval presentation of Jesus as a harsh judge. Period images emblematic of this portrayal of Christ are found most notably in Michelangelo's "The Last Judgment" (underwritten through the sale on Indulgences) and more recently in a revival piece at the heart of the altar of the Basilica of the Immaculate Conception in Washington D.C. Faced with a stern Jesus riding the rainbow in judgment and from whose mouth proceeded a double edged sword worshippers sought out the more inviting image of a woman and mother who would receive them in mercy.

[66] Phillip Melanchthon, *Apology of the Augsburg Confession*, article 21, 14.

[67] For more on this Reformation formulation see Timothy George, *Theology of the Reformers* 120, 125, 328.

[68] Martin Luther, The Ninety-five Theses, no. 62, 1517. See Henry Bettenson, *The Early Christian Fathers* (Oxford: Oxford University Press, 1956) 185-191.

[69] Luther did allow at least this one innocuous prayer for the dead "Dear God, if this soul is in the state so that it can still be helped, I pray that you would be merciful to it." WA 10, 3: 195; See also WA 12: 592-97.

recent inventions of Indulgences as well as the older practices of pilgrimages and relics and the still more ancient prayers and masses for the dead; the total collapse of the veneration for the saints and indeed their very remembrance in Protestant Churches was at hand.

The corrective theology of the Reformation broke the historic union, at least in Europe, among all members of the kingdom of God. Perhaps the most serious Protestant loss—one still not satisfactorily recovered—is the doctrine of the communion between pilgrims and saints, especially when we remember that the Reformation declared all Christians to be saints,[70] not just those who had been officially recognized, beatified, and/or canonized.

So, while the theology of the Church's true treasury may have been corrected, Protestant Christians remain bereft of a satisfactory explication of their creedal claim that "we believe in the Communion of Saints" Hence there is a Protestant need for a recovered doctrine of the Communion of Saints as including the dead no less than the living.

---

[70] "When we have repudiated this foolish and wicked notion about the name "saints" which we suppose applies only to the saints in heaven, and on earth to hermits and monks who perform some sort of spectacular work let us now learn from the writings of the apostles that all believers in Christ are saints." See Martin Luther, *Luther's Works: 55-Volume American Edition*, ed. Jaroslav Pelikan and Helmut T. Lehman (Fortress Press, 2002) vol. 27:83.

Part Two: Envisioning A Creedal Eschatology

Chapter Three

What Happens When We Die?

Primary to formulating a descriptive Protestant theology of the Communion of Saints is the explication of a Christian eschatology[1] that best allows for the fellowship described in the creedal statement. The questions of What happens when we die? and What can we know of life after death? are indeed important ones. Some would argue that religion itself rises out of the collective human anxiety surrounding the thought of our imminent mortality.[2] Such notions are common in our modern world where persons readily admit, at least theoretically, to the existence of eternity,[3] but stop far short of predicating their lives on its existence. Such lackluster answers to such fundamental questions moves Karl Barth to fittingly state "Eschatology, rightly understood is the most practical thing that can be thought."[4] Properly understanding our Christian hope, that is our future, eliminates the fears and anxieties of the present and helps us make evermore sense of the past.

Peter advised: "in your hearts, sanctify Christ as Lord. Always be ready to make a defense to anyone who demands from you an accounting of the hope that is within you; yet do it with gentleness and reverence.[5] So as theology has traditionally been defined as 'faith seeking understanding,'[6] eschatology can be described as 'hope seeking understanding;' that is, Christian hope in the Risen Christ being articulated in ways that make sense to believers and their cultural world.[7] From the beginning eschatology has

---

[1] Eschatology, from the Greek, *meaning* 'the Last Things' is the study of our final end and the realities associated with it, usually listed as death, judgment, heaven, and hell.
[2] See the preeminent arguments of Sigmund Freud in his *Totem and Taboo* (New York: Norton, W. W. & Company, Inc. 1913) and *Moses and Monotheism* (New York: Knopf Publishing Group 1938).
[3] According to the most recent Gallup Poll over 97% of Americans say they believe in God or a universal spirit, 90% believe in heaven, and 73% believe in hell. See *The Gallup Index of Leading Religious Indicators*, (Princeton, NJ: The Gallup Organization, 2005).
[4] Barth, *Dogmatics in Outline*, 154.
[5] 1 Pet 3:15-16.
[6] See Anselm's *Monologion* and *Proslogion*, trans Thomas Williams (Cambridge: Hackett Publishing Co. 1995).
[7] The influence of Marx, Freud, and Nietzsche, the so-called "great masters of suspicion" described by Hans Küng in his book *Does God Exist?* has so permeated modern culture that a seemingly systematic atheism has become the implicit premise

been present in the Creeds which profess Christ's future coming to judge the living and the dead and the Church's looking forward to the resurrection of the body and the life everlasting. These articles of the Creed affirm the two dimensions of Christian existence. Christians live in the present and look forward to the future in the light of the past. As the liturgical acclamation puts it: Christ has died, Christ is risen, Christ will come again!

As the creedal affirmation "we believe . . . in the Communion of Saints" expounds on its preceding affirmation "we believe . . . in the Church; so the proceeding affirmations "we believe in . . . the forgiveness of sins, the resurrection of the body, and the life everlasting" set the groundwork for understanding the Communion of Saints. That is, we believe in the existence of, and our communion with, the saints, out of and because, we believe in everlasting life, resurrection, and forgiveness. To deny the saints is to tacitly deny their, and in some way our own, forgiveness, resurrection, and life in God. So the Creed itself assumes within its affirmations a basic Christian eschatology. A brief exploration of them will frame a minimum Christian eschatology from within which the Communion of Saints functions. Let us consider the last first.

---

for understanding all human life and history. For Karl Marx, religious hope is a fundamental misplacement of vital energies that should be focused on this world into an otherworld of illusory expectations. Once people taste real truth and feel real freedom in this world, he thought, religion will be revealed as the illusion it is. For Sigmund Freud, religious hope is wish-fulfillment, an infantile projection expressing itself in the fantasy of the hereafter. It is a symptom of one's neurotic flight from the pain and burden of a genuinely adult existence. To this end, it forms the image of a father-figure who will keep us safe, and save us in the end. For Friedrich Nietzsche Christianity was the cult of negativity, in which the Christian conception of God was a contradiction of life itself as it declared war against nature, against the will to live, and the will to power. See Hans Küng, *Does God Exist. An Answer for Today*, trans Edward Quinn (New York: Vintage Books, 1981) 217-260; 262-337; 343-423.

Chapter Four

We Believe in . . . the Life Everlasting

Coinciding with their affirmation of the Communion of Saints the Church declares its belief in life everlasting, but just what the Church believes about life after death is difficult to depict. However if we are to ascertain what role the saints are to play in the life of the Church today we need some knowledge concerning their present state.

One may well conjecture, as will be explored later in this work, that the Church communes with the saints in a historical sense only, that is, the present Church inherits the legacy of the saints of the past. This is certainly true; the Church of today is indissolubly connected with its past members who have conveyed to their spiritual progeny their faith and works, both good and bad. However, the creeds self explication proclaims that this historical connection to the saints is not the totality of the apostles teaching concerning the communion. In its triumphant affirmation of the life everlasting, the Creed teaches that there is, in fact, life after death and by implication, that the saints who have died upon the earth are, in fact, not dead but alive in God. So the Communion of Saints is a fellowship of living persons that includes and encompasses all of history.

The Reality of Death

Physical death has spiritual significance not because of something dramatic the Christian knows or expects will happen at the hour of one's death but precisely because one is ignorant of what will happen, and that has a distinct and discernable influence upon one's life. Fear and ignorance of the future beyond death combined with the intuition that there are things which, if not done now in this life can never be done, profoundly affect one's life in the world. In the end, however, Christians do not ascribe great finality to death but look beyond it, assured that God accompanies them even there and even then. Because of Christ's resurrection death is no longer ultimately significant for the way Christians live. Death's stinger has been removed. Mature Christians act responsibly, not out of fear of death and judgment, but from love of God.

Death remains, however, a matter of natural course and a universal human phenomenon. "It sets its seal upon the whole; it is the wages of sin. The account is closed, the coffin and corruption are the last word. The contest is decided, and decided against us. Such is death."[1] "When King David's time to die drew near, he charged his son Solomon saying: I am about to go the way of all the earth."[2] Christians believe that "death has passed to all;"[3] and that "it is appointed to mortals to die once."[4] The last event in each and every person's life is already foreknown: they all will die. This awareness of death, however, deepens life's significance.[5] As a sick person's prognosis is shortened, the importance of his remaining time is heightened. Because life is so limited it becomes by that measure more significant. Likewise because each moment of time passes away and cannot be replaced once gone, the death of each moment brings historical significance to one's life and to one's moral decisions within life. "Life puts every person to the test. Life itself is the examination."[6] And death is the final question.[7] Death warns us

---

[1] Barth, *Dogmatics in Outline*, 154.
[2] 1 Kings 2:2.
[3] Romans 5:12.
[4] Hebrews 9:27.
[5] Thanks to death, says John Chrysostom, we have "a myriad of opportunities for philosophical perseverance. For death convinces us, both when it is present and when we await for it, to be modest and to live with prudence and to be humble and to be spared from every evil." (*On Romans*, Homily 10,3 PG 60, 478.) Death, he said on another occasion, was "an important teacher of philosophy that instructs our mind, controls our passions, calms the waves of our stormy life and brings serenity! This is no ordinary teacher of philosophy that has been introduced into our life." (*To the Scandalized* 7 PG 52, 496) Finally he retorts, "What would happen, one wonders, if they [terrible sinners] lived with security and without the fear of death? What would restrain them from their irreverent and criminal deeds? What would extinguish their evil desire? (*On Psalm 110*, 1-2 PG 55, 280-281.4) For more Orthodox gleanings see *The Mystery of Death*, by Nikolaos P. Vassiliadis, trans Fr. Peter A. Chamberas (Athens: The Orthodox Brotherhood of Theologians, 1997).
[6] See Søren Kierkegaard, *The Gospel of Suffering* (New York: James Clark Co., 1892) 60-61.
[7] The possibility of death is an act of divine love and wisdom in the economy of human beings for this reason: If God had created human beings immortal, then they ought also to have been incapable of sinning. For, if while immortal, they had fallen into sin, evil would have existed eternally; and evil would have itself, become immortal. On the other hand, if God had indeed created human beings immortal and, therefore, incapable of sinning, then their freedom would have been curbed; they would not have been a free being. See Theophilos of Antioch's comments on the potential of paradisal Adam and Eve where he says "God created man neither mortal nor immortal, but susceptible to both conditions. Thus, if he were to incline himself toward those things that have to do with immortality, having kept the commandment of God, he would receive his reward of immortality from God and become god by grace. But if on the other hand, he would incline himself toward

to "be careful how we live, not as unwise people but as wise, making the most of our time."[8]

So "death is not merely the outward limit of life but permeates the whole course of earthly life."[9] Death accompanies all life and the events of life "are all deaths."[10] The living reality of the world maintains itself at the cost of other living things. Stars die and planets are born; things eat and are themselves eaten. Nature's surrender to termination is a reflection of what might be termed as the good or positive death revealed within the Trinity. That is, death rightly understood as the sacrifice of life, the original image of which "is in God as the gift of life flowing between Father and Son in the Spirit. For the Father gives his whole life to the Son, the Son gives it back to the Father, and the Spirit is the out flowing gift of life."[11]

Death then has two faces, on the one hand it is a fact of nature; as human beings rose up out of the matter of the universe, so we are destined to return to it; dust to dust. On the other hand it is the greatest enemy of human beings separating them from those we love, destroying their families, and terminating their earthly friendships. Through his resurrection, Christ both overcame the natural process of death and defeated death.[12] Christians participate in Christ's victory over death by first appropriating the freedom from the "fear of death"[13] which Christ has provided. This allows Christians to accept the positives deaths that are a part of everyday life and essential to physical, emotional, psychological, and spiritual growth.[14] Ultimately,

---

those things that are related to death, having disobeyed God, he himself would be the cause of his own death. For God created man free and the master of his will." (*To Autolycus* 11, 27 BEPES 5, 39 (25-31).

[8] Ephesians 5:15.

[9] Hans Urs Von Balthasar, *Theo-Drama: Theological Dramatic Theory* Vol. 5: The Last Act (San Francisco: Ignatius, 1983) 250.

[10] C. S. Lewis, in his best work, *Till We Have Faces: A Myth Retold*, explicates this truth in the words of the pre-Christian Psyche: "To leave your home – to lose you, Maia, and the Fox – to loose one's maidenhead – to bear a child – they are all deaths." (New York: Harcourt Brace & Company, 1956) 73.

[11] See Balthasar, *Theo-Drama: Theological Dramatic Theory* Vol. 5, 251.

[12] See 1 Corinthians 15:26-57; which reads in part "The last enemy to be destroyed is death."

[13] See Hebrews 2:14-15 which reads "He [Christ] himself likewise shared the same things, so that through death he might destroy the one who has the power of death, that is, the devil, and free those who all their lives were held in slavery by the fear of death."

[14] "God [the Son] did not impede death from separating his soul from his body according to the necessary order of nature, but has reunited them to one another in the Resurrection, so that he himself might be, in his person, the meeting point for

Christians experience Christ's victory over death in their own resurrection from the dead.[15] This "Christian hope is the seed of eternal life."[16] This is our hope: "if we have died with Christ we believe that we will also live with him . . . dead to sin and alive to God in Christ Jesus."[17]

The Triumph of Life

So in the Creed we affirm our belief in life beyond death; the resurrected life of which Jesus is the "first fruits,"[18] and in which Christians presently participate and will ultimately and fully experience at the Last Day. So though every person dies, our "future non-existence cannot be as our complete negation"[19] for God is for us. While the law of entropy assures us that all will die. Salvific resurrection beyond death is a supernatural event that is in no way guaranteed by the laws of the universe. Death and resurrection must be distinguished in content if not in time.

Death is a human affair, new life is God's affair, death is the innate end, new life is God's gift. In resurrection human beings are called into new life, pulled out of the grave by the hand of Christ, brought home by God's Spirit into God's all embracing love where we are ultimately accepted and saved. While this happens with death, or more precisely, from death, it is a separate event which is grounded in and relies upon God's action and God's faithfulness. The God of the beginning is the God of the end. The creator of human beings is the perfector of human beings. The almighty creator who called the world and its inhabitants into existence out of nothing calls from death, life. And so the end is at the same time a new beginning! It is God alone who serves for a human hope beyond death. Properly speaking human beings have no beyond, "nor do they need one, for God is [their] beyond."[20]

The Witness of the Resurrection in the Lord's Supper

This is the witness of the Lord's Supper, that though the Lord has ascended into heaven and sits at the right hand of the Father, we receive his

---

death and life, by arresting in himself the decomposition of nature produced by death and so becoming the source of reunion for the separated parts. (466 Gregory of Nyssa, *Orat. catech.* 16: PG 45, 52D.)

[15] See Acts 24:15; and John 5:29.
[16] Barth, *Dogmatics in Outline*, 155.
[17] Romans 6:8, 11*b*.
[18] 1 Corinthians 15:23.
[19] Barth, *Church Dogmatics* III/3, 611.
[20] Barth, *Church Dogmatics* III/3, 632.

flesh upon the earth, likewise though our flesh is upon the earth it is, in a mysterious way, already in heaven, at the right hand of God, in Christ.[21] In this way the Supper is a foretaste of and testimony to our life in the world (or age) to come, that we participate in even now upon the earth.

Jesus alluded to both the future and present aspects of the resurrected life when he said in refutation to the position of the Sadducees who denied the resurrection of the dead[22] "the hour is coming and is now here, when the dead will hear the voice of the Son of God and those who hear will live. . . . Do not be astonished at this; for the hour is coming when all who are in their graves will hear his voice and will come out."[23] Understanding both the present and future dimensions of the resurrected life will help us avoid the drastic extremes of a too collective eschatology on the one hand, that can be blamed for the social fanaticism of the Radical Reformation and its modern liberation counterparts; and a too individualistic Christian eschatology on the other, that can be blamed for what is often called "pie in the sky by and by" social passivity which Karl Marx keenly observed is "the opium of the people."[24]

What we believe in and look forward to in the life of the world to come is not simply survival after death, through procreation, contribution to a greater and better society, or as the rational result of having an immortal soul. Neither do we look forward to the perpetual repetition of mortal life through reincarnation.[25] "Survival is not salvation. Persistence in mortality is not glorification."[26] "Resurrection means not the continuation of this life, but life's completion. To this [person] a 'Yes' is spoken which the shadow of death cannot touch."[27] Our hope is that we might, individually as embodied creatures and together as God's people, conform to the full stature of the body of Christ and fully share in God's own life as does Jesus "the

---

[21] See Question 49 in the Heidelberg Catechism which states in part "What benefit do we receive from Christ's ascension into heaven?" "That we have our flesh in heaven as a sure pledge that he, as the Head, will also take up, his members, up to himself." In Schaff, *The Creeds of Christendom*, 3:323.
[22] See Mark 12:18-27; Matthew 22:23-33; Luke 20:27-36.
[23] John 5:25, 28-29*a*.
[24] Karl Marx, *Contribution to the Critique of Hegel's "Philosophy of Right"* in *Deutsch-Französische Jahrbücher* (Seiten: Wissenschaftliche Buchges, 1967) February, 1844.
[25] Reincarnation's strength lies in its affirmation that we must be somewhat like what we are now, that is living beings created of matter in a world in which we can relate and act if we are to be said to have life after death.
[26] Luke Timothy Johnson, *The Creed: What Christians Believe and Why It Matters* (New York: Double Day, 2003) 293.
[27] Barth, *Dogmatics in Outline*, 154.

pioneer and perfector of [our] faith."²⁸ We live in expectation of this age to come when all of creation is properly ordered under God and in right relationship with God and each other "so that God may be all in all."²⁹ This culminating state which is the goal of all creation and made possible only through the incarnation and resurrection of Christ Jesus is accurately called heaven.

What and Where is Heaven?

Heaven rightly understood is not "above" the world. It is obvious to modern persons who have sent their representatives to the moon that the hemispherical vault apparently lying above the horizon in which stars appear is not the exterior of the throne room of God as it was understood in biblical times,³⁰ although this allusion still retains a deep archetypical religious significance. Heaven's existence above the world is not spatial but essential. Heaven is transcendent above and free from the constraints of the world and indeed is the power of love which overcomes the world. But heaven rightly understood is not "beyond" the world either. God is not hidden in a spiritual or metaphorical sense outside the world in some other worldly beyond, but the world is hidden in God. Heaven then, rightly understood is not simply a place but a state, a mode of being. Since God is infinite, and to be located in a place of time is to be limited within its domain, heaven, if it is the abode of God, cannot be a place in the way that we usually think of place. "Heaven then is none other than the hidden, invisible, sphere of God, who is not withdrawn from the earth, but rather, perfecting all things for good, grants [to creation] a share in the divine glory and kingdom."³¹ God and heaven are in fact the same: "In the present God is the kingdom of heaven; in the future, heaven is God."³² The gospels themselves testify to this with their interchangeable usage of the term Kingdom of God in the Gospels according to Mark and Luke with Kingdom of Heaven according to Matthew.

Heaven exists because God became truly human in Jesus Christ and made space for human existence within the Triune God. Hence the incarnation has eternal significance. Christ is the unsurpassable event of God's self-giving to creation and the humanity of Christ is the medium through which creation shares in the divine life. It is the God-given relational

---

[28] Hebrews 12:2.
[29] 1 Corinthians 15:28*b*.
[30] See Psalm 103:19; Matthew 22:20-23.
[31] Hans Küng, *Credo: The Apostles Creed Explained for Today* (New York: Doubleday, 1992) 162.
[32] Ludwig Feuerbach, *The Essence of Christianity* (1841) trans. George Eliot (New York, 1957) 172.

space in which the life of true communion is lived. As the Son comes forth from and returns to the Father, so those in Christ share in the life-giving and life-surrendering intimacy of the Triune God, as "sons and daughters in Christ Jesus"[33] and brothers and sister of one another. So to be in heaven is to be in Christ for heaven is union with Christ. To see God face to face means seeing God "in the face of Jesus Christ"[34] who is the eternal mediator of the creations encounter with the creator.

Because Jesus is God, Heaven is the description of what happens when persons encounter Christ. This means that heaven is already present in its fundamental forms in the life of the baptized Christian. It is already the personal reality of those who are identified with and grounded in the historical death and resurrection of Christ Jesus. Whose resurrection was not just a return to or continuation of this life in space and time, but a new life which burst the dimensions of time and space. So as was said concerning the life in the world to come the same can be said of heaven, it is a reality both in the future and in the present, in the beyond and in the now. One is in heaven when and to the extent that one is in Christ; when we, individually as embodied creatures and together as God's people, conform to the full stature of the body of Christ and fully share in God's own life as does Jesus, our heavenly joy will be complete.

In heaven God totally permeates the human being "all in all" and the human being enters into boundless fulfillment. This activity of heaven has been traditionally described in three ways. First the beatific vision in which glorified persons eternally contemplate the Triune God.[35] Second, entering the life of love, wherein glorified persons will eternally live in a loving relationship with God in the way that God wants to be loved. And third, the worship of God, where glorified persons will eternally give glory to God as indeed John beheld in his apocalyptic vision. Each of these descriptions is valuable but none exhaustive of the eternal life.

Now if heaven exists because of Christ, and its being depends on Christ, then it must in some way involve all those who constitute the body of Christ. If God is to be all in all then all must be resurrected. If "in Adam all die" is the account of every human life, then so is "in Christ all shall be made alive."[36] "The resurrection, like death, concerns all."[37]

In heaven, then, the isolation of death has given way to an open society that fulfills all human community; a fellowship of uninterrupted self-

---

[33] Galatians 3:26.
[34] 2 Corinthians 4:6.
[35] See 1 Corinthians 13:8-13; Matthew 18:10; 1John, 3:2; and 2 Corinthians 6-8.
[36] See Romans 5.
[37] Barth, *The Resurrection of the Dead*, 166.

communication between all the members of the body and with its head in an imminent and intimate love which has no limit.

> The individual's salvation is whole and entire only when the salvation of the cosmos and all the elect has come to full fruition. For the redeemed are not simply adjacent to each other in heaven, rather in their being together, and in the one Christ, they *are* heaven. In that moment the whole creation will become song. It will be a single act in which, forgetfully of self, the individual will break through the limits of being into the whole, and the whole take up its dwelling in the individual. It will be joy in which all questioning is resolved and satisfied.[38]

This intimate fellowship, however, is not such a closeness that the "I", that is one's individuality, dissolves into the "we." In resurrection death is not reversed but overcome. So in heaven ones identity is not abolished or absorbed into God but remains particular and preserved but in this completely new dimension. One is not absorbed into the body of Christ but integrated into it as a vitally important member. So heaven is common for the Church but individual for each person. "Everyone sees God in [their] own way. Everyone receives the love offered by the totality in the manner suggested by their on irreplaceable uniqueness.[39] "To everyone who conquers I will give some of the hidden manna, and I will give a white stone, and on the white stone is written a new name that no one knows except the one who receives it."[40] In heaven God gives to each and every person his or her fulfillment in a way particular to that person, so that heaven is rightly called our reward. "There we shall be still and see; we shall see and we shall love; we shall love and we shall praise. Behold what will be, in the end, without end! For what is our end but to reach that kingdom which has no end.[41]

Heaven as the Divine Moment of Success in God's Self-communication to Creation

In envisioning a heaven in which Christ is the medium through which the blessed see God face to face we affirm that heaven is, in fact, the

---

[38] Auer Ratzinger, *Dogmatic Theology 9: Eschatology*, 238.
[39] Auer Ratzinger, *Dogmatic Theology 9: Eschatology*, 235.
[40] Revelation 2:17*b*.
[41] Augustine, *The City of God*, XXVII, 30.

divine moment in which God's self-communication to the world is wholly achieved. In his affirmation "God is love"[42] John reminds the believer that it is not we who first loved God but God who first loved us."[43] This is the determining feature of heaven as well. The creature's coming to be in God gains life from God's coming to be in creation.

Heaven then is primarily the culminating moment of success in God's self-communication to creation. The Trinity, giving itself to creation as self-communicating love, is an open circle of a divine communion. The divine three draw each and all into their own life of love. The dynamism of this divine communication reaches an irreversible moment of success in the destiny of each of person. In each of the saints, the divine mystery realizes its self-giving. Each of the blessed enters the joy of the Lord, because the Lord has entered into his own joy, in the actualization of the God-self in each one. If this is a minimum description of the when and where of heaven, the question remains, what is between heaven and earth?

What is Between Death and Eternal Life?

As we hear in the familiar parable of the beggar Lazarus and his rich counterpart, whom tradition has named Dives, we see what appears, on the surface, to be a fairly clear statement regarding what happens to persons when they die.[44] However, in the many years since Jesus taught that parable, Christians have sought to make sense of competing biblical texts to further define the intermediate state of the dead between their earthly passing and

---

[42] 1 John 4:8.16.
[43] 1 John 4:10.
[44] Luke 16:19-31. The story involves a certain rich man who was luxuriously clothed, sumptuously fed, and lived in an expensive house. In stark contrast, Lazarus, the poorest of the poor, a beggar and full of sores was unceremoniously dumped daily at the wealthy man's gate, hoping only for the crumbs that fell from the rich man's table. Any meager comfort that Lazarus enjoyed was provided by the foraging street dogs who licked his diseased and frail body. Finally, both men died and their state of affairs was dramatically altered. The rich man was subjected to agonizing torment while Lazarus was honored and comforted.

This text is commonly used as proof that both the righteousness and unrighteous dead consciously await resurrection and final judgment in an intermediate state where they possess perception of objects and creatures; sensations of torments, anguish, sorrow, and comfort; communication with other similarly conscious beings; recognition; volition; recollection; and emotion. Adherents conclude that theories which allow for the extinction of the wicked, or for soul-sleeping on the part of the righteous dead, are not consistent with the plain teaching of Christ.

their eternal judgment. In general Christians believe that all persons will die according to the flesh, and at the last, great, and glorious Day of the Lord we shall be judged by Jesus our Christ. The results include the possibility of banishment into utter darkness for some and most assuredly for the redeemed life everlasting with God, properly called heaven. This being said some concern remains about what happens between our physical death and the general resurrection.

Justin Martyr, writing early in the second century, explicitly states that the souls of the godly are in a good place, and the souls of the ungodly are in a bad place; there to stay until the judgment day. He rejects just as explicitly those who teach that one went straight to heaven or hell upon their death. He cautions his fellows not to account as Christians those who declare that there is no intermediate state of the dead.[45]

So what is that middle state of the dead? Is it a state of waiting either in bliss or torment? Is one's fate fixed at death so that there is no possibility of growth, maturity, or change after earthly death? Is the term "soul-sleep" appropriate terminology for those who rest in the grave? Or are the dogmatic statements of our Roman Catholic brethren who believe in the existence of Purgatory, an adequate description of their plight? Are any of these explanations entirely satisfactory?

Soul Sleep

The radical reformers such as some Anabaptists, and Anti-Trinitarians[46] revived the doctrines of both soul-sleep and soul-death, first popularized in the Italian Renaissance.[47] These self explanatory dogmas taught that between one's personal death and the general resurrection the soul slumbered in some "theological and eschatological, [but] not anthropological" manner[48] or either ceased to exist all together.[49] The latter

---

[45] See his *Apology* 18-20.

[46] The present day Watchtower movement claims: "The dead are shown to be 'conscious of nothing at all' and the death state to be one of complete inactivity" (*Aid to Bible Understanding*, Brooklyn, NY: Watchtower, 1971, 431).

[47] See George Huntston Williams, *The Radical Reformation* (Kirksville, MO: Sixteenth Century Journal Publishers, 1992) 21, 24, 104, 174, 186, 189, 191, 355, 400, 401, 562, 609, 675.

[48] Donald G. Bloesch, *Essentials of Evangelical Theology* (San Francisco: Harper & Row, 1982) 2:187.

[49] This theology of "soul death" was rejected by the Church as early as 250 AD. "While he (Origen) was so engaged (in something Eusebius described earlier), a new group appeared on the Arabian scene, originators of a doctrine far removed from

being formulated by those theologians who recognized that the sleep metaphor alone was not adequate to do away with all consciousness; seeing that one dreams, moves, and sometimes even walks in sleep. In his rejection of Purgatory, Luther finally settled on an intermediate state that was "a deep and dreamless state without consciousness and feeling"[50] from which death and resurrection were likened to going asleep and waking.[51] The coffin, he wrote, was "nothing other than our Lord Jesus Christ's bosom or Paradise,

---

the truth, namely, that at the end of our life here the human soul dies for a time along with our bodies and perishes with them; later, when one day the resurrection comes, it will return with them to life. At this crisis a synod was convoked on a large scale, and Origen was invited. On arrival, he opened a public debate on the question at issue, and argued so forcibly that he compelled those who had previously gone astray to change their views." (Eusebius, *History of the Church*, VI, 37, trans G.A. Williamson, Penguin Publishers, 1975)

In 1513, in connection with the eighth session of the fifth Lateran Council, Pope Leo X issued the Bull *Apostolici regimis* declaring, "We do condemn and reprobate all who assert that the intelligent soul is mortal" (*Damnamus et reprobamus omnes assertentes animam intellectivam mortalem esse*). The Bull went on to decree that "all who adhere to the like erroneous assertions shall be shunned and punished as heretics." The decrees of this Council, it should be noted, were all issued in the form of Bulls or constitutions. See H. J. Schroeder, *Disciplinary Decrees of the General Councils*, 1937, 483, 487). In 1520, responding to *Apostolici regimis* and in defense of 41 of his propositions, Luther cited the pope's immortality declaration, as among "those monstrous opinions to be found in the Roman dunghill of decretals" (proposition 27). In the twenty-seventh proposition of his *Defence* Luther said: "I permit the Pope to establish articles of faith for himself and for his own faithful—such are: That the bread and wine are transubstantiated in the sacrament; that the essence of God neither generates nor is generated; that the soul is the substantial form of the human body; that he [the pope] is emperor of the world and king of heaven, and earthly god; that the soul is immortal; and all these endless monstrosities in the Roman dunghill of decretals—in order that such as his faith is, such may be his gospel, such also his faithful, and such his church, and that the lips may have suitable lettuce and the lid may be worthy of the dish. (Martin Luther, *Assertio Omnium Articulorum M. Lutheri per Bullam Leonis X. Novissimam Damnatorum* (Assertion of All the Articles of M. Luther Condemned by the Latest Bull of Leo X), article 27, Weimar edition of *Luther's Works*, Vol. 7, 131, 132.

[50] Paul Althaus, *The Theology of Martin Luther* (Philadelphia: Fortress Press, 1966) 414.

[51] In a 1533 sermon Luther preached "We are to sleep until he come and knocks on the grave and says, 'Dr. Luther, get up.' Then I will rise in a moment and be eternally happy with him." 28, September 1533, W.A. 37: 151. See also Martin Luther, *Gospel Sermon, Twenty-Fourth Sunday after Trinity* in *Sermons of Martin Luther* 8 vols. ed. J. N. Lenker (Grand Rapids: Baker, 1988) 8, 372-374, where Luther explicates the ancient tradition of calling places of internment not graveyards but houses of sleep.

the grave as nothing other than a soft couch of ease or rest."[52] The English Bible translator William Tyndale, in his rejection of the invocation of the saints and an intermediate state revived the teaching of conditional immortality. Tydale argued that if deceased persons were already in heaven or hell then there would be no need for a resurrection.[53] In 1534 John Calvin wrote *Psychopannychia* in which he defended the concept of the intermediate state characterized by consciousness and watchful waiting.[54]

Classic arguments from scripture against these doctrines included Jesus' aforementioned story of the rich man and Lazarus in which both central figures seem to have kept their consciousness after death;[55] Jesus' promise to the penitent thief, "today you will be with me in Paradise";[56] and finally Paul's suggestion that he "would rather be away from the body and at home with the Lord."[57] Historically, tradition has interpreted those passages which portray the dead as sleeping[58] as analogical and not to be applied literally.[59]

---

[52] Martin Luther, *Christian Songs, Latin and German, for Use at Funerals* in *The Works of Martin Luther*, 6, 287.

[53] Against the Roman Catholic proponent Sir Thomas More, Tyndale wrote: "And when he [More] proveth that the saints be in heaven in glory with Christ already, saying, "If God be their God, they be in heaven, for he is not the God of the dead;" there he stealeth away Christ's argument, wherewith he proveth the resurrection: that Abraham and all saints should rise again, and not that their souls were in heaven; which doctrine was not yet in the world. And with that doctrine he taketh away the resurrection quite, and maketh Christ's argument of none effect. William Tyndale, *An Answer to Sir Thomas More's Dialogue* Parker's 1850 reprint, (Baltimore, MD: The Catholic University of America Press, 2000), Bk. 4, Ch. 4, 118.

[54] François Wendel, *Calvin: The Origins and Development of His Religious Thought*, trans Philip Mairet (New York, Harper & Row, 1963) 43, 287. Note also that "psyshopannychia" meaning "a watchful wake of the soul" was later erroneously appropriated as an umbrella term for both soul-sleep and soul-death. See also Williams, *The Radical Reformation*, 582-583.

[55] See Luke 16:19-31.

[56] Luke 23:43.

[57] 2 Corinthians 5:8.

[58] See Daniel 12:2; Matthew 9:24; John 11:1; 1 Corinthians 11:30; 15:511; and 1 Thessalonians 4:14.

[59] See John Chrysostom, *Baptismal Instructions* in *Ancient Christian Writers: The Works of the Fathers in Translation*, ed. J Quasten, J. C. Puimpe, and W. Burghardt, 44 vols. (New York: Paulist Press, 1946) 31, 176.

Immediate Reward of either Bliss or Torment

As mentioned in the previous chapter, the reformers, in their rejection of the clerical abuses connected with Purgatory preached a corrective theology that emphasized the forensic, legal, and objective aspect of salvation. Herein the righteousness of Christ is imputed or attributed to believers who, in him, are at peace with God and heaven bound. Through the power of Christ's Holy Spirit, and with the aid of Word and Sacrament these believers grow into the full stature of Christ, that is they mature toward perfection. The obvious truth, however, is that the problem of sin and moral imperfection remains in the lives of many, most, if not all believers at the time of their death.

The reformers in agreement with Paul and the traditional teaching of the Church believed that nothing impure or unholy can enter heaven.[60] Salvation, then, can be likened to a two-sided coin, heads being justification and tales being sanctification, wherein salvation is more than just forgiveness of sins but also a matter of comprehensive moral and spiritual transformation as Christians empowered by faith and their Baptism to live according to the law of love in obedience to Christ Jesus their Lord. This is what scripture calls holiness or sanctification. God forgives and transforms sinners; actually and eventually making them (not just calling them) righteous. This process of sanctification makes one truly fit to enjoy the beatific vision of heaven. But if persons cannot fully participate in the life of God until they are holy what becomes of those who are justified but not sanctified in this life; whose sanctification was begun in faith but their character not yet made perfect? Such people are not ready for a heaven of perfect love and communion with God and his saints but neither should they be relegated to hell. This is the fundamental difficulty that led to the formulation of the doctrine of Purgatory in the first place.

The reformers apparently concluded that either as one wakes from a long sleep on Doomsday or at the very moment of death salvation is fully accomplished immediately, and apparently painlessly, by a unilateral act of God. That is, those who were justified are sanctified, as they are glorified. Jonathan Edwards expressed this view eloquently when he wrote:
At death the believer not only gains a perfect and eternal deliverance from sin and temptation, but is adorned with a perfect and glorious holiness. The work of sanctification is then completed, and the beautiful image of God has

---

[60] 1 Corinthians 1:9: "Do you not know that wrongdoers will not inherit the Kingdom of God? Do not be deceived." See also 15:50; Galatians 5;19-21; Ephesians 5:5; Revelations 21:7, 8; 22:15.

then its finishing strokes by the pencil of God and begins to shine forth with a heavenly beauty like a seraphim.[61]

A distinction offered by John Wesley, the founder of Methodism, is his belief that moral perfection or entire sanctification is possible in this life. He taught that sanctification can be received in a moment of faith analogous to the way justification is accepted by faith.[62] At the same time, Wesley stressed a gradual and progressive growth in grace and holiness[63] which if not brought to fulfillment in this life takes place at the instant of death.[64]

Hence, the vast majority of Protestants maintain that either at the resurrection on the Last Day or instantaneously at death, one receives his/her full reward, either heavenly bliss or eternal punishment or at least a foretaste of that reward in a paradisial or sorrowful waiting place.[65] The ultimate reunification of body with soul serves primarily to amplify and enhance heavenly pleasure or hellish agony.[66]

This idea, though widely accepted, is not without its problems. The instantaneous sanctification of believers by the unilateral act of God seems to eliminate the believer's free participation in their own moral transformation. God takes human free will seriously, and patiently

---

[61] As quoted by Jerry L. Walls in "Purgatory for Everybody," *First Things* 122 (April 2002): 26-30.

[62] For a exemplary statement see his Sermon XLIII "The Scripture Way of Salvation" where he preaches of instantaneous sanctification "Expect by faith, expect as you are, expect it now." (John Wesley, *The Works of John Wesley*, Vol 6, Peabody, Mass: Hendrickson Publishers, 1991, 53.)

[63] See his sermon LXXXV "On Working Out Our Own Salvation" (Works, 6, 509.)

[64] See sermon LXXVI "On Perfection" (Works, 6, 412). Note also however, at the end of his own life, January 17, 1791, in what was probably his last sermon, Wesley taught "I cannot therefore but think . . . all those holy souls who have been discharged from the body, from the beginning of the world unto this day—will be continually ripening for heaven; will be perpetually holier and happier, till they are received into 'the kingdom prepared for them from the foundation of the world?'" ("On Faith" in Works, 7, 326) This Sermon is not included in "Wesley's Standard Sermons," the norm of faith and doctrine for the Methodists and their daughter Churches.

[65] For more on the particular and general judgment at death or on the Last Day see chapter six of this work entitled "We Believe in the Forgiveness of Sins."

[66] Dante, in canto XIII of his *Divine Comedy: Inferno* has those who committed suicide existing as plants of hell and awaiting the resurrection of their bodies that they may have returned to them what they robbed themselves of, not "to dwell within again" but to be "hung with every one fixed on the thorn bush of its wounded shade." For the best translation see Robert Pinsky's *The Inferno of Dante* (New York: The Noonday Press, 1994) 105-107.

recognizes that even those persons walking in the light of his love and grace do so sporadically making inconsistent progress toward their ultimate goal. This lack of necessary cooperation explains to a large degree the perplexing array of evil still in the world. So while it is God who enables, elicits and empowers our transformation, our synergistic cooperation with his will is necessary. If this is the way God sanctifies Christians in life, it is reasonable to think God will continue to respect his gift of our freedom and require our cooperation in the next life as well until our perfection is finally achieved. "Indeed, the point should be put more strongly than this. If God is willing to dispense with our free cooperation in the next life, it is hard to see why he would not do so now, particularly in view of the high price of freedom in terms of evil and suffering."[67]

Purgatory

Purgatory is part of traditional Roman Catholic theology which developed in a process of clarification in which the Church held that although ones fundamental life decision was finalized and fixed at death one did not necessarily reach ones final destiny strait away.[68] While Roman Catholic history testifies that God has revealed his power in weak human vessels who have grown, even in this life, into "the measure of the full stature of Christ."[69] Experience also teaches that the great majority of persons exiting this life have not yet attained that sublime ideal set before us by our Lord: "be perfect as your Father in heaven is perfect."[70] but remain inadequate and immature.

Whereas some suppose that is surely within the power of God to interpose directly his grace and mercy in a seemingly magical way in order to purify persons from their faults and prepare them for union with God; Roman Catholics reject this scheme on the basis that it conflicts with God's justice and his stipulation that persons cooperate with grace. On the other hand, it would be contrary to God's mercy if persons whose hope is in Christ are eternally banished from his sight if they have not completely "purified themselves as he is pure.[71] From this line of reasoning Roman Catholics derive that there must be some possibility of purifying the soul after death.

---

[67] Jerry L. Walls, "Purgatory for Everybody" *First Things* 122 (April 2002): 26-30.

[68] In fact, it can be argued that no one, save Jesus and the Holy Spirit, is ever fully united to God. Because God is infinite and human beings finite our participation in the eternal and abundant divine life will be a dynamic involvement of ever increasing intensity and ever deepening ecstasy.

[69] Ephesians 4:13.

[70] Matthew 5:48.

[71] 1 John 3:3.

This state of purification is traditionally called Purgatory and was defined by the Church Councils of Lyons (1274), Florence (1439), and Trent (1534).[72]

The councils saw this process of purification present in the Scriptures. Earliest, in the pious thoughts and honorable actions of Judas Maccabeus recorded in 2 Maccabees 12:39-45[73]. Therein Judas, praying that their sin be wholly blotted out, provided Jerusalem with a sin offering on behalf of heroic soldiers who fell fighting for their faith while they had under their tunics sacred tokens of idols which the Law forbade Jews to wear.[74] This suggested that even in the Old Testament sins could be forgiven after death. Further support was lent by the words of Jesus as he warned that some sins "will not be forgiven in this age nor in the age to come"[75] alluding then that some sins would be forgiven in the coming age.[76] Jesus also speaks of one being thrown into prison where "you will never get out until you have paid the last penny" thus implying that the debts of sin that remain unsettled must eventually be paid.[77] Finally, Paul writes of a teacher who builds on the one foundation, which is Jesus Christ, with wood, hay, and straw rather than gold or silver. On the Day, fire will test the work each builder has done. "If the work is burned up the builder will suffer loss, the builder will be saved, but only as through fire."[78]

Purgatory is the name of that negative process whereby the faults, blemishes, and vices that remain because of the imperfection of ones earthly life are finally removed or purged. The removal of these defects is thought to be effected through passive punishment. This punishment is not a satisfaction of sin, for this was attained by Christ through his sacrificial death, but a satisfactory suffering which is necessarily attached, by the law of God's

---

[72] The Council of Trent, while upholding the notion of Purgatory left open the question of place and nature while warning against vain curiosity, superstition, and of course the quest for profit but maintained that "the souls consigned thereto may be helped by the prayers of the faithful." See Trent, Sess. 25 De Purg.

[73] This is part of the Apocrypha, canonical in Roman Catholicism, non-canonical among most Protestants, and of ambiguous authority in Anglicanism.

[74] See 2 Maccabees 12:43 ff.

[75] Matthew 12:32.

[76] Gregory the Great (540-604) built upon Jesus' words saying "As for certain lesser faults, we must believe that, before the final judgment, there is a purifying fire. He who is truth says that whoever utters blasphemy against the Holy Spirit will be pardoned neither in this age nor in the age to come. From this sentence we understand that certain offenses can be forgiven in this age, but certain others in the age to come." As quoted in the *Catechism of the Catholic Church* (United States Catholic Conference, 1994) no. 1032, 269.

[77] See Matthew 4:26.

[78] 1 Corinthians 3:11 ff.

justice, to even the least sin. It is likened to the refining process of fire by which straw, dirt, and other impurities are burned away leaving only the purest gold, silver, or precious stones.[79] One may extrapolate the warnings of Paul to apply not only to teachers but to all Christians; for all must base their lives upon Christ, and yet in our moral weakness we construct an imperfect work.

Whether or not Purgatory is characterized by real fire cannot be known. It is perhaps best to think that the stiffest penalty meted out to those in Purgatory is the recognition that that they are by their own fault long excluded from blessed vision of God (union with God). As they move through the purgatorial process, gradually turning away from themselves and opening their hearts more and more to God, the bitterness of their separation from God becomes greater and greater. In this way, the pains of purgation are ever-increasing and evermore cleansing. "It is the pain of homesickness for their Father; and the further their purification proceeds the more painfully their souls are scourged by its rods of fire."[80]

It is important to note that Purgatory is not a temporary hell full of mere punishment, pain, and wrath but it is the entranceway to paradise, the porch of the heavenly mansion, a thoroughfare into the New Jerusalem on which there is no standing still and every hurting step brings one closer to God. The pain of sin most egregiously felt by those in Purgatory is accompanied by the joy and sure expectation of the blessed hope. In this those suffering through Purgatory are fundamentally different from those in hell who have no further hope, for though they have pain, their "pain will turn into joy."[81]

History of the Concept of Purgatory

The concept of Purgatory or an intermediate state after death for the purpose of purification developed early in the history of the Church. Both Clement of Alexandria (150-215) and Origen (185-254) both taught those who had died without time for penance would be "purified by fire" in the next life. Augustine (354-430) also suggested purification for sins was necessary before entering into the joys of the next life.[82]

---

[79] See Malachi 3:3 ff; 1 Corinthians 3:2 ff.
[80] Karl Adam, *The Spirit of Catholicism* (New York: The Crossroad Publishing Company, 1997) 104.
[81] John 16:22.
[82] Augustine argues "that some sinners are not forgiven either in this world or in the next would not be truly said unless there were other [sinners] who, though not forgiven in this world, are forgiven in the world to come" *The City of God*, XXI, xxiv.

The practice of praying for the dead was widespread in the Church by the fourth century. This liturgical practice drove theology to explain what purpose such prayers served. So the central feature of Purgatory is the idea that the dead in some way suffer and that this suffering can be alleviated by prayer. It was Tertullian in his essay *On the Soul* who attached the factor of guilt to the suffering of Purgatory. Commenting on Jesus advice to "come to terms quickly with your accuser while you are on the way to court . . . or you will be thrown into prison . . . [from where] you will not get out until you have paid the last penny"[83] Tertullian thus interpreted the time between death and resurrection as a time of imprisonment in which the soul pays to the last penny in order to free itself for resurrection. On the basis of this rationale Purgatory becomes a necessary state for most everyone; the exception being the martyrs who died for their faith. In dealing with weaker Christians, those who did not have the courage to die for their faith during times of persecution but gave in to the demands of the pagan state and denied Christ, the Church established a penitential way of purification that allowed those persons to reenter the Church.[84] Cyprian of Carthage, who died in 258, suggested that this penitential way of purification existed not only in this world but in the world to come[85] and thus the base doctrines of Purgatory were formulated.

By the time of Origen the doctrine of Purgatory is clear. Building on Paul's discussion of the judgment in 1 Corinthians 3, Origen theologizes that when a baptized Christian dies with un-confessed sins he or she is condemned to a fire which burns away the lighter materials, and prepares the soul for entrance into the kingdom of God, where nothing defiled may enter. For if on the foundation of Christ you have built not only gold and silver and precious stones; but also wood and hay and stubble, what do you expect when the soul shall be separated from the body? Would you enter into heaven with your wood and hay and stubble and thus defile the kingdom of God; or on account of these hindrances would you remain without and receive no reward for your gold and silver and precious stones? Neither is this just. It remains then that you be committed to the fire which will burn the light materials; for our God, to those who can comprehend heavenly things, is called a cleansing fire. But this fire consumes not the creature, but what the creature has built; wood, and hay and stubble. It is manifest that

---

Similar interpretations are given by Gregory the Great, *Dial.*, IV, xxxix; Bede in his commentary on Augustine's text and Bernard, *Sermo* lxvi in Cantic., n. 11.
[83] Matthew 5:26.
[84] See page 17 of the work.
[85] See Cyprian of Carthage, *Letters*, 55, 20.

the fire destroys the wood of our transgressions and then returns to us the reward of our great works.[86]

In these words we see the proper content of the doctrine of Purgatory. Purgatory is best understood when it is understood in Christological way. The Lord himself is the judging fire which transforms us and conforms us to his own glorified body.[87] The burning flame that is the transforming power of the Lord himself "cuts free our closed-off heart, melting it, and pouring it into a new mold to make it fit for the living organism of his body."[88]

In this line of thinking we see that Purgatory is not a place where one spends a quantifiable amount of time but a description of a transition from the earthly into the heavenly. Purgatory is not some "super-worldly concentration camp where [one] is forced to undergo punishment in a more or less arbitrary fashion." [89] Rather it is an inwardly necessary process in which a person becomes capable of Christ, capable of God, and thus capable of unity with the whole Communion of Saints.

If all die imperfect, and fulfillment involves perfection of all persons, what the Church traditionally calls sanctification, then the alternatives are: sudden transformation at death or a process of moral growth after death involving purgation from sin, that is, some version of Purgatory. So we see that Purgatory is the continuation, or better yet the ultimate fulfillment, of sanctification in the life to come. It is the doctrinal recognition that salvation by grace does not exonerate us from the need to be transformed but indeed empowers that transformation. Purgatory is the working out, in this world and in the world to come, the doctrine of penance.

Orthodox Toll Houses

The Eastern Church's reject the idea of punishment and or atonement taking place in the afterlife[90] and since the thirteenth century have

---

[86] Origen, *P.G.*, XIII, col. 445, 448.
[87] See Romans 8:29; and Philippians 3:21.
[88] Auer Ratzinger, *Dogmatic Theology 9: Eschatology*, 229.
[89] Auer Ratzinger, *Dogmatic Theology 9: Eschatology*, 230.
[90] During the 17th and 18th centuries, when the western influence over the Churches of the East was at its height some Greek and Russian theologians, such as Gabriel Serverus, Peter Mogila, Patriarch Dositheos of Jerusalem (who later retracted his views) and Elias Miniati, while sidestepping the word "Purgatory" embraced a position relatively the same as the Roman view, including the notion of satisfaction made after death. This is not however represeative of the Orthodox tradition as a whole. See Timothy Ware, *Eustratios Argenti* (Oxford: Oxford University Press, 1964)

objected to what they consider to be the Roman Catholic theology of Purgatory. They do however practice intercessions for the dead by prayer, alms, good works, and most importantly the offering of the Eucharist for their repose. Orthodox tradition teaches that these prayers (a classification of all of the above) are heard by God in his mercy.

The Orthodox teaching of The Toll Houses corresponds more or less with the Western idea concerning the Particular Judgment and has some similarities with the Western theology of Purgatory. While not a dogma of the Church, tradition with early origins[91] speaks of a journey immediately following death where "the soul, accompanied by the guardian angel, passes through a series of twenty-two celestial toll or custom houses, each concerned with a different type of sin: idle talk, gluttony, sexual lust, jealously, sloth, and so on."[92] At each toll house the soul is meticulously examined with reference to that particular sin, spiritual luggage is inspected, and scrolls produced upon which the thoughts, words, and actions of ones life are recorded. With these the soul is confronted not only with shortcomings remembered but those long forgotten or never even noticed.

The teaching of the Toll Houses suggests in picture language that there is progress after death and that the essence of this progress is self knowledge. With the separation of the soul from the body all superficial trivialities are stripped away and only the essentials remain. The full implications of one's moral choices are made clear as one's life is revealed in full measure. In this sense, death is a moment of truth, a moment of clarification outside the categories of time and space. With the hustle and bustle of life finally quieted one is faced with what was there all along, yet most times ignored. It is not that once dead the human person is necessarily given a second chance to make a series of entirely new decisions and to therefore become an altogether different person; but they grow in self-awareness, understanding more and more clearly the substance, meaning, and consequences of their past acts. This self-discovery will undoubtedly be a bitter-sweet mixture of appalling sorrow and unexpected joy, a "sweet

---

148-151. The doctrine of Purgatory served as a dividing point at the attempted Eccumnical Reunions of Lyons in 1274 and Ferrara—Florence in 1439. See *Bull of the Union for the Greeks of 6. 7. 1439.*

[91] Toll House theology is associated with Origen, Athanasius, and Theodosius of Alexandria. A fully developed teaching was put forth by Gregory of Thrace in the tenth century. See G. Every, "Toll Gates on the Air Way" in *Eastern Churches Review* viii (1976) 139-151.

[92] Kallistos Ware, "'One Body in Christ' Death and the Communion of Saints" in *Sobernost*, ns 3 no 2 (1981) 179-191; 182.

wormwood of torments,"[93] in which one recognizes and grieves over one's failings while simultaneously beholding the wonder of joy divine forgiveness.[94]

This teaching where death signifies self-discovery and the confrontation with who we really are is closely related to the Western and Roman idea of a particular judgment, that is, a judgment of every individual human being at their death, which then conveys them to either hell or, through purgatory, heaven.[95] The particular judgment takes place sequentially before the resurrection and the Last Judgment which will reveal the final triumph of God and his redemptive work, "the final and decisive conquest of all evil and the revelation of the victory of the Lamb that was slain."[96]

Purgatory as Hospital not Prison

Protestants particularly object to three main features of what is generally understood as the Roman doctrine of Purgatory. First, that Purgatory is a third place somehow in conjunction with heaven and hell. Second, that persons in Purgatory suffer in physical, material fire. Third and most importantly, that these sufferings possess an expiatory or atoning value and through it the sufferers make satisfaction for their sins.

As regards the first objection, it is often pointed out that there is no mention of Purgatory in scripture. There is however much mention of the

---

[93] Dante's phrase in *Purgatory* 23. 86; also note how this idea of self-knowledge is expressed in Dante's own entrance into Purgatory where upon taking the first step upon a polished stone of white marble he "was mirrored there as [he] appeared in life." Dante, *Purgatory*, 9. 94.

[94] A similar approach to Purgatory comes from *Christ Among Us*, a Roman catechism now out of favor with the Vatican: "We are responsible and accountable for our sins, and we have a need within ourselves to make up for them. Purgatory is an attempt to express our need of eventual 'purification;' the growth of needed love we must undergo before attaining union with God, who is limitless Love. Purgatory is best described as the painful state or experience of encountering God after death, when we see him as he really is 'face to face' (1 Corinthians 13:12) and, by contrast ourselves as we really are, as sinful humans." Anthony Wilhelm, *Christ Among Us: A Modern Presentation of the Catholic Faith for Adults* (San Francisco, CA: HarperSanFrancisco, 1996) 413-414.

[95] See the *Catechism of the Catholic Church*, 1021-1022 (New York: Doubleday, 1995) 288-289.

[96] Anthony A. Hoekema, *The Bible and the Future* (Grand Rapids, MI: Erdmann's, 1979) 264.

purification of believers.[97] The *Catechism of the Catholic Church* claims that tradition has given "the name Purgatory to [the] final purification of the elect."[98] In this sense, the term place does not necessarily refer to a locality but the status of the departed. Such that the catechists can write "every sin . . . entails an unhealthy attachment to creatures, which must be purified either here on earth or after death in the state called Purgatory."[99] Furthermore, tradition insists that this purification is for "the elect," which is entirely different from the punishment of the damned."[100] So that Purgatory is not a third place between hell and heaven but the porch of heaven, populated only by the redeemed who are destined only for glory.[101] So, contrary to popular piety, as is often the case, the Church has not traditionally taught that Purgatory is a locality where souls are able work off their debt to God in order to enter heaven or from which those who do no such work fall into hell. But Purgatory is a description of the intermediate state itself wherein the redeemed respond to the particular judgment and cooperate with the sanctifying grace of God, a continuation beyond death of the work begun in life.

As regards the second objection, here the Church speaks biblically when referring to the "purifying fire"[102] of Purgatory.[103] Tradition goes on to say that these "punishments must not be conceived of as a kind of vengeance inflicted by God from without, but as following from the very nature of sin."[104] Thought of in this way, Purgatory is not about the past, as if one was under the legal punishments of the law but about the future, it is

---

[97] See among others: 1 John 3:3; "All those who have this hope in him, purify themselves as he is pure." 1 Peter 22; "Now that you have purified your souls by your obedience to the truth so that you have genuine mutual love, love one another deeply from the heart." Titus 2:14; "He it is that gave himself for us that he might redeem us from all iniquity and purify for himself a people of his own who are zealous for good deeds."

[98] *Catechism of the Catholic Church* 1031, 291.

[99] Ibid., 1472, 411.

[100] Ibid., 1031, 291.

[101] This theme is beautifully portrayed throughout *Purgatory*, the second part of Dante's great work *The Divine Comedy*, where all the inhabitants of Purgatory live in hope of heaven and do their penance with "rapid wings and pinions of immense desire." *Purgatory* IV, 29.

[102] *Catechism of the Catholic Church* 1031, 291.

[103] See among others, 1 Corinthians 3:13; "the work of each will become visible, for the Day will disclose it, because it will be revealed with fire, and the fire will test what sort of work each has done." and Hebrews 12:29; "For indeed our God is a consuming fire."

[104] *Catechism of the Catholic Church*, 1472, 411.

a place of rehabilitation and training for heaven where, as God's adopted children our relationship to God in Christ is not primarily legal but filial and familial. So the sufferings of Purgatory are like a bitter medicine a parent administers to a child for their own good. It is not a prison where we are punished but a hospital where we recuperate. The works performed, if it is right to call them works, are not reparations to God but more akin to therapy that prepares one for the life to come, thus its language should be one of restoration and cure.[105]

One would not however want to dismiss the fire of Purgatory as "only" or "just" a metaphor. The Eastern Orthodox tradition helps us here to understand that the purging or testing fires faced both within life and beyond death are the fires of God's love. "God's love is present everywhere; his wrath is none other than his love. The difference lies in our attitude, in the kind of response that we choose to give."[106] The divine fire of love is at the same time the uncreated light of God and the purifying fire of judgment. This formulation neatly solves two sometimes disconcerting theological problems: How can a God of love create a hell? and Are those in hell denied the love of God? If the uncreated energies of God are at the same time both the light of God's glory and the purifying fire of judgment then hell while real is uncreated. Developing this idea further Isaac the Syrian asserts "that even those in hell are not denied the love of God but by their own free choice experience as torment what the saint's experience as joy."[107]

Dante also, in his *Divine Comedy* views Purgatory as a state of purification by God's love. This is perhaps most clearly evident in that "hell is entered at night, Purgatory at dawn, and heaven at midday."[108] Thus Purgatory is a world between the sea and the stars in which one is gently prepared for the full light of the eternal day. Moreover, Dante carves his Mount Purgatory out of the scholastic theology of penance. Through precise symbolism, most clearly displayed in canto IX he shows in the three steps

---

[105] For a Roman Catholic treatment of Purgatory as restorative as opposed to penal, see Robert Ombres, OP, "Images of Healing: The Making of the Theology of Purgatory" in *Eastern Churches Review* VIII (1976) 22-86.

[106] Kallistos Ware, "One Body in Christ," 184. Note also that this position is somewhat of a contrast to the Roman Church whose *Catechism*, referred to above, claims the purification of the elect is "entirely different" from the punishment of the damned.

[107] Kallistos Ware, "'One Body in Christ,' 184. See also Vladimir Lossky, *The Mystical Theology of the Eastern Church* (New York: St. Vladimir's Seminary Press, 1997) 234.

[108] Robert Ombres, *The Theology of Purgatory* ("Theology Today" no 24: Dublin/Cork, 1978) 27.

that lead to Purgatory, the process therein, and foreshadows his own progress through the netherworld.

Dante envisions the entrance into Purgatory as a mythically elaborate confession scene. The "custodian who had not yet spoken"[109] represents the priest who is silent at the beginning of the sacrament of confession because it is the penitent who takes the first step. The stairs, the first "white marble, so polished and so clear that I was mirrored there as I appear in life. The second step . . . scorched . . . darker than deep purple . . . [and] the third . . . flaming red as blood that spurts from veins"[110] "represent the three parts of penance, contrition, confession, and satisfaction which united for a whole healing process."[111]

Contrition or true sorrow for sin is the first step of penance and thus the first step into Purgatory. The process begins with the seeing of one's true self as in a mirror and ends with the penitent as white and pure as the marble. The rough work and deep shame of confession turns the penitent deep purple. Finally, satisfaction, the third step, is flaming red as the zeal of love now motivates the heart of the penitent.

Dante devoutly kneels and asks humbly that the gate be unbolted "out of mercy."[112] The door-keeper opens the gates using the two keys he received from Peter who taught "rather to err in opening than in keeping this portal shut—whenever souls pray humbly."[113] So in splendid imagery Dante recreated the sacrament of penance in the entrance of Purgatory using Aquinas's approach that Purgatory is part of a person's return to God.

Catherine of Genoa (1447-1510) also wrote of Purgatory as the loving fire of God. In her treatise on the subject, generally thought to be an account of her spiritual life, she wrote that while still in the flesh, she was placed by the fiery love of God in Purgatory, which burnt her, cleansing whatever in her needed cleansing, to the end that when she passed from this life she might be presented to the sight of God, her dear Love. Catherine understood that in the state of Purgatory the soul, or one's true self, is drawn by God into his loving fire, where it is melted by the heat of the glowing love of God, which it feels overflowing it. Fully exposed to the light of God; they feel themselves drawn and led to it and to their full perfection. They are hindered however by sin, and they crave above all things to be unhindered; to approach that for which they instinctively crave. The burning away of sin is a far less pain that to see themselves going against the will of God whom

---

[109] Allen Mandelbaum, *Purgatory*, 9. 78.
[110] Allen Mandelbaum, *Purgatory*, 9. 94-102.
[111] John P. Marimon, "Purgatory Revisited" in *The Downside Review* 121-141 (1994).
[112] Allen Mandelbaum, *Purgatory*, 9. 110.
[113] Ibid., *Purgatory*, 9. 127-129.

they clearly see to be on fire with extreme and pure love for them."[114] The least vision of God, while not abating their pain, overbalances all woes and all joys that can be conceived.

As regards to the third objection, the ascription of any atoning or expiatory value to the suffering of those in Purgatory seems to "undermine the fullness of our Lord's redeeming sacrifice on the cross."[115] Medieval theology, as surveyed earlier,[116] developed a distinction between guilt and punishment so that while one's guilt may have been freely forgiven upon repentance there remained a temporal punishment to be paid, in this life or beyond.[117] It was this temporal punishment from which the papal power of the keys loosed one in association with an act of penance. The reformers rightly insisted, as did Orthodox theologians before them, that this distinction was misleading. If one's sins are freely and fully forgiven then why must one endure punishment for them? Christians, they claimed, are "baptized in the name of Jesus Christ for the remission of sins."[118] "Now where there is a remission of these [sins] there is no longer an offering"[119] required.

The mistake of the reformers was throwing out the purgatorial baby with its dirty bathwater of indulgences. On this point, the reformers thought it best not to reform but to reject, as Calvin wrote the "refutation of the doctrine of Purgatory is necessary . . . because with this ax it has already been broken, hewn down and overturned."[120]

A reformed Purgatory would rightly express the continuation beyond death of that sanctification which started before death. The middle state would be the final maturing process of the person, primarily a process of growing in the knowledge of God which in turn leads to self-knowledge. The terms of Purgatory would then be not those of merit and satisfaction but of capacity and charity, not of punishment but of loving and being loved.

---

[114] See *Catherine of Genoa: Purgation and Purgatory, the Spiritual Dialogue* (Classics of Western Spirituality Series) ed by Serge Hughes (New York: Paulist Press, 1979).
[115] John Calvin, *Institutes* III.5 (675).
[116] See page 29 of this work.
[117] The Councils of Lyons and Florence use the language of satisfaction and punishment although not the word expiatory.
[118] Acts 2:38.
[119] Hebrews 10:18.
[120] John Calvin, *Institutes*, 3. 5. 6, 675.

Soul Building

In his book *Death and Eternal Life*, John Hick offers a model of the after life in which the self-conscious ego or soul continues to exist after death and continues its trek to ultimate fulfillment. The basic thrust here is teleological, that is, focusing on a goal. Death does not divide existence into a short earthly life and an interminable after life, but ones life on earth is simply the first in a series of lives, each of which will terminate in a kind of death. Hick conceives of these future lives not horizontally directed into this world at a later date, as in reincarnation, but vertically directed, in which one re-becomes into another higher world. After some time in this next world, one will die again and enter into an interim psychological state of reflection until such time as it is drawn by better possibilities of existence or impelled by boredom and emptiness into another re-becoming. When one is re-embodied in this new and higher state it is not as an immature creature but as one fitting that world. Hick feels that Jesus' words concerning "many mansions"[121] or resting places point to his conclusions.

Hick teaches that God created human beings in such a way that they naturally respond to God and follow his will. So when a person is seeking their own fulfillment and perfection they innately turn to God. There is no need for God to coerce, for he implanted within them the inclination to fulfill his will. God's activity then is seen more like a psychologist who tries to remove inhibitions which prevent persons from truly fulfilling themselves.[122] Although God encounters a myriad of difficulties and resistance he continues his work of opening human beings to their full potentiality. The end goal of this soul building activity of God is to bring persons into a state where they are totally conscious of God, themselves, and others, so they might participate in a state of fellowship which closely corresponds to the state of the intertrinatarian fellowship in which there is distinction yet marked by unity. This final stage of humanity will be characterized by "a plurality of centers of consciousness, and yet these are not private but will include the others in a full mutual sharing, constituting . . . the complex collective consciousness of humanity."[123] People will share consciousness and yet remain distinct, thus completing the social dimension of the human community. In this state of complete development, embodiment will no longer be necessary and because there will be no more change the significance

---

[121] John Hick, *Death and Eternal Life* (London: William Collins Sons & Co. Ltd., 1976) 421. See also John 14:2.
[122] Ibid., 253.
[123] John Hick, *Death and Eternal Life*, 461-462.

of time will be eliminated.[124] Within this scheme Hick understands the realization of humanity as the body of Christ growing into its head and that it is in this "mystical body of Christ that humanity is to become; one in many and many in one."[125]

This description of life after death is ultimately unsatisfactory because it envisions in due course Christians earning their salvation as they cooperate with their natural, God-given inclinations, and become better and better persons through the soul-building process of continual re-embodiments into these higher realms. However, this idea does make important contributions to understanding the afterlife. First it envisions the soul doing something or going somewhere after death. Not to be merely punished or rewarded according to their deeds but to improve, to become better than they were. This relates to the inner desire of each individual to become more than they are, and our hopes, upon seeing an individual exit this world that they will finally be made or develop some way into the persons they were potentially. Second, it envisions humanity itself, not just the individual, becoming greater, that is, sort of evolving into an ultimate social state that seems the natural end to our cultural and collective momentum.

These two contributions are mirrored in traditional Christian teaching. Christ's resurrection revealed the completed work of justification accomplished on the cross and because he is "the first-fruits of those who have fallen asleep"[126] the future of all persons beyond death. While all persons were justified in Christ, it is through the working of the Holy Spirit that they are sanctified. If there is no opportunity offered after life to cooperate with the Spirit of Christ then the work of the Spirit is destined to remain eternally incomplete. If Christian hope speaks at all of the future, it means a future time when the perichoretic work of the Triune God, that is, the Father in election, the Son in redemption, and the Spirit in perfection will be complete. That each person as an individual and collectively as the Church will fellowship with God and participate in the Divine nature. Along this line one might then think of the soul-building process as an elaborated doctrine of Purgatory focusing not on the enduring punishment but on discarding vices and putting on virtue. This seems somewhat related to the Orthodox idea of "the toll booths"[127] one passes through on the way to enter heaven as

---

[124] Ibid., 463.
[125] Ibid., 462.
[126] 1 Corinthians 15:20.
[127] See page 96 of this work.

well as the mountainous vision promulgated so well in Dante's *The Divine Comedy: Purgatorio*.[128]

Purgatory for Protestants

So if salvation is to be complete and God's victory fully accomplished no one can be let off from the requirement of realizing perfect sanctity in cooperation with God's grace.[129] Those who fear theologies of works righteousness are quick to protest schemes which take ones cooperative role in one's own sanctification seriously enough to require Purgatory or something like it.[130] However, to insist that one must be fully matured by synergistically[131] cooperating with God before one can fully enter

---

[128] For the best current English translation of this classic work see Allen Mandelbaum's translation (New York: Bantum, 1984) which includes not only an abundance of invaluable notes, but maps, and Barry Moser's drawings of the penitents as well.

[129] In his article "No Heaven without Purgatory," in *Religious Studies* 21.4 (1985): 427-456, David Brown argues that because human beings exist in time, their transformation must be a cooperative endeavor within time. Time is necessary for one to fully understanding the various layers of sin, to come to terms with self-deception, to discern truth, and to allow it to transform one's character. His claim that there is no shortcut to sanctity mirrors the earthly pilgrimage to perfection whereupon it may seem that persons have abrupt and radical conversions but upon closer examination such turnarounds more often have important antecedent causes that led up to and prepared their way. In addition, true virtue, the internal change of character and not just outward behavior, is achieved over a period of time and through numerous moral choices, often in the face of adversity. So, if human beings are essentially temporal, "[their] capacity for moral perfection is likewise. No clear sense attaches to the claim that a human being could become instantaneously virtuous, morally perfect, and so, if God is to respect our nature as essentially temporal beings, He must have allowed for an intermediate state of Purgatory to exist."

[130] One example among many is the evangelical Baptist theologian Millard Erickson, who writes "In both this life and the life to come, the basis of the believer's relationship with God is grace, not works. There need be no fear, then, that our imperfections will require some type of post-death purging before we can enter the full presence of God." Millard J. Erickson, *Christian Theology* (Grand Rapids, Michigan: Baker Book House, 1983) 325.

[131] Within New Testament reference, synergism is the idea of being "workers together with" God (2 Corinthians 6:1), or of working "out your own salvation . . . for it is God who works in you" (Philippians 2:12, 13). This is not a cooperation between "equals," but of finite human beings working together with Almighty God. Synergism does not suggest working for, or earning, salvation. God gives salvation

God's presence is not a denial that grace is the basis of one's relationship with God. For indeed, God's grace is precisely that which takes the initiative and empowers transforming growth.

The problem is that the Protestant terms of salvation are primarily forensic ones where grace is seen first and foremost as forgiveness apart from its enabling work of sanctification. Forgiveness alone, in this legal model, does not change one in a subjective sense. So even if persons respond in loving gratitude to God's free gift, at the time of their death, many if not most, will remain imperfect lovers of God and others. Forgiveness itself does not eliminate the shortcomings of the body or mind. Indeed, the more one understands one's justification the more one realizes that the most pervasive and deadly sins are those of the spirit. These sins cannot be cured by receiving a new and better body at the resurrection. Other remedies are needed, and as C. S. Lewis writes, these other remedies most probably involve pain.

> Our souls demand Purgatory, don't they? Would it not break the heart if God said to us, "It is true, my son, that your breath smells and your rags drip with mud and slime, but we are charitable here and no one will upbraid you with these things, nor draw away from you. Enter into the joy"? Should we not reply, "With submission, sir, and if there is no objection, I'd rather be cleansed first"? "It may hurt, you know."—"Even so, sir."[132]

Lewis realizes that moral transformation is essentially painful and that the pain involved is not some arbitrary punishment that God attaches to

---

by His grace, and one's ability to cooperate also is a grace. Therefore, persons respond to salvation through cooperation with God's grace in living faith, thanksgiving, righteous works, and rejection of evil (James 2:14-26).

[132] C. S. Lewis, *Letters to Malcolm: Chiefly on Prayer* (New York: Harcourt, Brace, Jovanovich, 1973) 108-9. Lewis goes on in his letter "I assume that the process of purification will normally involve suffering. Partly from tradition; partly because most real good that has been done me in this life has involved it. But I don't think the suffering is the purpose of the purgation. I can well believe that people neither much worse nor much better than I will suffer less than I or more.... The treatment given will be the one required, whether it hurts little or much.... My favorite image on this matter comes from the dentist's chair. I hope that when the tooth of life is drawn and I am 'coming round,' a voice will say, 'Rinse your mouth out with this.' This will be Purgatory. The rinsing may take longer than I can now imagine. The taste of this may be more fiery and astringent than my present sensibility could endure. But . . . it will [not] be disgusting and unhallowed."

it; but intrinsic to the growth progress itself.[133] It can be said to be a universal principle of life that for some joy set before them, living things endure pain and therefore grow. This is especially true if the definition of pain includes anxiety. Maturity, then, both produces and requires a higher threshold for one's own pain and the pain of others. Never to allow others the gift of anxiety is to inherently retard their growth.

Lewis makes this point beautifully in *The Great Divorce* where the grass of heaven hurts the feet of the ghosts from the gray town (a purgatorial place for those who choose to leave it, a hellish one for those who choose to remain.) "Reality is harsh to the feet of shadows."[134] Becoming conformed to the life of heaven is uncomfortable for sinful persons. But the promise is given that those who persevere will eventually become more substantial, and thus more comfortable, and at home in heaven.

Purgatory then enables persons to come to terms fully with reality. Confrontation with the love of God makes one aware of one's own failed love relationships. It unmasks selfishness, and unresponsiveness, and in doing so brings its own kind of suffering, not as something inflicted by the beloved other, but as a pain somehow inherent in the loving response we wish to make. As love inspires and summons forth the best self, it also brings into awareness one's resistance to it: possessiveness, self-absorption, manipulation, violence, fear and so on. In such a sense, one becomes aware of one's unworthiness in the face of such a gift. "Show me a lover and he will understand"[135] Augustine preached. A true lover understands the pain of not being completely and fully for the other.

Again Lewis gives us an excellent example of how this might look. In his crowning work, *Till We Have Faces* Queen Orual in an experience somewhat between life and death is moved to write what might be called a life review to make her case before the gods. During this time of examination, introspection, and analysis, she comes to see her life as the gods

---

[133] The use of pain is the grounds for much popular resistance to doctrine of Purgatory. While this may be an understandable consequence to the vividly horrifying depictions of Purgatory purveyed in sermons and devotional literature of the past "it smacks of the sort of cheap grace, pervasive in much popular contemporary piety, which implies that mere mental assent to some basic Christian doctrines is all that is necessary for salvation. On this picture, salvation is a perfectly painless thing that requires nothing of the believer." Jerry L. Walls, "Purgatory for Everyone" in *First Things* 122 (April 2002): 26-30.
[134] C. S. Lewis, *The Great Divorce* (New York, The Macmillan Company, 1946) 43.
[135] Augustine, *Homily on St John's Gospel* 26, 4 in *The Nicene and Post Nicene Fathers of the Christian Church*, Vol. 7, ed by Philip Schaff (Grand Rapids, Michigan: William B. Eerdmans Publishing Company, 1956) hereafter referred to as NPNF.

do. She begins to understand the depth of her sin and how even her love was selfish and destructive. This painful recognition of her own ugliness enables her finally to see the beauty of sacrificial love within her world and at last in herself. It is by this process that she matures into a real person before the gods; "for how can they meet us face to face till we have faces."[136]

Philosopher Richard Purtill has taken up Lewis's paradigm with his suggestion that the period between death and resurrection will be a time of reading one's life like a book in what he calls Godlight. This Godlight would enable one to see the full force of how one's sins affected others. "The only adequate Purgatory [being] to suffer what you made others suffer—not just an equivalent pain, but that pain, seeing yourself as the tormentor you were to them. Only then could you adequately reject and repent the evil."[137] By the same token, in Godlight we will see with love even those who have hurt us, because God sees them with love. In the grace of Godlight God's perfect love will illumine all things and God's work to redeem from sin and unite all persons to him and each other will be fully revealed. This new insight, not only into ones own moral choices but into God's gracious love and saving power allows a commentary of sorts to be written in appreciation of and as a correction to our earthly lives, so that even a life of folly and waste could be the foundation of a glorious commentary much better than the book.

With his *Confessions,* Augustine provides the epitome of this purgatorial model. Remembering that the salvific process of sanctification after death is but a continuation of that which is started in this life, and that Augustine with his mother Monica "attained to a slight degree"[138] a vision of the Wisdom that is God while at Ostia, he then set about the long task of "recalling himself and encountering himself . . . things past . . . and future actions . . . as though they were actually present."[139] Through this prayerful exercise Augustine writes a commentary on his life that is better than the book, finally summarizing his life in these words:

> Too late have I loved you! Behold you were within me, while I was outside: it was there that I sought you, and, a deformed creature, rushed headlong upon the things of beauty which you have made. You were with me, but I was not with you. They kept me far from you, those things which, if they were not in you, would not exist at all. You have called to me, and have cried out, and have shattered

---

[136] C. S. Lewis, *Till We Have Faces* (New York, Harcourt Brace & Co. 1956) 294.
[137] See Richard Purtill, *C. S. Lewis's Case for the Christian Faith* (San Francisco: Harper & Row, 1981) 101.
[138] Augustine, *Confessions,* 222.
[139] Augustine, *Confessions,* 237.

my deafness. You have blazed forth with light, and have shone upon me, and you have put my blindness to flight! You have sent forth fragrance, and I have drawn in my breath, and I pant after you. I have tasted you, and I hunger and thirst after you. You have touched me, and I have burned for your peace.[140]

Thought of in this way, even though it may be a painful experience, Purgatory could be described as a state of joy, remembering that the New Testament repeatedly teaches Christians to rejoice in adversity that purifies faith.[141] This is not to trivialize the pain of Purgatory, but rather to point out that it ought to be dreaded no more than the pain of moral transformation experienced in earthly life; and like that beginning be viewed as a gracious gift of love.

So Purgatory then expresses the Christian hope that the patient love of God for all on their pilgrim journey will have its own way and finally bring them to completion. This purification in life and after death is always to be understood within the perspective of God's free gift of grace. In his redeeming love God does not pretend that evil is good, that imperfection is fulfillment, or that believing persons have arrived at their best selves, rather he works for the reality of our total transformation. Purgatory is one's unfinished existence being possessed by the living flame of the Spirit and the final exorcism of the demons that have driven one's life.

This approach goes a long way in meeting traditional Protestant objections to the doctrine of Purgatory. The problem of abuses has been addressed and dealt with. More notably, we see that Purgatory does not compromise the free gift of God but is a consequence of his sheer grace as it inspires human freedom to a complete and wholehearted conversion. The Reformers were right in their insistence that Purgatory in no way diminishes the all-sufficiency of the grace of Christ. Finally, Purgatory is not dolorism, that, is salvation wrought by sheer suffering.[142] Though there is suffering in Purgatory it is suffering born out of love and one's unreserved surrender to the Spirit. Any interpretation of God's love as merited or appeased by suffering would abolish Christian hope and turn eternity with such a God into a fearful prospect. The life of faith is described in the scriptures as a

---

[140] Ibid, 254-255.
[141] See Matthew 5:12; Philippians 2:17.
[142] Paul Tillich complained that, "In Catholic doctrine, mere suffering does the purging. Besides the psychological impossibility of imagining uninterrupted periods of mere suffering it is a theological mistake to derive transformation from pain alone instead of from grace which gives blessedness within pain." Paul Tillich, *Systematic Theology*, vol. 3 (Chicago, IL: University of Chicago Press, 1963) 417.

"walk thru the valley of the shadow of death."[143] In this Christian walk a certain amount of suffering can be expected if not assured. It is not this suffering, however, nor the willing acceptance of it, that atones for our sin or makes us acceptable to God. We are justified, sanctified, and glorified only by the person and work of Christ.

Death Itself as Purgatory

The experience of death itself may provide one with their final purification. As the world of sense and its confusing turmoil grow still, as loneliness and helplessness press down upon them, as their awe deepens before the approach of the great reality and their sense of guilt intensifies by the coming judgment, they cry in the terrors of death with purer inwardness and more profound trust to the merciful God. As a child in unquiet sleep reaches put for the loving hand of its mother, even so do they grope after God, the life of their life. And so there springs up within them an ardent love of their Father, a love that is ready to relinquish life gladly, a perfect love. In such ardor all sin dies, every evil inclination is extinguished and every penalty. The soul enters into the joy of the Lord.[144]

In these terms of Christian tradition, Purgatory implies a particular judgment at the moment of death.[145] This moment of truth is not so much a judgment passed on us by God, but the realization of the truth not only about ourselves but incarnate in what we are. In death human beings are stripped of their self-deceit. Their sin in fully revealed and they are exposed for what they were and are,[146] what they have decided to be, what they stand for, and what, through the process of life, they have become. In dying, we come to, as if awakened from a semi-self consciousness. Death is the ultimate moment of personal truth.

Ladislaus Boros, SJ in his book *Mysterium Mortis* suggests that the death experience is an opportunity for growth unsurpassed by any other event because it is the most exquisitely personal moment of anyone's

---

[143] Psalm 23:4

[144] Karl Adam, *The Spirit of Catholicism* (New York: The Crossroad Publishing Company, 1997) 102.

[145] In thinking of Purgatory an encounter with the risen Lord, and a definitive entry into the death of Jesus, the language of a moment of purification and perfect contrition seems appropriate and speculation of temporal duration makes little sense.

[146] See Barth, *Church Dogmatics* III/3, trans. G. W. Bromiley and R. J. Ehrlich (Edinburgh: T & T Clark, 1960) 86.

temporal existence.[147] The decision open to a person in death is to affirm or deny that death is beyond righteousness, retribution, and understanding. When all of these things are given up, then death is one's first and last chance to embrace the utter humanness of one's condition. But, by the same sign, it is one's first and last chance to know that in choosing to affirm the complete loss demanded by death, there is transformation toward one's prototype—the God-man, and there is also the joy of transformation; the passionate joy of gaining in loss that which is lost in gain. When a person mourns and affirms the final loss of their life time, they finally know in abundance the joy which follows the thousand deaths that accompany everyday living. They know the full meaning of Paul's words: "What you sow does not come to life unless it dies."[148]

Christians enter into eternal life through Baptism and resurrection. Baptism is our identification with the death of Christ and the beginning of our resurrection, "a way out of the labyrinth of death."[149] So in a sense, death completes what began in Baptism, it is the final entry into the dying of Christ himself. Our union with Christ in death reveals the fact that we are still refusing to die.[150] In the depths of selfishness and lovelessness Christ now appears as "the way."[151] Death and corruption have become the path to eternal life for "Christ united to himself all through which death reaches"[152] and through his own death he has overthrown death itself. In his descent into death, hell, and separation from God, he now summons the dying to the death of a final self-surrender in this dying they participate fully in the mystery of Christ's death, his self-emptying for the life of the world. He who has died for us, now dies in us, and we die in him. In this way each individual existence becomes a passion for God and Purgatory becomes pure faith; the loving but dreaded letting go of anything less than a totally Christened existence.

Purgatory as the Fire of Christ's Holy Spirit

It may well serve Christian theology to think of physical death, Purgatory, and even judgment, as we will soon explore, as one great event.

---

[147] See Ladislaus Boros, *The Mystery of Death*, trans Gregory Bainbridge (New York: Seabury Press, 1973).
[148] 1 Corinthians 15:35.
[149] Gregory of Nyssa, Or. *Catechetica Magna*, cap. 35, *P.G.* XLV, 88 ff.
[150] The exception to this would be the martyrs who meet death willingly in and for faith; as such the martyrs are said to bypass Purgatory. However, within this way of thinking we would say that their death was their Purgatory.
[151] John 14:6.
[152] Gregory of Nyssa, Or. XXX (Theology IV), 21, *P.G.* XXXIV, 132 B.

In this dying to God the whole person, body and soul, is judged, purified, healed, illuminated, and perfected by God through Christ Jesus. In this sense Purgatory is not a time or place but an encounter with God. "Purgatory is God himself in the wrath of his grace"[153] It is "the encounter of the unfinished person, still immature in his [or her] love, with the holy, infinite, and loving God; an encounter which is profoundly humiliating, painful, and therefore purifying."[154]

In this decisive encounter with Christ each person is confronted with the definitive form of humanity and personhood. One becomes aware of oneself being made "through him,"[155] for him, "in him."[156] In this encounter is becomes piercingly apparent that a great deal of one's existence is yet outside him, not yet for him, not yet subjected to him. Christ is the judgment passed on our life. The tension between what we obviously are and what we most love and desire to be is the root of the purifying suffering of Purgatory. Christ looks upon those who come to him with unreserved love and absolute graciousness.[157] His gaze, however, judgingly burns to the innermost parts of that human existence. So at the same time, encountering God in Christ's eyes of fire is both the highest fulfillment of a person's capacity for love and also the most fearful suffering one's nature can bear.

The fires of purification both in this life and in the life to come can be brought together in a new appreciation of the flame of the Holy Spirit.[158] This, above all, is the fire of Purgatory. Through every stage of life and beyond life the flame of the Spirit possesses and transforms our existence creating, redeeming, reconciling, liberating, and purifying. The work of the Spirit is to conform baptized persons to the crucified Christ that they might rise with him.

---

[153] Hans Küng, *Eternal Life? Life After Death as a Medical, Philosophical, and Theological Problem*, trans. Edward Quinn (New York: Doubleday & Company Inc., 1984) 139. Flannery O'Connor has a similar statement in her best novel *The Violent Will Bear It Away*, when the protagonist, having been through a violently painful experience that produced within him growth and maturity hears the command: "Go warn the children of God of the terrible speed of mercy." Flannery O'Connor, *The Violent Will Bear It Away* (New York: The Noonday Press, 1955) 242.

[154] G. Greshake, *Starker als der Tod, Zukunft – Tod – Auferstehung – Himmel – Holle – Fegefeuer*, (Mainz, 1976) 93, as quoted in Hans Küng, *Eternal Life?* 139.

[155] John 1:3.

[156] John 1:4.

[157] The mystic Marie des Vallées who was granted a day in hell by God writes: "God's love is more terrible, and better understands how to make us suffer, than his justice." Émile Dermenghem, *La Vie admirable et les révélations de Marie des Vallées d'après des textes inédits* (Paris, Plon-Nourrit et Cie, 1926) 73.

[158] Luke 3:16; 12:49; Acts 2:3; I Thessalonians 5:19

Just as in life, each transformation implies a death; the death of the old self and the rebirth of the new self. The great mystic John of the Cross testified to the dark night of suffering when the glaring objects of secure little worlds become dark in the radiance of ultimate light.

> The dark night is an inflowing of God into the soul, which purges it from ignorance and habitual—natural and spiritual—imperfections. . . . In this state God mysteriously teaches the soul the perfection of love, without its doing anything and without its understanding the nature of the infused contemplation. For what produces such striking effects in the soul is the loving wisdom of God, which by its purifying and illuminating action prepares the soul for the union of love with God. . . . But now the question arises: Why does the soul call the divine light dark? The answer is that for two reasons this divine light is not only for the soul night and darkness, but also affliction and torment. The first reason is the sublime grandeur of divine wisdom, which transcends the capacity of the soul and is therefore darkness to it. The second reason is the lowliness and impurity of the soul, and in this respect, divine wisdom is for the soul painful, bitter, and dark.[159]

In this sense, the fire of Purgatory is the Holy Spirit, penetrating, possessing, purging, purifying, and finally transforming all that we are.

Summary

In its Creed the Church establishes its belief in the reality of life beyond death. The sanctification of believing persons, which begins in the life below, is brought to completion in the life above. The saints are brought to perfection in, by, and through the grace of Christ Jesus the pioneer and perfector of faith. This final perfection of the saints is the continuation and completion of what began at Baptism where "though water and by the Spirit"[160] earthly persons are united to Christ's death,[161] "know his sufferings"[162] and glorified with him in heaven. The saints, then, are members of the Church, living with God, and being brought to perfection by

---

[159] John of the Cross, *The Dark Night of the Soul*, 2: 2; 5, trans. Kurt Reinhardt (New York: Frederick Ungar Publishing Co., 1957) 188-189.
[160] John 3:5; Acts 3:38.
[161] See Romans 6:1-11; 8:9-14
[162] 2 Timothy 1:8

God, who either await or perhaps have already experienced the resurrection of the body.

Chapter Five

We Believe in . . . the Resurrection of the Body

Jesus taught that God is "God, not of the dead, but of the living."[1] He spoke clearly of the resurrection of the dead and he linked that resurrection to his own person saying "I am the resurrection and the life."[2] Jesus raised persons from the dead[3] and he himself conquered the grave. So Christians believe and hope that just as Christ was truly risen from the dead and lives forever, "he who raised Christ from the dead will give life to their mortal bodies also."[4] For if it is "for this life only we have hoped in Christ, we are of all people most to be pitied."[5]

United with Christ in Baptism Christians, by the power of the Holy Spirit, already participate in the death and resurrection of Christ. In this sense they are already resurrected although "hidden with Christ in God;"[6] raised up with him and seated with him at the right hand of God. Christians look forward nonetheless to a definitive "Last Day"[7] "when the Lord himself we descend from heaven . . . and the dead in Christ shall rise."[8] Just as Christ was raised with his own body; for he testified to his disciples "look at my hands and my feet; see that it is myself; touch me and see," so too shall the dead be raised with their own bodies, yet they "will all be changed."[9] The perishable body will be made imperishable and the mortal will be made immortal.

So there will be both continuity and discontinuity in the resurrection. The body that is sown or buried today is not "the body that is to be, but a bare seed."[10] Within that seed is the essence of what it will become, but what it is to become in its maturity is far greater than the seed itself. As an acorn

---

[1] Mark 12:27.
[2] John 11:25.
[3] Mark 5:22-43; John 11:1-44.
[4] Romans 8:11.
[5] 1 Corinthians 5:19.
[6] Colossians 3:3.
[7] John 6:39-40; 44; 54; 11:24.
[8] 1 Thessalonians 4:16.
[9] 1 Corinthians 15:51.
[10] 1 Corinthians 15:37.

holds within it the kernel of a mighty oak tree so the earthly body relates to the spiritual body.

From its earliest proclamation Christian faith in the resurrection from the dead has met disbelief and opposition[11] but despite the ancient mockery of Greek philosophers and the modern mockery of skeptics, the Church continues to proclaim the resurrection of the body. Our bodies, which are an important part of our selves, will not be completely destroyed in the end. As they participated in Baptism, the other Sacraments, and the Christian life on earth, so they will enjoy, with our souls, eternal life in heaven. For this reason Christians do not seek to escape the body but to "redeem the body."[12] This view is at variance with reincarnation, which teaches that the body is a mere vehicle of the soul, one of many such vehicles which the soul will use and discard. Christians will not lay aside their sacred flesh[13] but it will be transformed. Like a butterfly emerging from its chrysalis, transcending its old form with an unimaginably new and greater form which will freely participate in what is yet the invisible and inconceivable sphere of God. This is our hope: not that we will become angels, God, or part of God, but that we in our created bodies will become incorrupt, powerful, and honorable, and that we "will be initiated into a realm of peace with God."[14]

Dualism

Traditionally Christianity has made a distinction between the body and the soul.[15] This is in large part motivated by the doctrine of the after-life and a belief in an intermediate state. That is, a period between death and the resurrection wherein ones personal identity survives. Such reasoning usually

---

[11] Acts 17:32; 1 Corinthians 15:12-13.

[12] Romans 8:23.

[13] The ancient Christian practice of signing one's body with a cross is a physical, kinetic profession of faith in the Trinity and salvation through the cross of Christ Jesus. It is a prayer of the body and a reminder that our bodies are sacred, consecrated to God as living temples.

[14] Barth, *Credo*, 166.

[15] As to the definition of the word *soul*: "The Church affirms the continuity of the spiritual element in [human beings] after death, an element which is endowed with consciousness and will, so that the human 'I' continues in being. In order to refer to this element the Church employs the term soul. [The Church] is aware that the word soul appears in the bible with varying significations. Yet it insists that there is no solid reason for rejecting this term. Much more it is considered a verbal instrument which is simply unavoidable for retaining the Church's faith." Auer Ratzinger, *Dogmatic Theology 9: Eschatology*, 245.

follows this pattern: If the organism that is the body is clearly dead and returns to dust in the grave, and if the person is to somehow survive death to take up his or her body again at the resurrection; then that center of personhood that is called the soul must reside either with God in a state of blessedness or separated from God and the world in a state torment or waiting. This survival in the intermediate state avoids the loss of identity between the person in the grave and the person resurrected. Thus a human person is said to consist of a body, the organism, and a soul, the essential person or self.[16] The essential person is distinct; created from and can exist apart from the earthly organism.

Historically these beliefs in the intermediate state and the body-soul distinction have been taken to be the full meaning of scripture, confessed by the faithful, and defended by Christian philosophers and theologians. While the details of the intermediate state were not completely agreed upon especially between Roman Catholics and Protestants, for the most part there existed, until the twentieth century, a general consensus that there was one, and therein the soul survived awaiting the resurrection of its body.

In modern times, however, body-soul dualism has been criticized by theologians, biblical scholars, philosophers, and scientists, Christian and non-Christian alike. The materialistic and monistic anthropologies of Hobbes and Spinoza in early modern philosophy disapproved of the traditionally accepted body-soul dualism and proposed non-dualist theories of human nature.[17] As the rapid acceptance of Darwinian evolution undermined the belief in the soul as a distinct entity in the nineteenth century, brain physiologists and psychiatrists discovered a great deal of evidence indicating the dependence of mental and psychological states on the brain, thereby undermining the basis for the soul as a separate substance from the body.[18] In identifying

---

[16] Some theologians, called tricotomists, separate the person into three components: the spirit as the essential human self that relates to God; the earthy body, and the soul which mediates and conjoins the spirit with the material body. The trichotomistic view was popular among the Eastern Church Fathers of Greece and Egypt influenced by Plato, among them were Clement of Alexandria, Origin, and Gregory of Nyssa. See Louis Berkhof, *Systematic Theology* (Grand Rapids: Erdmann's, 1941, 1976) 191-192. Important for the purposes here is the common assumption in both trichotimism and dualism that persons continue to exist after physical death.
[17] See Thomas Hobbes, *Leviathan*, trans. C. B. MacPherson (London: Penguin Classics, 1982); and Benedicto Spinoza, *Ethics* (1677), trans. G H R Parkinson (New York: Oxford University Press, 2000).
[18] See Franz Alexander and Sheldon Selesnick, *The History of Psychiatry* (New York: Harper & Row, 1966) Ch. 10; and Gardner Murphy, *Historical Introduction to Modern Psychiatry* (New York: Harcourt & Brace, 1949) Part II.

apparent direct causal relations between brain functions and states of consciousness these scientists now argue that neurophysiology demonstrates the radical dependence, indeed, identity, between mind and brain and therefore deny the mind or soul as an incorporeal entity.

In addition, after their careful analysis of the biblical texts, some scholars have concluded that the biblical view of human nature is not dualistic after all but rather insistently holistic.[19] Following in form, Christian historians confirm that the roots of the traditional dualistic anthropology were nourished in the soil of a Hellenistic worldview and not so much by scripture as had been previously assumed. Chief among these was Adolf von Harnack who speculated that Greek dualism had trounced Hebrew holism leaving its indelible dichotomizing imprint on Christian theology.[20]

Finally, many devoted Christians have charged that the traditional body-soul distinction has given rise to other false dichotomies and harmful separations such as the separation of nature from grace, secular from sacred,[21] physical from spiritual, and social gospel from personal gospel.[22] These fruits of dualism distort the gospel and breed such spiritual evils as the neutral conception of secular culture, the destruction of the environment, slavery, male dominance, and sexism,[23] thereby preventing the complete salvation of humanity and of the whole creation.[24]

---

[19] See H. Wheeler Robinson, *The Christian Doctrine of Man* (Edinburgh: T & T Clark, 1911).

[20] See Adolf von Harnack, *Outlines of the History of Dogma*, trans. Edwin Mitchell (1893; reprint, Starr King Press, 1957); and Oscar Cullmann, "Immortality of the Soul or Resurrection of the Body?" first published as "Unsterblichkeit der Seele und Auferstehung der Toten," *Theologische Zeitschrift* (1956) in which he challenged what he regarded as a "Platonic" reading of the New Testament.

[21] See Theo Witvliet, *A Place in the Sun*, trans. John Bowden (Maryknoll, NY: Orbis, 1985).

[22] See Brian Walsh and Richard Middleton, *The Transforming Vision* (Downers Grove, IL: InterVarsity, 1984) Ch. 7, "The Development of Dualism."

[23] See Elisabeth Schuessler Fiorenza, "Feminist Theology as a Critical Theology of Liberation," *Theological Studies* (1975) reprinted in Gerald Anderson and Thomas Stransky, eds., *Mission Trends No. 4* (Grand Rapids: Eerdmans, 1979) 188-216.

[24] See Bishop Desmond Tutu, "Black Theology/African Theology – Soul Mates or Antagonists?" (1975) in Gayraud Wilmore and James Cone, *Black Theology, A Documentary History, 1966-1979* (Maryknoll, NY: Orbis, 1986).

Monism

Based on these new scientific discoveries and scholarly opinions, various forms of monism have been proposed.[25] Monism seeks to define or at least speak of a person as a distinctly whole being not a composition of a body and a soul. The question then arises concerning the shape of individual eschatology, that is, what happens when we die? There are two alternative strategies for viewing death and resurrection which avoid the intermediate state and its inherent commitment to dualism. "One is to affirm an immediate or instantaneous resurrection. The other is to hold that humans pass out of existence and remain nonexistent until the resurrection, when they are completely recreated by God."[26]

Immediate resurrection involves a transformation at the very instant of death, as one either passes into another dimension of time beyond earthy time or transcends time altogether. Depending on how one defines resurrection this might include the receipt of a new or renewed body, the conversion into a spiritual mode of existence, or some type of union with God. In any case, there is no intermediate state between one's death and resurrection and therefore no need to separate the body from the soul. Or is there? While there may be no need to separate the body and soul, they are separated nonetheless. According to this theory the essential self is resurrected instantaneously in a new body or form of existence, however there are still two bodies, the one wasting in the grave and the resurrected one whatever it may be. The essential self moves, albeit quickly, from one to the other, but it is still a transition. The only real difference between the intermediate state and the immediate resurrection is the absence of a temporal gap between the two bodies. The essential self in both cases is related to two bodies and therefore dualism is not requited. So the alternative of immediate resurrection upon close inspection actually fails to avoid dualism. It is dualistic in that it entails the continuous identity of one person in two bodies. The same person is separated from a dead, earthly body in the same instant that he or she is joined to a resurrected body.

Extinction–Re-creation assumes that when the body dies the whole person ceases to be. No spirit, soul, mind, or essence survives death. However at the future time of the general resurrection God will bring back

---

[25] See Augustus Strong, *Christ in Creation and Ethical Monism* (Philadelphia: Roger Williams Press, 1899) for an early approach.
[26] John W. Cooper, *Body, Soul, and Everlasting Life: Biblical Anthropology and the Monism-Dualism Debate*, (Grand Rapids, MI: Eerdmans, 1989) 106. I am greatly indebted to Dr. Cooper's work relating to the problem of dualism.

into existence, that is re-create, the very same person in some glorified form. According to this theory, because one is extinct there is no awareness of the passing time between death and re-creation so from the first person point of view it would seem instantaneous. Again because the intermediate survival was avoided the problematic existence of the soul was also avoided. Or was it? Whether it be immediately after death or eons later, if God re-created a new single mental-physical whole person constructed exactly and in every way the same as its dead predecessor would that be the same person? Or would it be more similar to the clones of today's popular since fiction movies? In monism persons are fundamentally related to and inseparably part of a specific and particular entity. If there is then an earthy body and a resurrected or re-created body then there must be two persons, not one and the same person, even if the two bodies are exactly the same and share the same memories. John Cooper, Protestant theologian and author of *Body, Soul, and Everlasting Life: Biblical Anthropology and the Monism-Dualism Debate* offers an intriguing illustration to make this point. Imagine that an oak tree died and decomposed and many years later one of its acorns was planted on the exact spot where the oak once stood. There the acorn grew absorbing all and only those atoms from the soil that belong to its parent tree, which it resembled precisely in size, shape, and appearance. Though the trees would be exactly similar, they would not be self-identical.[27] Because numerical identity, being someone, and exact similarity, being recognized as someone, are different properties, extinction–re-creation cannot guarantee that recreated persons are the same persons as there earthly prototypes. The alternative of extinction–re-creation fails to fully engage and resolve the obstinate problems of personal identity. While this may seem to be a hairsplitting speculation, it is not a mere academic exercise but has a direct bearing on one's assurance of their personal future resurrection.

Holistic Dualism

What is needed is a resurrection theory that is faithful to scripture and Christian Tradition while answering the concerns of science and philosophy. Such a scheme must provide at least: that the essential selfhood or core personhood survives after death; that in such a state one is capable of some sort of experience; that one is aware of oneself as the same person

---

[27] John W. Cooper, *Body, Soul, and Everlasting Life*, 170.

who lived upon the earth; and that all this is possible without the earthy organism which lies in the grave. Holistic Dualism[28] offers just such a design.

Materialistic monism proposes that persons are a set of human mental and physical capacities generated by the body which includes the brain. So that persons are said not to have bodies but to be bodies. Holism on the other hand presents persons as body-soul unities. Holistic-dualism describes personhood as "holistic" in a functional sense.[29] That is, it recognizes, for example, that the human mind and brain function as a unity, but without assuming that they are one and the same metaphysical substance. Persons are dualistic in that their essential selfhood can in some way survive after the earthly body has turned to dust.

Holistic dualism makes the claim that despite the "holistic" tone of Hebrew anthropology, there are at least two reasons why it should not be read as a pre-philosophical type of monism. First, the creation references offer an indisputably composite description of human nature. "God formed man from the dust of the ground and breathed into his nostrils the breath of life; and the man became a living being."[30] Second, human life is not regarded

---

[28] In his book, *Body, Soul, and Everlasting Life: Biblical Anthropology and the Monism-Dualism Debate,* Cooper surveys in detail biblical anthropology while carefully analyzing current trends in physiological, psychological, and philosophical theory. After outlining the historical background of the controversy Cooper presents an exegetical case for "holistic dualism" in both the Old and New Testaments, as well as in inter-testamental Judaism by arguing that the texts as a whole support his interpretation with less ambiguity than any of the other alternatives. For instance, while New Testament passages that indicate a future resurrection do not exclude the possibility of extinction and future re-creation, as suggested in John Hick's theology, they nevertheless rule out an immediate resurrection. Likewise, passages that support continued existence after death without excluding the possibility of immediate resurrection, put forth in the theologies of Wofhart Pannenberg, Karl Barth, and Hans Küng, nevertheless rule out extinction and re-creation. Hence, the traditional view comes out ahead.

[29] Holistic dualism recognizes that while scientists experimenting in modern brain physiology and psychology have made important discoveries they are by no means certain that a complete correlation between brain events and specific states of consciousness actually exists. In fact, such a correlation, even if it could be proved, would not necessarily demonstrate that experience is unilateral between brain events as causes and conscious states as effects. For we already know that persons can generate complex brain episodes by first forming a concept, such as meditating on God, or worrying about an exam. Consequently, the causality postulated on the basis of a pattern of regular association must move in both directions.

[30] Genesis 2:7.

as ceasing at death, but as having a continued ghost-like existence[31] in *Sheol, Abaddon*, or, in the *Septuagint, Hades*.[32]

Where the New Testament is concerned, a survey of passages that support a future resurrection (without necessarily excluding the alternative of possible extinction and future recreation[33]) seem to rule out an immediate resurrection; while passages that support continued existence after death (without excluding the alternative of immediate resurrection[34]) seem to rule out extinction and recreation. Hence, the dualist approach comes out ahead.[35]

Answering the concerns of committed Christians, holistic dualism need not be synonymous with the religious dualism that too often seeks to separate a sacred religious sphere from a value-free secular one, nor an axiological dualism that divides mundane menial activities from nobler spiritual ones, nor with the social dualism that divides male and female, black and white, civilized and barbarian, and the like. There is no reason why a holistic dualist cannot be opposed to such wrong-headed idealizations. In broad terms holistic dualism does not confine one to a single set of philosophical circumstances but allows for a wide range of various scientific, biblical, and philosophical interpretations under its umbrella.[36] So what does a reasonable paradigm of holist-dualism look like?

Following the metaphysical outline of Thomas Aquinas, Christian Personalism, as most recently and ardently promulgated in the Lublin Thomism of Pope John Paul II, regards persons as created substances whose nature is to act and thereby develop themselves. The whole person is not just a soul, mind, or consciousness but a soul, mind, or consciousness incarnate in the world. Therefore, persons are bodily beings complete with

---

[31] See Deuteronomy 18:11; Leviticus 19:31, 20:6; 1 Samuel 28; Isaiah 8:19

[32] See Genesis 37:35; Job 3:13, Ecclesiastes 9:10; Isaiah 14, 9-10, 38:18; Psalm 88:10-12, 115:17-18.

[33] This view is proposed by John Hick, *Death and Eternal Life* (San Francisco: Harper and Row, 1976)

[34] This view is held in a variety of forms by held by Wofhart Pannenberg, *What is man?*, trans. D. Priebe (Philadelphia: Fortress Press, 1970); Karl Barth, *Dogmatics in Outline* (New York: Harper and Row, 1959) Ch. 24; and Hans Küng, *Credo: The Apostles Creed Explained for Today* (New York: Doubleday, 1992) Ch. 6.

[35] For an exhaustive and definitive explication of the scriptures in question see John W. Cooper, *Body, Soul, and Everlasting Life*, ch. 5, 6, 7.

[36] While it is not necessary here to hammer out their nuances, compatible theories include dualistic interactionism, which itself ranges from a robust Cartesianism to a softer Aristotelian-Thomism, dualistic parallelism, dual aspect monism, idealism, and even qualified materialism. Some theories, of course, are easier to reconcile with Christian Scripture and Tradition than others.

feelings, instincts, emotions, consciousness, thoughts, and wills created to realize and develop themselves through their acts. It is only this type of person that "can be the causative subject of his [or her] act and an efficient cause of all human values."[37] Such persons do not develop themselves from nothing but have been made in the image of God and that gives them a definite nature. Because God is love, the goal or meaning of human personal existence is love. "Love is the source of all humanities various spheres of existence. Love understood in these terms, becomes the ultimate and fundamental principle of self realization of a man [or woman] as a 'person-act.'"[38] Not just the soul but the entirety of human existence, including the body, is created for love.[39] This is the basis of ethics, the foundation for the proper treatment of the environment, animals, cultural objects, and other human beings. Love is the summary of our duty to God, the basis for justice in human society, and the defining purpose of human nature. Love leads to happiness for happiness results from self fulfillment, and love is the purpose of human existence. God is love. God created us in his image. When we love we reflect the image and glory of God. Love is from God.

Summary

Using the insights of holistic dualism we can say that the saint's essential selfhood or core personhood survives after death. They are capable of some sort of experiences, and are aware of themselves as the same person who lived upon the earth. Finally, that all this is possible without the particular earthy matter which lies in the grave.

The Created Soul and the Resurrected Body

All matter was created out of nothing[40]—we are matter—to exist and not be matter is to be uncreated—to be uncreated is to be eternal—to be eternal is to be God—we are not God—therefore we must be and must always remain matter. This argument is not a materialist one, that is one that denies the existence of the spiritual but its claim is that the spiritual, the soul,

---

[37] Andrew Woznicki, *A Christian Humanism: Karol Wojtyla's Existential Personalism* (New Britain, CT: Mariel, 1980) 9.
[38] Ibid., 30.
[39] This integral unity of the soul and body self-actualizing in love is ultimately realized in human sexuality as an act of interpersonal love which brings forth new life. Inasmuch we clearly see love as the origin and goal of human life.
[40] For the foundational argument of creation *ex nilho* see Augustine, *Confessions*, books 12, 13.

the true self that survives the body though it may be immaterial by some definition is, in fact, a created thing. The scriptures refer to the immortality of human beings as "God's gift of eternal life;"[41] as such human beings should not be considered innately or inherently immortal.[42] "The doctrine of the immortality of the soul as a substance is of Platonist (an ancient Greek philosophy) and not of biblical origin."[43] This is the difference between the respective deaths of Socrates and Jesus. Socrates drank his hemlock with little concern and no tears because his soul, he believed, was immortal and the death of his body but a release to a better existence.[44] Jesus, on the other hand, did not "obtain his victory by simply living on as an immortal soul"[45] but conquered dreaded death by first actually dying in all senses of the word.[46] Without a real death there cannot be a real resurrection.

The scriptures help us in thinking of death parallel to sin.[47] While God did not make human beings sinful he did create them with the ability to sin. Likewise, while creating human beings able to die he made them also able to continue to exist as persons beyond the physical death of the earthly organism. So the created person-soul is not innately immortal but can receive the gift of eternal life from God within the resurrection. So the question becomes what relation will the soul have with the body at the resurrection?

Aristotelian-Thomism defines the soul as the form of the body. The human person is a unity of form and matter. The matter is the bodily material out of which a person is constituted while the form is the soul which organizes, directs, and energizes the matter to actualize the bodily person.

---

[41] Romans 6:23.
[42] John Calvin assumed the immortality of the soul in his *Institutes* and thereby influenced Protestant acceptance of the doctrine. See *Institutes of the Christian Religion* 1.5.5, 56.
[43] H. W. Robinson, "Hebrew Psychology" in A. S. Peake, ed. *The People and the Book: Essays on the Old Testament* (Oxford: Oxford University Press, 1995) 362.
[44] See "The Death of Socrates" in Plato's *Phaedo*, a good English translation with notes is by David Gallop (Oxford: Clarendon Press, 1975).
[45] Oscar Cullman, *Immortality of the Soul or Resurrection of the Dead? The Witness of the New Testament* (New York: McMillan, 1958) 25.
[46] Cullman further states his belief that Paul "surely met people who were unable to believe in this preaching of the resurrection for the very reason that they believed in the immortality of the soul." Ibid. 59.
[47] See Genesis 2:17; Ezekiel 18:4; 1 Corinthians 15:21, 22, 56; Romans 5:17; 6:21, 23; 8:6; James 1:15.

Seen this way the soul is a created system or code that organizes matter.[48] "The body is the visibility of the soul and the soul the actuality of the body."[49]

This helps us make sense of a curious problem posed by modern biology, that continuity of bodily substance is not essential to bodily identity. Biologists tell us that because of the body's natural processes of ingestion, digestion, and excretion the matter which makes up one's body changes a number of times during a normal life span. So that the matter that apparently gives a person continuous identity is not essential to that identity even in this life. Understanding this will allow one to extrapolate a circumstance where the soul, thought of here as a code organizing matter, can receive a new body, composed of matter totally unrelated to the dust in the grave, and yet keep its identity. Thus our resurrected body need not necessarily be the exact same matter as lies in the grave. However this does not exclude the soul from taking up that same matter as did Jesus when he left the tomb.[50]

This also helps one resolve the problematic possibility that the same matter has over the ages belonged to more than one person. As bodies decay and are returned to the ecosystem their matter may re-enter at some point the human food chain and be incorporated into someone else. This is

---

[48] See Norbert Wiener, *The Human Use of Human Beings* (Boston: Houghton Mifflin, 1950) 91; and John Hick, *Death and Eternal Life* 281-283.

[49] Auer Ratszinger, *Dogmatic Theology 9: Eschatology*, trans. Michael Waldenstein, (Washington D.C.; The Catholic University of America Press, 1988) 149.

[50] An important note is that Jesus' resurrected body still carried the scars of his crucifixion, and he seemed to make a point of showing them to his disciples. He displayed them in his initial appearance in the upper room, and then again, for Thomas' benefit in John 20:19-20. The fact that Jesus' scars remained indicates that his wounds are part of his essential identity, the form of who he truly is. In Jesus Christ, God was revealed as the direct target of all the hatred, hostility and cruelty that human beings are capable. As the ultimate victim of human evil, Jesus can offer real forgiveness of it. True forgiveness, then, is not sweeping things under the rug, pretending they did not happen, with some superficial pretence of a lost innocence being restored. The visible and irreversible scars of Jesus demonstrate that forgiveness is shown in the willingness to speak peace to those who have wounded you and to wish for and act for the best for them. Forgiveness is known in hearing the word of peace breathed by the victim of your own sin. Victory over every hatred and hostility is shown and known in the risen Christ who takes it all in his own flesh and refuses to return it in kind but rises above it, forever ensuring that tragedy cannot entomb love and hope. Cruciform Forgiveness, accepting the consequences of sin without reacting vengefully, is theorized as a model of the atonement by Fisher Humphreys in his book *The Death of Christ*, (Nashville: Broadman, 1978). John Killinger, in his *Jessie: a Novel*, (San Francisco, McCracken Press, 1993) presents his risen heroine bearing the glory of her scars.

certainly the case at the historic Oakwood Cemetery, in Waco, Texas, in which scores of pecan trees grow among the graves. In the fall of each year the families of the reposed are invited to harvest the pecans which in many cases are destined for a Thanksgiving pie. The Sadduceeic question is in danger of arising: "whose will it be in the resurrection?"[51] To think of the soul as the form of matter also allows persons who died neonatally, as infants, to be complete in their resurrection.

Thinking of the soul as the form of the matter which it is currently organizing, coupled with the modern Einsteinian understanding that even energy is matter ($E=mc^2$), provides a wide range of possibilities for contemplating the afterlife. This idea can also be used to clarify theoretically why the Bible depicts visions of the dead as quasi-bodily or ghost-like beings without faulting the ignorant worldview of the seer or author.

Such existence is not purely speculative thinking but observed quantum reality. Quantum physics is that latest science that tries to make sense of the apparent fact that neither the sub-atomic world nor the macro-cosmic world conforms to the mechanist patterns so uniformly observed in our middle-size world. As such quantum theory has put to an end the fantasy that, reality is like a pocket watch whose inter workings become apparent when taken apart. With its development it was discovered that the sub-atomic world did not behave the way that Newtonian physics had predicted and that in fact, in that tiny world waves turn into particles and particles turn into waves; what has mass one moment is pure energy the next, and none of it is predictable. So there exists a small precedence at least for thinking about our resurrected bodies in this new way.

The Moral Significance of the Body

The last point to make concerning the resurrection of the bodies of the saints is this: the resurrection restores to the body moral significance and empowers Christians to use their bodies in ways that would otherwise appear foolish. Christians surrender their bodies in martyrdom as witness to God's will in the face of idolatry, corruption, and oppression. Virginity and chastity likewise can become witnesses to God's creative power to produce new life apart from biology. Finally poverty in service to others gives witness that there is more to life than the consumption of the world. Raised with Christ, Christians, their whole person including their body, share in the dignity of belonging to Christ. This means that Christians treat their bodies with respect, and also the body of every other person. Christians recognize that

---

[51] See Matthew 22:28; Luke 20:33.

"the body is meant for the Lord . . . and the Lord for the body . . . The body is a temple for the Holy Spirit . . . therefore [they] glorify God in [their] bodies."[52] Resurrected with Christ, Christians need not fear nor detest their bodies. Perfected in Christ, the saints control their bodies without sin; their sin and sins having been forgiven by the same Christ who restores their bodies in the resurrection.

Summary

By its belief in the resurrection of the body the Church claims that the Communion of Saints is that community of persons, in this life and beyond this life, whom God has chosen for bodily resurrection to eternal life and upon whom, body and soul, God has lavished his free gift of justifying and sanctifying grace through Christ Jesus. The earthly echo of this act of God is Baptism and it is affirmed in the Creed as the forgiveness of sins.

---

[52] 1 Corinthians 6:13,19-20.

Chapter Six

We Believe in . . . the Forgiveness of Sins

The Creed offers no theory of sin nor does it propose a theory of salvation. It simply asserts that God entered human existence; the result of which is the forgiveness of sins.

Baptism is the initial witness or sign expressing the forgiveness of sins. The Apostle Peter preached to the crowd "Repent and be baptized, every one of you, in the name of Jesus Christ, so that your sins may be forgiven."[1] Likewise, Paul is told by Ananias "Get up, be baptized, and have your sins washed away, calling on his name."[2] In his letters Paul lays out a theology that intricately connects Baptism to the forgiveness of sins.[3] So we see that "the relevance of Holy Baptism is this, that we may our whole life long think upon the fact that we are baptized;"[4] and therefore that our sins are forgiven even if and especially when we do not feel as if they are. The ancient Church is so insistent on this point that the Nicene Creed modifies the older line to state emphatically "I acknowledge one Baptism for the remission of sins."[5]

The forgiveness of sins is the work of the triune God. The Son intercedes on the cross saying "Father forgive them;"[6] the Father forgives on account of the Son who fully forgives his debtors; they both pour out their Holy Spirit upon sinners that they might forgive themselves and each other. So Christ taught his followers to pray "forgive us our trespasses as we forgive those who trespass against us."[7] This does not mean human forgiveness compels God to forgive, but that our forgiveness of one another "is indissolubly linked with our hope and plea that God might expunge our debts too, from his account book."[8] But the forgiveness of sins means more than the mere cancellation of a past debt. It means also "the lifting of the weight

---

[1] Acts 2:38.
[2] Acts 22:16
[3] See Romans 6:1-8:3; 1 Corinthians 9-11; Ephesians 5:25-27.
[4] Barth, *Dogmatics in Outline*, 150.
[5] Philip Schaff, *The Creeds of Christendom*, Vol. 2, The Greek and Latin Creeds (Grand Rapids, Michigan: Baker Books, 1993) 59.
[6] Luke 23:34.
[7] Luke 11:4; see also Matthew 6:12.
[8] Hans Urs Von Balthazar, *Credo: Meditations on the Apostle's Creed* (New York: Crossroads, 1990) 89.

of sinful attitude and disposition that drags us downward."[9] Moreover, forgiveness is more than pardon for particular sins but it is an affirmation of God's love and acceptance of finite human beings and the active expression of God's desire to be in fellowship with them. On the cross "the Son presents to the Father, in his own person, the sin of the world that he has taken away, at the same time presenting to him in his body, his bride, the living sinner now stripped of sin."[10] The sins are remitted, separated from us, and taken away. "They are banished to the place where everything God does not want and condemns is; hell."[11]

As stated earlier, it is Baptism that initiates one into a community enlivened by the forgiveness of sins and therefore called to the practice of forgiveness. So in the Apostle's Creed, belief in the forgiveness of sins immediately follows belief in the Communion of Saints, for it is the forgiveness of sins which not only reunites sinners with God but also with each other. For just as persons are not whole when they have distanced themselves from God, so also they are not whole when they have distanced themselves from one another. Therefore Jesus said: "when you are offering your gift at the alter, if you remember that your brother or sister has something against you, leave your gift there before the alter and go; first be reconciled to your brother or sister, and then come and offer your gift."[12] So the community of saints is populated by those who not only have received the forgiveness of sins but who practice the forgiveness of sins, remembering their Lord's words: "if you forgive others their trespasses, your heavenly Father will also forgive you; but if you do not forgive others, neither will your Father forgive your trespasses."[13]

The association of Baptism with the forgiveness of sins helps one understand the Creed's affirmation of the holy catholic Church and its relationship to the Communion of Saints. The Church is holy, not because it is a community composed solely of holy people, but is regarded holy because it can make people holy, since in it there resides the grace thorough which all persons can find salvation; justification and sanctification. The Church is "the inclusive ark of salvation"[14] proclaiming and practicing the forgiveness of sins for all people, even those who have committed post-

---

[9] Luke Timothy Johnson, *The Creed* (New York: Doubleday, 2003) 281.
[10] Hans Urs Von Balthasar, *Theo-Drama: Theological Dramatic Theory*, Vol. 5, The Last Act, trans. Graham Harrison (San Francisco: Ignatius, 1998) 314-315.
[11] Ibid. 314.
[12] Matthew 5:23-24.
[13] Matthew 6:14-15.
[14] William Barclay, *The Apostle's Creed for Everyman* (New York: Harper and Row Publishers, 1967) 302

Baptismal sin (as explored earlier in this work.[15]) This forgiveness of sins becomes tangible in the sharing of the holy things, that is the sacraments, which we shall see is another aspect of the Communion of Saints.[16]

Hence the forgiveness of sins is the primary concern of the fellowship of the saints both upon the earth and in the hereafter. The kingdom of heaven is "a society of mutual forgiveness, renewed fellowship and intimacy, based on God's forgiving us and our forgiving one another."[17] The saints in heaven are those who sins have been forgiven and who sin no more. Their great concern is praise to God in Christ for this divine action and that the sins of their brothers and sisters on earth also be forgiven. The Communion of Saints is the mysterious connection of all persons, in this life and beyond, united in Christ who surrendered himself for the forgiveness of their sins.

"He Shall Come to Judge the Living and the Dead"

These words of the Creed are its only description of the blessed future beyond time. While the Church affirms the existence of a "life in the world to come" it does not so affirm the outright existence of a heaven or hell. What we affirm instead is the reality of forgiveness of sins attached to the last article concerning Christ, that, he comes to all people, living and dead.

The Three-fold Coming of Christ

This leads to the understanding of the return of Christ as a three fold event. The first return of Christ was his resurrection and appearances during the forty days of Easter. This created and proved the basis of faith and assures Christians that what remains of death has been deprived of its power. The extension of the last day "is to allow space before the kingdom comes to repent and believe the Gospel[18] on the basis of this event."[19] A second form of the coming of Christ is in the impartation of the Holy Spirit[20] which effectualizes his presence in the world, not least of all in the sacraments. The third and final coming of Christ is his future return which is "the goal of the history of the Church, the world, and each individual as he comes as the

---

[15] See "Penance" in Part One of this work, 17.
[16] See page 298 of this work.
[17] See his comments on the parable of the unforgiving slave (Matthew 18:23-35) in John Killinger, *You Are What You Believe: The Apostle's Creed for Today* (Nashville: Abington Press, 1990) 108.
[18] See Mark 1:15.
[19] Barth, *Church Dogmatics* III/3, 622.
[20] See Barth, *Church Dogmatics* IV/3, part 1, 293.

author of the general resurrection of the dead and the fulfiller of the universal judgment."[21] This three-fold return of Christ represents one event, "each containing the other two by way of anticipation of recapitulation."[22] The final return of Christ is the completion of what God in Christ began in the resurrection and continued in the outpouring of the Holy Spirit. At last "God will be all in all."[23]

The Final Coming of Christ

In this since eschatology is not about something but about someone. It is about Christ and about his coming. The second coming of Christ is not only "the restoration, but at the same time the universal and final revelation, of the direct presence of Jesus Christ as 'God-man' this was the content of the forty days after Easter."[24] "Resurrection is the carrying out of the accomplished reconciliation of man in his future redemption."[25] It reveals that Easter was not a chance miracle or a one time event but the sign of the end and the meaning of all history. As such the focal point of all truth is the end of time; as Pannenburg states in his Dogmatic Thesis on the Doctrine of Revelation: "Revelation is not completely apprehended at the beginning, but only at the end of revelatory history." It was this final self-revelation of God that will only occur at the end of time which was brought forward into time and history in the life, death, and resurrection of Jesus Christ.[26]

As the goal of time comes to an end, Christ will "make visible, finally and for all people, the decision taken in him—God's grace and kingdom as the measure by which the whole of humanity and every single human

---

[21] Ibid., 293.

[22] Ibid., 294.

[23] Barth, *Dogmatics* in Outline, 155.

[24] Barth, *Credo*, 121.

[25] Ibid., 166.

[26] Pannenberg further states that these truths can only be revealed in certainty at the end of time; "Only at the end of all events can God be revealed in his divinity, that is, as the one who works all things, who has the power over everything. Only because in Jesus' resurrection the end of all things, which for us has not yet happened, has already occurred can it be said of Jesus that the ultimate already is present in him, and so also that God himself, his glory, has made its appearance in Jesus in a way that cannot be surpassed. Only because the end of the world is already present in Jesus' resurrection is God himself revealed in him. Wolfhart Pannenberg, "Dogmatic Thesis on the Doctrine of Revelation," in *Revelation as History*, ed. Wolfhart Pannenberg (New York, NY: Macmillan, 1968) 125-58.

existence is measured."[27] "The situation is that the world derives unknowingly, and the Church derives knowingly, from Jesus Christ, from his work."[28] Those who do not see Christ, who remain outside the Church "who have no direct experience of him, are no less reconciled to God through him than others are."[29] Though the atonement is less visible to some, that does not make it less real.[30] Jesus Christ has come. He has spoken his Word and finished his work. This is the objective fact of salvation and it exists independently of any person's belief of it or in it. What remains is for the hiddeness of this fact to be fully revealed. God in Christ makes fully manifest what he has already accomplished. The revelation known now to the Church where Christ is present in Word and Sacrament will be fully disclosed to all persons living and dead in such a way that no one will any longer be able to deceive themselves concerning the reality of salvation.

The New Testament frequently describes this scene as "the Son of Man coming in a cloud with power and great glory."[31] These are metaphors which indicate complete revelation to come when the heavens will be opened and the Son will stand before us as the person he is, at the right hand of the Father, and together with the Holy Spirit the Triune God will be known to all his creation and all his creation will participate in the Divine community. This is the ultimate and universal manifestation of Christ. "Then for the first time it will become visible, that it is not a question of our Yes and No, our faith or our lack of faith"[32] but the "it is finished"[33] of Christ will come to light in full clarity to all. We are all on the way to meet this manifestation. It is in the future, but the future of that which has already taken place "once and for all."[34] So that the "Alpha and the Omega"[35] are the same thing, the same person, Christ Jesus, our savior and judge.

What Kind of Judge?

This being the case how should we understand the judgeship of Christ? One would do well to remember that a judge is not merely a person who rewards good and punishes evil but the person "who creates order and

---

[27] Barth, *Dogmatics in Outline*, 129.
[28] Ibid., 132.
[29] Barth, *The Epistle to the Romans*, 160.
[30] Ibid., 416.
[31] Luke 21:27.
[32] Barth, *Dogmatics in Outline*, 134.
[33] John 19:30.
[34] Romans 6:10.
[35] Revelation 1:8; 22:13.

restores that which has been destroyed."[36] If we think of Jesus in this way then the judge is the restorer and the restoration, or better yet, the revelation of this restoration, is the judgment. In this way the judgment is an event that should be anticipated with unconditioned confidence.

One might reply that this conception does not take judgment seriously. However, if God's grace and God's faithfulness are the rule by which all is to be measured then the terrifying visions of Last Judgment scattered throughout the New Testament are not meaningless.

That there is such a divine No is indeed in the judgment. But the moment we grant this we must revert to the truth that the Judge who puts some on the left and some on the right is in fact he who yielded himself to the judgment of God for me and has taken away all malediction from me. It is he who died on the cross and rose at Easter.[37]

Judgment as Revelation

Karl Barth famously wrote "rightly understood there are no Christians: there is only the eternal opportunity of becoming Christians."[38] Barth's theology gives us a useful paradigm in which to think about judgment. Barth considered God's chief activity that of free and sovereign self-revelation. That is, God is freely revealing himself and giving himself to his creation that it might participate in God's relationship of love. This concept of God's self-revelation contains within it the idea that the revealer and what is revealed are identical. God is both the subject and content of this self-revelation. The ultimate revelation of all that God is was brought into history by, in, and through Christ. He is the Word incarnate, the revealed God, in him we see the complete revelation of the likeness of God.[39] The incarnation of the eternal Word, Jesus Christ, is God's supreme self revelation.

The focal point of all truth is the person of Christ himself. Jesus Christ the Son, in his relation to his Father, is the eternal archetype and prototype of God's glory in his outward manifestation. As the God-man, Christ not only reveals the true nature of God but is also the eternal archetype and prototype of true humanity revealing the ultimate criterion for what it means to be a human person. As the eternal Son of God who became human in Jesus of Nazareth, who suffered and died on the Cross that sinful persons

---

[36] Barth, *Dogmatics in Outline*, 135.
[37] Ibid., 136.
[38] Barth, *The Epistle to the Romans*, 6th ed., trans. Edwyn C. Hoskyns (London: Oxford University Press, 1933) 321.
[39] Barth, *Church Dogmatics*, Vol. 1/2, 58.

may forever have fellowship with God, Jesus Christ is himself the realization of that resolve of God (within himself in eternity before the creation of the world) which is sometimes called the eternal decree of God or God's election. It is only in Jesus Christ and through him that God could carry out and has carried out his eternal plan in which he elects himself to fellowship with man and man to fellowship with himself.[40] In his resurrection Christ revealed the end and goal of all time and the future of humanity.[41]

So we can think of the condemnation and mercy of God as two sides of the same coin; one being the reverse of the other. God cannot have mercy on anyone without first sentencing them to condemnation.[42] So sinful humanity is rightly rejected by God in righteous judgment and abandoned "to eternal perdition."[43] However, this judgment has been diverted to Christ Jesus "and in that way averted from others."[44] Salvation in Christ then is truly universal, in that it is offered to all humanity without exception on the basis that Christ has already died for the sins of all humanity and suffered the punishment thereof. Hence Jesus Christ is both the elect and the reprobate on behalf of all. God "rejects, and therefore elects; he condemns and therefore is merciful. God conducts men down into Hell and there releases them."[45] There is no room for an eternal punishment not already endured efficaciously by Christ. The divine "No" is a prelude to the divine "Yes." In the person of Jesus Christ, we meet both God's "Yes" to us and his "No" in such a way that it is a mistake to try to hear the "No" independently. In this way, "Rejection is the shadow of election."[46]

"The death of Christ is concerned precisely with this benefit. It is a benefit rather than providing us with knowledge of God . . . provides us with

---

[40] Christ is the servant judge who is judged in our place and who empties himself, the royal man who is raised up by God. He is the true witness, the victor over all that opposes him, and the light of life which exposes evil as an "impossible possibility" which has no future. Specific aspects of sin are exposed by each aspect of Christ – pride resists accepting what God-become-man does for us; sloth refuses to take an active part in the new life given by Christ; falsehood resists and distorts the witness of Christ, and so on. The way of human salvation is justification by grace through which the Christian community is gathered, in love through which the community is built up, and in hope, which sends the community out as witnesses in word and life.

[41] Barth, *The Resurrection of the Dead*, trans. H. J. Stenning (New York: Fleming H. Revel Company, 1933) 134.

[42] Barth, *Church Dogmatics*, IV/I, 501.

[43] Barth, *Church Dogmatics* II/2, 346.

[44] Ibid., 346.

[45] Barth, *The Epistle to the Romans*, 393. See also 1 Peter 3:19.

[46] Barth, *The Epistle to the Romans*, 401.

the assurance that [God] knows us."[47] So the revealing work of Christ and the judging work of Christ are in a sense identical. "This is the judgment, the light has come into the world"[48] says Christ. But people love darkness rather than light, for the light of God's self revelation exposes their evil deeds. So "we are not saved by our knowledge of God [but] our knowledge brings us under judgment.[49] Revelatory judgment exposes to persons the true God and their true selves. As Emil Brunner writes:

> Nothing further is needed but that the divine light should pierce [one's] being so that what is hidden—like the eternal parts of a body under x-rays—becomes visible. This again is a metaphor implying full disclosure of what has hither been concealed. 'It comes to light'—that is the essence of the judgment. It is revealed—not for God: for how could anything ever have been concealed from him?—but for ourselves. We shall stand naked and exposed according to the truth of our being, with no concealing raiment. . . . The sole decisive thing is the fact of manifestation. [50]

This judgment manifestation of that which is hidden includes also a separation. God's self revelation creates a crisis of decision which permits no neutrality or indifference. But this decision is not a matter of choosing between two possibilities, as if one's salvation rested solely upon ones choice for or against God. It is not left up to one's so-called free choice whether or not one belongs to God. God's self revelation means that God has already chosen us. God confronts us with the unequivocal demand that we recognize and endorse God's prior decision in Christ that we belong to him. To us is entrusted and expected "merely the echo, the subsequent completion, of the decision which has already been made"[51] about us and for us. Our decision for God is an answer to the Word of God which accepts us unconditionally. The essential meaning of judgment is the ultimate manifestation of the truth that it is God's decision and not our's which determines eternal life or eternal death.[52]

In this picture God's activity is revelation and judgment is a person's response as one sees themselves as they really are. God however is not out

---

[47] Ibid., 162.
[48] John 3:19.
[49] Barth, *The Epistle to the Romans*, 393.
[50] Emil Brunner, *Eternal Hope*, (London: Lutterworth, 1954) 176.
[51] Emil Brunner, *Eternal Hope*, (London: Lutterworth, 1954) 178.
[52] For an intriguing explication of the judgment scenes of the Gospels see Brunner, *Eternal Hope*, 180.

of the picture since it is only by an act of divine grace that one can come to this self-knowledge in which true judgment is possible. The very nature of sin requires self concealment and self justification. As long as one lives in the world and has their senses intact one can delude oneself with illusions of guiltlessness. However the final coming of Christ to judge the living and the dead will put an end to self delusion. In this way, the coming judgment, whether at the end of time or immediately following death, is good news. The good news of the apocalyptic stories is that the judge is none other than Jesus and this is the hope of all those who rely on him.

Upon death it becomes impossible for us to continue to deceive ourselves. Stripped from our senses we can only see ourselves, we see who we were, who we are, and what we have become. The light which enables this introspective sight is the light of God. "The face of the judge radiates a divine light that illuminates the very depths of our hearts, and we shall have no other accuser but our own sins, thus made present to us."[53] Augustine writes "There is a certain divine power whereby everyone is reminded of all that he [or she] has done, good or evil. ... This divine power is called a 'book' in which we read, as it were, what is set forth in it."[54]

Judgment then can be regarded as judgment upon oneself in light of the divine truth of what God has done for us in Christ Jesus. It is when we are confronted with ourselves and the divine act of love on the cross that we are forced to admit that we fall utterly short of God's glory. To this ultimate confrontation between our life and the life of Christ we can only respond with Peter's words "Depart from me, for I am a sinful man."[55] This self judgment however is not the final judgment, for God in Christ Jesus is the final judge of the living and the dead. And "in Christ the Trinity is bent on reconciling the world to God. In this perspective, therefore, even if a [person] tries to exclude [themselves] from it in order to be in [one's] own private hell, one is still embraced by the curve of Christ's being."[56]

The Pilgrims' Progress

Judgment in this manner, is not necessarily a single event. If one's faith emphasizes immortality in such a way that the human person reacts and develops beyond death in a manner similar to that in the world, judgment

---

[53] Basil, *On Psalm 33*, 4 (PG 37, 964.)
[54] Augustine, *The City of God*, 20, 14.
[55] Luke 5:8.
[56] Hans Urs Von Balthasar, *Theo-Drama: Theological Dramatic History, Vol. V: The Last Act*, (San Francisco, Ignatius Press, 1983) 304.

will likely be seen as a gradual process of becoming aware of the truth. But if one's faith emphasizes the moment of death as the moment of truth, judgment is more likely to be seen as a dramatic crisis point in which all is suddenly revealed. It is quite likely that both the dramatic moment and gradual changes have their place in judgment, for no single event is ever entirely unrelated to what goes on before and after it.

So judgment is a part of life and a part of life after death where at the crisis point or points the revelation of God is more and more piercing and the purging, changing, and correction are likewise more and more radical. "Confronted by Jesus, [human beings] must die, they must die daily."[57] Judgment is part of growth and development and is designed to move one closer and closer to God, to bring one to maturity, to develop persons into what they were created to be. For God is not indifferent, but loves. He desires that persons choose the way of life, and indeed participate in the divine life itself. The biblical analogy serves well here, in which one might be considered a tree and God a dresser. Through various judgment events we are pruned and directed until there comes a point when the direction of growth is so firmly fixed that no fundamental alterations remain to be made. The element of striving, with its anxiety that breeds uncertainty is removed, and peace and serenity take over. With the last corrections having been made perfection becomes reality within an existence where growth is never stagnated.

Such a view of judgment requires that we "reject the traditional doctrine, both Catholic and Protestant, of the inalterability of the souls state beyond death, the doctrine that there can be no 'second chance' of salvation beyond this life, no new and different moral decisions, and no personal growth and development in response to further experiences."[58] "God forbid that [we] should limit the time for acquiring faith to the present life. In the depth of the divine mercy there may be opportunity to win it in the future."[59] While the eternal direction of the saved is fixed at death, the ultimate condemnation of those who know not Christ is not so necessarily decided.

For the divine person-making process to be brought to completion it follows "that responsible life must continue through bodily death."[60] Life after death then must be a continued growth toward maturity and selfhood, which when grasped brings the Christian into a new and complete

---

[57] Barth, *The Epistle to the Romans,* 108.
[58] John Hick, *Death and Eternal Life* (Louisville, KY: Westminster/John Knox Press, 1994) 238.
[59] Martin Luther, in a letter to Hasen von Rechenberg in 1522, as quoted in Harry Buis, *The Doctrine of Eternal Punishment* (Grand Rapids, Michigan: Baker, 1957) 74.
[60] John Hick, *Death and Eternal Life,* 238.

relationship with God. In this pilgrim's progress one continues in one's restless search for the fullness and richness of God[61] and along this journey there will be both times of amazing growth and times of apparent barrenness.[62] "As the arrow, loosed from the bow by the hand of the practiced archer, does not rest till it has reached the mark, so [human beings] pass from God to God. [God] is the mark for which they have been created; and they do not rest till they find their rest in him."[63]

This analogy of a journey makes clear the impracticality of compartmentalizing life beyond death into the convenient regions of hell, Purgatory, and heaven, with all the dead suitably assigned blessed, faithfully departed, or damned. The analogy of the journey puts every Christian who departed on their way to salvation in essentially the same sort of condition. "On that road their will be so to speak, some far ahead and some lagging behind, some bounding forward, some finding it a struggle, some seeing efficiently ahead to avoid obstacles, others being struck by them."[64] So the pilgrim's progress goes. While we recognize that the peace and assurance of those at journey's end, within the grasp of perfection, constitute a more abundant quality of life than those who follow behind still touched by doubt, fear, and pain, we cannot define the particular point where one changes to the other.[65] This means then that although Purgatory may no longer be envisioned as a place where the departed go for a specified time, its validity in articulating the cleansing fire of this life and the next cannot be dismissed.

Hell likewise becomes not a place where God sub-humanly and everlastingly tortures the wicked without hope of deliverance but the valid articulation of a condition wherein there is no growth or development and therefore no hope of escape; a seemingly endless nightmare of pain and loss, but one which cannot be eternal for God in his great love can intervene and indeed only the action of God can win through and transform the situation. Hell, in this case, is not a place wherein one is thrown but a state, both in this

---

[61] It is important to remember as Augustine has taught us that the language we might use expressing our "restless search" for God is relative and should in no way deny the greater truth that God was and is ever drawing us unto him. See *Confessions*.
[62] John Bunyan's *The Pilgrims' Progress* captures the changing moods of this journey well.
[63] Barth, *The Epistle to the Romans*, 438.
[64] Michael Perham, *The Communion of Saints* (London: SPCK, 1979) 105.
[65] This point is beautifully literalized in Dante's *Purgatory* where suffering souls are translated out of their anguish at an unexpected moment that can in no way be defined in association with their works, and is punctuated by the song of the Church's liturgies and the sound of heavenly bells. See Dante Alighieri, *The Divine Comedy, Purgatory*, trans. Mark Musa (New York: The Penguin Group, 1984).

life and in the world to come, in which one may gradually drift or suddenly fall into a paralyzing deadness from which rescue is needed.

To resist one's true destiny and reject loving fellowship with God is certainly hell. In this description hell is that state where one is thoroughly off course. It is a figurative term for those who have refused to accept the only viable option, and have veered off the pilgrim's way onto a route that leads to a "dead" end or even more hellishly, that goes in the opposite direction of that intended for them. Just as life on earth has its "hells" Christians may do well to describe hell as an intermittent experience beyond the grave into which our God of rehabilitation descends to put things back on course.

So Purgatory can be thought of as the condition of departed persons who are going in the right direction but still have some obstacles to overcome. Unlike those in hell, there is no need for a dramatic change of course, but rather perseverance and patience. Heaven is the grasp of perfection graciously granted to those who have finished the course. To reach this condition persons must travel a long road whether in this life or beyond it. But at last they shall behold the vision of God and therefore shall rest in a state of complete trust, free from all anxiety and fear. Furthermore, because one's growth and maturity is brought about not only in relationship with God but with ones neighbor as well[66] there will be a sort of incompleteness and the victory of Christ will not be full until the abundant life of the heavenly kingdom is shared by all.[67] So not only will each unique life of every individual person come under the judgment of God but every tribal, political, national, and religious, institution, tradition, or authority will come under the Judgment of God in Christ as well. The full and final consummation and true happiness of humankind can come about only if all persons, present, past, and future share in this happiness. Thusly the happy ending of all human history and or every human's history can come only with an encounter with the manifest reality of God.

What is Hell?

Can there be a God of mercy from whom mercy to the dead is excluded? Can there be a God of peace and reconciliation who perpetuates a lack of peace and reconciliation? Can there be a God who commands love

---

[66] See Luke 10:27-28.
[67] See Hans Urs Von Balthasar, *Dare We Hope "That All Men Be Saved"* (San Francisco: Ignatius Press, 1996) and John Ballie, *And The Life Everlasting* (New York: C. Scribner's Sons, 1934) 249ff.

of enemy but who takes vengeance on his enemies for all eternity? Is it a contradiction to accept God's love and mercy and at the same time the existence of hell as a place of eternal punishment and torment?[68] Or, if God did take time to create a realm called hell would it be without residents? For, after all is said and done, "a blessed communion with God and others in heaven is one image of the ultimate state which could be nicely complemented by an image of an empty hell."[69]

In his *Peri Archon*, Origen first proposed the hypothesis that given the logic of God's relationship with history, universal reconciliation must be its destined end. Origen hoped that in and through divine suffering, the reality of evil is taken prisoner and overcome so triumphantly that it ultimately ceases to exist. Following him in this hope were a long line of Church Fathers including Gregory of Nyssa, Didymus the Alexandrian, Diodore of Tarsus, Theodore of Mopsuestia, Evagrius Ponticus, and Jerome of Bethlehem—who assumed that the punishments of hell were imposed only for a time. However, the synod held against Origen in Constantinople, in 543 AD defined the punishment of hell as being "temporally unlimited

---

[68] Annihilationism is the teaching that persons who die outside of the boundaries of salvation will suffer, not eternal conscious punishment in hell, but eternal non-existence, commonly called the second death. At the heart of its theological arguments (supported by exegetical criticism which gives careful attention to the apocalyptic genre of the majority of texts that deal with judgment and the eternal states together with the varied and clearly metaphorical nature of the language used to describe them) for annihilationism is the concept of immortality. Based on the premise that "according to Scripture, only God possesses immortality," annihilationists reject the immortality of the soul as a dualistic, Platonic intrusion on Christianity that has replaced the biblical teaching of the resurrection of the body at the end of time. Human beings are, therefore, inherently and naturally mortal and immortality is, potentially, communicated or conferred to humanity exclusively in God's gift of salvation in Jesus Christ (John 20:31). As Stott puts it, "he reveals it and gives it to us through the gospel" and it is received only at the eschaton (1 Corinthians 15:53), thus allowing the corollary that the unredeemed who do not receive the gift of immortality via salvation are simply extinguished at death. See John Stott, *Evangelical Essentials* (Downers Grove, Illinois: InterVarsity Press, 1988) 313-320.

[69] Keith Randall Schmitt, *Death and the After-Life in the theologies of Karl Barth and John Hick: A Comparative Study* (Amsterdam: Rodopi, 1985) 207.

and of eternal duration."⁷⁰ Centuries later Dante envisioned the inscription above hells portal to read "Abandon all hope, you who enter here"⁷¹

There is a sense however, in which hell itself is an articulation of hope. Hell is the expression of the Christian hope that anticipates a state in which evil will be finally revealed for what it is and brought to nothing. As a theological reality, hell represents God's ultimate judgment on evil; it is the divinely imposed limit to evil's destructive capacities. It is the point where evil is not only contained and rendered impotent, but made to serve the higher purpose of a good creation, where the anti-Christ is vanquished, and where evil has to face itself for what it is in the light of God. In that radiance there will be no pretence, no evasion, no compromise, and no further subversion of the good. The language of hell prohibits any representation of God's love as tolerance of evil or compromise with it.

God does not simply overlook sin, but rather in Christ God has overwhelmed it. The cross graphically demonstrates both the horridness of sin and evil and the powerful love of God. To suggest that an individual sin, or the collective powers of this world might in some way hamper the redeeming work of Christ is to suggest that in his resurrection Christ was not the victor and that somehow evil is more powerful than God. In Christ God achieved an overwhelming triumph of grace that no one or no thing can render ineffective. The decision of ones salvation and ultimate destination rests with God alone. To place that decision, in whole or in part, on a human being is to condemn them to an eternity of futile seeking and searching, which may well be considered a fair portrayal of hell.

Many passages in the Bible indicate a reconciliation of all and mercy on all. For instance Paul wrote to the Romans, "For God has imprisoned all in disobedience so that he may be merciful to all."⁷² Likewise, Paul envisioned a final state when all things are made subject to Christ.⁷³ In the fullness of time the mystery of God's saving purpose will be realized; he will "gather up all things in him, things in heaven and things on earth."⁷⁴ And "neither death nor life, nor angels nor rulers, nor things present nor things to come, nor height nor depth nor anything else in all creation will be able to separate us from the love of God in Christ Jesus."⁷⁵ Christian hope is based

---

⁷⁰ See *The Seven Ecumenical Councils of the Undivided Church*, trans H. R. Percival, in Nicene and Post-Nicene Fathers, 2nd Series, ed. P. Schaff and H. Wace, (repr Grand Rapids MI: Wm. B. Eerdmans, 1955), XIV, 300 - ff.
⁷¹ Dante, *Inferno*, 3:7.
⁷² Romans 11:32.
⁷³ See 1 Corinthians 15:27-28.
⁷⁴ Ephesians 1:9-10; see also Philippians 2:10; Colossians 1:20.
⁷⁵ Romans 8:38-39.

on the limitless possibilities of God, to whom all things are possible.[76] Though such passages can hardly be presented as proof texts for the universality of salvation, each in its own context points to a superabundance of divine grace and mercy that surpasses and surprises all human calculation. Within such hopefulness heaven and hell are not the simple alternatives we often present them to be.

The New Testament statements concerning hell are not attempts to convey information about the realm of the underworld to satisfy curious imaginations but seek to present to the here and now the essential seriousness of God's claim in Christ Jesus and the ultimate urgency of his call to repentance. In this sense "Hell is not so much a threat to be hurled at other people but a challenge to oneself."[77]

On the one hand, superficial universalism that regards all people as saved does not take serious the significance of individual moral decisions and personal responsibility. Moreover, it ignores the sovereignty of God who is required to save no one, especially the unwilling. On the other hand, the predetermination of some to blessedness and others to damnation as asserted by John Calvin's double predestination goes against God's universal will of love and mercy in which he desires to save everyone, even the unwilling.

Those in danger of too flippantly passing over the immense seriousness of their personal responsibility are warned by a possibility of a twofold outcome that their salvation is not guaranteed. Likewise, those in danger of loosing all hope in the face of the immense seriousness of their personal responsibility are encouraged by the possible salvation of everyone, even them, even from hell.

So, hell figures in Christian discourse as the language of fear and threat. While this type of language can be easily abused, it plays a part in motivating genuine human realization and response, even though it is not the most mature motive. Conscience is many times energized to the true good by fear of failure, self-destruction, and disgrace. The quality of such fear is not merely servile, but takes seriously the precariousness of human freedom, and recognizes that the universe is not a giant automatic salvation machine. The threat of hell is simply the acknowledgment that human beings can choose an ultimate self-enclosed lovelessness as their final state. If eternal life "is the highest possible development of all duration within the absolute

---

[76] See Matthew 19:26; Mark 10:27; Luke 18:27.
[77] Auer Ratzinger, *Dogmatic Theology 9: Eschatology*, 217.

vitality of God; [then eternal death] is complete withdrawl to the point of shriveling into a disconsolate immovable now."[78]

Thus, no recognition of human freedom is realistic if it does not allow for the possibility of eschatological tragedy.[79] Free human agents can opt for themselves, against God, and do so definitively; not as an accident but as a seemingly irrevocable choice into which they have put the whole deliberate weight of their lives. Not to allow for this possibility of ultimate self-enclosure is to make God the manipulator of a fundamentally illusory freedom. If salvation were automatic, the new creation would, in the end, be populated by automatons.

The nature of this tragedy has been hauntingly evoked in Dostoyevsky's *The Brothers Karamazov*, where Father Zossima intones "What is hell? It is the suffering that comes from being unable to love."[80] Equally poignant, C. S. Lewis puts forward the utterly banal character of ultimate selfishness when he writes:

> To love at all is to be vulnerable. Love anything, and your heart will certainly be wrung and possibly be broken. If you want to make sure of keeping it intact, you must give your heart to no one, not even to an animal. Wrap it carefully round with hobbies and little luxuries; avoid all entanglements; lock it up safe in the casket or coffin of your selfishness. But in that casket - safe, dark, motionless, airless - it will change. It will not be broken; it will become unbreakable, impenetrable, irredeemable. The alternative to tragedy, or at least to the risk of tragedy, is damnation. The only place outside heaven where you can be perfectly safe from all the dangers and perturbations of love is hell.[81]

So hell is not simply something that happens from the outside; nor is it something that God imposes on us afterwards for our misdeeds, but human beings themselves, within their own freedom, condemn themselves

---

[78] Hans Urs Von Balthasar, *Dare We Hope "That All Men Be Saved"* (San Francisco: Ignatius Press, 1996) 133.

[79] It is interesting to note that while the Church has solemnly declared the canonized saints to be in heaven, no one has been solemnly declared to be in Hell. Anyone tempted to indulge in such exercises of eschatological damnation, may do well to pay heed to the suggestion that the surest way of going to hell is to arrogate to oneself God's final judgment on the personal worth of others.

[80] Fyodor Dostoevsky, *The Brothers Karamazov*, Part 2, Book 6, Chapter 3, i (New York: Alfred A. Knoph, 1990) 322.

[81] C. S. Lewis, *The Four Loves* (London: Collins, 1963) 121.

through their sin. Their greatest torment is that they know heaven is present or real because of the light of God but that they can never reach it because they are unwilling to come into heaven by grace but seek instead to make it on their own. Hell is the mode of existence of a human being who is satisfied in his/her self, for all eternity; who has nothing more and desires nothing more than them self. "There is no tragic grandeur about hell, because fundamentally there cannot be any 'place', which is hell."[82]

If this human self-damnation and remoteness from God (as a state, not a place) "is made definitive by death, [then] indeed, deliberate self-enclosure is hell, or, as the bible calls it, the 'second death.'"[83] In the end, however, hell finds its place only within the actuality of a larger mystery: "God was in Christ reconciling the world to himself."[84] In its Creed the Church declares that Jesus descended into hell. With these words the Church hopes that the redeemer is "God with us"[85] even when we are furthest from God.

So the Saturday between Good Friday and Resurrection Sunday is called Holy. On Holy Saturday the Church recalls:

> the descent of the dead Jesus to hell, that is (put very simply) his solidarity in the period of non-time with those who have lost their way from God. Their choice—with which they have chosen to put their I in place of God's selfless love—is definitive. . . . Into this finality (of death) the dead Son descends, no longer acting in any way, but stripped by the cross of every power and initiative of his own . . . He is . . . dead together with them. And exactly in that way he disturbs the absolute loneliness striven for by the sinner: the sinner who wants to be "damned" apart from God, finds God again in his loneliness, but God in the absolute weakness of love who unfathomably in the period of non-time enters into solidarity with those damning themselves. . . . Only in absolute weakness does God will to mediate to the freedom created by him the gift of love that breaks from every prison and every constraint; in his solidarity from within with those who reject all solidarity. [86]

---

[82] Ladislaus Boros, *We are Future,* 129.
[83] Referring to Relation Rev 20:14 in Josef Ratzinger, *Introduction to Christianity* (San Francisco: Ignatius Press, 1975) 217.
[84] 2 Corinthians 5:19.
[85] Matthew 1:23.
[86] Von Balthazar, "Mysteries of the Life of Jesus VI: Resurrection" in *The Von Balthazar Reader* (New York: Crossroads Publishing Company, 1997) 153.

Jesus ... "descended into hell."

Christ's decent into hell is both a journey of suffering, as the last act of humiliation, and a journey of triumph, as the first act of exaltation. It is best understood as a symbol of the possibility of salvation for pre-Christian and thus non-Christian humanity and indeed all the dead.[87]

Jesus' descent into hell is an article of the Creed from the fourth century.[88] As such, it at least expresses the full human character of Jesus' death. He is God with us not only on the surface of life, not only in the experience of life's mortal agonies, but in going down into the underworld of the dead. The truly incarnate becomes flesh right to the end. In solidarity with all who have lived and died, he tastes death. He is subject to the power of the last enemy;[89] and goes to that point where all earthly relationships cease, either with God or with anyone else. His death is shrouded in alienation, despair, and unredeemed self-enclosure. He dies as one accursed,[90] condemned by the Law of Israel, rejected by his own people,[91] and abandoned by the Father,[92] with his prayers apparently unanswered. Jesus disappears into the region of utter lostness, utter silence, and utter darkness, into hell.[93]

Jesus is no glorious victor at this point, for he has been subjected to the power of death. He is no emissary sent into the realm of death with an announcement of victory. He goes into this world of alienation as one who

---

[87] J. N. D. Kelly in his great work *Early Christian Creeds* 3rd ed. (New York: Longman Publishing Group, 1972) 371-377, documents how "the decent into hell became more and more strongly a symbol of victory over the devil and death, and thus of the redemption of mankind as a whole." As early a Gregory of Nyssa, the lost sheep that Christ goes out in search of and delivers back to the ninety-nine (the un-fallen angels) is considered humanity as a whole. For this and other patristic examples see H. de Lubac, *Catholicism: Christ and the Common Destiny of Man* (San Francisco: Ignatius Press, 1988) Ch. 1.

[88] For an exhaustive look at the phrase "descended into hell" and its inclusion into the Creed see J. N. D. Kelly, *Early Christian Creeds*, 3rd ed. (New York: Longman Publishing Group, 1972) 371-377.

[89] 1 Corinthians 15:26.

[90] Galatians 3:13.

[91] John 1:11.

[92] Matthew 27:46; Mark 15:34.

[93] For an excellent historical critical treatment of the development of the concept of hell including a multi-layered exploration of the Hebrew *Sheol*, the Greek *Hades*, the New Testament *Gehenna*, and the Latin *Infernos* see Jon E. Braun, *Whatever Happened to Hell?* (Nashville, TN: Nelson, 1979); see also Jerry L. Walls, *Hell, the Logic of Damnation* (Notre Dame, IN: University of Notre Dame Press, 1992).

bears the whole weight of the world's alienation. His surrender to the Father takes him to a point of abandonment to the power of death, "to the end."[94] His cry form the cross, "My God, My God why have you forsaken me?"[95] echoes in all the deaths of defeated persons who have trusted in an apparently powerless God.

In this total abandonment, Jesus becomes God's mercy on the dead and the irretrievably isolated. His descent to this depth, the point furthermost from God, is the incarnation of the divine love present even in isolation. The Son, in refusing to be anything but the one given for the life of the world, is the revelation of the Father rejecting any relationship to the world other than that expressed in the free gift of the Son. The Son dies for sinners by being dead with them. The reality of definitive estrangement and ultimate alienation is now open to another presence, the only presence that could possibly penetrate it, the Father so loving the world as to give his only Son. In this way, the Son

> disturbs the absolute loneliness striven for by the sinner: the sinner who wants to be damned apart from God, finds God again in his loneliness, but God in the absolute weakness of love who unfathomably in the period of non-time, enters into solidarity with those damning themselves. The words of the Psalm 'I will make my bed in the netherworld; thou art there' (Psalm 139:8) thereby take on a totally new meaning. And even the cry, 'God is dead' as the self-made decree of the sinner for whom God is something done away with, takes on a totally new meaning objectively established by God himself.[96]

The dammed in their disobedience turn away from God and run into the lonely darkness. The Son in complete obedience descends into that darkness and places himself in the way of the dammed, "so that even in turning [their] backs on God, [they] still find the Son in front of them and must go toward him. Thus . . . sinners can move toward God, albeit unawares or reluctantly."[97] In this fullness of redemption "God in Christ reconciles the world to himself, not counting their trespasses against them.[98]

---

[94] John 13:1.
[95] Matthew 27:46; Mark 15:34.
[96] Balthazar, Hans Urs Von, *The von Balthasar Reader* (New York: Crossroad, 1982) 153.
[97] Balthazar, Hans Urs Von, *Theo-Drama V, The Last Act*, 311.
[98] 2 Corinthians 5:19.

Ultimately, hell or the realm of death is not annihilation or final isolation but is enfolded within the self-emptying of the Son. In this way, the point most distant from life and from God is also in Christ. In his decent into hell Christ makes the state of being dead a sort of Purgatory. In their self imposed isolation the dammed discover that they are not alone. Confronted with the dead Christ they are both, judged and called; judged as unconditional love exposes human self-centeredness, pride, and sloth for what it is; and called into the new life of God through his Son.

Making Captivity a Captive

The motif of Christ's victory over Satan is a chief and common understanding of Christ's work on the Cross.[99] It was prominent among the patristics and mentioned in various forms in *The Golden Legend of the Passion of the Lord*, which quotes Augustine as saying, "The redeemer came and the deceiver was vanquished; and what did the redeemer do to the one who had caught us? He held out a mousetrap, his cross, and baited it with his blood."[100] On Holy Saturday our Lord opened a way out of eternal alienation and into heaven. Because of this act of Christ, death itself now becomes a purifying event. Before there was only "the place of being dead, [but by] descending into this, Christ has thrown open the entranceway to the Father."[101]

Many verses of the New Testament celebrate Christ's communion with the dead, and his lordship over the realm of death. Christ "fills all things,"[102] "descended to the lower parts of the earth"[103] "and made captivity itself a captive."[104] He holds "the keys of death and of hell."[105] To his name "every knee shall bend in heaven and on earth, and under the earth."[106] The one who came down from heaven has come up from the abyss[107] and against his Church "the gates of hell will not prevail."[108] His reign will subdue the

---

[99] See Gustav Aulen, *Christus Victor* (New York: The Macmillan Co.) 1931.
[100] See Jacobus de Voragine (1275), *The Golden Legend*, trans. William G. Ryan (Cambridge: Princeton University Press, 1993).
[101] Balthazar, Hans Urs Von, *Credo*, trans David Kipp (New York: Crossroad, 1990) 54.
[102] Ephesians 4:10.
[103] Ephesians 4:9.
[104] Ephesians 4:8.
[105] Revelation 1:18.
[106] Philippians 2:10.
[107] Romans 10:6-8.
[108] Matthew 16:18; see also 27:51-53.

power of death, the last enemy.[109] After his death, he preaches to the "spirits in prison"[110] and "even to the dead."[111] Freed "from death because it was impossible for him to be held in its power"[112] Jesus is not only "the firstborn of all creation"[113] but "the first-born from the dead."[114] "In him all the fullness of God was pleased to dwell, and through him God was pleased to reconcile all things, whether on earth or in heaven, by making peace through the blood of the cross."[115]

After his death on the cross on Friday, Christ descended into the abyss, where he remained Saturday; on Sunday he was resurrected triumphant over death and hell.[116] This victory of Christ annihilated hell and death, and destroyed the kingdom of the devil. By descending into hell Christ illumined it entirely with the light of his presence. Unable to prevail against this holy invasion hell surrendered. In the words of John Chrysostom,

---

[109] 1 Corinthians 15:26-29.

[110] 1 Peter 3:18-22.

[111] 1 Peter 4:6. The Roman Church's *Office of Readings for Holy Saturday*, by an unknown Greek homilist, envisions Jesus sermon to the dead to partly read: "'Awake, O sleeper, and rise from the dead, and Christ will give you light.'" I am your God, who for your sake have become your son. Out of love for you and for your descendants I now by my own authority command all who are held in bondage to come forth, all who are in darkness to be enlightened, all who are sleeping to arise. I order you, O sleeper, to awake. I did not create you to be held a prisoner in hell. Rise from the dead, for I am the life of the dead. Rise up, work of my hands, you who were created in my image. Rise, let us leave this place, for you are in me and I am in you; together we form only one person and we cannot be separated. . . . See on my face the spittle I received in order to restore to you the life I once breathed into you. See there the marks of the blows I received in order to refashion your warped nature in my image. On my back see the marks of the scourging I endured to remove the burden of sin that weighs upon your back. See my hands, nailed firmly to a tree . . . my side has healed the pain in yours. My sleep will rouse you from your sleep in hell. The sword that pierced me has sheathed the sword that was turned against you . . . Rise, let us leave this place. The enemy led you out of the earthly paradise. I will not restore you to that paradise, but I will enthrone you in heaven. . . . The bridal chamber is adorned, the banquet is ready, the eternal dwelling places are prepared, the treasure houses of all good things lie open. The kingdom of heaven has been prepared for you from all eternity." See PG 43, 439, 462f.

[112] Acts 2:24.

[113] Colossians 1:15.

[114] Colossians 1:18.

[115] Colossians 1:19-20.

[116] See Revelation 1:18 where Christ says "I was dead, and see, I am alive forever and ever, and I have the keys of death and of Hades."

He who was held prisoner of it, has annihilated it. By descending into hell, he has made hell captive. He angered it when it tasted of his flesh. . . . It was angered for it was abolished. It was angered, for it was mocked. It was angered, for it was slain. It was angered for it was overthrown. It was angered, for it was fettered in chains. It took a body, and met God face to face. It took earth, and encountered heaven. It took that which was seen, and fell upon the unseen. O death, where is your sting? O hell, where is your victory?[117]

Christ's victory over hell, traditionally called "the harrowing of hell,"[118] inspired Dante in his *Inferno*, to describe a hell of "still unbolted and open"[119] gates, "rubble and scattered stone"[120] broken by a great earthquake when "a mighty one descended . . . arrayed with a crown of victory"[121] to rescue "our first parent, and his son Abel, and other shades who dwelled in limbo"[122] Luther picked up this great theme as he preached "the Lord

---

[117] John Chrysostom, "Easter Sermon," trans. Isabel F. Hapgood, *The Bible and the Holy Fathers for Orthodox*, ed. Johanna Manly, (Menlo Park, California: Monastery Books, 1990), 11

[118] This harrowing of hell is the Christian doctrine whereby Christ after his death on the cross and decent into hell, breaks down its gates, and rescues the saints from the clutches of Satan. The dogma is very early in the history of theology going back to the fourth century. (See the Arian formularies of the Fourth Creed of Sirmium of 359 and those of Nike and Constatanople in 360 in Phillip Schaff's, *The Creeds of Christendom* vol. 3 (Grand Rapids: Baker Books) 1931.) The textual evidence for the doctrine lays in three scant verses: 1 Peter 3: 18-20, which states, "alive in the spirit . . . he went and made proclamation to the spirits in prison, who in former times did not obey; Matthew 27:52, which states at Jesus' death, "earth shook, the rocks were split, the tombs were opened, and many of the saints who had fallen asleep were raised . . . and after his resurrection they entered the holy city; and finally, Luke 23:43, where Jesus says to Dismus, "today, you shall be with me in Paradise." *The Gospel of Nicodemus* includes a scene where Satan and the prince of Hell order the gates of Hell to be "fastened with bars of iron, lest they be taken captive . . . be bound, and have no power." For all the demons of Hell feared that Christ would enchain them in the same fetters in which they held the saints. (See *The Gospel of Nicodemus (the Descent into Hell)* 15; 15; 17. 16:4 quoted here from Frank Crane, *The Lost Books of the Bible* (Iowa Falls, IA:Word Bible Publishers) 1926, 83.) It also is a fulfillment of the protoevagelium of Genesis 3:15, the Lord said to the serpent "I will put enmity between you and the woman . . . you will bruise his heal but he will crush your head."

[119] Dante, *Inferno*, Canto 8, 67.

[120] Ibid., Canto 12, 93.

[121] Ibid., Canto 4, 29.

[122] Ibid.

Christ—the entire person, God and man, with body and soul, undivided—had journeyed to hell, and had in person demolished hell and bound the devil."[123]

The Eternal Fire of Hell

Inscribed over the portal to hell, Dante beheld the words, "Justice moved my high maker, in power divine, wisdom supreme, love primal. No things were before me not eternal; eternal I remain."[124] Hell itself claims that it is both eternal and made from love. Nevertheless, Christians have long tried to reconcile their image of a wrathful God who condemns persons to the everlasting fires of hell with the New Testament message that "God is love."[125] Isaac the Syrian writes that "there is no person who will be deprived of God's love, and there is no place which will be devoid of it . . . the very same divine love which is a source of bliss and consolation for the righteous in paradise becomes a source of torment for sinners, as they cannot [or will not] participate in it and they are outside of it." Isaac claims that the love of God toward the ungodly is itself the torment of hell.[126] This is the torture of the dammed, that though they do not love God, God loves them. So the fires of hell are made of the love of God.

Isaac basis his argument on the biblical claim that when the New Jerusalem comes, there will be no night, nor will there be any sun or moon to give light[127] but the glory of God shall illumine everything. This is a reference to the uncreated light of God. Similarly, the fires of hell are said to burn forever;[128] however, if this were physical fire, when all its fuel was consumed, it would burn out. Thus the fires of hell must also be the uncreated fire of God, who is often described as a consuming fire[129] and whose throne is said to stand in the midst of fire.[130] This does not mean that

---

[123] Martin Luther in a sermon preached at Torgau in April 1533, as quoted in Frederich Loofs, "Descent to Hades" in *Encyclopedia of Religion and Ethics*, ed. James Hastings (Edinburgh: T. & T. Clark Publishers, 1995) 4:657. For more on later Lutheran acceptance of this teaching see Benjamin Warfield, *The Plan of Salvation* (Grand Rapids, Michigan: Erdmann's, 1942) 81-84.
[124] Dante, *Inferno*, Canto 3, 19.
[125] 1 John 4:8.
[126] Isaac of Nineveh, *The Ascetical Homilies of Saint Isaac the Syrian*, "Homily 84" (Boston, MA: The Holy Transfiguration Monastery, 1984) 198.
[127] Revelation 21:22-25.
[128] Revelation 14:9-11, 21:8, 20:10.
[129] See Hebrews 12:29, Exodus 24:17, Isaiah 33:14.
[130] Ezekiel 1.

the images of hell in scripture[131] should be dismissed. Quite the contrary, they must be considered with the utmost seriousness for they point to something more, not less, horrible than their literal descriptions convey.

Thought of in this way, hell is not a place of punishment created by God but the very radiance of God's love which both warms and gives joy to the faithful but burns and torments the wicked. Augustine wrote "If I would not confess it to you . . . I would be hiding you from myself, not myself from you."[132] So persons who in earthly life preferred "darkness rather than light because their deeds were evil,"[133] will, in the next life find no such darkness, and will be unable to hide from that light which they hate. Bathed in the everlasting light of God's love, which they rejected but cannot escape, their own conscience, like a "never-dying worm,"[134] shall torment them.

Beholding the radiance of the glory and love of God, no one will be able to hide from it, and the conscience of each person, like an open book, will judge them. As indeed, our Lord says: "I do not come to judge anyone who hears my words and does not keep them, for I came not to judge the world but to save the world. The one who rejects me and does not receive my word has a judge; on the last day, the word that I have spoken will serve as judge."[135] The faithful, recounting the sins from which they were delivered by the love and mercy of God, will understand progressively and exponentially more, how great a salvation they have received and how great is the love of God that has accepted them and blotted out their sins. The wicked will understand, to the same extent, how great a salvation they have rejected and how great a love and mercy they have scorned. For them, this radiant love and glory of God, from which they can no longer hide, will become like "burning coals heaped on their heads."[136] The righteous receive the same fire as spiritual illumination and are filled by it with unspeakable joy and exaltation. For them it is the rays of the Sun of Righteousness which shall heal them of all that they lack, and produce in them growth in perfection and knowledge for all eternity for "the day is coming, burning like an oven, when all the arrogant and evildoers will be stubble; the day that comes shall burn them up . . . but for you who reserve my name the sun of righteousness shall rise, with healing in its wings."[137]

---

[131] Matthew 5:22; 7:23; 8:12; 10:28; 18:9; 13:42; 22:13; 25:41; Mark 9:42; 48; Luke 13:17; 16:22-23; 2 Thessalonians 1:9; Hebrews 10:29-31; Revelation 14:9-11; 20:15.
[132] Augustine, *Confessions*, 10, 2, 229.
[133] John 3:19.
[134] Mark 9:48.
[135] John 12:46-48.
[136] Romans 12:20.
[137] Malachi 4:1-2.

Dostoyevsky's voice again rings true: "We are all in paradise, but we do not want to know it."[138] The damned end up in the same place as the saved; what is heaven to one is hell to another. "For indeed our God is a consuming fire."[139] The wheat will be gathered into the barn, but the chaff will be burned away.[140] The blessed embrace this purifying fire of God's love and to them it is supreme bliss. The damned reject it and to them it is supreme torture, but the fire burns on, whether perceived as life giving warmth or destructive pain. It is the reality that is God, the fire of his love.[141] In this sense, even hell is heaven. In fact, "everything is heaven. Earth is heaven as a seed. Purgatory is heaven's kindergarten. Heaven is heaven accepted. [And] hell is heaven refused."[142]

God, who is love, is not unaffected by the refusal of divine love, but continues to absorb its horrible consequences. The reaction to God to the existence of hell "is one of pain . . . God, . . . so to speak, find[s], a brand burned into his flesh: we can guess that it is in the form of the cross. Our pain in the face of hell would then be only an echo of his pain."[143]

As Purgatory Is the Porch of Heaven, Sin Is the Porch of Hell

Paul wrote in his letter to the Romans: "Now that you have been freed form sin and enslaved to God, the advantage you get is sanctification. The end is eternal life."[144] The preceding part of this work analyzed the doctrine of Purgatory in this way.

---

[138] Fyodor Dostoevsky, *The Brothers Karamazov*, Part 2, Book 6, Chapter 2, a (New York: Alfred A. Knoph, 1990) 288.
[139] Deuteronomy 4:24; Isaiah 33:14; Hebrews 12:29. The teaching that guilt already contains within itself its own punishment has been handed down from Augustine who articulated it in his Confessions (I, 12, 19). See also Karl Barth, *Church Dogmatics* II/2 (Edinburgh: T&T Clark Ltd, 2004) 413-57 where he lays out his argument entitled "God's Mercy and Justice" wherein he contends that if the identity of God as a "consuming fire" () is to be maintained, then it is this very flaming love-justice of God that consumes those who hatefully oppose it.
[140] See Matthew 3:12.
[141] See C. S. Lewis, *The Great Divorce*, 69, where he writes "Every state of mind, left to itself, every shutting up of the creature within the dungeon of its own mind – is, in the end, hell. But heaven is not a state of mind. Heaven is reality itself. All that is fully real is heavenly."
[142] Peter J. Kreeft, *Everything You Ever Wanted to Know about Heaven but Never Dreamed of Asking* (San Francisco: Harper & Row Publishers, 1982) 139.
[143] Gustave Martelet, S. J. *L'au-delà retrouvé: Christologie des fins dernières* (Paris: Desclée, 1974) 189.
[144] Romans 6:22.

Purgatory . . . expresses the Christian hope that the patient love of God for all on their pilgrim journey will have its own way and finally bring them to completion. [And that] this purification in life and after death is always to be understood within the perspective of God's free gift of grace. In his redeeming love God does not pretend that evil is good, that imperfection is fulfillment, or that believing persons have arrived at their best selves, rather he works for the reality of our total transformation.[145]

Further stated was that "judgment is a part of life and a part of life after death . . . designed to move one closer and closer to God."[146] As this occurs the revelation of God is increasingly piercing and purging. This is the spiritual growth Paul calls sanctification. Its end is eternal life, God's free gift in Christ Jesus.[147] It is a major theme of this work that a Christian's participation in the life of God through Christ begins in this life, with Baptism, and continues to its ultimate fulfillment after death. In this life it is referred to as holiness, sanctification, and spiritual growth; beyond this life it is known in terms of Purgatory. These are not, however, two separate things or events but one glorious act of God bringing his adopted children to maturity. This allows the Church to say that sanctification and therefore Purgatory is the porch of heaven.

If this is the case, then likewise, sin is the porch of hell. Sin is that which attempts to lead one away from God and therefore sabotages one's fulfillment and completion. One could imagine Adam and Eve walking in the garden with God, the more they endure God's gaze, the more real they are, for God is the source of all being.[148] Adam becomes "less real, less authentic, less solid and substantial after the fall when he hid from God. God could hardly see him, when he called, 'Where are you?'"[149] Fading into the darkness, Adam was moving closer to the hell of hearing "I never knew you."[150] "Hiding from God, he then hid from Eve, by covering his nakedness and by passing [to her] the blame."[151] Sin pushes persons away form God and away from each other and into the abyss that is hell.

---

[145] See page 112 of this work.
[146] See page 148 of this work.
[147] Romans 6:23.
[148] See Acts 17: 28 and Genesis 2:7.
[149] Genesis 3:9.
[150] Matthew 7:23.
[151] Peter J. Kreeft, *Everything You Ever Wanted to Know about Heaven but Never Dreamed of Asking* (San Francisco: Harper & Row Publishers, 1982) 139. See also Genesis 3:12.

Emerging from one's freedom and then eating away that freedom, hellish sin is the spiritual cancer that grows from within to devour its host. Hell is not thrust upon us from above as the punishment for sin but "hell is sin itself in its consummation."[152] This moves Paul to write: "When you were slaves to sin . . . what advantage did you get from the things of which you now are ashamed? The end of those things is death."[153] Hell is spiritual suicide and sin is its means. But God's free gift is eternal life in Christ Jesus. [God] says to each as he said to Mary: May my Spirit impregnate you with my life so that my Son can be born in you?[154] The annunciation is for all, not just Mary, for Mary is a type of the Church, that is, us.[155] If we repeat Mary's fiat, it is done; heaven enters the soul, Christ is reproduced in us. If not, not. And this not is hell.[156]

Christ stands at the door and knocks[157] but the door is controlled by the person on the inside. If the door remains closed it becomes the door of hell. Hell is the refusal of the divine guest.

Summary

Eschatology is practical theology because it proposes a framework for properly understanding our future while helping us make sense of the past. The creedal affirmations "we believe in . . . the forgiveness of sins, the resurrection of the body, and the life everlasting" set the groundwork for understanding the Communion of Saints. To deny the saints is to deny tacitly in some way theirs and our forgiveness, resurrection, and life in God. Hence eschatology is present in the Church's anticipation of Christ's future coming to judge the living and the dead and in the Church's looking forward to the resurrection of the body and the life everlasting.

Within these affirmations the Creed itself affirms the two dimensions of Christian existence: in this life and beyond; in time and out of time; on earth and in heaven; below and above. Christ fills all in all. The Church is Christ's body. The saints are all those persons baptized into Christ, who forgives their sin and leads them, through judgment, to perfection in him. At the consummation they will share the life of God forever.

---

[152] Ibid., 135.
[153] See Romans 6:21.
[154] Luke 1:29-33.
[155] For more on this concept see *Documents of Vatican II*, "Decree on The Church," Chapter 2, ed. Walter M. Abbott (New York: Crossroad, 1989, c1966).
[156] Peter J. Kreeft, *Everything You Ever Wanted to Know about Heaven but Never Dreamed of Asking* (San Francisco: Harper & Row Publishers, 1982) 136.
[157] Revelation 3:20.

When the Lord comes in glory, death will be no more and all things will be subject to him. But at the present time some of his disciples are pilgrims on earth, while others have entered the life of glory. All the saints, upon the earth and beyond, in varying degrees and in different ways, share in the same love of God and love for each other; and they all join together to sing the one hymn of glory to God. All, indeed, who are in Christ and who have his Spirit form one Church and in Christ are bound together.

Part Three: Envisioning A Saintly Communion

Chapter Seven

We Believe . . . in the Church

This book rests on the assumption that those who die in Christ never really die but live triumphantly with God. The preceding part attempted to provide a framework wherein one could imagine existence beyond the grave. It called those persons, in this life or beyond, who are on the road of salvation, their ultimate destiny secure in Christ, saints. It is to these pilgrims that Paul addressed his letters.[1] The saints are holy not in themselves but because they are in Christ. Their holiness has nothing to do with their own personal merit but everything to do with the holiness of Christ imputed to them.[2] They are called by a holy God into communion with God and with each other in, by, and through Christ Jesus the Son, not because they are holy but "to be holy."[3] This redeeming, renewing, and regenerating work takes place in the Church.

The Church is one. This is succinctly made manifest in the Creed's reference to "the Church" and not churches. As there is "one body and one Spirit . . . one hope . . . one Lord, one faith, one Baptism, and one God and Father of all,"[4] so there is one Church. The Church is "the body of Christ, the fullness of him who fills all in all."[5] Belief in the Church affirms the baptized person's position within the body of Christ. Belief in the Communion of Saints affirms baptized person's relationships to one another within Christ's body. These mutual relationships of faith, prayer, and love span the gap of time, space, and eternity.

Is There Any Biblical Basis For This Idea?

Christian belief, in all matters, looks to the Bible. One interpretive approach to the scriptures sees the earliest sketch of the Communion of Saints doctrine in the Kingdom of God of the synoptic gospels. Here the kingdom is not an individualistic creation or a purely eschatological

---

[1] See Romans 1:4; 2 Corinthians 1:1; and Ephesians 1:1.
[2] See Romans 4:1—5:21.
[3] 1 Corinthians 1:2.
[4] Ephesians 4:4.
[5] Ephesians 1:22.

conception but an organic whole[6], which includes within in its bonds of love[7] all the children of God[8] on earth and in heaven,[9] and even the angels themselves.[10] When one reads the parables of the kingdom[11] one perceives not only its corporate nature but also the continuity which links together the kingdom in our midst and the kingdom that is to come. The account of the Old Testament saints who were raised with Christ and appeared to many is a pronouncement of the penetration of God's grace beyond the pale of death.[12] The accounts of the transfiguration, where Moses and Elijah appear to Jesus and his disciples, depict the linkage of saints above with saints below through a common faith in the Lord Jesus.[13]

Jesus compared this communion to a vine and its branches. Jesus is the vine and his followers are the branches who are grafted on to the vine (at Baptism) by the vinedresser who is the Father. Insofar as they abide in the vine the branches bear fruit. Unfruitful vines are cut off or wither away.[14] In his letter John expands this organic and life-giving union of the vine and its branches to all those who "walk in this light as he is in the light;" these have "fellowship with one another;[15] this fellowship is an extension of their true fellowship "with the Father, and with his Son, Jesus Christ."[16]

It is this fellowship that enables them to be sharers "of the inheritance of the saints in the light,"[17] and to come to "the assembly of [God's] firstborn children who are enrolled in heaven."[18] The saints are all in the one family of the one Father wherein racial, class, and gender distinctions are superseded, for in Christ "there is neither slave nor free, male nor female."[19] The saints above surround those below as "a great cloud of witnesses"[20] encouraging them to lay aside sin and look to Jesus the perfector of faith.

---

[6] See Matthew 13:31.
[7] See Matthew 22:39.
[8] See Matthew 19:28 and Luke 20:36.
[9] See Matthew 6:20.
[10] See Luke 15:10.
[11] See Matthew 13 for an example.
[12] See Matthew 27:51-53.
[13] See Matthew 17:1-13; Mark 9:2-13; Luke 9:28-36.
[14] See John 15:1-8.
[15] 1 John, 1:3, 7.
[16] See John, 14.
[17] Colossians 1:12.
[18] Hebrews 12:23.
[19] Galatians 3:28.
[20] Hebrews 12:1.

In his conception of the mystical body, Paul repeatedly speaks of the one body whose head is Christ,[21] whose life energy is love,[22] and whose members are the saints, not only of this world, but also of the world to come.[23] Since Paul speaks of Christ as the first-born within a large family, and of the glorification of the elect in the same connection, it is clear that he regards all those whom Christ has redeemed, those perfected and those striving after perfection, those here upon the earth and those in the world to come, as members of that same body.[24] In an alternate metaphor Paul proclaims the faithful as members of the household of God, citizens with the saints, laid upon the foundation of the apostles and prophets with Christ Jesus as the cornerstone in whom the whole structure is joined together as a holy temple in the Lord.[25]

The One Body of Christ

The Church, as the body of Christ, has many members yet it is one body. Paul wrote to the Corinthians, "Just as the body is one and has many members, and all the members of the body, though many, are one body, so it is with Christ. If all were a single member, where would the body be? As it is, there are many members, yet one body."[26] Through Christ, its head, "the whole body [is] joined and knitted together by every ligament with which it is equipped, as each part, working properly, promotes the body's growth."[27]

In his letter to the Ephesians, the apostle goes on to write that every loving person baptized into the Church has a special function to fulfill within the body. "For as in one body we have many members, and not all the members have the same function, so we, who are many, are one body in Christ, and individually we are members one of another. We have gifts that differ according to the grace given to us."[28] Every part is important to the health of the whole, and for each there is a particular gift of grace. All the members of the body are necessary although in different ways, and in light of their ultimate purpose, their functions cannot be arranged in any precise order or merit. "The head cannot say to the feet, 'I have no need of you.' On the contrary the members of the body that seem to be weaker are

---

[21] Colossians 1:18
[22] Ephesians 4:16
[23] Ephesians 1:20; see also Hebrews 12:22.
[24] Romans 12:4-5; 1 Corinthians 12:26-27; Romans 8:29-30.
[25] Ephesians 2:19-22.
[26] I Corinthians 12:12
[27] Ephesians 4:15, 16.
[28] Romans 12:4-6a.

indispensable."[29] No gift then is a purely personal possession and every blessing belongs to all. Gifts, blessings, and special functions within the Church find ultimate meaning and purpose in their close relationship to the complete organism.

Mere fulfillment of this task alone, however, does not complete the practice of communion. For "as one member suffers all suffer together with it; and if one member rejoices all rejoice with it."[30] Over and above their personal and special functions, the saints are bound together into intimate community by the fellowship and sympathy of sorrow and joy. Being members of Christ, the saints stand before God individually but not as an isolated unit. Christ uses each member individually and "through all the members, therefore, his body is made full. The head is fulfilled and the body becomes perfect when we are all combined and gathered into one."[31]

In a previous section concerning holistic dualism[32] this work posited the human person as a unity of form and matter; the matter being the bodily material out of which a person is constituted and the form being the soul which organizes, directs, and energizes the matter to actualize the bodily person. This line of thinking was applied to the Church by Origen who wrote:

> should we think of [the Church] as an organ of its head or should we think of the head as an aspect of the body of a person, so the whole Church of Christ is Christ's body in that he ensouls it with his Godhead and fills it with his Spirit. Or perhaps it should be interpreted another way. But even if [this] is true, the more human part of it is by itself a subservient aspect of the whole body, while the divinity that gives life to the whole Church is, as it were, the divine power that enlivens it.[33]

The Communion of Saints is the community of persons, baptized by the Spirit of Christ into the one body of Christ, wherein they exist individually as members and communally sharing all their spiritual goods. This communal sharing is not only among faithful and loving Christians upon the earth, but with all those who are united with God and those who await that blessed union. The Communion of Saints then embraces the whole mass of

---

[29] 1 Corinthians 12:21-22.
[30] I Corinthians 12:26.
[31] John Chrysostom, "Homily on Ephesians" 3.1.20-23 in *Interpretatio Omnium Epistularum Paulinarum*, ed. F. Field (Oxford: Clarendon, 1849-1862) 4:129.
[32] See page 126 of this work.
[33] Origen, "Epistle to the Ephesians" in *The Journal of Theological Studies* 3:401.

the redeemed, who in their various stages of growth are unified through their one head Jesus Christ into one family, one fellowship, and one body.

The One Priesthood of Christ and the Priesthood of All Believers

There is but one priesthood in the Church. It is the priesthood of the Head, the God-man, Christ Jesus, who redeemed us through his whole life, but especially his sacrificial death upon the cross and his glorious resurrection. The priesthood of the body that is "of all believers"[34] is a true priesthood only in, by, and through Christ its head.

As pure being God is the eternal form of all beings. Human beings are created in the image of God to reflect his glory and virtue. Christ is the supreme instance of a human being "fully alive."[35] Likewise, Christ is the eternal form of the Body of Christ. It is from this eternal form that the Body of Christ attains its determinate structure, shape, and manner. In the grace of Christ the members of the body are identified as "a chosen race, a royal priesthood, a holy nation, God's own people. In order that [they] may proclaim the mighty acts of him who called [them] out of darkness into his marvelous light."[36] Thusly, Christ's "incarnation is the foundation of the Church's unity and Pentecost is the affirmation of the multiplicity of persons within the Church."[37]

The priesthood of Christ is thus imparted to the Christian by the Spirit first through Baptism and then Confirmation and for some Ordination. Every Baptism is a consecration to the priesthood of Christ, for in Baptism one is removed from the profane world and appropriated to Christ. In Christ we are both justified and sanctified and thus made fit to perform the acts of worship and service belonging to the vocation of the child of God. Confirmation intensifies the Christians priesthood in Christ in that it empowers the Christian to actively participate in the building of the temple of God. Ordination sets apart some Christians as special ministers within and to the Body of Christ.

The sacramental identification which each Christian has with Christ and the conjunction of the priesthood of all the whole Body with the priesthood of Christ is the spring from which flows the supernal streams of fellowship in prayer, faith and love.

---

[34] See 1 Peter 2:5, 9.
[35] Irenaeus in his monumental work composed about 185AD wrote "Man fully alive is the glory of God." *Against Heresies* (Lib. 4, 20, 5-7; SC 100, 640-642, 644-648).
[36] 1 Peter 2:9.
[37] Vladimir Lossky, *The Mystical Theology of the Eastern Church* (New York: St. Vladimir's Seminary Press, 1998) 176.

Christological Errors are Ecclesiastical Errors

If the Church is the body of Christ then all that can be asserted or denied about Christ can be well applied to the Church inasmuch as it is a theandric organism, that is, a created nature united to God through the Son, having two natures, two operations, and two wills, at once inseparable yet distinct. This being the case, the ancient Christological heresies come to life anew in reference to the Church. It is the old Nestorian error that thus arises to divide the Church into two distinct beings: on the one hand the heavenly and invisible Church, alone, true, and absolute; on the other hand, the earthly Church or churches, imperfect and relative, wandering in the shadows, human societies seeking to draw, so far as possible for them, to transcendent perfection.[38]

Replacing Traditional Terminology

Traditionally theologians have divided the Church into three sections: the Church Militant comprising Christians who are living upon the earth, the Church Suffering or Expectant comprising those Christians presently in Purgatory, and the Church Triumphant comprising those who are in Heaven. The term militant has a primary meaning of serving as a soldier in the military but acquired the secondary meaning of to struggle or to make an effort, which is the intended sense when speaking about the Church. Suffering is a reference to the painful purging of sin that prepares one to enter fully into God's presence, and triumphant refers to sharing fully in the triumph of Christ over sin and death, as Chrysostom preached "Oh how high he has raised the Church! For, as if he were lifting it by some stage machine, he has led it up to a great height and installed it on that throne. For where the head is, there is the body also."[39] For the purposes of this work and out of the Protestant sensitized purgatorial theology constructed in previous sections, these historic terms have been abandoned in favor of the descriptors: the Church Below and the Church Above.

---

[38] See Vladimir Lossky, *The Mystical Theology of the Eastern Church*, 186.
[39] John Chrysostom, "Homily on Ephesians" 3.1.20-23. in *Interpretatio Omnium Epistularum Paulinarum*, ed. F. Field (Oxford: Clarendon, 1849-1862) 4:128-129.

The Church Below

The saints[40] upon the earth, that is within space and time, are a "chosen people . . . a holy nation"[41] proclaiming the mighty acts of Christ. Their "struggle is not against enemies of blood and flesh, but against the rulers, against the authorities, against the cosmic powers of [the] present darkness; the spiritual forces of evil."[42] They are the merchants seeking the one pearl of great value,[43] rejoicing over the treasure found hidden in a field.[44] Christ painted their picture in vivid phrases as he preached his sermon on the mount. They are the poor in spirit who place their total dependence upon God and in so doing become spiritually rich. They mourn over their sins and the suffering of humanity and look forward to the comfort of the age to come. In their meekness they surrender to the control of God and God gives them true self-control. In their hunger and thirst for righteousness they recognize the presence of God and his Kingdom as the most important thing in their lives. In grateful response to God's mercy upon them they are merciful to others. Their hearts are undividedly devoted to the worship and service of God. They proclaim and share God's peace with those around them, participating in the work of God's Son and becoming, by God's grace, children of God themselves. For all these things the world does not reward them but persecutes them as indeed Jesus was persecuted. This persecution they gladly accept. They are a light for the world, a challenge to the present culture of death, a holy city built upon a hill for all to see.[45]

The Church Above

Persons pass into heaven directly and mediately by the road of purgation. The redeemed come into the presence of the Lamb and of him who sits upon the throne, and behold the Lord their God face to face. In this beatific vision they contemplate the Holy Trinity. Finally delivered from all selfish limitations and raised above all earthly anxieties, they live the great life of God, within that sphere of love which their life on earth has traced out. This true life is not one of idle stagnation but of superabundant activity of the senses, mind, and will. Incorporated into the glorified humanity of

---

[40] See Romans 1:7, 8:27; 1 Corinthians 1:2; Ephesians 3:8, 4:12; 2 Thessalonians 1:10; Jude 3.
[41] 1 Peter 2:9.
[42] Ephesians 6:12.
[43] See Matthew 13:46.
[44] See Matthew 13:44.
[45] See Matthew 5:1-16.

Jesus the glorified saint participates in the divine life of the Godhead itself. The meaning of all existence, all power, all beauty, all peace, and all truth are inexhaustibly present in God and to the saints in an eternal now.

The Spirit of Jesus, the Head of the body, is manifested in all his saints in the full assortment of their particular lives and according to the various degrees that each individual soul, with its own unique gifts and call, has received and used Christ's gift. The one ideal of a saintly person is thus embodied in a countless variety of forms while at the same time each complementing the other in such a way as to form together the one ideal of perfect sanctity that is the body of Christ "grown up in every way into him who is it's head."[46]

The Litany of the Saints[47] reminds worshippers of this celestial hierarchy.[48] At the center of the glorified universe is the throne of the Holy Trinity, then Mary, the mother of God, then the angelic choirs, then the forerunner of the Christ, John the Baptizer, then Joseph the step-father of the Lord, then the patriarchs and the prophets, then the apostles, disciples, and witnesses to the gospel, then the holy martyrs, bishops, confessors, priests, Levites, monks, hermits, virgins, and widows. The whole of redeemed humanity, all the saints of God, orbiting the Sun of Righteousness in concentric circles of glory and grace, "a great multitude that no one could count from every nation, from all tribes, and peoples, and languages . . . robed in white with palm branches in their hands . . . crying out with a loud voice, 'salvation belongs to our God who is seated on the throne and to the Lamb.'"[49] The true Kingdom of God is not God alone but God and the totality of all the members whom Christ their head generously raises through

---

[46] Ephesians 4:15.
[47] The Litany of the Saints or *Litaniae Sanctorum* is a sacred prayer of the Roman Catholic Church, used both in the Western and Eastern Rites. It was prescribed by Pope Gregory the Great in 590 for a public procession of thanksgiving which took place on the cessation of the plague which had devastated Rome. In a somewhat different form it was in use at a much earlier date, as it is mentioned by Basil in the fourth century and by Gregory Thaumaturgus in the third. It is a prayer of invocation to God, Jesus, the Blessed Virgin Mary, and all the martyrs and saints upon whom Christianity was founded. It is most prominently sung during the Easter Vigil and in the liturgy for Holy Orders. Following the invocation of the saints, the Litany concludes with a series of supplications to God to hear the prayers of the worshipers. See "Litany of the Saints" in *Encyclopedia of Catholicism*, ed. Richard P. McBrien (San Francisco: HarperSanFrancisco, 1995) 772.
[48] This "heavenly hierarchy" is an orderly description of the heavenly community, not an attempt to place persons on a ladder of patronage as will be shown to be a corruption of the Communion of Saints doctrine. See page 216 of this work.
[49] Revelation 7:9-10.

sanctifying grace from the abysmal ruin of their sins into the divine life and all its blessings.

The Roman Catholic emphasis on the Incarnation (reinforced by the doctrine of transubstantiation) produces a tendency to think of God as the Word made flesh, together with all of his members, who are united to him by faith and love in a real unity. The God of the saints is a "God who with a veritable divine folly takes up into himself the whole creation that culminates in human nature, and in a new unheard of supernatural manner, 'lives in it,' 'moves in it,' and in it 'is.'"[50] In this mode of thinking the saints are not just lofty exemplars of holy behavior but living members of the Body of Christ through which they acquire not only moral but religious importance. Like the apostles and prophets who are "the foundation upon whom they are built"[51] the saints are the co-workers of Christ,[52] his wedding guests,[53] his servants,[54] his friends,[55] and his glory.[56] They are knit together to one another and above all to Christ whose bodily welfare depends upon "each part working properly."[57]

The Two Dimensions of the One Church

The two dimensions of the Church inform two supernal streams of faith, hope, and love within the one Church. These vital movements compromise and make fruitful the Communion of Saints.

The first could be said to be horizontal, that is, within the members of the Church below. The many members of the Church below exchange among themselves gifts of love, mercy, forgiveness, peace, and help which produce fruitful hubs of life through which earthy fellowship is continually renewed. Until well into the fifth century the Communion of Saints was primarily perceived in terms of the earthy fellowship among members of the Church.[58] This mysterious inner life of the Church was what Paul had

---

[50] Acts 17:28, as quoted in Karl Adam, *The Spirit of Catholicism* (New York: The Crossroad Publishing Company, 1997) 109.
[51] Ephesians 2:20.
[52] See 1 Corinthians 6:1.
[53] Matthew 9:15.
[54] Matthew 10:24.
[55] John 15:14.
[56] 2 Corinthians 8:23.
[57] Ephesians 4:16.
[58] See Nicetas Bishop of Remesiana, "*Explanatio Symboli Habita ad Competentes*" in A. E Burn, *Niceta of Remesiana, His Life and Works* (Cambridge; Cambridge University

especially in mind when he wrote of the process whereby the fellowship of Christ organically "grows into a holy temple in the Lord . . . a dwelling place for God."[59]

The second stream could be described as vertical, that is, between the members of the Church above and the Church below. In a historic sense this is simply the working out of the horizontal stream after some participants in it pass beyond the veil. Their fervent love and witness continues to flow to the members of Christ on earth and then returns above in countless rushing brooks to the blessed in heaven.

Press, 1905) np. See also C. H. Turner, "Niceta and Ambrosiaster" in *Journal of Theological Studies*, 7 (1906), 203-19, 355-72.
[59] Ephesians 2:21-22.

Chapter Eight

The Communion of Faith: Fellowship in Redemption

Faithfulness as the Historical bond of the Church

Fellowship in faith means that all members of the Body of Christ loyally profess one and the same faith, preserved and passed on to them through the tradition of the Church. They share the same luminous vision, the same effective rule, and the same fruitful source of spiritual life. Nicetas (c. 400), missionary bishop to what is now Romania and the former Yugoslavia regions, and the writer of the great hymn, *Te Deum,* shows in his work the first evidence that "the Communion of Saints" was actually being affirmed as part of the creedal formula, he wrote:

What is the Church but the congregation of all saints? From the beginning of the world of the patriarchs, prophets, martyrs, and all other righteous people who have lived, or are now alive, or who shall live in time to come, compromise the Church, since they have been sanctified by one faith and manner of life, and sealed by one Spirit, and so made one body, of which Christ is declared to be the head, as the scripture says . . . So you believe that in the Church you will attain the Communion of Saints.[1]

The Communion of Saints is the relationship of all holy people of all ages, including all the company of heaven, which is anticipated and partially realized in the community of saints on the earth.

Our Common Identity: Called to Be Saints

Through their sharing in the supper of the Lord early Christians were formed by the Holy Spirit into a new and vital company of friends of the crucified and risen Christ, with the responsibility to bear his good news to the world. At the heart of this message was the graciousness of God, which led them to a sense of identity as holy people, called saints by God in his grace.

---

[1] See J. N. D. Kelley, *Early Christian Creeds* 3rd ed. (London: Longman, 1972) 391, emended for inclusively.

The notion of a community of holy people sharing holy things is rooted in the Jewish tradition, where liberated from bondage and chosen for covenant, the Jewish people are constituted as Gods holy people, sharers in Gods own holiness. As the Lord spoke on the mountain "tell the Israelites: you have seen what I did to the Egyptians, and how I bore you on eagles wings and brought you to myself. Now therefore, if you obey my voice and keep my covenant you shall be my treasured possession among all peoples. Indeed, the whole earth is mine, but you shall be for me a priestly kingdom and a holy nation."[2] The Israelite's new relationship with God was not won by their great works of virtue or merit but is given them as a free gift. "It was not because you were more numerous than any other people that the Lord set his heart on you and chose you, for you were the fewest of all peoples, It was because the Lord loved you."[3] The gift of God evokes thanksgiving and an ethical duty to live worthy of the calling expressed in the divine mandate: "I am the Lord your God who brought you up from the land of Egypt, to be your God; you shall be holy, for I am holy."[4]

Early Christians drew upon this biblical theme to articulate their own identity as a holy people chosen by God to participate in God's own holiness, through the Son, and by the Spirit. The heart of their self understanding was not their own achievements or works but the work of God in Christ in which they participate through the waters of Baptism and the bread and cup of salvation. These are the gifts of God for the people of God and the chief means by which "The grace of the Lord Jesus Christ, the love of God, and the communion of the Holy Spirit [come to] all."[5] It is this gift of the Holy Spirit which makes God's chosen people holy. The same life-giving Spirit who raised Jesus from the dead is poured out in them and they are clothed with Christ,[6] and transformed into the very image of Christ.

It is these persons whom Paul greets in his letters: "To all God's beloved in Rome, who are called to be saints;"[7] "To the Church of God that is in Corinth, to those who are sanctified in Christ Jesus, called to be saints;"[8] "To the saints in Christ Jesus who are at Philippi;"[9] "All the saints greet you."[10] The saints are all those people sharing in the death and resurrection

---

[2] Exodus 19:3*b*-6.
[3] Deuteronomy 7:7-8.
[4] Leviticus 11:45.
[5] 2 Corinthians 13:14.
[6] See Galatians 3:27-28.
[7] Romans 1:7.
[8] 1 Corinthians 1:2.
[9] Philippians 1:1.
[10] 2 Corinthians 13:12; see also 1:1; 8:4; and 9:1.

of Jesus Christ. They form a community; chosen, beloved, called, redeemed, gifted, and sent by God to proclaim the good news to the world. The consecrating gift of God brings with it the responsibility to live worthy of its calling, that is, in gratitude and lament, praise and repentance, and in deeds of love, mercy, and justice. Though struggling amid the sinfulness of the world and their own hearts, the saints are in fact holy people.

Participation in the Communion of Saints involves recalling and being encouraged by Christian heroism and sanctity in every age. Moreover, the saints are the links in the chain by which believers are reminded of their spiritual origins in the Christ Event. Here the recollection and commemoration of saints in an annual cycle of celebration is a continuing expression of the Communion of Saints. In following the calendar, the Church first practices, commemoration; remembering and honoring the dead. Second, the Church encourages imitation; following the examples of our forerunners in the faith. Third, the Church looks forward to the consummation; that time of which Protestants are so fond of singing when Christ the bridegroom, and his bride the one Church are together forever and the marriage supper of the lamb is celebrated. These practices recognize the inspiration of the Holy Spirit in all the saints and are a particular and concrete expression of our participation with them in the mystical body of Christ that is the one Church.

Commemoration

Jesus taught us saying 'whosoever does the will of my Father in heaven is my brother and sister and mother."[11] What they are to the Lord they should be also to us. The saints are our spiritual sisters, brothers, and mothers whom we identify as apostles, prophets, and friends of God; whose example we welcome as righteous;[12] and in whom we recognize the glory given to them by Christ.[13]

Through the gospel they passed on to us, the Church has fellowship with the apostles. John wrote in his first letter "We declare to you what we have seen and heard so that you also may have fellowship with us; and truly our fellowship is with the Father and his Son Jesus Christ."[14] This fellowship with, and connection to, the apostles in and through the gospel of Christ Jesus is not interrupted by death or rifted by space or time.

---

[11] Matthew 12:50.
[12] Matthew 10:41.
[13] John 17:22.
[14] 1 John 1:3.

Just as one who has studied the whole of a subject has an understanding of its elementary parts so those who have reached heaven have involvement in what they have gone through and they do not cease to be participants in the life of the Church on earth. While it may be said of the apostles and prophets that at their death they put off the earthly body they did not put off the Church body. They not only were but they also remain the foundation upon which the household of God is built, with Jesus Christ himself as the cornerstone.[15] So even after their death they continue to be in communion with believers upon earth. "If you conquer, I will make you a pillar in the temple of my God, you will never go out of it."[16] "All the saints are our elder brothers in the one house of the heavenly Father, who have departed from earth to heaven, and they are always with us in God, and they constantly teach us and guide us to eternal life by the means of the Church services, mysteries, rites, instructions, and Church decrees, which they have composed."[17]

We Grasp the Living Christ by Means of the Living Church.

In Christ the Divine and the human, God and humanity were joined permanently together. The Gospel of John describes the event: "And the Word became flesh and lived among us and we have seen his glory, the glory of the Father's only Son, full of grace and truth."[18] But how does one come to believe in Jesus, that is, have faith in the Son of God. One might be tempted to say that one derives faith from the scripture. However, faith in Jesus existed before the Gospels or Letters were written. We can though look to the scripture to reveal the manifestation of faith.

Matthew's Gospel relates Simon Peter's confession of faith at Caesarea Philippi where he answers Jesus' question "But who do you say that I am?" by saying "You are the Christ the Son of the Living God." To this statement of belief Jesus responds "Blessed are you Simon son of Jonah! for flesh and blood has not revealed this to you but My Father in heaven."[19] Understanding the reality of Jesus' messianic and divine identity, "the mystery that [was] hidden throughout the ages and generations but now has been

---

[15] Ephesians 2:20.
[16] Revelation 3:12.
[17] John of Kronstadt, "What Does It Mean to Believe in the Church? Thoughts about the Church and the Orthodox Divine Services" in *The Spiritual Counsels of Father John of Kronstadt*, ed. W. Jardine Grisbrooke (New York: Attic Press, 2000) 92.
[18] 1 John 1:14.
[19] See Matthew 16:13-20.

revealed to [the] saints," and placing our trust in it involves a divine illumination.

At the beginning of Christian faith neither the scripture nor human reason brings one to faith in Jesus the Christ but the grace of God alone. [20] Jesus said, "no one can come to me unless drawn by the Father who sent me."[21] The resurrected faith of the apostles was not a human work but an experience of the life giving Spirit of God breathed into the Church at Pentecost. Belief and faith in Christ come to the world and to the individual Christian as it came to the apostles, through the living Word and the quickening of the Spirit.

The Holy Scriptures

Those "who were from the beginning eye-witnesses and servants of the Word"[22] proclaimed the gospel and gave testimony to Christ "in Jerusalem, in all Judea and Samaria, and to the ends of the earth."[23] They penned the historical records of Jesus' life and the Acts of the Apostles. Some wrote letters to both individuals and communities wherein they laid down Christian teaching and gave instruction for the Christian life in answer to the questions and special circumstances of those to whom they wrote.

It is important to remember that these written communications were supplementary to the apostles oral preaching,[24] either as confirmation of it or as preparation for it, and in none of them are claims made of an exhaustive exposition of the Christian faith. This emphasis caused Paul to tell his protégé Timothy "what you have heard from me through many witnesses entrust to faithful people who will be able to teach others as well."[25] In fact so much emphasis was placed on preaching and so little on writing that some apostles left no writing whatsoever and some of the apostolic letters have disappeared.[26]

Thus the Christian community, incorporated into the living Word and animated by the Holy Spirit grew up around the apostles teachings. By Baptism one was initiated into this spiritual fellowship and in Confirmation ones admission was sealed and perfected. The literary records were not the

---

[20] See also Matthew 11:25; 1 Corinthians 1:18-25; 2:6-16.
[21] John 1:44.
[22] Luke 1:2.
[23] Acts 1:8.
[24] For the classic defensive of this treatise see C. H. Dodd's, *The Apostolic Preaching and Its Developments* (New York, Harper & Row Publishers, 1964).
[25] 1 Timothy 2:2.
[26] See 1 Corinthians 5:9; Colossians 4:16.

primary means of bringing the Good News of Jesus to human persons but rather the fellowship of faith based on the apostles preaching and animated by the Holy Spirit.

So the New Testament writings point beyond themselves to the life of the Church from whence they came. They are not an independent source of revelation but stand within the life of the Church which already existed before the apostolic scriptures were written. Accordingly the Bible has no autonomous authority disconnected from the faith of the Church. Not even the Gospels are comprehensive and complete portrait of the person and work of Christ. Without the living tradition of the Church essential elements of this picture would remain hidden from our view. Furthermore, without the teaching of the Church we could never hope to achieve historical or religious sympathy with Jesus. In light of this reality Augustine ungrudgingly wrote "I would not believe the Gospel, did not the authority of the Church move me."[27]

The One Faith

This fellowship of faith, hope, and love which grew out of apostolic preaching and was invigorated by the Holy Spirit spread ever wider over the world. The apostles entrusted the Gospel message to disciples commissioned and appointed by them to oversee the Christian community. From these disciples to the present day runs a continuous line of preachers fulfilling the apostolic commission. Stemming from the root of the historical Jesus, and blossoming along the vine of these historical preachers grew the fruit of their preaching: the space-time fellowship of the faithful, that is, the universal Church on earth.[28]

Over time the external structures of this community became more fully organized and indeed larger and more visible. But it is the same Church and so in a true sense the Church as a whole, as one organism, that has seen

---

[27] Augustine of Hippo, *Against the Manicheans* c. V, in *St Augustine the Writings Against the Manicheans and Against the Donatists: Nicene and Post-Nicene Fathers of the Christian Church*, Part 4, ed. Phillip Schaff (Whitefish, Montana: Kessinger Publishing, 1997, 2004) np.

[28] A practical suggestion for realizing this connection to the saints in one's own life is to sketch out a spiritual family tree. This identifies persons who are important in helping one develop in the faith. In listing and connecting those persons and in turn the persons who influenced them one quickly discovers a vast network of Christian parents and siblings, the vast majority of whom are already dead, who contributed in bringing one to the faith. See Alister McGrath, *I Believe: Exploring the Apostles' Creed* (Downers Grove: IL, InterVarsity Press, 1997) 108.

Jesus, stood beneath his cross, and experienced his resurrection. In this way, it is the Church that brings us into the closest historical relation to Jesus by not only pointing out that his life, work, and message is recorded in cherished documents but experienced in the lives of generations past, many in whom the divinity of Christ blazes forth in external manifestation, and in thousands of millions in our own time who are the sons and daughters of God, brothers and joint heirs with Christ, filled with his Spirit of new and abundant life.

The Fellowship of Faith Defines and Continually Reforms the Teaching of the Church

The doctrines of the Church are contained within its sources of revelation, that is, Tradition and Scripture. It is not, however, always explicitly expressed in its specific content but implicitly contained within other truths. Sometimes a seemingly lengthy process is needed to make these truths plain and visible. More than two hundred years passed before the New Testament canon was fixed; more than three hundred years passed before the doctrine of the Trinity was settled; and more than six hundred years passed before the Church set forth exhaustively the central Christian teaching of the person of Jesus, the God-man.

With the help of theologians who mine implicit truths from the deposit of faith, the active authority of the organizational Church guards and promulgates its teachings. In their passive authority, the faithful, hear, obey, and prove, by their moral and religious experiences, these same manifold and profound truths. In their mutual participation, both elements join to form the maternal organism that is the fellowship of faith wherein the Church's teachings are brought to maturity and given definition. In this sense every new teaching is the child not only of the Church below, upon the earth, but the Church above, in heaven, who fostered and nurtured it until its time came, and of the illuminating and empowering Spirit of Christ which gave it life. In this way "we are enriched in [Christ,] in speech and knowledge of every kind" and the testimony of Christ "is strengthened among us."[29]

The Life of Love

Love is the most precious fruit of the Communion of Saints on earth. As Augustine wrote, "Love is the motive weight of the Christian

---

[29] 1 Corinthians 1:5-6.

being."[30] Christians "love one another."[31] This love is characterized by the strong realization that we are bound to one another in joy or in sorrow, not merely by the natural bonds of humanity but by the supernatural kinship that comes through our communion in the Body of Christ our Head. This love, so beautifully depicted in Paul's letter to the Corinthians[32] produces a feeling of mutual responsibility and demands acts of service and deference to others. It is characterized by a sentiment of solidarity in which one first looks to the whole and then comes back to the individual and to itself only from and in relation to the whole. It is a love that sees with deep reverence in every member of Christ, not only a sister or brother, but Christ himself.

"This love is the lifeblood of the body of Christ, which welling forth out of the heart of the God-man, flows through the whole body and gives it form and strength and beauty."[33] Christ our Lord is love incarnate and his Body in an incarnation of that same love in all who are incorporated into Christ. The Body of Christ will not be fully mature or complete until love, the soul of all virtues, has become the dominate principle of living and dying in all its members. For this is how the world recognizes Christ's disciples, they love one another.[34]

In the Communion of Saints there are no limitations of space and time. "From out of the remote ages of the past, from civilizations and countries of which the memory is now only faintly echoed in legend, the saints pass into his presence and call him brother and enfold him in their love."[35] Christians are never alone. Christ their Head is with them and along with Christ all the holy members of his body in heaven and on earth.

Within the members of the Body of Christ there is a solidarity and partnership of the faith. The solidarity of the faith manifests itself in the apostolic tradition of the Church affirmed in its creeds, written in its scriptures, proclaimed by its preachers, and lived by its saints. It is the special task of the community of the Church to attest to the truth of the Church's proclamation by living it. Every life that is lived in faith is a persuasive and inspiring incarnation of the Church's proclamation. It is "a demonstration

---

[30] Confessions 13, 9.
[31] See John 13:34; 15:12; Romans 13:8; 1 Thessalonians 4:9; 1 Peter 1:22; 1 John 3:11; 1 John 4:7; 2 John 5.
[32] See 1 Corinthians 13.
[33] Karl Adam, *The Spirit of Catholicism* (New York: The Crossroad Publishing Company, 1997) 139.
[34] See John 13:34-35 and Ephesians 4:4-6.
[35] Karl Adam, *The Spirit of Catholicism*, 140.

of Spirit and of power."[36] More effective than the "lofty words of wisdom"[37] the life of faith is the most convincing proof of Christianity. "In the flame of the Spirit there is living unity between those who have gone and those who remain on earth."[38] The saints attest the Gospel before the world and communicates their living faith to the weaker members of the Body of Christ.

The Great Cloud of Witnesses

Throughout the Old Testament certain persons are singled out as individuals who embody the values of the community in an exceptional way; Able, Noah, Abraham and Sarah, Isaac, Jacob and Rachel, Joseph, Moses, Miriam, Joshua, Deborah, David, Solomon, Job, Isaiah's suffering servant, Ester, and a myriad of prophets, to name a few. Their witness encouraged others to be strong in the faith and their memories were honored with alters, tombs, and monuments,[39] a practice depicted even in Matthew's Gospel.[40]

Early Christians were "convinced that neither death nor life, nor angels nor rulers, nor things present nor things to come, nor height nor depth, nor anything else in all creation, [could] separate [them] from the love of God in Christ Jesus [their] Lord."[41] No one who died was lost but "the God in whom [they] believed, who gives life to the dead"[42] would likewise bring them to new and abundant life, just "as Christ [had] been raised from the dead, the first fruits of those who have died"[43] and a pledge already given of coming life for all people and for the world.

This act of hope in the faithfulness of God deduced the syllogism: "If living persons shared in the life of God, and if the dead were likewise still clasped by the living God, then both the living and the dead were united to each other, forged into one community by the same vivifying Spirit."[44] The destructive power of death is unable to sever the bonds of the Communion

---

[36] 1 Corinthians 2:4.

[37] 1 Corinthians 2:1.

[38] Eberhard Arnold, *Inner Words*, ed. Emmy Arnold, ed. (Rifton, New York: Plough, 1975) 165.

[39] See Joseph Fitzmyer, "Biblical Data on the Veneration, Intercession, and Invocation of Holy People" in George Anderson, *The One Mediator, the Saints, and Mary* (Minneapolis, Minnesota: Augsburg Fortress Publishers, 1992) 135-147.

[40] See Matthew 23:29.

[41] Romans 8:35-39.

[42] Romans 4:17.

[43] 1 Corinthians 15:20.

[44] Elizabeth A. Johnson, *Friends of God and Prophets* (New York: The Continuum Publishing Company, 1998) 65.

of Saints, for these bonds are the grace, love, and community of God's own being. Thus grew the idea that the community of God's chosen people extends not only across spatial boundaries to include those living in different lands at the present moment, but also extends across time boundaries to include those living in different historical periods. "For whether we live or whether we die, we are the Lord's. For to this end Christ died and rose again, that he might be the Lord of both the living and the dead."[45]

Veneration

As was the case in the Old Testament, within the New Testament community certain individuals are singled out as noteworthy and described as "highly favored,"[46] "full of grace,"[47] "full of faith and the Holy Spirit,"[48] and "living blamelessly."[49] Special reverence was paid to the martyrs, those who died for their faith. In John's Revelation a beatitude is pronounced over them: "Blessed are the dead who from now on die in the Lord . . . they will rest form their labors, for their deeds follow them."[50] In the letter to the Hebrew's the author provides a powerful example of venerating the memory of our forbearers in the faith while evoking a solidarity between the Old and New Testament saints and flowing into an exhortation of the whole community to find courage and heart for their journey.

> Now faith is the assurance of things hoped for, the conviction of things not seen. Indeed, by faith our ancestors received approval. . . . By faith Abel offered to God a more acceptable sacrifice than Cain's. . . . By faith Enoch was taken so that he did not experience death. . . By faith Noah . . . built the ark. . . . By faith Abraham obeyed when he was called . . . received power of procreation . . . offered up Isaac. . . . By faith Isaac invoked blessings . . . on Jacob and Esau. By faith Jacob . . . blessed each of the sons of Joseph. . . By faith Joseph . . . gave instructions about his burial. By faith Moses was hidden by his parents . . . left Egypt . . . kept the Passover . . . passed through the Red Sea. . . . By faith the walls of Jericho fell. . . . By faith Rahab the prostitute did not perish.

---

[45] Romans 14:7-9.
[46] Luke 1:28.
[47] John 1:14.
[48] Acts 6:5.
[49] 1 Thessalonians 2:10.
[50] Revelation 14:13.

> And what more should I say? For time would fail me to tell of Gideon, Barak, Samson, Jephthah, of David and Samuel and the prophets—who through faith conquered kingdoms, administered justice, obtained promises, shut the mouths of lions, quenched raging fire, escaped the edge of the sword, won strength out of weakness, became mighty in war, put foreign armies to flight. Women received their dead by resurrection. Others were tortured, refusing to accept release, in order to obtain a better resurrection. Others suffered mocking and flogging, and even chains and imprisonment. They were stoned to death, they were sawn in two, they were killed by the sword; they went about in skins of sheep and goats, destitute, persecuted, tormented—of whom the world was not worthy. They wandered in deserts and mountains, and in caves and holes in the ground. . . . God had provided . . . that they would not, apart from us, be made perfect.
>
> Therefore, since we are surrounded by so great a cloud of witnesses, let us also lay aside every weight and the sin that clings so closely, and let us run with perseverance the race that is set before us, looking to Jesus the pioneer and perfecter of our faith, who for the sake of the joy that was set before him endured the cross, disregarding its shame, and has taken his seat at the right hand of the throne of God.[51]

Here the faithful dead are proposed not only as exemplars to be imitated but as a multitudinous throng of faithful followers of God whose journey Christians are called upon to share and continue. The living memory of these victorious persons and groups inspires those presently running the race to "run in such a way that [they] may win it.[52]

God's glory is so creative and so pervasive that it does not only shine in the face of God's only begotten Son alone but is reflected also in all those who in Christ have become God's children. The glory of Christ Jesus, who is himself "the reflection of God's glory and the exact imprint of God's very being illuminates the countenances of the blessed with unfading radiance. "So we love them as countless dewdrops in which the sun's radiance is mirrored."[53] We venerate them because in them we see God. Seeing as God is in them, we are confident that they can and will help us, because where God is there is our help.[54] They do not help us through their own strength but by the strength of God.

---

[51] Hebrews 11:1—12:2.
[52] I Corinthians 9:24.
[53] Karl Adam, *The Spirit of Catholicism* (New York: The Crossroad Publishing Company, 1997) 117.
[54] Psalm 33:20; 46:1; 4:17; 115:9.

The Martyrs

Martyrs, from the Greek word meaning witnesses, were those Christians who resisted pressure to recant their faith in Christ Jesus as Lord and God, even to the point of torture and death. Within the first three centuries of Christian history, before Constantine legalized Christianity with his Act of Toleration, persecution was the norm. As the number of witnesses increased they began to be recognized as a distinct group within the community. Jesus himself was the first martyr,[55] "the faithful witness, the firstborn of the dead."[56] Following Jesus' death on the cross the martyrs participate in his suffering as Christ suffers in them. In this way they become icons of Christ, re-presenting Christ to the world.[57] Strengthened by Christ's Holy Spirit they allow their bodies to be broken and their blood to be poured out, for the sake of Christ and his gospel. In so doing they become a living Eucharist. What began in them at their Baptism now comes to fulfillment; they are buried with Christ to be raised with him in glory.[58] Hence, the martyrs are assumed to be, not in purgatory or an intermediate place of waiting, but beholding God face to face. Stephen, the first martyr, proclaimed at his death, "Look, I see the heavens opened and the Son of Man standing at the right hand of God."[59]

Because the martyrs themselves were sacraments their bodily remains belong to the realm of the sacred. Whenever possible they were carefully collected and buried or entombed with dignity. This too, follows the paradigm of Jesus as martyr, whose body was begged by Joseph or Arimathea, wrapped in linen and buried in a newly hewn garden tomb, to where the women would return with spices and ointments.[60] On the yearly anniversary of their death, the day of their new birth in heaven, pilgrims would gathered at the graves of martyrs for a nightlong vigil that ended with the Lord's Supper celebrated at dawn. As the anniversaries of various martyrs

---

[55] While Jesus is the first, that is preeminent martyr, Abel murdered by his brother Cain, should perhaps be considered first in biblical chronology. Genesis 4:10 provides a cryptic allusion to the fact that God hears the cry of those martyred from the very beginning and responds to their blood. God says to Cain, "Listen, your brother's blood cries out to me from the soil." This literary device, the part for the whole, is indicative of the whole Communion of Saints.

[56] Revelation 1:5 and 3:15.

[57] See John Downing, "Jesus and Martyrdom," *Journal of Theological Studies* 14 (1963) 279-293.

[58] Romans 6:4.

[59] Acts 7:56.

[60] Luke 23:50-56.

in a region or city were celebrated on the appropriate day, a liturgical calendar of the saints developed. As the stories of the martyrs spread or their devotees moved to another region so would their commemorations despite the absence of their tombs. Small shrines put up on or near their graves would eventually develop into Churches.

The earliest evidence of such veneration is from "The Martyrdom of Polycarp," beloved bishop of Smyrna who was burned to death after terrible torture in the second century. His followers wrote to their sister Churches: Thus at last, collecting the remains that were dearer to us than precious stones and finer than gold, we buried them in a fitting spot. Gathering there, so far as we can, in joy and gladness, we will be allowed by the Lord to celebrate the anniversary day of his martyrdom, both as a memorial for those who have already fought the contest and for the training and preparation of those who will do so one day.[61]

It bears noting that from the very beginning the Church has differentiated between the reverence given to the saints called veneration and the reverence offered to God alone called adoration.[62] In a defining letter, the Church at Smyrna insisted that they

> could never abandon Christ, who suffered for the redemption of those who are saved in the whole world, the innocent one dying on behalf of sinners. For him we worship as the Son of God. But the martyrs we love as disciples and imitators of the Lord, and rightly so because of their matchless affection for their own king and teacher. May we too become their comrades and fellow disciples.[63]

Augustine later preached: "Venerate the martyrs, praise, love, proclaim, honor them. But worship the God of the martyrs."[64]

So, Jesus is the first martyr; "the faithful witness [martyr] the first born of the dead.[65] Martyrs are the ideal disciples because they followed Jesus

---

[61] "The Martyrdom of Polycarp" 18, in Herbert Musurillo, *The Acts of the Christian Martyrs* (Oxford: Clarendon Press 1972) 17.

[62] The second Council of Nicaea in 787, against the iconoclast, established the fundamental difference between the veneration of saints and the worship due to God alone.

[63] At first, the authorities prevented the Church from gathering the bones of their beloved Polycarp, erroneously reasoning that they would then shift allegiance from Jesus to their martyred bishop. "The Martyrdom of Polycarp" 17 in Herbert Musurilo, *Acts of the Christian Martyrs* (Oxford: Oxford Universtiy Press, 1954) 16-17.

[64] Augustine, *Sermons,* 273.9 (8:21).

[65] Revelation 1:5; 3:14.

even to the point of death.⁶⁶ Condemned, tortured, bloodied, and executed, men and women graphically and physically entered into the dying of the crucified Jesus. In their suffering for "Jesus' sake and for the gospel"⁶⁷ they entered into his passion. They were strengthened by Christ's Spirit which gave them courage in torment, and boldness and freedom of speech. Faithful to God until the end they become a living word testifying to the truth and hope of the faith; a striking source of encouragement for believers and attraction to the Christian way for pagans. The symbolic power of their sacrificial deaths unleashed powerful forces that galvanized resistance and energized commitment among an oppressed community.⁶⁸

The Common Martyrdom of All Christians and the Role of Hagiography

The common martyrdom of all Christians is the "strict discipleship"⁶⁹ empowered by the Spirit, about which Paul wrote when he said "those who belong to Christ Jesus have crucified the flesh with its passions and desires. If we live by the Spirit, let us also be guided by the Spirit."⁷⁰ "Put away your former way of life, you old self, corrupt and deluded by its lusts, and be renewed in the spirit of your minds, and clothe yourselves with the new self, created according to the likeness of God, in true righteousness and holiness."⁷¹ This "old self was crucified with [Christ] so that the body of sin might be destroyed, and we might no longer be enslaved to sin."⁷² It was the white martyrdom of asceticism that equipped believers to withstand the red martyrdom of persecution.

---

⁶⁶ See the collection of literature in Herbert Musurillo, ed. *The Acts of the Christian Martyrs* (Oxford; Oxford University Press, 1972) and John Downing, "Jesus and Martyrdom," *Journal of Theological Studies* 14 (1963) 279-293.
⁶⁷ Mark 8:35; Matthew 10:39, 16:25, Luke 9:24, see also John 13:38; John 15:21; Acts 9:16; 1 Corinthians 9:23; 1 Peter 3:14; 1 John 2:12.
⁶⁸ See Lawrence Cunningham, *The Catholic Heritage* (New York: Crossroad, 1983) 17.
⁶⁹ John Chrysostom, Homily on Galatians 5:24, in *Interpretatio Omnium Epistualarum Paulinarum*, ed. F. Feild (Oxford: Clarendon, 1849-1862).
⁷⁰ Galatians 5:24-25.
⁷¹ Ephesians 4:22-24.
⁷² Romans 6:6; see also Chrysostom's Homilies on Romans II in Phillip Schaff, *A Select Library of the Nicene and Post-Nicene Fathers of the Christian Church*, 2ⁿᵈ series, 14 vols. (Buffalo, New York: Christian Literature, 1887-1894, reprint Peabody, Mass: Hendrickson, 1994) 1 11:409, where he preaches "Paul does not say that we have been crucified but that we have been crucified *with him*, thus liking Baptism with the cross.

The early martyrs prepared for their inevitable trials by a routine of ascetic practices designed to fortify them against the devastating effects of sever and cruel pain. Tertullian, for example, exhorted his readers to prepare for prison by fasting and abstaining from water until gone was all anxiety about eating. They should "enter prison in the same state as most people who were leaving. What they would suffer there would not be any penalty but the continuation of their discipline."[73] The ascetic life trained one for prison and prison trained one for the final interrogation, which, if the training was complete, would end in death when the torturer realized efforts at indoctrination were futile. "As the desert had been the training ground for the final witness of the prophet, the prison was the training ground for the martyr."[74]

Through strict disciplines of severe fasting, abstinence, and prayer, undergirded by a worldview focused exclusively on the cross of Christ, the martyrs were able to avert the psychic disintegration and world breakdown common to torture victims. Cyprian instructed would-be martyrs to turn each instrument of torture and the pain into a means of uniting themselves to the passion of Christ and reconfiguring their own bodies to the cross. Wooden clubs should hold no terror, for the wood of the cross brought salvation. Chains ought not weigh their feet down but should be ornaments. Sparse clothing ought to recall they were clothed with Christ. The shaved head of humiliation ought to tell them Christ was truly their head. Lying on the cold, hard ground should remind them of being in bed with Christ.[75]

Coping devices such as preparatory fasting, altered states of consciousness, and the reconfiguring of the meaning of pain enabled martyrs to accept and even non-masochistically welcome torture to the point of death as the continuation and ultimate fulfillment of their discipline and integration into the cross and life of Christ. These Christians used ascetic practices to break the link between the disintegration of the mind and of the body and thereby "turn the tables on the torturers. Whenever a torturer inflicted a

---

[73] Tertullian, *De Ieiunio* CCL 21255-77, as quoted by Tilley, Maureen Tilley, "The Acetic Body and the (Un)Making of the World of the Martyr," *Journal of the American Academy of Religion* 65 (1991) 473. Tilley remarkably argues that "the evidence refutes the common claim that asceticism, or white martyrdom, was a substitute for red martyrdom, which Christians adopted once their religion was legalized and they were no longer persecuted. See also The Suffering Self: Pain and Narrative Representation in the Early Christian Era (Routledge 1995); Brent Shaw, "Body/Power/Identity: The Passions of the Martyrs" *Journal of Early Christian Studies* 4 (1996).

[74] Tertullian, Ad Martyras CCL 1:1-8, as quoted by Tilley, 474.

[75] Cyprian, *Epistuala(e)* 76.2.1 and 77.3, CSEL3/2:1-841 as quoted by Tilley, 474.

punishment designed to deconstruct the mind of the martyr through the deconstruction of the body, the opposite effect was achieved."[76] Instead of mental breakdown, physical torture brought psychological fulfillment. Hence, "asceticism logically and practically preceded martyrdom. In fact, it made martyrdom possible."[77] Early Christians learned these methods through the testimonies of survivors, and the hagiographical sermons and stories about the martyrs. When times of persecution ended, the way of the martyr continued to be honored. Those who followed in it were recognized as holy; especially those who led a celibate life, were wise teachers, astute Church leaders, or cared for the poor, sick, and infirmed, even though they may not have suffered a violent death.

Partners in Faith and Hope

Living Christians remembered and honored their contemporaries who had been known and loved in this life and who had died for the faith. They looked up to the dead as a great cloud of witnesses who encourage the community in the struggle to be faithful disciples. Their lives are remembered with profound gratitude because of how their life and death witness to Christ, the cross, and the work of the Holy Spirit, nourishing the faith of the rest.

This mutual interaction between the saints below and departed above form a circle of friendship centered on and around the graciousness of God in Christ. As Christ gave himself to the Father by giving himself for the world, so the cruciform saints give themselves to Christ and in doing do become a gift to the community of faith. The community of faith receives the example, remembers the sacrifice, and gives thanks to God. This is the veneration of the saints. It is participation in a collegial fellowship of grace, discipleship, and thanksgiving, where the living and the departed, the struggling and those beyond struggle, are companions, co-disciples, and partners in faith and hope, witnessing to one another and being carried along by the same saving grace poured out in Christ Jesus. The martyrs above and the struggling below, Augustine proclaimed "all serve the one Lord, follow the same teacher, accompany the same leader. We are joined to the one head, journey to the

---

[76] Maureen Tilley, "The Acetic Body and the (Un)Making of the World of the Martyr," 475.
[77] Ibid.

same Jerusalem, follow after the one love, embrace the same unity."[78] "When we pay honor to the martyrs we are honoring the friends of Christ."[79]

Paradigmatic Figures

Within the great cloud of witnesses particular persons are recognized by the common spiritual sense of the community as witnessing to the truth and hope of the gospel and/or to the transforming power of the Holy Spirit in a particular time and place. These persons are what popular tradition refers to as saints. Theologically, they have no spiritual advantage over the rest of the community who are saints in the biblical sense, but the convergence of historical conditions and their own distinct gifts give them a beneficial function within the wider circle of pilgrims. These paradigmatic figures are saints by and for others. They belong to and reflect the community that loves and venerates them.

The community itself is aware of its Spirit-filled life and its understanding of the gospel. It encounters the dramatic witness, narrative memory, or artistic icon, of a real person and in that encounter it recognizes the image of God reflected in a genuine, living, and particular way that is compelling and attractive. The recognition of paradigmatic saints is a discernment of the Spirit. The saints themselves are gifts of the Holy Spirit to the community, just as the holiness of a saint is a gift of the Holy Spirit to that person.

A paradigmatic "saint is a person so grasped by a religious vision that it becomes central to his or her life in a way that radically changes the person and leads others to glimpse the value of that vision."[80] These saints correct and enlarge the community's moral vision in times of temptation and infidelity to the call to holiness. "Faithfulness cannot be sustained by good theories and static traditions. It takes good people. So when a faithful one raises up among us and we are able to hear and recognize the goodness of

---

[78] Preaching a century after persecution had ceased on the feast day of Sts Perpetua and Felicity, Augustine, Sermon 280.4 6, trans. William H. Schewring, *The Passion of Perpetua and Felicity, together with Sermons of Saint Augustine upon these Saints* (London: Sheed and Ward, 1931) 49-51.

[79] Augustine, 332.1, in *The Works of St. Augustine: A Translation for the 21st Century*, part 3: *Sermons*, 10 vols. ed. John Rotell, trans. and notes by Edmund Hill (Hyde Park, New York: New City Press, 1990-1995) vol. 9:194.

[80] Laurence Cunningham, *The Meaning of Saints* (New York: Harper & Row, 1980) 65.

this person's judgment upon us, we call this extraordinary person a saint and the miraculous transformation in us, the work of God."[81]

So by naming these saints the community itself catches a vision of holiness and becomes itself a little more holy. The saints distill the central values of the community in a concrete and accessible form. The direct force of their example acts as a catalyst in the community, galvanizing recognition that, yes, this is what we are called to be. Because Christianity is a way of life, their concreteness leavens and nurtures the moral environment, drawing others to produce their own creative fidelity. The strange wholeness and integrity of these persons lures the community evermore into the encompassing logic of a life for God and in God, in the process strengthening the network of relationships among all. Their religious passion fuels the community's forward movement. In the light of their memory all are encouraged to walk the path of life: "one fire kindles another."[82]

The early reformers attempted to retain the honor given to the saints by recognizing them as living stories of God's grace, instructing us by the example of their bold faith. Confident that their destiny in God strengthens the hope of Christians below the *Augsburg Confession* states:

> "It is also taught among us that the saints should be kept in remembrance so that our faith may be strengthened when we see what grace they received and how they were sustained by faith. Moreover, their good works are to be an example for us."[83]

Likewise *The Second Helvetic Confession* declares:

> We do not despise the saints or think basely of them. For we acknowledge them to be living members of Christ and friends of God who have gloriously overcome the flesh and the world. Hence we love them as brothers, and also honor them; yet not with any kind of worship but by an honorable opinion of them and just praises of them. We also imitate them. For with ardent longings

---

[81] Davis Matzko, "Postmodernism, Saints, and Scoundrels," *Modern Theology* 9 (1993) 35, n. 35

[82] Elizabeth A. Johnson, *Friends of God and Prophets: A Feminist Theological Reading of the Communion of Saints* (New York: Lexington Publishing Company, 1998) 239; finally quoting William James, *The Varieties of Religious Experience* (New York: Longmans, Green, 1923), 358.

[83] Philip Melanchthon, *Augsburg Confession* 21:2, in *The Book of Concord*, ed. Theodore Tappert (Philadelphia: Fortress Press, 1959) 297.

and supplications we earnestly desire to be imitators of their faith and virtues, to share eternal salvation with them, to dwell eternally with them in the presence of God, and to rejoice with them in Christ. And in this respect we approve of the opinion of Augustine in *De Vera Religione:* 'Let not our religion be the cult of men who have died. For if they have lived holy lives, they are not to be thought of as seeking such honors; on the contrary, they want us to worship him by whose illumination they rejoice that we are fellow-servants of his merits. They are therefore to be honored by way of imitation, but not to be adored in a religious manner,' etc.[84]

The saints are to God like stained glass is to sunlight. Light from the sun is white, but when passed through a prism or colored glass, it's constitution becomes evident: the many colors that combine to form its radiance dance varied hues and textures to reveal the hidden perfections of the original light beam. So it is with the saints. Their lives and their faith show the perfections of God's holiness shining through our human weakness. By contemplating and honoring their goodness, we come better to know and revere the overawing holiness of God.

The Blessed Virgin Mary

Chief among these paradigmatic saints is the Mother of God,[85] through whom the Word of God came into the world, the Blessed Virgin Mary. The central importance of the Virgin Mary in Christian tradition is rooted in the scriptures. She is, in the words of her cousin Elizabeth, "the mother of my Lord."[86] Luke's gospel tells her story most fully.[87] He writes of Gabriel's Annunciation to Mary; that she had found favor with God and

---

[84] *The Second Helvetic Confession* 5.026, quoted from *The Constitution of the Presbyterian Church (U.S.A.), Part I, Book of Confessions;* (Louisville, KY: Geneva Press, 1996).

[85] The teacher Nestorius preferred the title *Christotokos*, "the bearer of Christ" over the long used Marian title *Theotokos*, "the bearer of God" because he considered the divinity of Christ and humanity of Christ to function as two separate and divided parts, intrinsically unrelated to one another. The Council of Ephesus (431) deemed this portrayal of a divided Christ as heretical and recognized the title *Theotokos*, God-bearer, as an orthodox way to describe Mary. The use of the title was not to exalt Mary unduly but to confess Christ completely, to assert the divinity and unity of her Son, Jesus, to affirm that the beloved Son of the Father was "born of a woman"— God manifested in the flesh (1 Tim. 3:16). See

[86] Luke 1:43

[87] See Luke 1:26ff; cf. Matthew 1:18ff.

was to conceive by the Holy Spirit and bear a child whom she would name Jesus. He would be called the Son of God.[88] Mary responded in obedience: "Here I am, the servant of the Lord, let it be with me according to your word."[89] Her humble acceptance of the Word set the tone for the rest of the New Testament and became the foundation for centuries of Marian devotion.

When she visits Elizabeth, John the Baptizer leaps for joy in his mother's womb at the sound of Mary's voice.[90] Along with Gabriel's greeting, the *Ave Maria* and Mary's poetic response, the prayer-song known as the *Magnificat*,[91] the Visitation confirms that the events for which Mary was chosen are indeed God's fulfillment of "all that the prophets had spoken."[92]

From the time of Irenaeus, Christian apologists have opposed the Gnostic heresy by pointing out Mary's significant place in salvation history.[93] The historical Mary provided a biblical case for Christ's human nature as well as divine nature, over against the Gnostics' spiritualization of Christ. The phrase "conceived by the Holy Spirit, born of the Virgin Mary" drives this point home about the two natures of Christ and the purity of his birth in the Apostles' Creed, the Chalcedonian Definition, the Old Roman Baptismal Creed of Hippolytus, and the Niceno-Constantinopolitan Creed, among others.

The veneration of the apostles, prophets, and martyrs of the early Church expanded to all the saints by the third century. In the fourth century, the veneration of the Virgin Mary was greatly promoted by the Nestorian controversies. As virginity was a high ascetic ideal in the early Church, Jerome, Ambrose, and Augustine, celebrated Mary as the premiere example of virginity as a spiritual vocation.[94] Always mindful that "Mary was the

---

[88] Luke 1:35-37.
[89] Luke 1:38.
[90] Luke 1:39-56.
[91] Because it begins *"Magnificat anima mea Dominum"* or "My soul magnifies the Lord."
[92] Acts 10:43; Christians in search of links between Jesus' birth and Old Testament prophecies focused early and often on Mary's virgin conception (cf. Luke 1:34). Matthew, in his telling of Jesus' birth (1:22-23), brings the promise in Isaiah to bear on Jesus: "Behold, a virgin shall conceive, and bear a son, and shall call his name Immanuel" (7:14). In this way the virginity of Mary becomes a crucial indication for early believers that Jesus was the long expected Christ.
[93] The formula offered by Irenaeus, that Mary is a "second Eve," becomes the standard in Marian literary typology. See *Against Heresies*, Lib. 5, 19, 1; 20, 2; 21,1: SC 153, 248-264. See also Jaroslav Pelikan, The Emergence of the Catholic Tradition (Chicago: University Chicago Press, 1971) 71-81.
[94] Since very early in the history of the church Christians have dwelt devotionally on Mary's virginity, often insisting that her virginity was never violated throughout her

temple of God, not the God of the temple, and therefore he alone is to be worshipped who is working in his temple."[95] Ambrose instructed his flock in the adoration that is offered to God alone and the veneration given to the Blessed Virgin and to the saints. Later, Thomas Aquinas among others spoke of Mary as the model saint for those called to study scripture because she willingly accepted God's Word and became the receptacle for God's Word made flesh.

Protestants, then, can honor the Virgin Mary as an otherwise obscure Jewish girl who became, through the work of the Holy Spirit and by her willing obedience, the instrument of divine grace. Through her, the divine majesty and unapproachable holiness of God joined the frail impermanence of fallen humanity. She is the chosen vessel of the Incarnation and a special vehicle of God's grace in giving Jesus to the world.

Just as Protestants feel free admire the apostle Paul and celebrate his life and accomplishments for the sake of the gospel, as well as his service and contributions to the Church, and never feel as though they are worshipping Paul, so Protestants can rightly revere Mary. A vestige of such Marian devotion in Protestant Churches is the religious play or Christmas pageant, which entered into medieval Christian tradition with Francis's devotion to the crèche.[96] By the light of candles on Christmas Eve young Protestant girls are dressed as Mary, and in particularly brave congregations, place a live baby into the manger. While it is certainly good to keep this part of the devotion in their worship, Protestants need to continue it with serious reflection on the meaning of the Incarnation which should naturally go beyond singing "Silent Night" once a year.

The two most notable statements Mary makes in the Gospels, first: "Let it be with me according to your Word,"[97] and second, "Do whatever he tells you,"[98] are exemplary of Christian discipleship. Her posture of humility and surrender anticipate her Son's prayer in the garden, "Not my will but yours be done," and proclaims to all believers the stance they are called to take before God.

---

life. Like other Marian themes, this one had its zenith in the medieval period. See Luigi Gambero, Thomas Buffer, *Mary and the Fathers of the Church: The Blessed Virgin Mary in Patristic Thought* (Ignatius Press, 1999); see also Jaroslav Pelikan, *Mary Through the Centuries : Her Place in the History of Culture* (New Haven, CT: Yale University Press, 1998).
[95] Ambrose, *De Spiritu Sancto III*, 11:80 in PL 16, 837.
[96] Timothy George, "The Blessed Virgin Mary in Evangelical Perspective" in *Mary: Mother of God*, ed. Carl E. Braaten (Grand Rapids, MI: Eerdmans, 2004).
[97] Luke 1:38*b*.
[98] John 2:5.

It is unreasonable to think of Paul as a doorway to Christ but Mary as a snare. As Protestants honor Paul in his apostolic sufferings, so they can honor Mary who "all generations [are to] call blessed"[99] as she willingly offered up her own cherished Son, and like no one else on earth, felt the sword that pierced the side of Christ pass through her own soul.[100] Mary stands as our premier example of justification by faith alone, because she believed so purely in the gospel and as a truly faithful disciple of her Son, Jesus the Christ. She was, of course, a witness to his miraculous birth, but also to his sacrificial death. She was the one disciple who did not flee when all the other disciples did so. She stayed and accepted the burden of being under the shadow of the cross to the very end. When believers suffer or behold the suffering of those they love they can look to Mary who remained faithful and obedient even in those grim, dark, and lonely hours.

Mary was also among those in the Upper Room upon whom the Holy Spirit fell with power on the Day of Pentecost.[101] Her distinct faithfulness to Christ, her Son, and his word, up to and beyond the cross, declares to Protestants that the true faith can and will be preserved, even in one individual, and for this she should be considered the mother of the remnant church.

Christ "desire[s] each one of [us] to show the same earnestness in realizing the full assurance of hope . . . not to be sluggish . . . but to be imitators of those who through faith and patience inherit the promises."[102] The Annunciation, then, is to all, not just the Blessed Virgin Mary, for Mary is a type of the Church and therefore the ultimate example for all. God says to each of us as he said to Mary: "Let my Spirit impregnate you with my life so that my Son may be born in you." When we repeat Mary's fiat, it is done; heaven enters the soul and Christ is reproduced in us. Paul's words encapsulate what has become the core of Marian devotion: "Be imitators of me, as I am of Christ."[103]

Canonization

Early on, the veneration of specific saints was deeply rooted in the memory and popular piety of the local community, who would, with the approval of their bishop, extol their shining example and name them aloud

---

[99] Luke 1:48.
[100] Luke 2:35.
[101] Acts 1:14ff.
[102] Hebrews 6:11-12.
[103] 1 Corinthians 11:1, cf. 1 Corinthians 4:16.

at the Eucharist on the anniversary of their death. If the appeal of the martyr or holy person was particularly remarkable or universal, other local congregations would follow suit and the saint would be "spontaneously canonized."[104]

Once the local people had recognized a holy person, and their local bishop had allowed their naming at the Eucharist, many times the Pope was asked to recognize the saint and remember him or her at the altar in Rome. This effort to enhance the dignity and popularity of the local saint was commonplace by the tenth century. Gradually, and paralleling the growth of papal power, the making of saints came under the jurisdiction of the Holy See and its lawyers. In 1170, Alexander III decreed that no one, regardless of his or her reputation for holiness or wonder-working, could be venerated locally without papal authorization. However, his decree by no means spelled an immediate end to Episcopal canonizations, nor did it quench the popular thirst for new cults. In 1234, Pope Gregory IX published his *Decretals*, or collection of pontifical laws, in which he asserted the absolute jurisdiction of the Roman Pontiff over all causes of saints and made it binding on the universal Church. Since saints were objects of devotion for the entire Church, he reasoned, only the pope, with universal jurisdiction, possessed the authority to canonize. From this point on the canonization process became increasingly fastidious.[105]

Inevitably the centralized bureaucratic process became politicized and commercialized. The list of canonized saints grew increasingly favorable toward powerful religious orders, bishops, priests, and upper-class aristocrats, especially those politically allied with the Pope. The process was inherently "biased against lay persons in general and women in particular, and prejudiced against the full and legitimate use of human sexuality by both women and men."[106]

On the positive side papal recognition and certification promoted careful scrutiny to ensure the orthodoxy and authenticity of the persons the whole Church venerates; preventing saints from "springing up from the fertile imagination of hagiographers like so many spring mushrooms"[107] which was too often the case in the early medieval period. Provincialism,

---

[104] Lawrence Cunningham, *The Meaning of Saints* (New York: Harper & Row, 1980) 45.
[105] Kenneth Woodward, *The Making of Saints: How the Catholic Church Determines Who Becomes a Saint, Who Doesn't and Why* (New York: Simon & Shuster, 1990) 67.
[106] Elizabeth A. Johnson, *Friends of God and Prophets: A Feminist Theological Reading of the Communion of Saints* (New York: Lexington Publishing Company, 1998) 103.
[107] Ibid, 59.

nationalism, and racial and ethnic prejudices were subtly challenged when saints of one country or culture were lifted up for appreciation by the Church in a different country or culture.

Negatively, however, the saints became an evermore elite group venerated for their heroic virtue and power to produce impressive miracles.[108] Eventually, the very word "saint" shrunk in popular Christian usage to refer only to those who have been officially named so through the canonization process. This obscured the theological meaning of the term which embraces all persons made holy in Christ, living and dead, and essentially rarified the ideal of Christian holiness to the point where common believers reject their true identity with the pronouncement "I'm no saint."

The purpose of canonization is to determine who among the deceased has given such evidence of a holy life that the living may venerate them in public worship. There must be some mechanism for this. Both Anglican priest Michael Perham in his book *The Communion of Saints* and United Methodist Bishop Clifton F. Guthrie in his book, *For All the Saints* offer a new paradigms for inclusion of such figures into protestant Church calendars.[109]

The Rise of the Patronage System

In her book *Friends of God and Prophets: A Feminist Theological Reading of the Communion of Saints*, Elizabeth Johnson suggests two distinctly different patterns of the Christian community's relationship with the martyrs and other holy persons who had died. The first and earliest envisions an egalitarian community that names the holy dead as companions and friends, who form an inspiring cloud of witnesses in the one Spirit; surrounding the living with lessons of encouragement and faithfulness. The second, a later development, envisions a patriarchal community that casts certain privileged dead into

---

[108] A miracle after death is generally seen as proof that the saint is in heaven as opposed to purgatory. The need to have this objective standard of holiness, however, has tended to skew the significance of miracles out of proportion to their true importance. The lessons of encouragement read in a life well lived or testimony in times of great struggle have validity apart from any wonders worked before or after death, which may actually serve to distract from the activity of the Spirit. See John Paul II, *Apostolic Consitution Divinus Perfectionis Magister* (promulgated on January 25, 1983) and Richard P. McBrien, ed. *HarperCollins Encyclopedia of Catholicism* (San Francisco: HarperSanFrancisco, 1995) 219.

[109] See Michael Perham, *The Communion of Saints* (London, SPCK, 1980) 114 ff; and Clifton F. Guthrie, *For All the Saints: A Calendar of Commemorations for United Methodists* (Akron, OH: Order of Saint Luke Publications, 1995) XIII-XVI.

positions of patronage; intercessors before the distant throne of God obtaining good things for needy petitioners.[110]

Augustine, preaching on the festival days of the martyrs, provides the vocabulary for the partnership model of the friends of God and prophets.[111] "Let us be companions in believing" he proclaims, "let us be companions in seeking."[112] Here is the call to every individual person and all persons together to belief, faith, and holiness. One is re-born into this life of the Spirit at Baptism and is continually nourished in it at the Lord's Table. These means of grace incorporate one into the body of Christ and make one's own body a temple of Christ's Spirit. Each person becomes holy and together they become a holy people. Speaking to the newly baptized about the bread and wine Augustine declares: "If you receive them well, you are yourselves what you receive."[113]

Remembering the saints who have passed on to us the faith, and especially those who testified to its power through their martyrdom is a communal act of identity. "You are the people of God . . . you are members of Christ . . . you are in communion with the members of the apostles, in communion with the shrines of the holy martyrs scattered throughout the world."[114] The martyrs stand out because they remained steadfast during sever testing, though it was not them but Christ in them, and that same Spirit is still faithful. The Church cherishes their legacy by means of festivals, celebrated on the day they suffered and gave us their "lessons of encouragement."[115]

To remember, examine, and believe what the martyrs set before us and then embody it in our selves is the truest celebration of their life witness. In response to their great example the saints below emulate, imitate, and

---

[110] A cursory study of a map of the United States illustrates how compelling devotion to saints was to the early explorers. Most settlements and cities were named after some patron saint during the pioneer days of the Franciscan missions, and especially of the less affluent Jesuit missions.

[111] Johnson is quick to point out that while Augustine's sermons reveal a strong grasp of the value of the companionship model, his legacy is ambiguous, as later in his life Augustine "showed great interest in miracles and other accoutrements of the patronage relationship, especially after relics of the first martyr, Stephen, were transferred from Palestine to North Africa." Elizabeth A. Johnson, *Friends of God and Prophets: A Feminist Theological Reading of the Communion of Saints* (New York: Lexington Publishing Company, 1998) 81.

[112] Augustine, *Sermons*, 53.13 (2:73).

[113] Ibid., 227.1 (6:254).

[114] Ibid., 137.15 (4:382).

[115] Ibid., 273.2 (8:17).

follow in the footsteps of the saints above. "As companions in the faith the martyrs gave their own lives; in response, the community matures in its own life of love in accord with the contours of their witness."[116] "As we reflect on all this, let us be on our toes to imitate the martyrs, if we want the feast day we celebrate to be of any use to us."[117] Sometimes the lesson is clear and particular as is the case with Stephen: "It is above all in the matter of loving our enemies that he is to be followed and imitated."[118] More often they inspire us by the general mood and manner of their lives. They did what they did by the abundant outpouring of the grace of God and "the fountain is still flowing, it has not dried up."[119]

Since the affairs of everyday life cast us into circumstances where we are tested, persecuted, and suffer, we can draw strength from the witness of the martyrs. For example, a person may endure martyrdom on their sickbed, struggling to remain faithful against the varied temptations that illness brings. Perhaps one faces economic martyrdom because the faith disallows them to participate in an unjust system or plan. To them the witness of ascetics offer valuable lessons. Every situation of human life is an opportunity to trust God, show courage, and love.

A free-flowing reciprocity occurs between the saints above and the saints below. The saints above give the Church their lives and testimony. The saints below respond by remembering and honoring them. In the celebration of their festivals they teach us the faith and inspire us on our journey with their lessons of encouragement. After listening to their story we rejoice in their victory, draw hope from their witness, sing in gratitude to God, and follow their example.

> The living and the dead together are [the] holy people of God at different stages of the journey; each one gives and receives what is appropriate, while the whole group of friends of God and prophets is centered on the incomprehensible mystery of divine love poured out in Jesus Christ for the sake of the world.[120]

"We honor the martyrs, and with the martyrs [we] worship God."[121] Gratitude and joy compel the Church to commend the departed saints with

---

[116] Elizabeth A. Johnson, *Friends of God and Prophets*, 82.
[117] Augustine, *Sermons*, 302.7 (8:304).
[118] Ibid., 314.2 (9:127).
[119] Ibid., 315.8 (9:133).
[120] Elizabeth A. Johnson, *Friends of God and Prophets: A Feminist Theological Reading of the Communion of Saints* (New York: Lexington Publishing Company, 1998) 85.
[121] Augustine, *Sermons*, 273.3 (8:18).

whom they share a common humanity, history, struggle, and faith to contemporary interest.

Is the Veneration of the Saints a Pagan Influence on Christianity?

Veneration has commonalities with pagan hero-worship.[122] Both venerate (that is respect, esteem, and honor) the historical achievement of the said figure and revere in him or her the manifestation of the divine in human form. This is not, however, a particularly pagan impulse but one that is commonly human and therefore universally valid. The difference lies in that paganism eradicates the boundaries between the divine and human, cultivating polytheism. This cultivation is foreign to Christianity and repugnant to the body of Christ.[123] Far from promoting its development, paganism can be seen to have impeded the veneration of the saints for fear of returning to polytheistic impulses.

Relics of Saints

With the emergence of Constantinian peace and the building of great Churches and Cathedrals[124] the desire arose to have a martyr's body under

---

[122] For the best study on the history of the dogma in the pre-Constantinian Church see J. P. Kirsch, *The Doctrine of the Communion of Saints in the Ancient Church*, trans. John R. M'Kee (Willits, Georgia: Eastern Orthodox Books, n.d.).

[123] This relates to the Eutychian error of the mixed nature, see page 181 of this work.

[124] The French social historian Philippe Ariès called attention to the conflict between Christian and secular assumptions about death in his classic *The Hour of Our Death*. Ariès argued that virtually every non-Christian culture, including Judaism, treated the dead as unclean. They sought to banish the dead to the margins of society, burying the dead outside of town, and regarding those who handled the dead as ritually unclean. Christians acted in a way that was unprecedented in the classical world. Rather than burying their dead away from their population centers, they put them at the center of their lives. They were able to do this because of their central story, which was always recited at burials. As Christians moved into less settled areas in northern Europe they brought this new sense of the place of the dead with them. In some cases Christian graveyards were older than both the churches set in their midst and the towns that surrounded them. In fact, many times, the sequence of events gave priority to the graves: a local saint was buried at a certain spot. Other Christians chose to bury their dead in the same location in the hope that the sanctity of the saint would have a positive effect on their dead. At some point a rich family would build a small shelter in which family members could be protected from the weather while visiting the graveyard. They and others would eventually expand the shelter into a chapel. A town would then grow up around the chapel. Graves were thus at the

the altar, or if that was not possible, a portion of the body. This led to the moving and exchanging of relics as some martyr's remains were moved to grand Churches thought to befit their dignity or to certain communities that held their memory to be exceptionally forming in some way. Because at the very heart of the Communion of Saints is the sharing in holy things, the martyr's remains were shared. This allowed their continuing witness to be especially present in a multitude of places and kept the precious remains from being totally lost in an unforeseen tragedy.[125]

In its reaction to the popular piety of the medieval Church, early Protestantism was infatuated with anxiety over idolatry. Horrified reformers saw stained glass windows adorning the largest Cathedrals and even the smallest Churches and the faithful praying before spectacular paintings, statues, and images. Not only did people pray before the images but they lit candles there and sometimes even dressed the images up and carried them about in parades.[126] There were similar displays of the consecrated Host.[127] Every Church boasted the relics of saints,[128] or at least objects that claimed

---

very center of some of the Christian communities that formed in northern Europe. See Philippe Ariès, *The Hour of Our Death* (New York: Barnes & Noble Books, 2000) n.p. See also Peter Brown, *The Cult of the Saints* (Chicago: University of Chicago Press, 1982) 69-75, where he suggests that the graveyards that were on the margins of classical society suddenly became great centers of Christian pilgrimage and activity as Christians built massive new building projects in what had been graveyards. It was not always immediately evident what was city and what was burial place.

[125] This became particularly important in the Middle Ages, as holy places were toppled by the Muslims, many of the saint's relics moved west into Europe. The relics were moved into protectorate communities who would subsequently benefit from the pilgrimage trade.

[126] The Galleria Doria Pamphili in Rome contains the treasures of the members of the Doria family, a Roman family that began to prosper when a family member was elected pope (Innocent X) in 1644. There are a number of valuable art works in the collection, but the family's most treasured possession was not a painting or a statue, it was the body of a saint. It was kept in a glass coffin and was carried around by members of the family when they traveled. The bodies of the saints were not something unclean and therefore to be avoided, but signs of God's power in the world.

[127] This fear of idolatry contributes to the suspicion of the Sacraments as well, even though prayers, hymns, sermons, and scripture also depend of the material – the human voice, breath, and body. Nor do we have access to them apart from our bodies for we perceive them through our senses.

[128] Wealthier Churches maintained vast collections, the incentive for which was to assure those who venerated them a correspondingly immense period of Indulgence. "In Halle, Cardinal Albrecht of Brandenburg managed to accumulate 39,245,120 years." (Bernd Moeller, Piety in Germany around 1500" in *The Reformation in Medieval*

to be knucklebone of a saint,[129] or a piece of the true cross.[130] The first preaching of the Reformation was often the denunciation of these forms of popular religion, which seemed to the reformers to split and scatter the devotion owed to God alone.[131]

The starting point for Christianity, however, is the doctrine of incarnation that "the Word became flesh and lived among us, and we beheld his glory."[132] The conviction that the Word has become flesh leads us also to affirm that the Spirit is manifest in material things such as water, bread, and wine, as well as holy people. As stated earlier, since the Church is the body of Christ it is subject to the same errors. A spirituality disassociated from materiality not only denies both the doctrines of creation and incarnation but veers in the direction of Docetism. This is the early Christian error that claimed Christ only seemed to be human.

Images of the Saints

Jesus Christ is "the image of the invisible God"[133] in whom "the whole fullness of Deity dwells bodily."[134] Having the images of Christ Jesus or other members of our family in Christ is a bit like carrying the photograph of a loved one, in that such an image helps to call to mind that person and

---

Perspective by Steven E. Ozment [Chicago: Quadrangle Books, 1971] 55. The post Vatican II *General Instruction of the Roman Missal* §266 states "The custom of putting relics of saints under an altar to be dedicated is to be retained. But it is important to verify the authenticity of such relics."

[129] The Pardoner of *The Canterbury Tales* abused his position by selling some papers which he claimed if people bought, their time in purgatory would be shortened after death; he sold them for very high price. He also claimed that he had Virgin Mary's veil, which would have been 1330 years after Mary died. He also claimed that he had St. Peter's sail and said the pig bones, he always carried with him, were relics of St. Peter. Chaucer also criticized him by implying him as a homosexual by referring him to a gelding or a mare. See Geoffrey Chaucer, *The Canterbury Tales*, trans. David Wright (Oxford: Oxford University Press, 1998) lines 659-714.

[130] In *The Innocents Abroad*, Mark Twain noted that as he and his fellow travelers crossed Europe, "we find a piece of the true cross in every old church we go into, and some of the nails that held it together. I would not like to be positive, but I think we have seen as much as a keg of these nails." (New York: Penguin Group, 2002) 53.

[131] See Carlos M. N. Eire, *War Against the Idols: The Reformation of Worship from Erasmus to Calvin* (Cambridge: Cambridge University Press, 1986).

[132] John 1:14.

[133] Colossians 1:15.

[134] Colossians 2:9.

one's love for them. But it is much more than that, while the image itself is a mere thing "the honor rendered to an image passes to its prototype [and] "whoever venerates an image venerates the person portrayed in it."[135]

The veneration of images is not a violation of the First Commandment, for the transcendent God who revealed himself to Israel, the "Author of all beauty"[136] permitted and even commanded the making of images that pointed symbolically toward salvation by the incarnate Word; such was the bronze serpent,[137] and the ark of the covenant.[138] Based on such reasoning the seventh ecumenical council at Nicaea (787) upheld the making and honoring of holy images and icons of Christ, the Virgin Mary, the angels, and all the saints. By becoming incarnate, they surmised the Son of God had introduced a new economy of images in which representational art now propagates the gospel. It provides confirmation that the Word of God truly became a human being and that this reality was not imaginary. The more the cross, the books of the gospels, other sacred objects, images of Christ, the apostles, the martyrs, and the saints are seen, the more those who see them are drawn into their story, and remember and long for those who serve as their models.

Hagiography

The term hagiography means holy writing and has come to refer to the full range of Christian literature which concerns the saints. The scope of which includes the lives of the saints, collections of miracle stories, accounts of the discovery or movement of relics, bulls of canonization, inquests held into the life of a candidate for canonization, liturgical books, sermons, visions, and the like. These works were composed in both the official clerical languages and the vernacular languages of the day. Written from at least the middle of the second century, the Middle Ages was a particularly fruitful time for the composition of these texts. [139]

The very penning of such a story serves as evidence that its subject has received some form of public honor. The continued use of such

---

[135] Basil, *De Spiritu Sancto* 18:45, PG 32, 149C.

[136] The Wisdom of Solomon 13:3.

[137] Numbers 21:4-9; John 3:14-15.

[138] Exodus 25:10-22.

[139] Unfortunately no adequate general guide to the history, study, and use of hagiography exists in English. The best introduction to research in hagiographic sources currently available is Jacques Dubois and Jean-Loup Lemaitre, *Sources et méthodes de l'hagiographie médiévale* [Sources and Methods of Medieval Hagiography] (Paris, 1993) which includes an extensive, but largely Francophone, bibliography.

chronicles implies that its subject has received paradigmatic status from the community. Because they were venerated long after their deaths and thus after living memory of them had faded, the texts were needed by the community to pass on their witness.

The most common type of hagiography is *The Lives of Saints*, which record the actions that formed and demonstrated their holiness.[140] Excerpts from such lives were often read publicly as part of the liturgical celebration of a saint's feast. The aim of hagiographers was not to produce a biography in the modern sense, but rather to portray a saint as an exemplar of the Christian life. In doing so, they sought to show how the saints themselves had imitated holy norms, particularly those provided by the life of Christ and previous saints. Just as they encouraged their audience to imitate the example of the saints, so too they employed the literary models offered them by the Bible and by earlier hagiographic works. Stories, themes, and motifs were repeated from the life of Christ to the life of a saint, and from the life of one saint to that of another, each hagiographer adapting a traditional pool of material to the needs of the narrative at hand. Hagiographers even went so far as to repeat phrases and whole passages verbatim from earlier works. The effect, largely intentional, was in part to subsume the particularity of a given saint's life into a generalized type of sanctity, such as the martyr, the virgin, or the holy bishop, thus aiding the moral and didactic purpose of life-story.

The records of the lives of the saints become a template of Christian virtue, a map of the way to salvation. Just as epics such as Beowulf or the Norse sagas provided a key to understanding the ideals of Germanic culture, so too the works of holy writers help to unlock the ideals of early and medieval Christianity.

How to Read the Lives of the Saints

One way to read the lives of the saints is to consider them a continuation of the Acts of the Apostles. They are a record of the acts of Christ, in and through the lives of his followers by the power of his Holy Spirit.

In them is found the same gospel, the same life, the same truth, the same righteousness, the same love, the same faith, the same eternity, the same power from on high, the same God and Lord. For the Lord Jesus Christ is

---

[140] In addition to exemplary conduct hagiographers also included the miracles which God performed through the saints. Such miracles did not only occur during the lives of the saints, but also posthumously at their tombs or otherwise in relation to their relics.

the same yesterday and today and for ever;[141] the same for all peoples of all times, distributing the same gifts to all who believe in him.[142]

The lives of the saints bear witness to us that true spiritual life begins when we live in Christ, and Christ lives in us, right here on this earth. The life of Christ on earth did not end with his ascension into heaven, nor with the martyrdom of the apostles, but his life continues to this day in his Church, and is seen most brilliantly in paradigmatic saints. All believers, in their own spiritual lives, are to enter into that continuing, never-ending life.

So, one reads the lives of the saints looking to them as examples. Christians desire to grow in the likeness of Christ and to have that likeness shine in them. For this to occur, they look to the saints to see real, practical examples of how to live. In this way the lives of the saints are applied practical theology. The saints are proofs and illustrations of the reality of Christ. They are transformed human beings, proof positive that people are redeemed, purified, illumined, transformed and recreated by Jesus Christ. Furthermore, the lives of the saints are applied ethics, in that they are embodiments of the life of holiness and virtue that is possible in Jesus Christ; they are embodiments of the life of grace.

The Church below finds great encouragement in the witness of countless Christians of every age whose lives give evidence that the Christian God is a God who acts in each generation and is acting still. I addition to acquiring confidence, when the Church meditates on the witness of the saints and also the fellowship of all Christian people, both living and dead, it places itself under divine judgment: if God was able to great things through these faithful ones of the past, how will the Church respond to God's divine initiative today?

Hymn Singing

The Church of England maintained many of the traditional perspectives regarding the saints such as the observance of the feast days of biblical saints and some martyrs[143] culminating in the grand celebration of All

---

[141] Hebrews 13:8.
[142] Justin Popovich, *Orthodox Faith and Life in Christ* (Belmont, MA: Institute for Byzantine and Modern Greek Studies, 1994) n.p.
[143] While some ancient martyrs were revered along with the noteworthy Churchman Thomas Becket and the great Cranmer, beginning in 1563 Foxe's *Book of Martyrs* connected those of the early Church to the real and sometimes imagined martyrs of the Protestant and finally English Reformation. Foxe's books were largely regarded as a quasi-official defense of the Church of England as long as the Catholic powers seemed to threaten its security. The eighteenth century witnessed new editions

Saints Day. In the eighteenth century, John and Charles Wesley transformed the spiritual atmosphere of the Church of England with the warmth and light of the Methodist revival. Methodism rediscovered the inherent power of the Communion of Saints as a fellowship across time and space in their local societies. They met regularly to hold members accountable for their activities, encourage holy living, and engage in corporate acts of confession and good works. John Wesley believed and taught that the members of the Church have fellowship with the triune God and also "with all the living members of Christ on earth, as well as all who are departed in his faith and fear."[144] This belief was honored in a spirited celebration of All Saints day every year, "a festival [he] dearly love[d]."[145] Wesley's journal entry for 1765 reads "November 1, Monday was a day of triumphant joy, as All Saints Day generally is—how superstitious are they who scruple giving God solemn thanks for the lives and deaths of his saints!"[146] The collect for All Saints Day, used by Wesley in his services, was taken from the 1662 *Book of Common Prayer* and expresses the Wesleyan perspective on the comradeship of the Communion of Saints. It reads:

> O Almighty God, who had knit together thine elect in one communion and fellowship in the mystical body of thy Son Christ our Lord, grant us grace so to follow thy blessed saints in all virtuous and godly living that we may come to those ineffable joys which thou has prepared for those who unfeignedly love thee; through the same Jesus Christ our Lord, who lives and reign with you and the Holy Spirit, one God, now and forever. Amen.

In his journal entry for November 1, 1766, Wesley confided "On this day in particular, I commonly find the truth of these words 'The Church triumphant in his love, their mighty joys we know; They praise the lamb in hymns above,

---

abbreviated from the larger collection of Protestant martyrologies. For example, in 1750 John Wesley published a version of Foxe's work in his *Christian Library* with enough excerpts and gory woodcuts to sustain the view that the English were a chosen people and an elect nation, destined to be locked in conflict with the papists. The mediation of Foxe to a wider readership was evidenced by anti-Catholic propaganda of the period, especially at key moments such as the Salzburg expulsions of Protestants in 1731 and the Jacobite rebellions in 1715 and 1745.

[144] John Wesley, "Letter to a Roman Catholic," cited in Geoffrey Wainwright, "Wesley and the Communion of Saints," *One in Christ* 27 (1991) 334.

[145] John Wesley, *Journals*, ed. Nehemiah Curnock (London: Epworth Press, 1938) 5:236.

[146] Ibid., 4:190.

And we in hymns below."[147] Those words written by his brother Charles, one of the greatest hymn writers in the English language, reveals the essentially doxological character of the Wesleyan practice of the Communion of Saints. United by the one Christ into one holy community that transcends space, time, and even death all who are alive in the Spirit form one great choir; singing God's praises; proclaiming the message of his Son; and advancing Christian holiness. Charles Wesley's great funeral hymn captures this sense of transcendent solidarity between the living and the dead with stunning power.

> Come, let us join our friends above who have obtained the prize,
> and on the eagle wings of love to joys celestial rise.
> Let saints on earth unite to sing with those to glory gone,
> for all the servants of our King in earth and heaven are one.
>
> One family we dwell in him, one church above, beneath,
> though now divided by the stream, the narrow stream of death;
> one army of the living God, to his command we bow;
> part of his host have crossed the flood, and part are crossing now.
>
> Ten thousand to their endless home this solemn moment fly,
> and we are to the margin come, and we expect to die.
> E'en now by faith we join our hands with those that went before,
> and greet the blood-besprinkled bands on the eternal shore.
>
> Our spirits too shall quickly join, like theirs with glory crowned,
> and shout to see our Captain's sign, to hear this trumpet sound.
> O that we now might grasp our Guide! O that the word were given!
> Come, Lord of Hosts, the waves divide, and land us all in heaven.[148]

The vision expressed in this great hymn assures those who sing it that they too are part of this blessed community, the one family, the one Church above and beneath, being guided to heaven by Christ Jesus.

The outstanding and prolific Baptist hymn writer Isaac Watts penned a similar theme in his "Am I a Soldier of the Cross? It sings:

> Am I a soldier of the cross, a follower of the Lamb,
> and shall I fear to own his cause, or blush to speak his name?

---

[147] Ibid., 5:191.
[148] Charles Wesley, Come, "Let Us Join Out Friends Above" in *The United Methodist Hymnal* (Nashville, TN: The United Methodist Publishing House, 1989) 709.

> Must I be carried to the skies on flowery beds of ease,
> while others fought to win the prize, and sailed through bloody seas?
>
> Are there no foes for me to face? Must I not stem the flood?
> Is this vile world a friend to grace, to help me on to God?
>
> Sure I must fight, if I would reign; increase my courage, Lord.
> I'll bear the toil, endure the pain, supported by thy word.
>
> Thy saints in all this glorious war shall conquer though they die;
> they see the triumph from afar, by faith they bring it nigh.
>
> When that illustrious day shall rise, and all thy armies shine
> in robes of victory through the skies, the glory shall be thine.[149]

Watts' hymn recognizes the comradeship between the saints above, who fought to win the prize, and those below, who are continually inspired by their faithfulness and final victory. He leads his singers to anticipate their own spiritual martyrdom and envisions the saints above anxiously awaiting that illustrious day when all the saints, together and victorious, give glory to God.

Recalling the victory of the saints is a great encouragement for Christians still combating their way throughout the trials of the world below.[150] Thomas Howard, author of *Evangelical Is Not Enough* recalls a rousing hymn from his youth, *Art Thou Weary, Art Thou Languid,* when he writes:

---

[149] Isaac Watts, "Am I a Soldier of the Cross? in *The United Methodist Hymnal*, 511. This hymn is also partly included in *The Baptist Hymnal* (480); sadly however, excised are the fifth and sixth verses, which specifically reference the saints above.

[150] For more examples see Ignaz Franz, "Holy God, We Praise Thy Name," *The United Methodist Hymnal,* 79; Thomas Shepherd, "Must Jesus Bear the Cross Alone," 424; Fred Pratt Green, "Rejoice in God's Saints," 708; and Lesbia Scott, "I Sing a Song of the Saints of God," 712, particularly popular with children when it intones: "They lived not only in ages past; there are hundreds of thousands still./ The world is bright with the joyous saints who love to do Jesus' will. / You can meet them in school, on the street, in the store, / in church, by the sea, in the house next door; / they are saints of God, whether rich or poor, / and I mean to be one too."

After speaking for six exquisite verses about the difficulties of following Jesus, the hymn concludes, "Finding, following, keeping, struggling / Is he sure to bless? / Angels, prophets, martyrs, virgins / Answer, Yes." I was overwhelmed by this picture. What solace! What encouragement! I was in an ancient lineage, and all of these forerunners knew everything I had experienced, and all of them could testify, "Keep going! It is worth it! Praise God!"[151]

The doxological thrust inherent in so many of the hymns which express the Communion of Saints creates a "musical iconography" which "enacts the presence of the saints so that the joy of heaven may be known upon the earth."[152] With them, motivated by them, and under their watchful gaze, the saints below are heartened as they sing, and together in one chorus with the saints above, place their faith in, and sing their song to Christ their Lord. It will be considered in a following chapter that some hymns are actually invocations of the saints.

All Saints Day

The reality of the Communion of Saints is brought to the liturgical consciousness of the Church on All Saints Day, November 1, or on the nearest Sunday in many Protestant Churches.[153] This is the day when the Church recalls that "great multitude with no one could count, form every nation, from all tribes and peoples and languages . . . and all the angles . . . and all the elders . . . who have washed their robes and made them white in the blood of the lamb;"[154] "God's Children . . . purifying themselves as he is pure;"[155] and following Jesus according to the beatitudes.[156] The collect of this joyous feast acknowledges the solidarity of all the saints above and below and asks for the gift of the Holy Spirit that those below might follow the example of those above and ultimately share their destiny:

---

[151] Thomas Howard, *Evangelical Is Not Enough: Worship of God In Liturgy and Sacrament* (Ignatius, San Francisco, 1984) 58.
[152] Geoffrey Wainwright, "Wesley and the Communion of Saints" in *One in Christ* 27 (1991) 332-345.
[153] The Eastern Churches observe All Saints Day on the Sunday after Pentecost.
[154] Revelation 7:9-17, the first lesson on All Saints Day in the Revised Common Lectionary.
[155] 1 John 3:1-3, the second lesson on All Saints Day in the Revised Common Lectionary.
[156] Matthew 5:1-12, commonly referred to as the Beatitudes is the Gospel lesson on All Saints Day in the Revised Common Lectionary.

> Almighty God, you have knit together your elect in one communion and fellowship in the mystical body of your Son Christ our Lord: Give us grace so to follow your blessed saints in all virtuous and godly living, that we may come to those ineffable joys that you have prepared for those who truly love you; through Jesus Christ our Lord, who with you and the Holy Spirit lives and reigns, one God, in glory everlasting. Amen.[157]

The Eucharist prayer of the United Methodist Church for All Saints (and memorial occasions) names a litany of biblical saints including the Virgin Mary, but regrettably leaving off any mention of the sects founder John Wesley or his brother Charles, who are both considered paradigmatic saints in the Anglican communion. It reads:

> It is right, and a good and joyful thing, always and everywhere to give thanks to you, Father Almighty, Creator of heaven and earth, God of Abraham and Sarah, God of Miriam and Moses, God of Joshua and Deborah, God of Ruth and David, God of the priests and the prophets, God of the apostles and martyrs, God of Mary and Joseph, God of our mothers and fathers, God of our children to all generations. And so with your people on earth and all the company of heaven, we praise your name and join in their unending hymn. Holy, holy, holy . . . .[158]

Such prayers remind us that "in the course of the world's history an innumerable multitude has already been drawn into the eternity of God before us, so that we are the late-comers. And the realization of this should generate hope and consolation in us, courage and trust."[159]

Official saints have their own day on the calendar so when the Church celebrates All Saints it especially remembers that great host of anonymous saints whom the world only counted for taxes and whom the institution has lost track but who nonetheless are found in the eternal flock of the Good Shepherd who looses no one.[160] We thank God for "the poor and the little ones who were great only in God's eyes. Those who go

---

[157] *The Book of Common Prayer* (The Seabury Press, 1979) 245.
[158] *The United Methodist Book of Worship* (Nashville, Tennessee: The United Methodist Publishing House, 1992) 74.
[159] Karl Rahner, "All Saints," *Theological Investigations* 8, trans. David Bourke (New York: Seabury Press, 1977) 29.
[160] See John 18:9.

unclaimed in any of the rolls of honor belonging to the Church or to world history."[161]

All Saints also remembers those persons whom we have personally known and loved, who created us as human beings, who nourished us in the faith, and helped us on our pilgrimage of life. Like our immediate family this is our immediate cloud of witnesses whose faces are held in living memory. Entrusted to God's mercy they are "our" saints. In remembering them we highlight the value and dignity of all members of the community.

As the great festival of the victory of grace All Saints is our day to. In its celebration we not only commemorate the saints above but we remember that we are all saints; made holy in Christ and by his Spirit. The living Church itself is a company of saints that praises and thanks God for his merciful grace and supports the rightful self-affirmation of all its members as saints. And we look to a future All Saints celebration when our lives too will be celebrated, even if anonymously.

All the dimensions of saintly remembrance are intertwined on this great feast day. On All Saints Day they belong to us and we belong to them and because of the God that binds us, together we can do more than any of us had dreamed we could do alone.

Summary

The saints cannot justify us. "The power of awaking souls to [eternal] life belongs to God alone."[162] The saints cannot sanctify us. Sanctification is the new life in God and can therefore be obtained only through God himself who is Divine Life. The divine life, that is, sanctification comes through Jesus alone by the Holy Spirit and not through or by the saints. But the saints play a role in the work of redemption—as witnesses not redeemers; as helpers not saviors; as intercessors not advocates.

Christ alone has procured salvation. Yet the saints, above and below, direct persons to Christ in order that they can find their salvation in him. They reveal in their lives that spiritual reality that links every believer to God. Through their words and deeds the saints—past, present, and future—participate in the passion and victory of Christ.[163] They do not add to Christ's

---

[161] Karl Rahner, "All Saints," *Theological Investigations* 8, 26.
[162] Augustine, *Sermons* XCVIII, 6.
[163] Colossians 1:24.

all-sufficient atoning work, "but they participate in his present passion as he battles the forces of evil in the world."[164]

By grace the saints are privileged to communicate the fruits of Christ's sacrifice to the world, through the historical preaching of the gospel and the administration of the sacraments, the true treasury of the Church. Through their teaching, example, and prayers they contribute to the up-building and outreach of the kingdom of God. Their communion, itself, is a means of grace; a channel through which the grace of Christ is poured out upon the world by the power of his Spirit, apart form whom they can do nothing.[165]

---

[164] Donald G. Bloesch, *The Last Things: Resurrection, Judgment, Glory* (Downers Grove, Illinois: InterVarsity Press, 2004) 169.
[165] John 15:5.

Chapter Nine

The Communion of Hope: Fellowship in Prayer

The Christian life is not solitary but social. Christians belong to a family. Love of God and love of neighbor are indivisible. "As God is love, so the Holy Spirit in the saints is love."[1] If one is united with God, then one is united with all those who love God. So there is a sort of connection or circulation of love between, in, and through all the members of the body of Christ and its head. This community of mutual love expresses itself in mutual prayer: we pray with each other and for each other.

This community of mutual love and prayer embraces the living and the dead in a single unity. We are all alive in Christ; by virtue of whose resurrection death is no longer an impassible barrier. God is the God of the living, not the dead.[2] God is the God of those who struggle upon the earth and the God of those who have died and yet live in him. Because in Christ there is no division between the living and the departed the living continue to pray for the departed and trust the departed to pray on their behalf.

While living upon the earth Christians pray for one another and request to be remembered in each other's prayers. Not to continue to pray for the departed or ask for their prayers suggests that they have either ceased to exist or become somehow unconnected to the community of love which is the family of God.

Questions of satisfaction and merit become irrelevant when prayer is seen as the expression of mutual love that binds together the members of the body of Christ. "Jesus Christ himself is the one and only propitiation for our sins and not ours only but for the sins of the whole world."[3] Therefore our prayers for the dead do not help them do penance for their sins and neither do their prayers for us draw on some treasury of merits for our benefit but we pray for each other because we are members of one family. Mutual prayer is the fruit of our love for each other. And not even death can separate us from the love of God which is in Christ Jesus our Lord.[4]

---

[1] Archimandrite Sophrony, *The Undistorted Image* (London, 1958) 163.
[2] Matthew 22:32.
[3] 1 John 2:1, 2.
[4] See Romans 8:38-39.

Prayer Is the Spiritual Bond of the Church.

Prayer is the expression of the Church's life and the spiritual bond of its members with God and with each other. It is the breathing of the Church and the atmosphere in which it lives. Prayer connects each member of the Church to the heavenly Father, the members of the earthly Church with each other, and the Church below with the Church above. Within this connection there is no loss of individuality and yet a great interdependence so that the all are "individually members one of another",[5] sharing blessings,[6] suffering,[7] and prayers.[8]

Our Father and Our Common Priesthood

The perfect example of prayer, of course, is the Lord's Prayer[9] in which Jesus himself teaches us that prayer is the very form of the Church's life, the chief mechanism of its activity, and the power of its overcoming. The model prayer Christ taught begins "Our Father." With these words Christ joined together all who pray them into a single unity and directed them to appeal out of this unity to their common Father. The Church prays then not in the name of any individual, save Christ, nor as the mere sum of all individuals, but as a holy fellowship, as a priestly unity, as the visible priesthood of Christ.

There is but one priest and one sacrificial offering of the new covenant.[10] Christ's role as reconciler of sinners is unique. However, Christ's one priesthood is not exclusive; it brings into being a plenitude of participation in itself both by the whole people of God. Sinners are made partakers in the death, resurrection, and saving mission of Jesus. The one priesthood of Christ does not exclude but includes all believers baptized by water and the Spirit. They are empowered not to substitute or supplement

---

[5] Romans 12:5.
[6] 1 Corinthians 13:13.
[7] 1 Corinthians 12:26.
[8] Ephesians 6:18.
[9] "Our Father in heaven, hallowed be your name. Your Kingdom come, your will be done, on earth as in heaven. Give us today our daily bread. Forgive us our sins, as we forgive those who sin against us. Lead us not into temptation, but deliver us from evil. For the kingdom, the power and the glory are yours, now and for ever. Amen." See Matthew 6:9-14 and Luke 11:2-4.
[10] Hebrews 10:12-14.

the redemptive work of Christ but to share in it enabled and energized in particular places and at particular times by the Spirit of Christ.

In this way every Christian participates in the one priesthood of Christ. In this intercessory role the Church community is called in the scripture "a holy priesthood,"[11] "a royal priesthood,"[12] and "a kingdom of priests."[13] So it is not each individual Christian that prays but the mystical Christ, as Paul wrote, "it was not I, but the grace of God within me."[14]

The fruits then of this prayer belong to all who are in Christ. As a chosen generation and royal priesthood, the members of the Body of Christ, not only within public worship, but even in their private life, pray not for their own needs alone but for all the redeemed in Christ. The priestly unity of all Christians is nowhere more powerfully and obviously realized than in the Eucharist, where Christ our High Priest sacramentally re-presents his sacrifice offered on Calvary once and for all. This great prayer of thanksgiving will be explored in the next chapter of this work.

We Should Pray for Each Other

We pray for ourselves and we pray for others. Prayer for one another articulates, communicates, and conveys mutual love between the members of the Church. Since love never fails[15] it is fitting and indeed necessary within the "royal law of love"[16] that the pilgrim church pray not only for themselves but for the saints beyond and likewise for the saints beyond to pray for the pilgrim Church below.

That we should pray for one another is a common theme throughout the scripture. Prayers of intercession for others are commonly mentioned in the Old Testament where the prophets especially occupy a mediatory role between God and the chosen people.[17] Moses is perhaps the most prominent example of this intercessory role. God initiated the relationship when through the burning bush God revealed himself, his will to save his people, and his desire that Mosses be his messenger.[18] Moses speaks with God often and at length, "as one speaks to his friend,"[19] and to Moses was "entrusted

---

[11] 1 Peter 2:5.
[12] 1 Peter 2:9.
[13] Revelation 1:5.
[14] 1 Corinthians 15:10.
[15] 1 Corinthians 3:18
[16] James 2:8; see also Matthew 5:44; 12:31, Luke 10:27.
[17] See Jeremiah 42:2; Baruch 1:13; and 2 Malachi 1:6.
[18] See Exodus 3:1-10.
[19] Exodus 33:11.

all [God's] house."[20] Moses prayed constantly for the people whom God had called to be his own, and for individuals such as for the healing of Miriam.[21] Primarily Moses interceded after his people's apostasy when he stood in the breach before God to turn away his wrath and save his people.[22]

David, the shepherd king "after God's own heart,"[23] prays for his people and prays in their name. At the dedication of the house of prayer built by David's son Solomon, the king stands before the altar of the Lord and spreads out his hands to heaven and entreats the Lord on his own behalf, on behalf of the entire people, for foreigners, and for future generations, that their sins be forgiven and their daily needs be met, so that the world may know that God is the only God.[24]

The prayers of the temple, the Psalms, are both personal and communal and express concern for those who are praying, for the whole people of God, for all nations, and all creation. The prayers of the prophets, while at times an argument or complaint, are characterized by a hopeful intercession that awaits and prepares for the intervention of the Savior God into history.[25]

In the intertestamental period, Judas Maccabeus inspired his troops by relating to them a recent dream in which he was given a vision of the prophet Jeremiah, introduced to him by Onias the high priest, as one who "prays much for the people and the holy city."[26] After the battle Maccabeus sends to Jerusalem to "provide for a sin offering" for those who had fallen in battle after plundering gifts offered to idols. "In doing this he acted very well and honorably taking account of the resurrection."[27]

Mutual prayer is certainly consistent with the New Testament teaching of Jesus, who in Luke's gospel enjoins believers to pray for their enemies.[28] The parallel passage in Matthew suggests that to pray for someone is to confer a benefit upon them. Therefore, children of the heavenly kingdom are expected to perform this labor of love for one another above

---

[20] Numbers 12:7; see also 8 which reads "With him I speak face to face, clearly, not in riddles," and 3 "Now the man Moses was very humble, more so than anyone else on the face of the earth."
[21] Numbers 12:13-14
[22] Ps 106:23; see also Exodus 32:1—34:9.
[23] 1 Samuel 13:14.
[24] See 1 Kings 8:22-56.
[25] See Amos 7:2, 5; Isaiah 6:5, 8, 11; and Jeremiah 1:6; 15: 15-18; 20: 7-18.
[26] 2 Maccabees 15:14.
[27] 2 Maccabeus 12:39-46.
[28] Luke 6:28.

all else, and in so doing they resemble their heavenly Father.[29] Jesus himself said to his disciple Peter "I prayed for you, that you would not fail."[30]

James, the brother of the Lord, exhorts the faithful to pray for one another.[31] In many passages in Paul's letters we find allusions to mutual intercessions. To the congregations in Rome, Philippi, Thessalonica, and Colossae, Paul writes that he remembers them in his prayers while he assures the Colossians that their mutual relationship with Epaphras has resulted in many prayers on their behalf, not only by Epaphras but by Paul and his comrades.[32] Moreover, Paul asks those to whom he writes to pray for him, and attributes his accomplishments to their prayers.[33] Thus among his exhortations to the Ephesians we find "persevere in prayer for all the saints."[34] Paul included in his first letter to his protégé Timothy instructions for the common prayer of the congregation which urged "supplications, prayers, intercessions, and thanksgivings be made for everyone, for kings and all who are in high positions."[35]

Following the longstanding Old Testament pattern fulfilled in the teaching and example of Jesus, the apostles and early Christians clearly believed that their intercessions for one another were effectual and useful. They were obviously convinced that by such intercessions they were able to gain divine assistance for others in the same way they could attain it for themselves through their own prayers. This notion of a life of mutual love and prayer, combined with the idea of an intimate union existing between all members of the Kingdom of God, both living and dead, and the representation of that union as the one body of Christ form the basis of the Communion of Saints doctrine.

The Living and the Dead Inhabit the Same Kingdom

According to the teaching of Jesus, the Kingdom of God includes not only participants who are alive on earth but those who have gone on into the life to come as well. On Christ's return at the end of the age, "the

---

[29] Matthew 4:44-45.
[30] Luke 22:42.
[31] James 4:16.
[32] Romans 1:9-10, 10:1-2; Philippians 1:3-5; Colossians 1:9, 4:12, 2 Thessalonians 1:11.
[33] Romans 15:30-32; 2 Corinthians 1:9-11; Philippians 1:19; Colossians 4:2-3; 1 Thessalonians 5;25; 2 Thessalonians 3;1; see also Hebrews 13:18.
[34] Ephesians 6:17-19.
[35] 1 Timothy 2:1-4.

righteous shall shine like the sun in the kingdom of their Father."[36] Those described as blessed will go into the Kingdom prepared for them from the foundations of the world.[37] Christ speaks of the present and future kingdoms of heaven without distinction.

In Paul's attempt to abrogate the ignorance of the Thessalonians concerning the Kingdom of God he assures them in his first letter that the dead in Christ are by no means left out.[38] Moreover, in the writings of the apostles the Kingdom of God is many times alluded to in expressions which portray the life of its members upon the earth as a participation in the heavenly kingdom save only that their full and perfected participation therein is reserved for the world to come. In this sense, Paul speaks of his being rescued from the lion's mouth and saved for the heavenly kingdom. Moreover, Peter exhorts the faithful to confirm their call and election with goodness in order that they not stumble but be provided entry into the eternal kingdom.[39]

We Should Pray for the Dead

The Church prays for all who have died asking forgiveness of their sins remembering that there is no person without sin for "all have sinned"[40] and "if we say that we have no sin we deceive ourselves and the truth is not in us."[41] Regardless of the how good or righteous a person may seem to have lived, at their death the Church prays for them as Paul ask of his spiritual children "beloved, pray for us."[42]

The scriptures contain examples of petitions made on behalf of the faithfully departed. Elijah and Elisha prayed for dead children respectively, bringing them back to life.[43] Similarly, Jesus interceded for the resuscitation of Lazarus[44] and Peter for the resuscitation of Dorcas.[45] Paul instructs Christians to "persevere in supplications for all the saints;"[46] all necessarily including the departed. In addition, Paul writes of the early practice of

---

[36] Matthew 13:40-43.
[37] Matthew 23:34.
[38] 1 Thessalonians 4:13-18.
[39] 2 Peter 1:3-11.
[40] Romans 3:23.
[41] 1 John 1:8.
[42] 1 Thessalonians 5:25.
[43] See 1 Kings 17:20-22; 2 kings 4:32-34.
[44] See John 11:38-34.
[45] See Acts 9:36-41
[46] Ephesians 6:18.

"receiving Baptism on behalf of the dead,"[47] implying that those on this side of death can help those on the other side. Finally, in his second letter to Timothy Paul issues a prayer for his dead comrade when he writes: "May the Lord grant mercy to the household of Onesiphorus, because he often refreshed me and was not ashamed of my chains . . . may the Lord grant that he will find mercy from the Lord on that day!"[48] It is clear that Paul is speaking about Onesiphorus in the past tense, in that while he asks for blessings upon his household, for Onesiphorus he asks for mercy of the last great Day of the Lord. From this we conjecture that Onesiphorus is dead and Paul prays for him still.

When we pray for those who have died, we do so "not for any juridical reasons, but simply because we and they want to belong to the same family. No other justification is either possible or necessary. Such prayer is the fruit of our love for each other: for death cannot sever the bond of mutual love and mutual prayer that links together all the members of Christ's body."[49]

Sepulchral inscriptions dating as early as AD 71, give evidence that Christians prayed for one another beyond death. Brief prayers without any formal address to God such as *"pax tibi"* (peace to thee) inscribed upon a grave marker are simple expressions of the hope that some benefit, such as peace, refreshment, life, light, eternal life, or union with God, would come to the one there laid. Epitaphs addressed directly to God frequently requested the forgiveness of sins and sometimes asked passersby to pray for the interred.[50]

The early liturgies of the Church are in harmony with its monuments. In both East and West, the Church remembered the dead in its public prayer. The Liturgies of James, Basil the Great, John Chrysostom, and Gregory confirm this. Comparable references are found in the Roman, Spanish, and Gallican liturgies as well as in the separated churches; the Jacobites, Copts, Armenians, Ethiopians, and Syrians. The Liturgy of James, considered to be the oldest surviving liturgy developed for general use in the Church provides the typical example:

---

[47] 1 Corinthians 15:29.
[48] 2 Timothy 1:16-18.
[49] Kallistos Ware, "'One Body in Christ': Death and The Communion of Saints," *Sobornost/ECR* 3:2 (1981), 179-191.
[50] See J. P. Kirsch, *The Doctrine of the Communion of Saints in the Early Church*, 39-44; as well as his other works on monumental inscriptions.

> Remember, O Lord, the God of spirits and of all flesh, those whom we have remembered and those whom we have not remembered, men of the true faith, from righteous Abel unto today; do thou thyself give them rest there in the land of the living, in thy kingdom, in the delight of Paradise, in the bosom of Abraham, Isaac and Jacob, our holy fathers, from whence pain and sorrow and sighing have fled away, where the light of thy countenance visiteth them and always shineth upon them.[51]

Eusebius writes in *The Life of Constantine*, that at his entombment "a vast crowd of people together with the priests of God offered their prayers to God for the Emperor's soul with tears and great lamentation."[52] Finally, as we have already noted throughout this work Augustine speaks many times of prayers for the dead, such as when he preached: "The universal Church observes this law, handed down from the Fathers, that prayers should be offered for those who have died in the communion of the Body and Blood of Christ, when they are commemorated in their proper place at the Sacrifice"[53]

The Problem of Prayer

The fundamental problems inherent to the whole question of intercessory prayer come to a head when we consider prayer for the dead. Prayer for the dead presents the problem of "what we are trying to do when we pray" in its most acute form.

> When we pray for the departed are we asking God to do things he has already determined either to do or not to do, so that our prayer can have no effect upon the issue one way or the other? Are we asking God to change his mind as to the fate of, or the treatment in store for, particular [persons]? Are we assuming that, in default of our prayers, God will not do the good things for which we are asking? Or that unless we pray he will not do these things effectively or quickly, so that our prayers have the power to intensify or speed up God's action.[54]

---

[51] See Irénée Henri Dalmais, *Eastern Liturgies*, trans. Donald Attwater (New York: Hawthorn Books, 1960) n.p.
[52] *Vita Constantius*, IV, lxxi, in *PG*, XX, 1226.
[53] Sermon, clxxii, 2, in *PL*, XXXVIII, 936.
[54] Ian Ramsey, ed. *Prayer and the Departed* (Grand Rapids: Eerdmans, 1971) 17.

These deep-seated questions arise in relation to prayer for the living as well as for the dead. At any level the workings of intercessory prayer are a mystery. We do not understand how a living person's prayer is effectual for another living person. The relationship between the act of praying, the free will of other persons, and God's providence and grace are beyond are comprehension. However, we know from personal experience that prayer between living persons is effective and we continue to pray for one another.[55] Likewise we do not know precisely how our prayers benefit the dead, but it does not follow that we should cease praying for them. Similarly, we do not know exactly how the saints are aware of our prayers, however we can rest in the confidence that they share the "mind of Christ."[56]

Guidelines for Praying for the Dead

Because "men and women will pray for the dead, especially the dead to whom they have been close in this life, the task of the Church must therefore be to provide them with words to say and ideas to articulate."[57] While very specific prayers for the dead that envision their exact needs seems presumptuous, plainly and solemnly naming the dead before the all-loving God, in confidence that he will do what is best, is enough to overcome our ignorance regarding their state or precise needs. "We do not pray for them because God will otherwise neglect them. We pray for them because we know he loves and cares for them, and we claim the privilege of uniting our love for them with God's."[58]

---

[55] The anecdotal experience of Christians across the millennia is now being backed up by scientific study, see "Positive Therapeutic Effects of Intercessory Prayer in a Coronary Care Unit Population," *Southern Medical Journal* (volume 81, pages 826-829, 1988); Harris, W.S., Gowda, M., Kolb, J.W., Strychacz, C.P., Vacek, J.L., Jones, P.G., Forker, A., O'Keefe, J.H., and McCallister, B.D. "A Randomized, Controlled Trial of the Effects of Remote, Intercessory Prayer on Outcomes in Patients Admitted to the Coronary Care Unit, 1999" *Arch Intern Med.* 159:2273-2278; Cha, K.Y., D. P. Wirth, and R. A. Lobo, "Does Prayer Influence the Success of in Vitro Fertilization–Embryo Transfer? Report of a Masked, Randomized Trial, 2001" *Journal of Reproductive Medicine* 46:781-787; among others. When considering such scientific work, one should keep in mind that the need for proof is contrary to very definition of faith, which "is the substance of things hoped for and the evedense of things not seen" (Hebrews 11:2).

[56] 1 Corinthians 2:16.

[57] Michael Perham, *The Communion of Saints* (London: SPCK, 1979) 111.

[58] William Temple quoted in *Prayer and the Departed: A Report of the Archbishop's Commission on Christian Doctrine*, chair. I. Ramsey (London: n.p., 1971) 90.

So prayers for the dead should seek for them deliverance from death and hell through the merits of Christ alone who gives rest and peace. Such prayers do not exclude the saints above as not in the same need as others or the un-faithful dead as beyond God's love and grace. Since we do not know the exact needs or condition of the departed, such prayers express our belief that God will do what he alone can know needs doing, along with our trust in God's forgiveness; thus assuring that our prayers do not drift into an unconditional immortality doctrine. As we thank God for the expression of his power in the lives of the saints and the encouragement that it gives us, we ask for grace to imitate them, as we anticipate the resurrection and acknowledge the incompletion that exists until the final consummation that is to come.

The Anglican Catechism endorses prayers for the dead "because we still hold them in our love and because we trust that in God's presence those who have chosen to serve him will grow in his love, until they see him as he is."[59] In this spirit the Church prays "Grant them your peace; let your perpetual light shine upon them; and, in your loving wisdom and almighty power, work in them the good purpose of your perfect will; through Jesus Christ our Lord."[60] Another prayer reads "We also bless thy holy name for thy servants departed this life in thy faith and fear; beseeching thee to grant them continual growth in thy love and service."[61]

Praying for the Faithfully Departed and the Lost

When we pray for the faithfully departed we need not pray for their redemption or justification, since this has already been accomplished in the gift of Christ Jesus.[62] We may however, pray for their continual progress toward final glory, since, as has already been surmised, there is spiritual growth beyond the grave, where "the Lamb will be their Shepherd and . . . guide them to springs of the water of life,"[63] and where "seated with [God] in heavenly places in Christ Jesus, . . . in the ages to come [the Father] might show the immeasurable riches of his grace in kindnesses to [them] in Christ Jesus."[64]

---

[59] *Book of Common Prayer* (New York: Church Hymnal Corporation, 1979) 862.
[60] Ibid 504.
[61] As quoted in E. R. Hardy, "The Blessed Dead in Anglican Piety," *Sobornost* 3, no 2 (1981) 173.
[62] See Romans 3:24-25.
[63] Revelations 7:17.
[64] Ephesians 2:6-7.

It has traditionally been said that the saints are enjoying perfect bliss. Just what perfect bliss is, is not exactly known, but it consists at least of a complete knowledge of the purged self and therefore complete self-affirmation[65] and a full knowledge of God's acceptance of one into the divine life. But, as already stated, such bliss is only possible in relation to others. Until all can together achieve perfection, even those nearest to God are not in such a state of perfection that they have ceased to grow. If they are still growing and moving forward, they are likely to welcome the prayers of their fellow travelers on the way. In fact, those saints ahead value and desire the Church's prayers to a greater extent in relation to their greater knowledge of its effectiveness. So if prayer for the dead is seen chiefly as an expression of love within the Christian fellowship, such loving prayer will naturally extend to and for the faithfully departed and even the great heroes to the faith.

We can and should pray for all people even those in hell. The Eastern Orthodox Churches pray at the Vespers of Kneeling on the Eve of Pentecost Sunday for those suffering in hell that their torments might be relaxed. Many Orthodox pray for the actual release of those in hell believing that Christ's "descent into hell shattered the eternal bars and revealed the way of ascent for those who dwell in that lower world."[66] The gates of hell stand open, they believe, until the last judgment so that no one is as yet irretrievably condemned. [67]

Teresa of Avila wrote that the saints above pray not only for the saints below but for all those who suffer, even the lost:

> If we see someone, especially someone who is our friend, in desperate straits or in great suffering, then we are overcome, apparently as a natural reaction, by compassion, and if [their] pains are severe, then we feel them most vividly. But to see a soul condemned for all eternity to the torment of all torments, who could bear such a thing?[68]

---

[65] See John Stott, *The Cross of Christ* (Downers Grove, IL: InterVarsity Press, 1986) 276.
[66] See "The Service of Kneeling for Whitsunday" in *The Service of the Blessing of the Waters of Epiphany; The Service of Kneeling for Whitsunday* (Williams and Norgate 1917) 76.
[67] See Kallistos Ware, "'One Body in Christ': Death and The Communion of Saints," *Sobornost/ECR* 3:2 (1981), 190.
[68] Teresa of Avila, *The Life of Saint Teresa of Avila by Herself*, trans. J. M. Cohen (London: Penguin Classics, 1988) ch. 32.

In our prayers we may hope for the final reunion of all souls, even the lost. An appropriate prayer is: God have mercy on their souls. We have already investigated the biblical hope that God's grace reaches beyond death.[69]

The Church Benefits When She Prays for the Dead

In praying for the dead the Church intercedes for them just as for the living on account of the sacrifice of Christ on the cross, which was offered for the deliverance of all. On the earth it is not known with certainty to what lot each person has been subjected to in death but the prayer of love can never be profitless. If those whom we love have entered the Kingdom of Heaven then they unite in our prayer for them with a prayer for us. If our prayers are powerless to help them they are not harmful to us but return to us as Christ has said in Matthew's gospel "let your peace return to you."[70] John Damascene wrote "If anyone wishes to anoint a sick man with myrrh or some other sacred oil, first he becomes a partaker of the anointing himself and then he anoints the sick one. So also everyone who struggles for the salvation of his neighbor, first receives the benefit himself, and then offers it to his neighbor."[71]

The Dead Pray for Us

The key to understanding prayer for the dead and to understanding intercessory prayer as a whole is the idea of mutuality. The living and the dead belong together. This mutuality implies that not only are the living concerned with the dead but that the dead are concerned with the living. So we are not to be content only to pray for them but we ask them to pray for us. "In such prayer, while they lived on earth, they both displayed and consecrated their love towards us. Doubtless that ministry of love continues. . . . It is in the mutual service of prayer, our prayer for them and theirs for us, that we come closest to them." [72]

Prayer does not cease but increases and is exalted in the heavenly kingdom. Scripture clearly states that angels can help us and pray for us.[73] We have similar scriptural ground for believing the glorified saints can help

---

[69] See 1 Peter 3:19-20; 4:6.
[70] Matthew 10:13.
[71] As quoted in Father Michael Pomazansky, *Orthodox Dogmatic Theology*, trans. Hieromonk Seraphim Rose (St. Herman of Alaska Brotherhood, 1994) 314.
[72] William Temple quoted in *Prayer and the Departed: A Report of the Archbishop's Commission on Christian Doctrine*, chair. I. Ramsey (London: n.p., 1971) 90.
[73] See Genesis 48:16; Daniel 9:20-23; Zechariah 1:12; Luke 1, 2 ; Acts 1:10-11.

us as well. Paul refers the Galatians in their difficulties to "the Jerusalem above . . . our mother."[74] Peter writes "I will make every effort so that after my decease you may be able at any time to recall these things."[75] In John's revelation the souls of the martyrs pray to God after death. From under the altar they cried out with a loud voice pleading for the vindication of God's justice for those who had endured persecution.[76] The impact of these heavenly prayers upon the earthy Church is seen in angelic sealing of the servants of God which gives them "protection in and through death."[77] In other passages the revelator envisions the twenty-four elders and then angels offering to God the prayers of the saints.[78] Within these pictures of the highest heaven the spirits who serve God are aware and mindful of their counterparts upon the earth and present their prayers as an offering before God on the heavenly altar.[79] Finally Malachi looks forward to the coming of the prophet Elijah who will "reconcile parents to their children and children to their parents."[80]

The Church Below May Request the Prayers of the Church Above

Often, perhaps when life is troubling, one asks a relative or close friend to pray on one's behalf. It is very good that persons ask others to pray for them and their needs and also to offer reciprocal prayers. Praying to the saints is analogous to asking a friend to pray on one's behalf. One can still pray directly to Christ, but one's friend is also praying. Not only does prayer benefit the receiver, but also the person who prays: it draws us all into closer union with Christ and with each other.

Because person-to-person intercession among the living is in no way seen as being in conflict with prayer to Christ "who always lives to make intercession for them"[81] "at the right hand of God"[82] Christians extended their prayers for each other into heaven, believing that joined with the risen Savior the saints above continue to pray for those who were still struggling

---

[74] Galatians 4:26.
[75] 2 Peter 1:15.
[76] Revelation 6:9-10.
[77] See Revelation 7:1-8; 8:1-5; and Adela Yarbro Collins, "The Apocalypse," in *The New Jerome Biblical Commentary* (Englewood Cliffs, New York: Prentice Hall, 1990) 1005-1006.
[78] Revelation 5:8; 8:3-4.
[79] Jesus also spoke in reference to this type of heavenly ministry in Matthew 18:10.
[80] Malachi 4:5; see also Revelation 11:1-13.
[81] Hebrews 7:25.
[82] Hebrews 10:12.

on the way to their joy. In this way "an invocation of any saint, [below or above,] is always an invocation of all the saints, i.e., an act by which we take refuge in faith in the all enfolding community of all the redeemed."[83] So from very early in the Church's history the saints were believed to be praying for the living[84] and could be asked to do so.[85]

Spiritual Communion Not Spiritual Communication

The Communion of Saints must not be confused with spirit communication or necromancy which is clearly forbidden in the scripture.[86] This kind of activity pertains to the realm of darkness and has a shadow existence in regard to the true Communion of Saints which concerns real interaction between the faithful above and below. The Old Testament account of the medium at Endor who brings back Samuel from the dead serves only to attest to the reality of a world beyond from which, with a special permission of God, the departed may appear to the living, and even manifest things unknown. However, the art or science of evoking the dead, is due to the agency of evil, and the means inadequate to produce the expected results. As the aforementioned story attests, the medium herself was surprised and terrified at the appearance of the dead prophet. Such activity is forbidden in the scriptures because they are the practices of pagan religions and the authority of the oracle is opposed to that of prophet which the Lord's has raised up to reveal his divine will.[87]

---

[83] Karl Rahner, "Why and How can we Venerate the Saints," *Theological Investigations* 8, trans. Davod Bourke (New York: Seabury, 1977) 23.

[84] 2 Maccabees 15:14; Matthew 18:10; Revelation 5:8; Revelation 8:3-4.

[85] For the most complete historical examination of the subject see J. P. Kirsch, *The Doctrine of the Communion of Saints in the Ancient Church*, trans. John R. M'Kee (Willits, Georgia: Eastern Orthodox Books, n.d.); for later development see Peter Brown, *The Cult of the Saints: Its Rise and Function in Latin Christianity* (London: SCM Press, 1981).

[86] See Leviticus 19:26, 31; Deuteronomy 18:9-14; Isaiah 8:19-22; 19:3; Acts 16:16-18.)

[87] See Deuteronomy 18:9-15, which reads in part: "When you come into the land that the Lord your God is giving you, you must not learn to imitate the abhorrent practices of those nations. No one shall be found among you who . . . who practices divination, or is a soothsayer . . . or who consults ghosts or spirits, or who seeks oracles from the dead. For whoever does these things is abhorrent to the Lord . . . You must remain completely loyal to the Lord your God . . . do [not] give heed to soothsayers and diviners . . . the Lord your God will raise up for you a prophet like me from among your own people; you shall heed such a prophet."

The saints do not communicate through mediums but through Christ himself. The communion saints have with one another is derivative of their communion in Christ. As the saints above behold the face of God they hear the saints below in Christ. The saints below hear the saints above by the mediation of Christ. This inward hearing and seeing is generally not available to others but the truth of its content can always be verified within the called community. In some instances persons are granted a special dispensation of God's grace to see and hear more directly, as in the case of the first martyr, Stephen who beheld "the glory of God and Jesus standing at the right hand of God."[88]

Unspoken Requests

The absence of direct invocation should not be equated to a lack of belief in the Communion of Saints. For one can remember the saints, give thanks to God for their lives and witness, and hope to share their destiny without emphatically requesting their prayers. However, if one defines invocation rather more broadly to include seeking help from the saints in general and not just specifically through prayer, then even calling to mind the inspiring memory of a saint's luminous example would be a sort of invocation. That is, in doing do, one is unconsciously but not intentionally asking for guidance. The very act of "remembering the dead becomes a prayer even if it does not contain a specific petition to the saint."[89] The same could be said of looking to Paul's letters with a desire to discover some instruction for modern daily life. Frequently, one searches the scriptures for wisdom and knowledge and finds such in the writings of the apostles. Though they be in glory, we seek their help and find it.

Spoken Requests

From the earliest Christian centuries believers have not only made these unspoken requests of the saints above but have requested their prayers openly, audibly, publicly, and liturgically. While there was no official teaching that commended this practice it naturally arose out of early communal piety. The fellowship of the believers and their communion with one another through Christ's Holy Spirit kept their mutuality alive even though some had

---

[88] See Acts 7:54-60.
[89] Karl Rahner and John Baptist Metz, *The Courage to Pray* (New York: Crossroad, 1981) 86.

been planted in the grave. To pray for the dead and to request their prayers simply seemed a consistent and good thing to do.

The first evidence of such prayers comes form graffiti scratched on the walls of the Roman catacombs and in other cemeteries invoking the prayers of the martyrs or others outstanding members of the church there entombed, for example: "Vincent, you are in Christ, pray for Phoebe;"[90] and "Januaria . . . pray for us;"[91] "intercede and pray for your brothers and sisters;"[92] and "Paul and Peter, pray for Victor;"[93] "Paul, Peter, pray for Eratus;"[94] [Sentianus] "in your prayers pray for us, for we know that you are in Christ."[95] An ancient tomb of a Christian child proves it was not only the martyrs or heroic Christians who were invoked, as its inscription reads: "Child pray for your parents."[96]

Calling upon the dead in Christ for their prayers is a concrete expression of the mutuality of Christian fellowship and a way of remembering and calling upon the solidarity which exists in Christ between those still struggling below and those victorious above.[97] These latter are

---

[90] H. Delehaye, *Les Origines du culte des martyrs* (Bruxelles: Bureaux de la Societe des Bollandistes, 1912), 123.

[91] Ibid, 124.

[92] Ibid, 125.

[93] Josef Jungmann, "The Veneration of the Martyrs," in *The Early Liturgy to the Time of Gregory the Great,* Francis Brunner, tr. (Notre Dame: University of Notre Dame Press, 1959), 175-87:182.

[94] Ibid.

[95] Charles McGinnis, *The Communion of Saints* (St. Louis: B. Herder, 1912), 54, quoting Marucchi, *Elements d'archeologie chretienne,*Vol. 1, p.188.

[96] D Hardy, as quoted by Kallistos Ware, in "'One Body in Christ': Death and The Communion of Saints," *Sobornost/ECR* 3:2 (1981), 190.

[97] A slight distinction bears being reiterated rising out of the petitioner-patronage model of the Communion of Saints which became quickly entrenched as canonization was regularized. Roman teaching here posits that when the common voice of the Church testifies to the virtue and faithfulness of a departed Christian, persons are taught by their good example and place them as models or patterns to be imitated. When such a common conviction is further confirmed by special witnesses such as martyrdom, self-sacrificing service to God, the gift of healing, or especially miracles occurring upon their intercession (these seen as the Lord confirming the sanctity of the departed person and their place in heaven as opposed to purgatory) the Church remembers them in a special way. The prayers for the forgiveness of their sins gives way to praising their struggles in Christ, since "no one after lighting a lamp puts it under a bushel basket, but on a lamp stand, and it gives light to all the house" (Matthew 5:15) and petitions that they might pray for us, for the remission of our sins and for our moral advancement.

asked to remember before God their brothers and sisters who have not yet finished the race. That they too might obtain grace from Jesus Christ the only Savior and sole mediator that would make them good disciples, holy people, and witnesses to the uttermost should they be called next to give their lives for the sake of the gospel.

As the church began to honor their memory liturgically and then publicly so too did they invoke their prayers liturgically and publicly. Instead of overshadowing the person of Christ, for it is "in [Christ that] the other world acts on this, and this world on the other,"[98] these prayers served to strengthen the bonds between the members of Christ's body, in heaven and those upon earth, giving particular expression to the way those who are in Christ are related one to another.[99]

Such faith moved Cyprian to write in a letter to Cornelius Bishop of Rome: "If one of us goes before the other, let our love for one another be unbroken, when we are with the Lord: let our prayers for our brethren and sisters be unceasing."[100] Likewise, Origen dogmatically claimed: "All those fathers who have fallen asleep before us fight on our side and aid us by their prayers."[101]

Communion with the saints in prayer is the realization of the bond between Christians upon the earth and those in heaven. In the Church we "have come to Mount Zion, the city of the living God, the new Jerusalem, and to innumerable angels in festal gathering and to the assembly of the firstborn who are enrolled in heaven, and to God the judge of all, and to the spirits of the righteous made perfect and to Jesus, the mediator of the new covenant."[102] The faithful upon the earth are not separated from their dead brothers and sisters for "[God] is not the God of the dead but of the living for to him all of them are alive."[103]

---

[98] P.T. Forsyth, *This Life and the Next* (1918; reprint, London: MacMillan, 1964) 37.
[99] While Pope Leo XIII condemned a particular prayer in which the souls in Purgatory were invoked there exists no binding dogmatic statement on this subject; see Robert Ombres, *Theology of Purgatory*, 66.
[100] Cyprian in a letter to Cornelius Bishop of Rome (251-253) quoted in Henry Barclay Swete, *The Holy Catholic Church, The Communion of Saints* (London: McMillan, 1915) 222.
[101] Origen quoted by J. Paterson-Smyth, *The Gospel of the Hereafter* (Toronto: Musson, 1910) 121.
[102] Hebrews 12:22-24.
[103] Luke 20:38.

Criticisms in Opposition to the Practice

Three serious criticisms have been made in opposition to the practice of asking the saints above for their specific prayers or even direct favors. Classic Protestant critique judges such prayers to distort the basic structure of Christian faith by transferring the heart's trust from our merciful Savior, Jesus Christ, who is alone the unique mediator between God and human beings to others who are needed to bridge the gulf between the righteous Judge and unworthy sinners. The basic feminist critique of hierarchical relationships finds in such prayers the relationship of a weak petitioner dependent upon a powerful patron, implying that God does indeed "show partiality,"[104] limiting his access to a privileged few. Finally the critique of the enlightened and modern world claims to expose such prayers as spiritually deficient since there can obviously be no direct communication between the living and the dead; and to assume we have such a relationship with a host on invisible people is foolishness.

In answer to the reformers concern that Christ not be overshadowed in the transference of one's trust from Jesus Christ who alone is the merciful Savior to other persons who are needed to bridge the gulf between unworthy sinners and the just judge, the saints are not petitioned as intermediaries but addressed as co-disciples from whom we do not receive mercy, grace, or blessings of any sort, but ask them to aid us by their prayers as human beings united with us in the one and same communion. The saints cannot take the place of Christ in his role as the fountain of mercy; they can however point us to Christ. They do not add to but accompany the great work of redemption with their nurturing love and intercession. Christ Jesus, the only begotten Son of God, by his great sacrifice on the cross merited for us, once and for all, the grace and mercy of God so that they are ever-present to us and we need no saints to mediate these to us. "We honor them, and they pray for us; but neither they nor the Blessed Virgin Mary can give us any grace or show us any mercy. They can simply present our prayers to the Almighty and unite them to their own."[105]

In answer to feminists who fear patriarchal elitism that casts one into a dominant-subordinate relationship between pilgrim and saint, the practice of invocation activates mutual regard and provides a vehicle for leaning on and being supported by a particular, limited, and concrete expression of our

---

[104] For the opposite declaration see Peter's words in Acts 10:34.
[105] John F. Sullivan, *The Externals of the Catholic Church* (New York: P. J. Kennedy and Sons, 1959) 328.

solidarity with all God's people who remain with us in the Spirit, through the ages, and across the various modes of human existence.

In answer to enlightened agnostics we call upon the names of the saints who have gone before us as a way of acknowledging our inheritance of their legacy of faith and joining our lives and prayers with the lives and prayers of all people who hope in God. Resting on the creedal claims of the resurrection of the body and everlasting life, the practice of invocation does in fact assume a relationship with a host of invisible persons who are cognizant of what persons on earth are doing and saying. Calling on the cloud of witnesses for their prayer recognizes and actualizes our affiliation with one another where the courage, witness, and love of one person affects the whole body, just as one person's apathy and sin exercises a deleterious influence.

The principle paradigm on which to rely in the face of these critiques is to recall the clear example of scripture that encourages believers to pray for all human beings as well as for their specific needs. In his letters, Paul lovingly assures his churches "I always pray for you"[106] and requests of them: "brothers and sisters, pray for us."[107] Within the Communion of Saints, prayer is the key way of expressing love and concern for others.

If saints living upon the earth can and do ask each other for the encouragement of prayer then the saints living above certainly can as well. We do not request the prayers of the saints above because they are more compassionate, more disposed to aid us, or nearer to God than we are, for how could they be; since in God "we live and move and have our being."[108]

But our request of their prayers is a particular and tangible expression of the solidarity of all saints, in the Spirit, beyond boundaries and borders, across time and space, and despite the various modes of human existence. By requesting the prayers of the saints above, the saints below remember their Spirit filled witness and are simultaneously encouraged to struggle on to a sure and certain hope.

The Mistakes of the Patronage Model

In her book *Friends of God and Prophets*, Elizabeth Jonson lays out an argument for the development of what she calls the patron-petitioner understanding of the relationship between the living and dead in Christ. "In raw terms, the saints in heaven went from being primarily witnesses in a

---

[106] 2 Thessalonians 1:11.
[107] 1 Thessalonians 5:25.
[108] Acts 17:28.

partnership of hope to being primarily intercessors in a structure of power and neediness."[109] A diminished sense of being holy people and an increased sense distance felt between sinful, needy people and a holy and majestic God "cast the saints in the role of sponsors who could plead ones cause before the throne of God and even dispense favors in their own right."[110] The primary way one connected with the honored dead moved from remembrance and inspiration to intercession before God for physical and spiritual protection. Mirroring the courtiers of Constantinian Rome, the saints above became seen as mediators having their own spheres of influence and acting as benefactors in return for prayers, devotions, pilgrimages to their tombs, and reverence for their relics; the mother of the king having the best access of all.

The official theology of the Church increasingly proclaimed this notion of the saints and the Virgin Mary as advocates pleading causes before a stern, divine judge, as mediators, as go-betweens, as intriguers or wire-pullers at the court of Heaven—all metaphors were used. It is significant also that the saints themselves were arranged in a hierarchy, in both the liturgy and official iconography, the Virgin Mary as the arch-intercessor through whom the petitions of the other saints were directed.[111]

The Arian controversy[112] which led to a strong emphasis on the divinity of Christ had the subsequent effect of obscuring his human nature by which he is related to human beings as their brother. Christ who had mercifully died to save sinners was now ever more identified with the ruling power of God authorized and increasingly depicted as the judging Jesus riding on the rainbow, coming to justly weigh each person's good and bad deeds and assign a due destiny in heaven or more likely hell.

---

[109] Elizabeth A. Johnson, *Friends of God and Prophets*, 86.
[110] Ibid.
[111] Stephen Wilson, ed. *Saints and their Cults: Studies in Religious Sociology, Folklore, and History* (London: Cambridge University Press, 1993) 23.
[112] Arius denied that the Son is of one essence, nature, or substance with God the Father; he is not consubstantial (*homoousios*) with the Father, and therefore not like him, or equal in dignity, or co-eternal, or within the real sphere of Deity. The Logos which John exalts is an attribute, Reason, belonging to the Divine nature, not a person distinct from another, and therefore is a Son merely in figure of speech. As such Christ was to be esteemed neither truly divine nor truly human, neither God nor human; but a being intermediate between the two, the first and most exalted of creatures, who assumed a human body for the sake of humanity's redemption. The Creed adopted at the Council of Nicaea (325) defined orthodoxy and anathematized the Arian position.

Arising in response, the cult of the saints reclaimed the holy, gentle, and human face of heavenly love.[113] The saints would act as powerful mediators who would interceded for both material and spiritual blessings for poor, weak, and unworthy sinners. As human beings they could compassionately understand the struggles of the common people; and because they were not busy governing the universe they had time to care about individual devotees; finally because they themselves were redeemed, they could plead the cases of sinners before the harsh judgment seat of Christ.

Because of her maternal relationship with her Son and her demonstrated ability at the wedding of Cana[114] to persuade him to perform miracles for the benefit of others, the Mother of God was thought to be the best intercessor of all. Consequently, while the portrayals of her Son where progressively more callous the iconography of the Blessed Virgin was the epitome of sympathy and kindness. The ultimate result was a religious situation in which popular piety shifted the confidence and trust that should have rested in God's abundant grace in Christ to the saints.

These friends of God became regarded as patrons and mediators before God and Christ on behalf of other members of the Church, and could obtain grace and help by their prayers for the faithful, both living and dead. The saints were important above their role and exemplars as intercessors able to acquire spiritual aids and to give protection and deliverance. Origen was the first to write of this sort of invocation of saints:

> It is not improper to address these to saints, and two of them, I mean intercession and thanksgiving, not only to saints but also to men, but supplication only to saints , as for instance to some Paul or Peter, that they may aid us, making us worthy to obtain the power granted unto them for the forgiveness of sins.[115]

Further evidence is sparse until one hundred years later when it is found in the writings of Hilary, Basil, Gregory of Nazianzus, and Gregory of Nyssa.[116] Basil wrote that he called upon the holy apostles, prophets, and martyrs that by their intercession, "the good God may be propitious to me and that I may be granted redemption for my offenses."[117]

---

[113] See Peter Brown, *The Cult of the Saints; Its Rise and Function in Latin Christianity* (Chicago: University of Chicago Press, 1981).
[114] See John 2:1.
[115] Origen, *De Oritione* 14.
[116] Hilary, *Liber de Synodis* 92; Basil, *Ep*. II.cciii.3; Gregory of Nazianzus, *Oration* xxiv. 19; xliii.82.
[117] Basil, *Ep*. ccclx.

By the late fourth century the Church had acculturated the social dynamics of the patronage system[118] so that "just as the terrestrial patron is asked to use his influence with the emperor, so the celestial patron, the saint, is asked to use his influence with the Almighty."[119] Saints became increasingly important for there thaumaturgic powers, so much so, that by the sixth century miracles became the primary norm for legitimizing veneration. By 1500 the patronage system was complete. "That is, the responsibility of a particular saint for a particular group of the population or a particular emergency was fixed, and the practice of giving children the names of saints had also become commonplace."[120]

The patron-client paradigm which had become the predominate feature of medieval devotion to the saints became the main target of the Reformation critique that it diminished awareness of the gracious and compassionate love of God freely poured out in abundance in the person and work of Christ Jesus. As Martin Luther later recalled:

> Consider what we used to do in our blindness under the papacy. If anyone had a toothache, he fasted to the honor of Apollonia; if he feared fire, he sought St Lawrence as his patron; if he feared the plague, he made a vow to St Sebastian or Roch. There were countless other such abominations, and every person selected his own saint and worshiped and invoked him in time of need. In this class belong those who go so far as to make a pact with the devil in order that he may give them plenty of money, help them in love affairs, protect their cattle, recover lost possessions, etc., as magicians and sorcerers do. All these fix their heart and trust

---

[118] See Carl Lande, who defines the patron client relationship as "a vertical dyadic alliance, i.e., an alliance between two persons of unequal status, power, or resources each of whom finds it useful to have as an ally someone superior or inferior to oneself. The superior member of such a relationship is called the patron. The inferior member is called the client." in *Friends, Followers, and Factions*, ed. Stefen Schmidt, Laura Guasti, Carl Lande, and James C. Scott (Berkley: University of California Press, 1977) xx. He goes on to say that theses relationships are often pyramided upon each other, so that several patrons, each with their own sets of clients, are in turn the clients of a higher patron, who in turn in the client of a patron even higher than himself." Ibid, xxi.

[119] G. E. M. de Ste. Croix, "Suffragium: From Vote to Patronage," *British Journal of Sociology* 5 (1954) 46.

[120] Bernd Moeller, Piety in Germany around 1500" in *The Reformation in Medieval Perspective* by Steven E. Ozment (Chicago: Quadrangle Books, 1971) 55.

elsewhere than in the true God. They neither expect nor seek anything from him.[121]

The Corrections of the Reformation

Having rediscovered that the true treasury of the Church is the holy gospel of Gods free gift, the reformers pushed the insight that there is no need for subordinate mediators because the flood of divine grace is poured out from the cross of the one mediator, Christ Jesus, in whom there is no condemnation.[122] The reformers rightly saw that setting up a series of intercessors between ourselves and Christ dangerously detracts form the heart of the gospel's revelation that Christ alone is the bringer of God's mercy.

Luther wrote in his Catechism "What formerly you sought from the saints, or what you hoped to receive from mammon or anything else, turn to [Christ] for all this; look upon [Christ] as the one who wishes to help you and lavish all good upon you richly."[123]

Since none of the reformers claimed that mutual prayer between the living undermined the singularly unique mediation Christ Jesus, neither then should mutual prayer involving the departed.[124] The Apology of the

---

[121] Martin Luther, *Large Catechism* in *The Book of Concord*, ed. Theodore Tappert (Philadelphia: Fortress Press, 1959) 366.

[122] Romans 8:1.

[123] Martin Luther, *Large Catechism* in *The Book of Concord*, 366.

[124] As stated earlier in this work the reformers for the most part, especially Luther, settled on the conclusion that the souls of the dead are utterly separate and cut off from the world of the living. Their attacks on the Church's jurisdiction over souls in purgatory and on the venality of intercession for the dead led them to renounce the entire range of intercession for the dead, from prayers and masses for the dead to indulgences and pilgrimages. This was seen as the only way to assure that the abuses surrounding these practices came to a full stop; to disallow that the living could intercede for the dead in any way. If prayers for the dead were kept at all the pious practice was reduced to an agnostic prayer of submission to God's will.

Although, as we have previously explored, the doctrine of purgatory developed through penitential theology, prayer for the dead was the historical and theological foundation of purgatory. (See Le Goff, *Birth of Purgatory*, 52-95; Henry Charles Lea, *A History of Auricular Confession and Indulgences in the Latin Church*, Vol. 3: *Indulgences* (1896; repr. New York, 1968), 296-364; and R. J. Edmund Boggis, *Praying for the Dead: An Historical Review of the Practice* (London, 1913). Of the three main elements that composed the doctrine of purgatory, identified by Le Goff, (prayer for the dead, postmortem purification, and a distinct location for this purification), prayer for the dead was by far the oldest as it had been an integral part of the economy of salvation

Augsburg Confession makes this allowance in its claim that the saints may be intercessors but never propitiators.[125]

> I shall pray for you, I ask that you pray for me. As little as I doubt that your prayer is effective for me you should not doubt that my prayer will be effective for you. If I depart this life ahead of you—something I desire—then I must pull you after me. If you depart before me, then you shall pull me after you. For we confess one God and with all saints we abide in our savior.[126]

Both John and Charles Wesley were ardent believers in the Communion of Saints, which they celebrated as a means of giving additional comfort to those who were struggling in their pilgrim journey on earth. While accepting that God may work immediately upon the human soul, John Wesley taught that God makes use of "subordinate means,"[127] one of these being the prayers of faithfully departed. In this way the saints above minister to those who they have left behind. Disgusted with thee quid pro quo abuse of invocation Luther predicted, "When physical and spiritual benefit and help are no longer expected, the saints will cease to be molested in their graves and in heaven, for no one will longer remember, esteem, or honor them out of love, when their is no expectation of return."[128]

Answering Common Objections

One might argue that the saints cannot pray for us because they are in a state of rest in glory. While they are at rest from their trials upon the

---

since the second century. (See Robert Ombres O.P., "Latins and Greeks in Debate over Purgatory, 1230-1439," *Journal of Ecclesiastical History* 35 (1984), 1-14.) The reformers, in their denial of the efficacy of prayer for the dead, rejected the oldest element of purgatory first, and in doing so struck a blow at the root of the tree. Because the Medieval purgatory system was about intercession for the dead: a mystical or spiritual purgatory that separated the dead from the prayers of the living was a shadowy construction that was doomed never to become a living doctrine.

[125] Phillip Melanchthon, *Apology of the Augsburg Confession*, Article 21, in *The Book of Concord*, trans. and ed. Theodore G. Tappert (Philadelphia: Fortress, 1959) 229-236.

[126] Martin Luther as quoted in Bengt R. Hoffman, *Luther and the Mystics* (Minneapolis: Augsburg, 1976) 185.

[127] See *The Message of the Wesleys*, ed. Phillip S. Watson (New York: McMillan, 1964) 224-225; 228-230.

[128] Martin Luther, *Smalcald Articles* 2:28, in *The Book of Concord*, ed. Theodore Tappert (Philadelphia: Fortress Press, 1959) 297.

earth, they do participate in the work of intercession. The scriptural usage of the word rest carries with it the idea of joy in accomplishment or satisfaction in labor not cessation of all activity.[129] The saints will become like angels[130] who "worship [God] day and night within his temple."[131]

One might argue that the saints cannot pray for us because they are not aware of our circumstances. But the scripture presents numerous examples of persons while still living upon the earth see, hear, and know things inaccessible to ordinary understanding; such as Peter seeing into the heart of Ananias,[132] as well as seeing visions of the world above, and in the case of Isaiah and Ezekiel even to behold the image of God. Paul too was taken up into the third heaven in a mystical experience he could not fully recount. All the more are the saints in heaven capable of knowing what is happening on the earth and of hearing those who appeal to them since in heaven they are "like angels and are the children of God."[133]

In the parable of the rich man and Lazarus[134] Jesus suggested that Abraham, being within the heavenly realm, could hear the rich man who was suffering the torments of Hades despite the great chasm that separated them. The words of Abraham to the rich man concerning the fate of his brothers "they have Moses and the prophets, they should listen to them" implies that Abraham knew the history of the Hebrew people after his death.

The spiritual vision of the righteous in heaven is surely greater than it was upon the earth for Paul writes "Now we see in a mirror dimly, but then we shall see face to face. Now I know in part but then I will know fully even as I am fully known. The saints above are not omniscient but because they behold God face to face they see in God all the knowledge they need, and all that is relevant to them as their mature wills so desire, and so they see, in God, our prayers to them. Thomas Aquinas taught the Divine essence is the medium for knowing all things;[135] following Augustine's teaching:

---

[129] See Loraine Boettner, *Immortality* (Grand Rapids, Michigan: Eerdmans, 1956) 92.
[130] Luke 20:36.
[131] Revelation 7:15; see also 4:8.
[132] Acts 5:3.
[133] Luke 20:36.
[134] Luke 16:20-36.
[135] See *The Summa Theologica of St Thomas Aquinas,* Second and Revised Edition, 1920 trans. Fathers of the English Dominican Province (2000 Online Edition by Kevin Knight, accessed 5/2/2006); I, 12, 7,8; bound to the patronage model, Aquinas goes on to say: "Now it pertains to their glory that they assist the needy for their salvation: for thus they become God's co-operators, 'than which nothing is more Godlike,' as Dionysius declares (Coel. Hier. iii). Wherefore it is evident that the saints are cognizant of such things as are required for this purpose; and so it is manifest that

The spirits of the dead are able to know some things which happen here, which it is necessary for them to know. And those for whom it is necessary that something be known, not only the present or the past but even the future, — they know these things by the revealing Spirit of God, just as not all men but the Prophets, while they lived, knew not all things but those which the providence of God judged ought to be revealed to them. [136]

One might argue that the saints cannot pray for us because to do so would cause mental or spiritual suffering? The scripture speaks of the present passion of Christ distinguished from his atoning suffering[137] and of "the fellowship of his sufferings"[138] in which all the saints participate in Christ's continuing passion. Paul declared that "when one member suffers, all suffer together with it; if one member is honored, all rejoice together with it."[139]

One might argue that the prayers of the saints interfere with the unique mediatorship of Christ. "For there is one God, and there is one mediator between God and men, the man Christ Jesus."[140] Jesus is the one mediator between God and human beings but this does not prevent other people from acting as intercessors on our behalf.[141] In the same passage where the apostle speaks of Christ's unique mediatorship Paul writes: "First of all, then, I urge that supplications, prayers, intercessions, and thanksgivings be made for everyone. . . . This is right and acceptable in the sight of God our Savior who desires everyone to be saved."[142]

Jesus is the one mediator between God and humanity in two senses. First, he is the only God-man, and as such forms in his person the only and living bridge between earth and heaven. Jesus alludes to this type of mediatorship in John's gospel when he represents himself as Jacob's ladder.[143] Second, he is the mediator of the new covenant, written in his

---

they know in the Word the vows, devotions, and prayers of those who have recourse to their assistance."

[136] Augustine of Hippo, "On the Care of the Dead,"15, 18 in *PL* 40:591-610.
[137] See Acts 9:4-5; Ephesians 4:30; Hebrews 6:6.
[138] Philippians 3:10.
[139] 1 Corinthians 12:26.
[140] 1 Timothy 2:5; see also Romans 8:34, Hebrews 7:25, and 1 John 2:1.
[141] Paul also wrote in Romans 8:26-27 that "the Spirit intercedes for the saints according to the will of God." This certainly is not meant to detract from Jesus role as mediator and nowhere does the scripture say these tasks are reserved to Jesus or the Holy Spirit.
[142] 1 Timothy 2:1-3.
[143] See John 1:51.

blood, by which we obtain salvation.[144] Neither of these senses prevent intercessory prayer. In fact, Jesus himself describes this type of prayer as an essential part of being a child of God: "But I say to you, Love your enemies and pray for those who persecute you, so that you may be children of your Father in heaven."[145] The unique mediatorship of Christ no more prevents our brothers and sisters above from praying for us than it prevents our brothers and sisters below from praying for us.

One might argue that the better plan of action is to pray directly and only to Jesus. There is no doubt that Christians should pray directly to Jesus, and that, because we have Jesus as our high priest, we can "approach the throne of grace with boldness, so that we may receive mercy and help in the time of need."[146] However, asking others to pray with us is both appropriate and beneficial. Again Paul sets the example by repeatedly asking for others to pray on his behalf. "I appeal to you, brothers and sisters, by our Lord Jesus Christ and by the love of the Spirit, to join me in earnest prayer to God on my behalf."[147] "You also join in helping us by your prayers, so that many will give thanks on our behalf for the blessing granted us through the prayers of many."[148] "Pray in the Spirit at all times . . . for all saints. Pray also for me . . . an ambassador in chains."[149] "For I know that through your prayers and the help of the Spirit of Jesus Christ this will turn out for my deliverance."[150] "Pray for us also, that God will open to us a door for the word, to declare the mystery of Christ, on account of which I am in prison."[151] "And one more thing, prepare a guest room for me, for I am hoping through your prayers to be restored to you."[152]

One might argue that Paul is asking the saints below to pray for him not the saints above, we should then confine our request to the saints below.[153] We should join our brothers and sisters in Christ in prayer and ask

---

[144] See Hebrews 8:6, 9:15, 12:24.
[145] Matthew 5:44-45.
[146] Hebrews 4:16.
[147] Romans 15:30.
[148] 2 Corinthians 1:11.
[149] Ephesians 6:18-20.
[150] Philippians 1:19.
[151] Colossians 4:3.
[152] Philemon 22.
[153] This was the argument of Vigilantius against whom Jerome wrote: "You say in your book that while we live we are able to pray for each other, but afterwards when we have died, the prayer of no person for another can be heard; and this is especially clear since the martyrs, though they cry vengeance for their own blood, have never been able to obtain their request. But if the Apostles and martyrs while still in the

them to pray for us. As we shall see later, requesting the prayers of the saints above is in no way a requirement for Christian living. However, requesting the prayers of the saints above is good and useful.[154] Pilgrim Christians are afflicted with a lack of knowledge and discernment, as well as weariness, distractions, interruptions, and lack of fervor in prayer, this is not the case with our glorified counterparts. "The prayer of the righteous is powerful and effective."[155] The saints above are being perfectly sanctified in Christ, as such their prayers should have correspondingly powerful effects. Loving perfectly "We must believe that the saints who have died possess love in a far higher degree towards the ones engaged in the combat of life than those who are still subject to human weakness and involved in the combat along with their weaker brethren"[156]

Three Ways the Church May Invoke the Saints

"The saints in each generation, joined to those who have gone before, and filled like them with light, become a golden chain in which each saint is a separate link, united to the next by faith, works, and love. So in One God they form a single chain that cannot quickly be broken."[157] We access this strength in a variety of ways; through Church architecture, martyr chapels, stained glass windows, icons, sculptures, home altars, lives of the saints, calendars of holy people, hymns, writings, teachings, movies and tapes of live addresses of paradigmatic figures, gatherings on anniversary days, and so on. All of which can be loosely be defined as some sort of prayer, especially if "prayer is the raising of ones mind and heart to God or the

---

body can pray for others, at a time when they ought still be solicitous about themselves, how much more will they do so after their crowns, victories, and triumphs." Jerome, "Against Vigilantius," 6 in *PL* 23:339.

[154] The Council of Trent laid down guidelines to reform the most egregious abuses connected with the veneration of the saints but gave the subject no systematic theological analysis but simply referred to the practice as "good and useful." See the full text in *Cannons and Decrees of the Council of Trent*, trans. H. J. Schroeder (St. Louis: Herder, 1941) 214-217. See Carl J. Peter, "The Communion of Saints in the Final Days of the Council of Trent" in *The One Mediator, the Saints, and Mary: Lutherans and Catholics in Dialogue VIII*, ed. George Anderson et al. (Minneapolis: Augsburg Fortress Press, 1992) 219-233.

[155] James 5:16.

[156] Origen, "On Prayer," 11, 2 in *PG* 11, 452C.

[157] Kallistos Ware, *The Orthodox Church* (Harmondsworth, England: Penguin Books, 1963) 260.

desiring of good things from God."[158] The saints below give particular expression to their prayers in communion with the saints above in at least three ways that do not focus on petitioning from them special favors.

Thanksgiving

The great cloud of witnesses leads us not only to "lay aside every weight and sin"[159] but to look ahead to the joy that is set before us, and in doing do give praise and thanks "to the Father of lights; the giver of every good and perfect gift."[160] An example of a prayer that gives thanks for saints both known and unknown, beyond and in our midst, and acknowledges that the radiant light of their holiness is the fire of the Holy Spirit is found *The Oxford Book of Prayer*:

> We than thee, O God, for the saints of all ages; for those who in times of darkness kept the lamp of faith burning; for the great souls who saw visions of larger truth and dared to declare it; for the multitude of quiet and gracious souls whose presence has purified and sanctified the world; and for those known and loved by us, who have passed from this earthly fellowship into the fuller light of life.[161]

Another in that same volume recognizes in the finite, mortal, but visible lives of the saints the image of the God. Being encouraged by their perseverance the church below so shines:

> O King, eternal, immortal, invisible, who in the righteousness of thy saints has given us an example of godly life, and in their blessedness a generous pledge of the hope of our calling, we beseech thee that, being compassed about by so great a cloud of witnesses, we may run the race that is set before us, and with them receive the crown of glory that fadeth not away; through Jesus Christ our Lord.[162]

Thanking God for the saints who form the community's heritage sets the feet of saints below on the right path. The testimony of their victory

---

[158] John Damascene, Defide orth. 3, 24: *PG* 94,1089C.
[159] Hebrews 12:1.
[160] James 1:17.
[161] Anonymous, in *The Oxford Book of Common Prayer* ed. George Appleton (Oxford: Oxford University Press, 1985) 168.
[162] Ibid.

encourages the still struggling that the same Spirit who inspired them will kindle the sacred fire in their lives too. The whole community of God rejoices together as John Chrysostom wrote of the martyrs:

> They suffered and we rejoice, they struggled and we leap for joy; their crown is the glory of all, or rather the glory of the whole Church. How can this be? you will say. The martyrs are our parts and members. 'And if one member suffers all members suffer with it; if one member is honored all rejoice with it.'[163] The head is crowned and the rest of the body rejoices. One becomes a victor in the Olympic Games and the whole people rejoices and receives him with great glory. If at the Olympic Games those who do not in the least participate in the labors receive such satisfaction, all the more can this be with regard to the strugglers of piety."[164]

Lament

The ancient prayer of lament, flung in outrage and grief to God, cries out for justice, relief, and explanation. It arises out of our witness or memory of tragic death and destruction: violence, torture, war, genocide, famine, or natural disaster. When we solemnly remember those who died senseless deaths deprived of dignity "we gather them into our common memory and hope, they become more than faceless, forgotten individuals but enter into a living history as an impetus to forge a different future for others."[165]

The ringing of Church bells at 1:07 pm on August 6, the AIDS quilt, the Vietnam War Memorial in Washington D.C. all serve to creatively preserve the identity of the dead while defying the tendency to reduce victims to mere statistics, and allow for grief rituals that ultimately stimulate awareness and resistance to the cause of their deaths. In remembering all the saints the Church gives voice to the massive, anonymous dead. Its prayer becomes a social force confronting the structures of injustice and violence. In the face of their suffering, the Church laments the plight of our sinful world and listens to their testimony. They "speak [to us, they] have the right to do so—[they] who have suffered and lost [their] lives. We have the duty to listen to [their] testimony."[166] Such disorienting remembering will

---

[163] 1 Corinthians 12:26.
[164] John Chrysostom, "Eulogy for the Holy Martyr Romanus".
[165] Elizabeth A. Johnson, *Friends of God and Prophets* (New York: The Continuum Publishing Company, 1998) 249.
[166] John Paul II, "Visit to Mauthausen," *Origins* 18, no. 8 (July 7, 1988) 124.

ultimately lead us back to the praise of God, for the cross of Jesus introduces a hope that transforms death into life, suffering into victory, despair into hope, and lament into praise.

The Litany of the Saints

Naming the names of saints is one way we can remember the saints, proclaim our solidarity with them in Christ, commend their witness to the community, and perhaps join their prayers. This energizing prayer, usually sung in a rhythmic cadence, originated in the Eastern Church in the fourth century as a prayer, not of the clergy, but of the laity.[167]

Singing ones way through the Litany of the Saints on a festal occasion such as the Easter Vigil brings to consciousness the fact that the Church is much more universal than a particular congregation gathered at a particular time. Our ancestors in the faith, all of whom had their hearts set on Christ, form a great cloud of witnesses that widens the assembly. Now forever with God, their lives and prayer are of benefit for those below who are still on their journey. Summoning the memory of particular ones by name out of the unnumbered multitude brings the memory and hope of their lives before our eyes while repeated references to all stretches the company beyond the horizon. Asking them to pray for us has the effect of strengthening bonds of persons today with whole holy people of God throughout time, thereby deepening union with God in Christ. As the movement of the litany swings from Christ, to the saints, and back to Christ implies, it is not a matter of the saints functioning as intermediary patrons but of everyone connected in mutual regard in the great company of friends of God. Many times the litany is done at Baptisms where joining together the saints below with those above creates a welcoming community around those about to be initiated into the holy communion.

A variation of such a litany, inclusive of names suitable to the purpose of the gathering can have a similar vivifying effect. The traditional response "pray for us" may be changed to one more symbolically or theologically appropriate for the group, such as "be with us" or "to you O God we give thanks." A litany in celebration of our spiritual foremothers used in some Methodist Mother's Day observances reads:

---

[167] See Louis Weil, "*The History of Christian Litanies*," Liturgy: Journal of the Liturgical Conference 5, no. 2 (Fall, 1985) 33-37.

On this Mother's Day we give thankful praise
    for valiant women of faith,
  who are a living testimony that God is God in all.
Praise be to God for these women whose lives give us hope:
Eve—the first woman,
    mother of all the living, soul of the human race.
Praise be to God for our mothers.
Sarah—heart of the covenant, mother of nations,
    who conceived laughter in her old age.
Praise be to God for our mothers.
Rebecca—woman of ingenuity,
    achieving her own purposes in a patriarchal world.
Praise be to God for our mothers.
Rachel—who waited seven years, seven days,
    waited for love, waited for life.
Praise be to God for our mothers.
Mary—Mother of God, a woman, one of us.
Praise be to God for our mothers.
Elizabeth—who proved one is never too old
    to have her dream come true.
Praise be to God for our mothers.
Anna—prophet at prayer in the Temple
    when Jesus was offered to God,
    who from that moment preached Jesus,
    proclaiming salvation to all.
Praise be to God for our mothers.
Suzanna—mother of John and Charles,
    and preacher of righteousness.
Praise be to God for our mothers.
For our own mothers who have given us life and love,
    our sisters in the faith.
Praise be to God for our mothers.
Who shall find a valiant woman?
Look! We are all around you.
Praise be to God!

    The litany can also be crafted to celebrate universities or milestones of particular congregations or groups. The gift of the litany to be endlessly adaptable makes it appropriate for all churches and assemblies. In whatever form it takes the litany surrounds the Church with the cloud of witnesses.

Other Invocations

Hail Mary

The Hail Mary[168] is perhaps the best example of how invocation should be used.[169] This intently scriptural prayer begins with two salutations to Mary, using first the praising words of the annunciating angel Gabriel, "Hail . . . the Lord is with thee; blessed art thou among women;"[170] and second that of her cousin Elizabeth, who repeats "Blessed art thou among women" and adds "and blessed is the fruit of thy womb."[171] At its climax the prayer names the fruit of Mary's womb, Jesus, and then, following Elizabeth, proclaims Jesus to be God by using Mary's definitive and ancient title, Theotokos, Mother of God.[172] The prayer then goes on to make the request "pray for us sinners now and at the hour of our death."

This is a private prayer to a single saint. It preeminently recalls the Savior Jesus, the gift of God, who blessed Mary his mother by becoming incarnate through her whom he also redeemed. Mary's life is remembered as a pilgrimage of faith and her holiness a direct result of Jesus being born in her. Therefore she is saluted as a preeminent member of the church, and as the church's most excellent model of faith, love, and service. In the petition, the believer requests the prayers of this paradigmatic member of the Communion of Saints to pray "for us," that is for all the saints below, in their continuing pilgrimage of faith and at the final time of testing, the hour of our death. The petition lacks many specifics trusting that the prayer from above will be in accord with God's will.

Thus the Hail Mary expresses both the interrelated Communion of Saints below, in that the petitioner requests prayer "for us," and the interrelated Communion of Saints below with those above, in that the prayers are requested from one preeminent member of the redeemed community, Mary, for wayfarers who are still on the journey. Such a prayer unites the one who prays it more closely to Christ through the recognition our fellowship in him with Mary, his mother and faith-filled disciple. The Rosary is a biblically inspired, rhythmic contemplative prayer which combines the recitation of the

---

[168] Hail Mary, full of grace, the Lord is with thee. Blessed art thou among women, and blessed is the fruit of thy womb, Jesus. Holy Mary, Mother of God, pray for us sinners now, and at the hour of death. Amen.
[169] See Gerard Sloyan, "Marian Prayers," in *Mariology*, Vol. 3, Juniper Carol, ed. (Milwaukee: Bruce Pub. Co., 1960), pp. 68-73.
[170] Luke 1:28 (KJV).
[171] Luke 1:42 (KJV).
[172] Luke 1:43.

Apostles Creed, the Lord's Prayer, and the Hail Mary with quiet and systematic meditation upon the salvific events of Christ's life. Beyond its educatory value, such a prayer leads the believer to turn away from the distractions of the world, and with the saints above worship and adore the saving Christ.

Hymn Singing

Hymns combine poetry, music, and theology into singular vehicles of worship. Through hymns believers pray, evangelize, witness, educate, and convey important historical and cultural facts. In a powerful way, singing unites individuals into a single body. Singing one's national anthem, for example, at a sports event, can bring together thousands of strangers into a stadium of persons united in a common gesture of respect and honor. Similarly, communal singing in Christian worship gathers the many individuals present and makes them into a visible expression of the one body, united in Christ, offering a single prayer of praise and thanksgiving to God.

In its hymns the Church not only interprets the scripture and gives aid to memory, but it binds believers together in singular expressions of joy or sorrow, and praise and prayer. Augustine once commented, "Those who sing pray twice."[173] Certainly one could simply speak throughout worship without music, as one can even worship without speaking, however, sacred music is itself a prayer giving theology wings so that it may "counted as incense before [God] and . . . as an evening sacrifice."[174] Much more than entertainment or background music, sacred singing is prayer. Putting prayer into music not only helps to unite believers in the prayer they make, it also gives a unique expression to their prayer that words alone cannot achieve.

As the Lord's Prayer demonstrates praise and petitions addressed to God is the very definition of prayer. So when the Church sings "Holy, Holy, Holy! Lord God Almighty" it is offering a collective prayer of praise and thanksgiving to "God in three Persons, the blessed Trinity."[175] This one action of praise occurs both below, by those blinded by their sin, and above, by those adoring God face to face. Singing unites the saints below in mutual worship, and in doxologically and theologically correct forms, to the worship of heaven.

---

[173] Augustine, *Enarrations on the Psalms* 72, 1.
[174] Psalms 141:2.
[175] Reginald Heber, "Holy, Holy, Holy! in *The United Methodist Hymnal*, 64. See also *The Baptist Hymnal*, 2. A favorite hymn, sung to a tune appropriately named NICAEA.

A hymnic witness to the connection between earth and heaven is found in J. A. L. Riley's hymn "Ye Watchers and Ye Holy Ones." Here, it is not the saints above who are inspiring the saints below, but the saints below enjoining the praise of the heavenly host:

> Ye watchers and ye holy ones, bright seraphs, cherubim, and thrones,
> raise the glad strain, Alleluia!
> Cry out, dominions, princedoms, powers, virtues, archangels, angels' choirs:
> Alleluia! Alleluia! Alleluia! Alleluia! Alleluia!
>
> O higher than the cherubim, more glorious than the seraphim,
> lead their praises, Alleluia!
> Thou bearer of th' eternal Word, most gracious, magnify the Lord:
> Alleluia! Alleluia! Alleluia! Alleluia! Alleluia!
>
> Respond, ye souls in endless rest, ye patriarchs and prophets blest,
> Alleluia! Alleluia!
> Ye holy twelve, ye martyrs strong, all saints triumphant, raise the song:
> Alleluia! Alleluia! Alleluia! Alleluia! Alleluia!
>
> O friends, in gladness let us sing, supernal anthems echoing,
> Alleluia! Alleluia!
> To God the Father, God the Son, and God the Spirit, Three in One:
> Alleluia! Alleluia! Alleluia! Alleluia! Alleluia![176]

This hymn is not only an example of a prayer of praise to God but in it the saints below invoke the saints above. The text of the hymn forms an extolling prayer addressed to the saints above, encouraging their praise of God. In fact, its second verse is addressed to Mary, remembering her *Magnificat*, and acknowledging her leadership in the heavenly choir. This recognition that the saints on earth and in heaven sing one song of praise and call upon one

---

[176] John Athelstan Laurie Riley, "Ye Watchers and Ye Holy Ones" in *The United Methodist Hymnal*, 90.

another to extol the greatness of the God and salvation through Christ is a common theme in Protestant hymnody.[177]

Evident in ancient hymns such as the "*Kyrie Eleison*," the saints below join the saints above in their common prayer for all people, in all places, at all times: "Lord, have mercy. Christ, have mercy. Lord, have mercy."[178] Beyond their common prayer, other Protestant hymns, such as The Church's One Foundation" concedes that the saints above continually pray for the Church struggling below. The saints in heaven pray for the saints on earth. It sings:

> Though with a scornful wonder we see her sore oppressed,
> by schisms rent asunder, by heresies distressed,
> yet saints their watch are keeping; their cry goes up, "How long?"
> And soon the night of weeping shall be the morn of song. [179]

Finally, in its hymns the Church looks forward to the great consummation, when through the work of Christ, the saints below, will dwell together with the saints who have gone before them. Charles Wesley anticipated this hope as he wrote:

> Eternal, Triune God, let all the hosts above,
> let all on earth below record and dwell upon thy love.
> When heaven and earth are fled before thy glorious face,

---

[177] See Philipp Nicolai, "Wake, Awake, for Night Is Flying," *The United Methodist Hymnal*, 720; and William J. Irons, "Sing with All the Saints in Glory, *The United Methodist Hymnal*, 702.

[178] "Lord, Have Mercy," in *The United Methodist Hymnal*, 482, 483, and 484. This hymn is considered the oldest vestige of Greek worship retained in the modern Church's liturgy, see William J. Reynolds and Milburn Price, *A Survey of Christian Hymnody* (Carol Stream, IL: Hope Publishing Company, 1999) 10.

[179] Samuel J. Stone, "The Church's One Foundation," *The United Methodist Hymnal*, 545. See also Brian Wren, "Christ Loves the Church," *The United Methodist Hymnal*, 590. In their hymn, "Hail, Thou Once Despised Jesus," John Bakewell and Martin Madan offer an interesting corrective to poor pre-reformation doxology which overemphasized the intercessions of the saints in heaven for those upon the earth. They move the focus clearly on Jesus' intercession as they sing: Jesus, hail! Enthroned in glory, / there forever to abide; / all the heavenly hosts adore thee, / seated at thy Father's side. / There for sinners thou art pleading; / there thou dost our place prepare; / thou for saints art interceding / till in glory they appear. See *The United Methodist Hymnal*, 325.

sing all the saints thy love hath made thine everlasting praise.[180]

On the night he gave himself up for us, Christ sang hymns with his disciples.[181] When the Church is gathered to hear God's Word, to eat the Bread of Life and drink from the Cup of Salvation, its prayers reflect the joy and depth of the profound mystery of faith. Joined with one another in Christ, the songs of prayer and praise, above and below, are one. In this way the Church fulfills the words of Paul who instructed the saints: "sing together psalms, hymns, and spiritual songs"[182] as you await the coming in glory of the one whose death you proclaim.

The Church Prays with All the Heavenly Host

The scriptures contain many stories that teach that the community of the faithful is aided by angelic visitors through whom God may reach us and teach us.[183] In the Old Testament the prophet Daniel is consoled and strengthened by an angel with whom he conversed.[184] The psalmist sings of angels who do the Lord's bidding.[185] Zechariah also spoke with angels.[186] The definitive example of the New Testament is The Blessed Virgin Mary, who responded to the angel Gabriel's announcement with these words of faith "Behold, I am the handmaid of the Lord, let it be to me according to your word."[187]

Remembering that the word pray means to make a request we can see the Psalms contain invocations of angels: "Bless the Lord, O you his angels, you mighty ones who do his bidding, obedient to his spoken word. Bless the Lord, all his hosts; his ministers that do his will."[188] And again

---

[180] Charles Wesley, "Maker in Whom We Live," *The United Methodist Hymnal*, 88. See also Ignaz Franz, "Holy God, We Praise Thy Name," 79; Robert Lowry, "Shall We Gather at the River," 723; Charles Wesley, "Lo, He Comes with Clouds Descending," 718; Samuel J. Stone, "The Church's One Foundation," 545; Emily D. Wilson, "When we all get to Heaven," 701; and Frederick Lucian Hosmer, "Forward Through the Ages," 555, a particularly strong message of our solidarity with all the saints, giving new words to a much loved but oft neglected tune.
[181] Matthew 26:30.
[182] Colossians 3:16.
[183] See also Revelation 10:9-11; 14:6-7.
[184] Daniel 10:2-21.
[185] Psalm 103:19-22.
[186] Zechariah 6:1-8.
[187] Luke 1:38.
[188] Psalm 103:20-21

"Praise the Lord. Praise the Lord from the heavens; praise him in the heights! Praise ye him, all his angels; praise ye him, all his hosts!"[189] One can surmise since the Psalms were prayed when Jesus himself went to synagogue, the angels may be addressed or enjoined in prayer.

John Wesley welcomed assistance form both angels and saints, though he believed glory and power to ultimately reside in God alone. "May we probably suppose that the spirits of the just, though generally lodged in paradise, yet may sometimes, in conjunction with the holy angels, minister to the heirs of salvation? May they not sometimes, on errands of love, revisit their brethren below?"[190]

For What do the Saints Above and the Heavenly Hosts Pray

The intercessory prayer of the saints is best understood in correlation the Lord's Prayer. [191] The payers of the saints are the expression of their fervent desire that the name of God be hallowed and the will of God accomplished upon the earth as it is in heaven. The model prayer Christ taught begins "Our Father." With these words Christ joined together all those who pray them into a single unity and directed them to appeal out of this unity to their common Father with whom we are already seated "in the heavenly places in Christ Jesus."[192]

The first series of petitions carry us toward God for God's own sake; they are for "thy name . . . thy kingdom . . . and thy will." These three supplications are already answered in the saving work of Christ, but we await their final fulfillment in hope, for God is not yet "all in all."[193] The second series of petitions join all God's holy people together and concerns their most immediate needs; they are "give us . . . forgive us . . . lead us not . . . and deliver us."

So close is the bond of love within the family of God that none are fully perfected apart from the others. The saints pray in communion with all their brothers and sisters that all be delivered from every evil, present, past, and future, by the one who "is the first and the last . . . alive forevermore . .

---

[189] Psalm 148:1-2.
[190] *The Message of the Wesleys*, ed. Phillip S. Watson (New York, MacMillan, 1964) 224.
[191] "Our Father in heaven, hallowed be your name. Your Kingdom come, your will be done, on earth as in heaven. Give us today our daily bread. Forgive us our sins, as we forgive those who sin against us. Lead us not into temptation, but deliver us from evil. For the kingdom, the power and the glory are yours, now and for ever. Amen." See Matthew 6:9-14 and Luke 11:2-4.
[192] 2 Corinthians 5:2.
[193] See 1 Corinthians 5:28.

. and has the keys to death and hell."[194] They pray that all might have the discernment to take "the way out" [195] when they are tested and not the path that leads to sin. With bold confidence they pray for the forgiveness of sins and for the material and spiritual nourishment that is the gift of God. They ask that the loving plan of God for salvation in the life of the world below be realized as it is in the world above and that the final reign of God that was "brought near in Christ Jesus"[196] be made complete. They pray this that "the name of the Father will be glorified."[197]

So the saints, below and above, pray for the perfection not only of individuals in their own time but for the coming of the Kingdom of God. They join with the Holy Spirit eagerly awaiting and praying for the final appearing of Christ,[198] the resurrection of the dead, and the restoration of all things, when the end will be reached.[199] For God has provided something better so that they would not, apart form us, be made perfect."[200]

Recapitulation, Quantum Interconnectedness, and the Seamless Whole

Paul can be credited with the theology that contrasts Adam and Christ. He wrote in his letter to the Romans: "Therefore by the offence of one [Adam], judgment came upon all to condemnation; even so by the righteousness of one [Jesus], the free gift came upon all unto justification of life."[201] And to the Corinthians he wrote: "For as in Adam all die, even so in Christ shall all be made alive."[202]

In the latter passage Jesus is called by analogy and contrast the new or last Adam.[203] This is understood in the sense that as the original Adam was the head of all mankind, the father of all according to the flesh, so also Jesus constitutes the chief and head of the spiritual family of the elect, and potentially of all humankind, since all are invited to partake of his salvation. Thus, the first Adam is a type of the second. While the former transmits to

---

[194] Revelation 1:18.
[195] 1 Corinthians 10:13.
[196] See Luke 21:31.
[197] See John 12:28.
[198] Revelation 22:17.
[199] See 1 Corinthians 15:24.
[200] Hebrews 11:40.
[201] See Romans 5:12-20, 18 quoted here.
[202] See 1 Corinthians 15:45, 47.
[203] Christ is the last Adam inasmuch as "there is no other name under heaven given to men, whereby we must be saved" (Acts 4:12) and therefore no other chief or father of the race is to be expected.

his progeny a legacy of death, the latter, on the contrary, becomes the vivifying principle of restored righteousness.

Both the first and the second Adam occupy the position of head with regard to humanity. The first through his disobedience ruined and corrupted, as it were, in himself, the entire race, and left to his posterity an inheritance of death, sin, and misery. The other through his obedience, merited for all those who become his members a new life of holiness and an everlasting reward. It may be said that the contrast thus formulated expresses a fundamental tenet of the Christian religion and embodies concisely the entire doctrine of the economy of salvation.[204]

This new Adam theology was systematized early in church history and is traditionally referred to as the recapitulation model of the atonement.[205] It recognizes the significance of the incarnation as the beginning and foundation of salvation, and the resurrection as crucial because in it Christ is the "firstborn of the dead"[206] restoring to the human race the image of God that had been lost in Adam. The notion of this recapitulation was meticulously developed by Irenaeus who interpreted it both as the restoration of fallen humanity to communion with God through the obedience of Christ and as the summing-up (recapitulating) of all previous revelations of God in the Incarnation. Furthermore, Christ was said to recapitulate all the stages of human life and in doing so reverse the course initiated by Adam.[207] This great reversal was punctuated by the resurrection wherein the entire direction of creation, which seemed to be moving inescapably from life towards death, was reversed from death towards life. Jesus, the "pioneer of our faith,"[208] is the divine trailblazer leading the parade of creation in its ascension back to God.

---

[204] See James F. Driscoll, "Adam," *The Catholic Encyclopedia*, Vol. 1 (New York: The Robert Appleton Company) 1907.

[205] The prominence of new Adam theology can be traced through Origen's *Tractatus XXXV* (185); Irenaeus in *Against All Heresies* (200); Athanasius' *On the Passion* (296); Augustine's *Sermon on Time* (354) and Anselm's *Why the God-Man?* (1033). The theology was officially dogmatized by the Church in the Council of Trent Session 5 Cannons 1 and 2, which refer to Christ as *"the second Adam who restored mankind to the state of righteousness which had been lost by the first Adam."*

[206] Colossians 1:18.

[207] "When [Christ] was incarnate and became a human being, he recapitulated in himself the long history of the human race, obtaining salvation for us, so that we might regain in Jesus Christ what we had lost in Adam, that is, being in the image and likeness of God." Irenaeus, *Against Heresies*, 5. 1. 1. (PG 7; SC 100).

[208] Hebrews 12:2.

Irenaeus's recapitulation progresses beyond the idea of simply restoring humanity to a pre-fallen state towards the idea that redemption is the very fulfillment of creation itself. Arguing against the Gnostics who taught that the whole of the material world itself was the result of the fall from grace, the loss of perfection, Irenaeus claim that we are not saved from the world, but within and with the world. Offering us a view of creation and salvation history that fits surprisingly well with the contemporary understanding of an evolutionary universe.

In Irenaeus's theory Adam's sin is due to immaturity rather than maliciousness. Drawing on Paul's statement "I have fed you with milk and not solid food, for you were not able to take it"[209], he argues, that as a mother refrains from giving solid food to her child until they are able to receive it, so God could also "have endowed man with perfection from the beginning, but man was as yet unable to receive it, being as yet an infant."[210] The subsequent growth and development of humanity, nourished by the Spirit and fulfilled in the Son, is the growth towards the perfection of God.

> Humanity was created God's image: the Father being well pleased and giving the command, the Son acting and creating, the Spirit nourishing and giving increase, and humanity making gradual progress and so advancing towards perfection, coming closer, that is to say, to the Uncreated One . . . Now it was necessary that humanity should in the first instance be created; and having been created, should receive growth; and having received growth, should be strengthened; and having been strengthened, should abound; and having abounded, should recover; and having recovered, should be glorified; and being glorified, should see his Lord. For God confers incorruption, and incorruption brings us close to God.[211]

We have already explored the Christian affirmation of the resurrection of the body. Because we relate through our bodies to the rest of the created world our ultimate salvation implies the eventual sanctification of the material environment as well. If there is to be a "new heaven and a new earth"[212] then our human salvation leads to the redemption of the whole

---

[209] 1 Corinthians 3:2.
[210] Irenaeus, *Against Heresies*, 4. 38. 1. He further explains: "God had power at the beginning to grant perfection to man; but as the latter was only recently created, he could not possibly have received it, or even if he had received it, could he have contained it, or containing it, could he have retained it." *Against Heresies*, 4, 38, 2
[211] *Against Heresies*, 4, 38, 3.
[212] Revelation 21:1.

created order, which through us "will be set free from its bondage to decay and will obtain the freedom of the glory of the children of God.[213] This cosmic task is fulfilled in Christ "who is before all things and in whom all things hold together."[214]

Recent discoveries in the quantum field promises to upset previous notions of space and time. Scientist have proven that two particles separated by whole galaxies are in some way connected to each other so intimately that when the spin of one is changed the spin of the other reverses—wherever it is—instantaneously—using some form of communication that is faster than light. Extrapolating from this observance we can envision the entire universe not as a infinite multitude of particles and galaxies but a seamless whole. If this be the case and God in Christ became incarnate in this creation then all of creation is connected to him and possibly saved by him.

In relation to union with God the universe can be conceived as a series of concentric circles around a center which is occupied by the Church, the members of which are the children of God.[215] However, this adoption into God's family is not the final goal for there is yet a narrower circle within the Church, that of the glorified, those who have entered into a union with God. The Church then, is the sphere wherein the union of human persons with God is fully accomplished. Seen in this way the Church is the center of the universe, the sphere wherein all destinies are determined. All are called to enter the Church. The Church is enlarged and is compounded throughout history as it brings the elect into its fold and unites them with God. The world is subject to entropy and decay but the Church is continuously revitalized by the Holy Spirit the source of all life. In the end when all of us come to the unity of the faith and of the knowledge of the Son of God, to maturity, to the measure of the full stature of Christ"[216] the external world, having exhausted its vital resources will perish, but the Church will emerge in its eternal glory as the Kingdom of God. The Church will then be revealed as the true foundation of all persons raised up in incorruptibility to be united with God who will be all in all.

---

[213] Romans 8:21.

[214] Colossians 1:17.

[215] Impressively in his *Divine Comedy*, Dante envisions such a map of the destiny of the universe. Ultimately, he saw the new creation as consisting of two conical stadiums, the points of which turned on the axis point of the Triune God revealed in Christ Jesus. Each concentric circle of the stadium above was filled with the glorified saints illuminated and warmed by the light and live of God on whom they gazed face to face. Similarly but opposite the rebels below burn in a freezing darkness, with there backs turned from God, Satan forever under the feet of Jesus.

[216] Ephesians 4:13.

"Some will be united to God in grace, and some apart from grace."[217] Some will be united with God by the power of the Holy Spirit which they will have acquired in their interior selves; others will remain without, and for them the fire of the Spirit will be an external flame, excruciating to those who oppose the will of God. The Church is the sphere within which union with God takes place in our life upon the earth, and within which the union will be finally and unendingly consummated in the age to come. When this happens all the prayers of all the saints will be answered.

---

[217] Maximus, "Quaestiones ad Thalassium, LIX", *P.G.*, XC, 609 B. "Capedocian Theology and Oecon.," 4th century, 1312.

Chapter Ten

The Communion of Love: Fellowship at the Table

The Eucharist is the Physical Bond of the Church:
The Life Blood of the Mystical Body

    The Church is the mystical body of Christ, and the Communion of Saints (the communion of holy people in holy things) is the unity that holds its various and individual parts together and connects them with Christ their head. Much like a bodily system, each individual member, whether cell, tissue, or organ maintain its own identity and boundaries, while at the same time interconnect and interrelate with the others to form something far greater than they were alone and vivified by a by an even more mysterious life-giving Spirit.

    Paul set forth this image in his letter to the Ephesians,[1] where he wrote that the members of the Church are bound together by a supernatural life communicated to them by Christ through his word and sacraments.[2] Christ is the center and sole source of life to whom all are united, and who gives to each member gifts fitting their position in the body.[3] These graces equip each for their work and form the members into an organized whole, whose parts are knit together as though by a system of ligaments and joints.[4] Through these gifts and graces of Christ the Church has its growth and increase; growing in extension as it spreads through the world and growing in intensity as each and every individual believer develops in themselves the likeness of Christ, and comes to the full knowledge of the faith.[5]

    In virtue of this union of the head with the body, that is of Christ and his Church, which he fills with his Spirit, the Church is called "the fullness of him who fills all in all."[6] The union between the head of the body and its members is conserved and nourished by the Eucharist, which is itself

---

[1] Ephesians 4:4-13; see also John 15:5-8.
[2] Ephesians 4:5.
[3] Ephesians 7-12.
[4] Ephesians 16; see also Colossians 2:19.
[5] Ephesians 13-15.
[6] Ephesians 1:23.

a union of the heavenly and earthy. Through the sacrament of the table a believer's incorporation into the Body of Christ is both outwardly symbolized and inwardly actualized; "We being many are one body; for we all partake of the one bread"[7]

The sacraments were ordained and inaugurated by Christ and given to the church, along with a command to observe them. Jesus Christ is himself the ultimate sacrament. In the God-human the Divine and the created came together as God's fullness was revealed in a human being. The church is also sacramental in that it is both human in its members, and divine as they are filled with Christ's Spirit and together form his body; the visible, material instrument through which Christ continues to be made known and the divine plan is fulfilled. In this way, the Church participates in Christ's redeeming work.

Holy Baptism and Holy Communion are special means, instituted by Christ, through which divine grace comes to believers. Holy Baptism is that which initiates one into the body of Christ and through which we receive our identity and mission as Christians. Holy Communion is the sacrament that sustains and nourishes believers on their journey of salvation. The sacraments are sign-acts, which include words, actions, and physical elements that combine to both express and convey the gracious love of God. The sacraments make God's grace both visible and effective.

As early in Christian history as the day of Christ's resurrection believers recognized the presence of the risen Christ in the breaking of bread.[8] The long-established Jewish practice of taking bread, blessing and thanking God, and breaking and sharing the bread took on new meaning for the followers of Christ. When they were gathered in Jesus' name, the breaking of the bread and sharing of the cup became the primary means of remembering his life, death, and resurrection and of encountering the living Christ. Around the Lord's Table they experienced afresh the presence of their risen host and received sustenance for their lives as his disciples. The salvific events recalled in the Eucharist gave birth to the Church and the custom of the Eucharist became the characteristic ritual of the community and the central act of the Church's worship.

Beginning with the first half of the fourth century, Eusebius asserted that the primary manner of honoring martyrs was in the use of their tombs as altars upon which the Eucharist was offered.[9] There was sound theological reasoning for correlating the Eucharist and the saints, for the communion

---

[7] 1 Corinthians 10:17.
[8] Luke 24:13-35
[9] Eusebius, *Praepar. Evang.* XIII.ii.

meal was and is the most fundamental expression of the Church's unity. The body of Christ is not only the Church on earth but the whole Communion of Saints, living and dead, past and present, and to all generations. This understanding led John Chrysostom to mark the status of martyrs by naming them in the Lord's presence while his death was being celebrated, [10] thus establishing the calendrical commemoration of the saints in the public liturgy of the Church.

The Celestial Eucharist

In recognizing the saints at the Lord's Supper the Church is not only invoking their prayers but more importantly declaring the Church's participation in the celestial Eucharist which is beyond time and space. Here the Church recognizes the Eucharistic event as touching history, in that, the once and for all saving action of the Son took place in time, but that this action was not only a temporal event. The Son's submission to the Father in his acceptance of the cross for our redemption was an action in time that touches eternity. As one participates in the liturgy of the Lord' Supper one joins the whole company of heaven and take part in the celestial event: the glory given to the Father by the Son who redeemed the world; the lamb of God, slain before the foundations of the world, presented and glorified in heaven. In one chorus the Church below joins with those above to sing: "Through him, (Christ) with him, in him, in the unity of the Holy Spirit, all glory and honor is yours, Almighty Father, now and forever. Amen."

The celestial Eucharist is the eternal aspect of Christ's death; not just a memorial or reminder of the event. Because the action of Christ was not just an action in human events and worldly history but an action before and toward the eternal Father, it has an eternal aspect in glory; the witness of which are the wounds of his passion our Lord forever bears. The resurrection itself gives witness to the eternal aspect of the sacrificial event. It therefore can be remembered and re-presented now upon the earth.

In the Eucharist the Church is joined to the complete action of Christ, not simply in the past historical action, but in the eternal transaction between the Father and the Son which subsists in the celestial Eucharist. The worldly, human, and historical Christ event was the expression in time of the eternal movement of love between the Father and the Son, and as such can be not only remembered and commemorated but made truly present.[11]

---

[10] John Chrysostom, *In Act. Apos. hom.* XXI.4.
[11] Among the reformers, Luther argued that the statement by Christ in Matthew 26:26: "this is my body" was a literal expression of the real presence of Christ in the Eucharist akin to the Roman view, and thus that through the supper Christ gave

The Eucharist is a Transtemporal Expression of the Trinitarian Life

Our knowledge of God's being and life is derived through Jesus Christ. God's being, the immanent Trinity, and God's self revelation, the economic Trinity, are revealed in the person and work of Jesus Christ who makes the life of the God-head known. The Father eternally begets the Son, the Son gives his life back to the Father, and the life exchanged between them is the Holy Spirit.[12] The Son's Trinitarian mission was to take sinful death up into the sacrifice of life within God, thus extinguishing human death with the fire of eternal life. To accomplish this the Father breathed his Spirit upon the Virgin Mary who brought the Son into the world, on the cross the Son commended his Spirit back to the Father as he exhaled his last breath; the Father then raised up the Son, "having freed him from death, for it was impossible for him to be held in its power."[13] This divine respiration is the eternal archetype, the economic expression of the inner-Trinitarian relationship. The incarnation of the Son is the temporal expression of the Father's eternal attitude of love for the Son while the Son's self surrender unto death is the Son's temporal expression of his eternal attitude of love to the Father.

Within the life of the Trinity each person surrenders totally to the other. It begins above with the self-surrender of the Father, the ground of

---

forgiveness and comfort to his people. Zwingli, however, considered Jesus' words to be a metaphor and hence the "is" to mean "signifies." For Zwingli, the supper was not a means of Christ's grace, but a means by which the individual believer demonstrated his or her trust in Christ's grace alone. Zwingli's conception of a sacrament was principally informed by his understanding of "oath," particularly in terms of one's identity with and loyalty to one's community. For Zwingli the sacraments confirmed the believer's public allegiance to God and to the church. Baptism was the believer's public initiation into the community, which was demonstrated as valid through competent adult participation in Holy Communion. In this view, the sacraments are understood as enhancements of unity and commitment, public professions, and acts of solidarity and loyalty done throughout one's life, in the church. Luther charged his Swiss counterpart, whom he scornfully referred to as "Zwingle," with preaching "the real absence" of Christ in the Eucharist thereby creating a Nestorian Christology of the sacraments and Church. Luther went on to say: "Before I drink mere wine with the Swiss I shall drink blood with the pope." *Luther's Works*, XXXVIII. See also Timothy George, *Theology of the Reformers* (Nashville, TN: Boardman, 1989) 144-162; and W. P. Stephens, *The Theology of Huldrych Zwingli* (Oxford: Claredon Press, 1986).

[12] See Augustine, *The Trinity*. For other perspectives on the immanent Trinity see Gerald Bray, *The Doctrine of God* (InterVarsity Press 1993).
[13] Acts 2:24.

being and source of eternal life, and the divine response is from below as the Son surrenders himself to the Father in the Spirit. Each person in their own decline causes the other to rise. The Father expends himself in generating the Son. The world beholds this self-consumption in the consumed body of the Son which the Holy Spirit makes present to us that we might become one with it. Through the Holy Spirit the Son takes humanity into himself back to the Father. "To illustrate this connection the Father lends transtemporal divine forms of being to the Son's worldly existence in the Eucharist."[14] The Father continually generates the Son in his Eucharistic form. The Eucharist came into being through the Son's self surrender on the cross; "this was both the beginning of his Eucharist incarnation and the moment when his temporal existence was given participation in eternity."[15] In his acceptance of the Son's sacrifice the Father gives him resurrected life that is then communicated to the Church through the Eucharist, thereby integrating the world into his sacrificial Spirit[16] and assimilating creation into the life of God.

One interpretation is that through the Eucharist we become partakers in the divine nature of God.[17] When we eat and drink at the Lord's table Christ acts through his Spirit to make us his own body. We are joined to Christ in order to partake of divine life without confusion or division. Thus, eternity penetrates our finitude. Men, women, and children are invited to share in the Trinitarian life of God. Like Mary, we become God-bearers. The life of the Trinity flows and dwells in us through "the grace of our Lord Jesus Christ, the Love of God [the Father] and the Communion of the Holy Spirit."[18]

The Eucharist is Eternally Present in the Memory of the Father

The Eucharist re-presents the sacrificial death of Christ to the Church as the Church re-presents the sacrificial death of the Son to the Father. The Son "holds his priesthood permanently, because he continues forever. Consequently he is able, for all time, to save those who approach God through him, since he always lives to make intercession for them."[19]

---

[14] Hans Urs Von Balthazar, *Theo-Drama V, The Last Act* (San Francisco: Ignatius, 1998) 483.
[15] Ibid., 484.
[16] The Holy Spirit who was active in the Son becoming a human being is also active in communicating the Son's sacrificial mind and presence to those who receive him, so they can offer themselves as a living sacrifice in union with the Son to the Father.
[17] See 2 Peter 1:4; John 6:47-58; Revelation 3:20.
[18] 2 Corinthians 13:14.
[19] Hebrews 7:24-25.

"Seated at the right hand of the throne of the Majesty"[20] the Son forever bears his open wounds[21] before the Father and the Father forever exalts the Son giving "him the name that is above every name, so that at the name of Jesus every knee should bend, in heaven and on earth and under the earth, and every tongue should confess that Jesus Christ is Lord, to the glory of the Father."[22] Likewise, the body of Christ below re-presents before the Father the life, death, and resurrection of the Son. In this commemoration, God remembers, but not in the way we do, for the past is not lost to God. The once and for all redemptive action of the Son is eternally present to the Father in eternity and through the Eucharist present upon the earth. As believers are drawn into that action by Christ lifted up[23] they too are lifted up with him and exalted into the life of God.

The Eucharist is the Completion of the Incarnation and the Sign of the Resurrection

The Eucharist proclaims the fact that the incarnate Son of God lives eternally before the Father in his glorified body and blood and that the bread and wine are now vehicles for the eternal presence of that same Christ who lived, died, and rose from the dead for each of us, to be really present to each of us. Both the incarnation and the resurrection find their completion in the Eucharist which allows the risen Christ to be present throughout the world even while he subsists within the Holy Trinity. The glorified body of Christ is present to the Father, and saints in heaven, and this same body and blood are made really present on earth in the bread and wine of the sacrament. In this way the Eucharistic presence of Christ is an even more fitting expression of the glorified life than continued resurrection appearances would have been and eternally solidifies the communion of the heavenly and the earthly.

The Eucharist, while connecting the Church to the once and for all sacrifice of Christ, is also a foretaste of the Marriage Supper of the Lamb. Reminding the pilgrim Church that there is a consummation, still to come, and a greater joy, still to come, even for those who now have joy with God, for there is incompleteness until all are in fellowship with God and with them. So both the pilgrim Church below and the saints above look forward to the fulfillment of God's eternal kingdom.

---

[20] Hebrews 8:1.
[21] See Zechariah 12:10, John 19:37, Revelation 1:7.
[22] Philippians 2:9-11.
[23] See John 12:32.

In the sacramental life, believers attain true communion with their fellow Christians when that which is earthly is joined to that which is heavenly and the living join in chorus with those who have gone before. The culmination of our Christian life is realized in the eating and drinking of Holy Communion, the bread of life and the cup of salvation, the flesh and blood of one who died and yet lives, who brings life out of death, and who joins the living and dead in the eternal life of the resurrection.

The Communion of Holy Things

In the third section of the Apostle's Creed the Church affirms its belief in the Holy Spirit and the fruits of that same life giving Spirit: everlasting life, the resurrection of the body, the forgiveness of sins, the Communion of Saints, and the Church. The Latin language permits an intriguing ambiguity where our affirmation of the Communion of Saints is concerned. The *sanctorum* of the Creed's original language can be understood in two different ways. The traditional reading, which this work has thus far endorsed, interprets the noun to be the genitive form of the grammatically masculine noun *sancti*, meaning holy persons. In this case, the phrase is properly translated "the Communion of Saints" and affirms the Church's belief in the community of all holy persons, living and dead, below and above. *Sanctorum* may also be interpreted as the genitive plural of the grammatically neuter noun *sancta*, and thus be properly translated "the communion in holy things." In this case, the phase would refer to participation in those things made sacred by and through the power of the Holy Spirit, and which in turn make those who partake in them sacred. Specifically these are the sacraments: Baptism and the Lord's Supper (most properly called in this case Holy Communion.)[24] So, *communio sanctorum* signifies a communion in the holy: holy people and holy things in interrelationship.

---

[24] See J. N. D. Kelley, *Early Christian Creeds* 3rd ed. (London: Longman, 1972) 388-397, where he offers a persuasive argument that the term originated in the East, where it had the objective sacramental meaning, but as it migrated to the West its meaning was interpreted as more subjective and personal. Kelly writes that *koinonia ton hagion*, the Greek equivalent to the Latin *commmunio sanctorum*, was early and "firmly established in the East and bore the clear-cut sense of participation in the holy things, i.e., the Eucharistic elements. This makes it highly probable that the idea and the language expressing it originated in the East." (389-390) For further understanding see Wilhelm Breuning, "Communion of Saints" in *Sacramentum Mundi*, ed. Karl Rahner (New York: Herder & Herder, 1968) 1:391-394; Wolfhart Pannenberg, *The Apostle's Creed*, trans. Margaret Kohl (Phildelphia: Westminster, 1972) 144-159;

While the personal meaning has predominated the tradition of the West, the sacramental meaning has not been wholly absent. In his short essay on the Apostle's Creed, Thomas Aquinas, following Bonaventure and in agreement with Abelard connects both meanings in a unified vision where the holy sacrament of the table forms its recipients into a holy people. In this vein he wrote: "because all the faithful form one body, the benefits belonging to one are communicated to the others. There is thus a sharing of benefits (*communio bonorum*) in the Church, and this is what we mean by the Communion of Saints (*communio sanctorum*).[25] Aquinas explains that the goods shared compromise everything worthwhile done on earth by the members of the community; for the various gifts given to each person, when well used, strengthen and encourage the others. Most especially the goods shared include the sacraments which fill the Church with power flowing from Christ's passion.

The sharing of holy things and corporate solidarity mutually reinforce each other. There is no need to choose between the personal and sacramental meaning of the creedal phrase. The ambiguity of the phrase "allows us to see that holy people and holy things are inextricably linked in the one Spirit of God."[26] The elusive quality of its original meaning allows the Creed to covey a multi-layered reality: the holy people of God are grounded in the one Christ, filled with his one Spirit, and gathered into one community by their sharing in the holy things; the one faith, the one gospel, the one Baptism, the one Spirit active in each other's lives and witness, and chiefly the one loaf and one cup of Holy Communion.

The Holy Communion

The Eucharist is the heart of the Church—the nexus point where the past and future, the horizontal and vertical supernal streams, the Church above and below, the natural and the supernatural, the heavenly and the earthy, all come together in particular, concrete expression made real and present at the Lord's table. In the New Testament, there are at least six major ideas associated with Holy Communion: thanksgiving, fellowship, remembrance, sacrifice, action of the Holy Spirit, and eschatology. A brief look at each of these will help us better understand how God's holy people are interrelated through God's holy things.

---

[25] Thomas Aquinas, cited in J. N. D. Kelley, *Early Christian Creeds*, 394.
[26] Berard Marthaler, *The Creed* (Mystic, Connecticut: Twenty-third Publishing, 1987) 368.

Holy Communion is Thanksgiving

Holy Communion is an act of thanksgiving, hence the frequently used term Eucharist. The first Christians "broke bread at home and ate their food with glad and generous hearts, praising God and having the good will of all the people"[27] As the Church communes, it expresses joyful thanks for all God's mighty acts throughout history culminating in the salvific work of Jesus Christ and the ongoing work of the Holy Spirit. The whole mystery of the divine economy from creation to incarnation, especially the cross, the tomb, the resurrection, the ascension, the enthronement at the right hand of the Father, and the final glorious coming are gratefully proclaimed. Thus, in experiencing the reigning Christ in the sacramental celebration, the past, present, and future of the history of salvation are lived as one reality in the mystery of the Kingdom of God.

In naming the saints in prayer at the Lord's table, the Church gives thanks for the patriarchs and prophets who waited faithfully for Christ under the old covenant which Christ fulfilled. Likewise the Church gives thanks for the apostles, who were Christ's witnesses, who heard with their own ears, saw with their own eyes, and touched with their own hands concerning the Word of life.[28] They are the preachers of the new covenant in his blood,[29] who gave us the gospels[30] and letters,[31] "so that [we] may come to believe that Jesus is the Messiah, the Son of God, and that through believing [we] might have eternal life"[32] and "our joy may be complete."[33] They are "God's servants, working together"[34] to lay the foundation of the faith. We are the builders who have come behind them. Similarly, the Church gives thanks for the martyrs, who built upon the foundation laid by the apostles with the gold, silver, and precious stones of their lives faithfully lived and laid down "for the sake of the gospel."[35] Their testimony, proven through fire, inspires the Church that the same Spirit at work in them is at work in us, "joining us together into a holy temple in the Lord."[36] For it was not they who did these

---

[27] Acts 2:46-47.
[28] 1John 1:3; see also 1 Corinthians 15:6.
[29] Luke 2:22; see also Hebrews 9:15.
[30] See Luke 1:3.
[31] See Galatians 6:11.
[32] John 20:30.
[33] 1 John 1:4.
[34] 1 Corinthians 3:9.
[35] Mark 8:35.
[36] Ephesians 2:21.

great things but Christ who lives in them;[37] and "the fountain is still flowing, it has not dried up."[38] Lastly, the Church gives thanks for the more recently departed whose memory is cherished and whose labors are received as a sacred gift to local communities.

These thanksgivings can be specific, for instance, "for John the Baptizer and Elizabeth his mother," but they can also be more general, such as:

> Lord God, we thank you for our heritage of faith:
> For the patriarchs and prophets who prepared it for us;
> For the apostles and evangelists who brought it to us;
> For the martyrs and teachers who secured it for us;
> For the preachers and pastors who proclaimed it to us;
> For our families and friends who nourished it within us.
> Lord God, give us the will and strength to pass it on to others,
> For the glory of your name, through Jesus Christ our Lord.[39]

These more general thanksgivings have the added benefit of including the unknown or long forgotten pilgrim. The Liturgy of James provides the archetypical example from antiquity, of naming the saints, when practice was inculcated into every liturgy: "Especially we perform the memorial of the holy and glorious ever-virgin, the Blessed Theotokos. Remember her O Lord our God, and by her pure and holy prayers spare and have mercy on us."[40]

Holy Communion is Remembrance

Holy Communion is a remembrance, a commemoration, and a memorial that re-presents the past gracious acts of God and makes them truly present now, by the power of the Holy Spirit. In obedience to Christ's command to "Do this in remembrance of me"[41] the Church "eats the bread and drinks the cup proclaim[ing] Christ's death until he comes."[42]

---

[37] Galatians 2:20.
[38] Augustine, *Sermons*, 315.8 (9:133).
[39] Adapted from "Heritage Sunday" in *Chalice Worship* ed. Colbert S. Cartwright and O. I. Cricket Harrison (St. Louis, MO: Chalice Press, 1997) 193.
[40] Quoted in Michael Pomazansky, *Orthodox Dogmatic Theology* (Planitna, CA: Saint Herman of Alaska Brotherhood, 1994) 317.
[41] Luke 22:19; 1 Corinthians 11:24-25.
[42] 1 Corinthians 11:26.

Jesus Christ, who "is the reflection of God's glory and the exact imprint of God's very being"[43] is really present in Holy Communion. Christ's presence is a promise to the church and is not dependent upon recognition of it by individual members of the community. Through Jesus Christ and in the power of the Holy Spirit, God gathers his people and meets them at the table in the sacrament he has given to his Church. Christ is present in the community gathered in Jesus' name,[44] in the Word proclaimed and enacted, and in the elements of bread and wine.[45]

The Lord's Supper is the primary memorial action of the Christian community. Through it the community re-members and re-presents the incarnation, death, and resurrection of Christ Jesus. Christian remembrance of the saints is linked to this action, "for as many as have been baptized into Christ Jesus . . . have been baptized into his death [and] . . . his resurrection."[46] When the Church remembers the death and resurrection of Christ the Church is remembering also all those who are "in Christ."[47] Therefore, when proclaiming Christ's death, it is good and right to call to mind all the dead in Christ and all those for whom Christ died.

John Damascene (429 AD) claims the custom of remembering the dead at the Lord's Supper was established by "the disciples of the Savior and His holy apostles [who] sanctioned a commemoration of those who had died in the faith, being made in the awe-inspiring and life-giving mysteries."[48] According to the writings of Augustine the Eucharistic prayer included: the names of the martyrs,[49] the names of some of the faithfully departed,[50] with

---

[43] Hebrews 1:3.
[44] Matthew 18:20.
[45] 1 Corinthians 11:23-26.
[46] Romans 6:3-5.
[47] 2 Corinthians 5:17; Romans 8:1.
[48] John Damascene, *De his qui in fide dormierunt* 3, as quoted by Aquinas in *Summa Theologica*, 5.7.102.
[49] Sermon 159.1 "That is why, as the faithful know, Church custom has it that at the place where the names of the martyrs are recited at God's altar, we don't pray for them, while we do pray for the other departed brothers and sisters who are remembered there." (Hill 5:121) See also Tract John 84.1; (CCL 36:537.25-35); Sermon 297.3; *Civ Dei* 22.10; (CCL 48:828.18-26).
[50] Sermon 172.2: "It is not to be doubted that the dead can be helped by the prayers of the holy Church, and the Eucharistic sacrifice, and alms distributed for the repose of their spirits; so that God may deal with them more mercifully than their sins have deserved. The whole Church, I mean, observes this tradition received from the Fathers, that prayers should be offered for those who have died in the communion of the body and blood of Christ, whenever their names are mentioned at the sacrifice in the usual place, and that it should be announced that the sacrifice is offered for

the consecrated virgins coming first,[51] then the bishops,[52] and then a general commemoration of all the faithfully departed of the entire church;[53] as well as the names of the clergy and other bishops in the communion.[54] He states further "Of no small weight is the authority of the Church whereby she clearly approves of the custom whereby a commendation of the dead has a place in the prayers which the priests pour forth to the Lord God at His altar."[55]

Holy Communion is Sacrifice

Holy Communion is sacrifice because it re-presents but not repeats[56] the sacrifice of Christ. It is a type of sacrifice related to the atoning life, death, and resurrection of Christ that has made divine grace available to us. Through it believers present themselves in union with Christ "as a living sacrifice, holy and acceptable to God, which is [their] spiritual worship.[57]

> The belief that the Eucharist is a sacrifice is found everywhere. This belief is coupled with strong repudiations of carnal sacrifices; and is saved from being Judaic by the recognition of the elements as Christ's body and blood, of the union of the action of the Church on earth with that of Christ in heaven, and of the spiritual character of that whole priestly life and service and action of the community as the body of Christ which is a distinguishing mark of the Christian system.[58]

---

them. When, however, works of mercy are performed for their sakes, who can doubt that this benefits those for whom prayers are not sent up to God in vain? (Hill 5:252). See also *Civ Dei* 20.9 (CL 48:717.71-74).

[51] Augustine, *Sancta Virginitate* 45.46 (*CSEL* 41.3:290.10ff).

[52] Augustine, Sermon 359.6, stating the penalty for idolatry: "We will not recite his name at the altar among the bishops whom we believe to have been faithful and innocent." (Hill 10:204).

[53] Augustine, *Cura Pro Mort. ger.* 4.6 (*CSEL* 41.3:631.3-9).

[54] Augustine, Ep 78.4, referring to a priest under ecclesiastical judgment "His name should not be taken from the list of those mentioned at the Eucharist." (*CSEL* 34:337.16-18).

[55] Augustine, *Cura Pro Mort. ger.* 4.6 (*CSEL* 41.3:631.3-9).

[56] See Hebrews 9:26 that makes clear Christ does not suffer "again and again . . . but . . . he has appeared once for all at the end of the age to remove sin by the sacrifice of himself."

[57] Romans 12:1; 1 Peter 2:5.

[58] Darwell Stone, *A History of the Doctrine of the Holy Eucharist*, vol. 1 (London: Longmans, 1909) 54.

Holy Communion has been regarded as the distinctively Christian sacrifice from at least the closing decade of the first century. Following the prophet Malachi's exhortation to offer God the King and Lord a pure sacrifice[59] the instructions of the *Didache* urge believers to "assemble on the Lord's Day and break bread and give thanks, having first confessed your sins, that your sacrifice may be pure."[60] The elements of the sacrifice are the body and blood of Jesus. Joined to Christ's once and for all sacrifice "is the Eucharist itself, the great act of worship of Christians, their sacrifice. The writers and liturgies of the period are unanimous in recognizing it as such."[61]

Augustine refers to the Eucharist as "the sacrifice of our redemption, the sacrifice of the Mediator, the sacrifice of peace, the sacrifice of love, the sacrifice of the body and blood of the Lord, and the sacrifice of the Church.[62] However, he is quick to point out that "it is not new sacrifice added to that of the cross, but a daily, un-bloody repetition and perpetual application of that once and only sacrifice."[63] Christ Jesus the true mediator between God and human beings "is both the Priest who offers and the sacrifice offered. And he designed that there should be a daily sign of this in the sacrifice of the Church, which, being his body, learns to offer herself through him."[64]

Holy Communion is Grace

Holy Communion is a means of this grace through the action of the Holy Spirit;[65] whom the Father sends in Christ's name to teach the Church everything and remind it of all that Christ has said.[66] As the mystery of the Incarnation at Bethlehem was accomplished by the power of the Word of God and by the Holy Spirit, so also the mystery of Christ's being made really present in the Eucharist is accomplished through the action of Word and

---

[59] Malachi 1:10.

[60] *Didache* 14 in Henery Bettenson, *Documents of the Christian Church* (Oxford: Oxford University Press, 1963) 66.

[61] Kelly, *Early Christian Doctrines*, 196-198, 214.

[62] Augustine, Conf 9:32; Enchir 110; In Ps 21 Enar 2:28; In Ps 33 Enar 1:5; De civ Dei 10:20, as quoted in Darwell Stone, *A History of the Doctrine of the Holy Eucharist*, vol. 1 (London: Longmans, 1909) 1:113.

[63] Phillip Schaff, *A History of the Christian Church*, vol.3 (New York: Charles Scribner's Sons, 1910) 507 discussing Augustine, *Contr Faust Manich* 1.20.18.

[64] Augustine, *De Civit Dei* 10.20, in Phillip Schaff, *Early Church Fathers: Nicene & Post-Nicene Fathers* Series 1, 14 Vols, herafter called NPNF(New York: The Christian Literature Publishing Co., 1890) 6:102

[65] Acts 1:8.

[66] John 14:26.

Spirit. Jesus Christ is "the Word [which] became flesh and dwelt among us."[67] Parallel to the incarnation when the Holy Spirit came upon the Virgin Mary[68] so the power of the Most High overshadows the Eucharistic elements through which Christ becomes present.

As we encounter the risen Christ in Holy Communion and repeatedly receive his gift of divine grace, we are progressively shaped into his image. This spiritual growth is a lifelong process through which God shapes his people into a holy people; and the identity God has bestowed on us in our Baptism is fulfilled and completed.

The grace we receive through Holy Communion is spiritual nourishment. The Christian life is a challenging and arduous journey. To live faithfully and grow in holiness requires constant sustenance. The Spirit makes such life-giving food available in the sacrament of the table. As Jesus tells the crowd: "I am the bread of life. Whoever comes to me will never be hungry, and whoever believes in me will never be thirsty."[69] Gathered around the table again and again, believers are strengthened repeatedly and empowered to live as disciples and witnesses performing our ministry and mission, to continue Christ's work in the world; redemption, reconciliation, peace, and justice.[70] As we commune, we become aware of the worth and the needs of other people and are reminded of our responsibility.

In this way each Lord's Supper is a continuation of the feast of Pentecost. It is the renewal and the confirmation of the coming of the Holy Spirit who is ever present in the Church. The worshipping community earnestly prays: "Pour out your Holy Spirit upon us gathered here, and on these gifts of bread and wine, and make them be for us the body and blood of Christ, that we may be for the world, the body of Christ redeemed by his blood."[71] The consecrated gifts become a communion of the Holy Spirit and the Church a Spirit-bearer to the world.

Holy Communion is Fellowship

Holy Communion is the unifying fellowship of the church. Much more than an act of personal piety the sacramental meal unites us to Christ and to each other. "Because there is one bread, we who are many are one

---

[67] John 1:4.
[68] See Luke 1:35.
[69] John 6:35.
[70] 2 Corinthians 5:17-21.
[71] *The United Methodist Book of Worship* (Nashville, Tennessee: The United Methodist Publishing House, 1992) 38.

body, for we all partake of the one bread."[72] Wherever Holy Communion is celebrated, that local Church possesses the visible marks of the true Church; unity, holiness, catholicity, and apostolicity. These marks do not belong solely to the human gathering but are the eschatological signs given to the community through the Spirit of God. There is only one Christ. Wherever his Supper is celebrated he is wholly and fully present. In this way, present in each local Church, even if only two or three are gathered in Christ's name,[73] is the whole mystery of the universal Church, for the Lord, its head and living heart is present.

Christ our Lord is one and he desires that we receive him in unity with one another, with all human beings of all times and places, and with all creation.[74] On the night he instituted the sacrament of Holy Communion Jesus prayed to his Father for the unity of the Church that would be born of his suffering, death, and resurrection. He prayed that future disciples in the Church would be united as he and the Father were united.

> I ask not only on behalf of these, but also on behalf of those who will believe in me through their word, that they may all be one. As you Father are in me and I am in you, may they also be in us, so that the world may believe that you have sent me. The glory you have given me, I have given them, that they may be one, as we are one, I in them and you in me, that they may become completely one, so that the world may know that you have sent me and have loved them even as you have loved me.[75]

The Church's unity is a reflection of the unity of the Father with the Son, rooted in the nature of God and in Jesus' obedient love. The Father is in Jesus, and Jesus is in the Father. Through the sacraments Jesus is in us, and therefore "we have fellowship with the Father and with the Son Jesus Christ."[76] This communion is the gift of eternal life.[77] Jesus presented himself as the bread of life saying: "Those who eat my flesh and drink my blood have eternal life, and I will raise them up on the last day."[78] Life in union with Christ is eternal life. It is not only the promise of our being with Christ after physical death but it is our being in dynamic loving relationship

---

[72] 1 Corinthians 10:17.
[73] Matthew 18:20.
[74] See John 17:22; Ephesians 4:5.
[75] John 17:20-24.
[76] 1 John 1:3.
[77] John 17:2.
[78] John 6:52.

with Christ here and now. It is life that never ends because it is grounded in the everlasting love of God who comes to us in the sacraments. "This is eternal life: to know the only true God and Jesus Christ, whom [he] has sent."[79] The loving Christ who gathers us around his table and meets us there gives us the gift of eternal life. Just as the Father has sent the Son into the world, Jesus sends his disciples into the world.[80] So it follows that Christians should love one another as Jesus loves the Father and the Father loves the Son. This motivating power of God's love is the dominating expression of the Church's mission.

Sharing in the life of Christ and revivified by the gifts of the Holy Spirit, the Church becomes a manifestation of divine love. The sharing and bonding that occurs at the table exemplify the nature of the church and model God's will for the world. Believers cannot be in communion with the Lord if they are not in communion with each other. So Jesus instructs: "When you are offering your gift at the altar, if you remember that your brother or sister has something against you, leave your gift before the altar and go; first be reconciled to your brother or sister, and then come and offer your gift."[81] When we are gathered around the Lord's Table, we go to meet Christ and each other, to be one with Christ and each other. For this reason the mentioning in prayer of the names of the apostles and other paradigmatic saints, as well as current bishops or Church leaders remind us that the celebration of Holy Communion is not only a meeting of heaven and earth, but also a meeting of the Church then and now, and a meeting of the Church here and there. The gathering of the one Church around the one table of the one Lord is a visible sign of the unity of the Church.

Through the sharing of the bread and cup all members of the Christian community are saints, for they all participate in the holiness of God shared in, through, and by the life, death, and resurrection of Christ Jesus. Present day saints are in unity with the saints of the past. Time and space are transcended in the Church as in Christ's prayer, "not for these only but for all who will believe in me through their word, that they all may be one."[82] Those who have gone before us into the other world are in union with us in Christ; we are united with Christ below and they are united with Christ above and through Christ all the saints are united together.

In an apaphatic vision, Augustine heard God's voice from on high saying to him: "I am the food of grown men. Grow, and you shall feed upon

---

[79] John 17:3.
[80] John 17:18.
[81] Matthew 5:23-24.
[82] John 17:20.

me. You will not change me into yourself, as you change food into your flesh, but you will be changed into me."[83] In the normal process of eating, the human is the stronger being who takes things in and assimilates them to their self. The food is transformed to build the body and give life. In our relationship with Christ, he is the stronger being. When we truly communicate with Christ, we are assimilated into him. In becoming one with him, through him, we become one with the fellowship of all our brothers and sisters, who were given life through his food and transformed into his body.

Holy Communion is Eschatology

Holy Communion is eschatological. God's purpose for the world is revealed in the three part proclamation of the gospel: Christ has died; Christ is risen; Christ will come again. When the believers communes they share with and are bonded to the faithful gathered around the local table below and the saints above whom they join in the great feast. To participate below is to receive a foretaste of what awaits above; it is a pledge of heaven. On the night he gave himself up for us, Christ looked forward to this occasion and promised his disciples, "I will never again drink of the fruit of the vine until that day when I drink it new with you in my Father's kingdom."[84]

Holy Communion is our present token of the consummation yet to come. The Lord's Supper is not exclusively focused on Jesus' suffering and death, and our need of repentance. But it is linked, especially in Luke, to the great messianic banquet anticipated by Jesus who said "people will come from east and west, from north and south and will eat in the kingdom of God."[85] So the Lord's Supper is not only understood in terms of suffering, death, and penitence but in the post-resurrection terms of eating, drinking, and rejoicing with the risen Lord in expectant anticipation of the marriage feast of the Lamb.[86]

---

[83] Augustine, *Confessions*, 7:10:16, trans. John K. Ryan (New York: Doubleday, 1960) 171.
[84] Matthew 26:29; Mark 14:25; Luke 22:18.
[85] Luke 13:29.
[86] The grim piety imported into the Protestant service of Holy Communion from the often somber and penitentially centered medieval mass is slowly recovering a fuller understanding of the Sacrament of the Table as is reflected in the words of the 1961 *Directory of Worship* for the United Presbyterian Church USA: "The promise of Christ's presence in the midst of those who receive the sacrament witnesses to the reality of his resurrection from the dead and is a foretaste of eternal fellowship with him." *The Constitution of the United Presbyterian Church in the United States of America*, Part 2, *Book of Order*, 21.031.

"We are guests at the Lord's Table, which is not only an image; it is an event."[87] As guests we are no longer separated from our host. We eat his flesh and drink his blood and his flesh is true meat and his blood true drink unto eternal life in this midst of this present life. Through this meal he is in us and we are in him so that "in him our body is already in heaven."[88]

This messianic banquet is the time and place in which the heavenly joins the earthly. It is not simply a sacred drama or a mere symbolization of past events but it constitutes the very presence of God's embracing love, which purifies, enlightens, and perfects all "those who are invited to the marriage supper of the Lamb."[89] At the Lord's Supper we are reminded of what God has done for us in the past, experience what God is doing now, and anticipate what God will do in the future. We await that last great day, when Christ comes in final victory to bring all who are in Christ into the glory of that victory.

When believers eat and drink at the Lord's Table they are anticipating the heavenly banquet celebrating God's final victory over sin, evil, and death.[90] In the midst of the personal and systemic brokenness of the world in which they live, they yearn for everlasting fellowship with Christ and ultimate fulfillment of the divine plan. Nourished by sacramental grace, they strive to be formed into the image of Christ and to be made Christ's instruments for transformation of the world.

When the saints on earth are gathered around the table of the Lord to celebrate the sacrament of his holy institution, whereby and in which by the power of the Holy Spirit Christ is truly present in a real, personal, and living way, under the gaze of the Church above, to whom and with whom Christ is also present, the Church in one voice prays to heaven, "'remember these your servants . . . who have gone before us in faith and now rest in the sleep of peace' it is then that heaven and earth truly greet each other"[91] the Church above and the Church below, "meet in a holy kiss and the whole Christ with all his members celebrate a blessed love feast, a memorial of their communion in love, and joy, and pain."[92] In the eschaton, pain, suffering, and death will come to an end, but the work of adoration, celebration, and thanksgiving will continue. So the faithfully departed saints "wait until the

---

[87] Barth, *Dogmatics in Outline*, 155.
[88] Question 49, *Heidelberg Catechism*, as quoted in Barth, *Dogmatics in Outline*, 155.
[89] Revelation. 19:9.
[90] See Matthew 22:1-14; Revelation 19:9; 21:1-7.
[91] Karl Adam, *The Spirit of Catholicism* (New York: The Crossroad Publishing Company, 1997) 123.
[92] Ibid.

end of the world for us, the believers still on earth, to fulfill their ministry, their works, their crown, their joy."[93]

---

[93] Pierre-Yves Emery, *The Communion of Saints* (London: Faith, 1966) 126.

Chapter Eleven

Good and Useful

This book has argued that since it is confessed in the Creed, the Communion of Saints forms an inseparable part of the doctrine of God's saving grace to which those persons who profess the Creed entrust their lives. Further, it has established that implicit in the very practice of faith is the interweaving of the Communion of Saints. However, the question that remains whether the overt veneration of the saints mandatory for Christians, necessary for salvation, or an obligation of Church membership?

Public Liturgical Remembrance

Ostensibly, the Church venerates the saints in its public prayers and worship, chief among these being the celebration of the Holy Communion, also called the Lord's Supper. In this context the Church thanks God for the sinless life, sacrificial death, and victorious resurrection of Jesus Christ made really present at the table, around which the Church below is gathered for a foretaste of the great feast of the Lamb in which the Church above already partakes. With Mary, the apostle's, and all the saints, the Church below enjoys the real presence of Christ, praises God's glory, and sets their hope on sharing with the Church above in this glory forever.

In the singing of hymns, the Church below joins all the company of heaven praising the name of God and singing their unending hymn: "Holy, holy, holy, Lord, God Almighty, who was, and is, and is to come . . . you are worthy our Lord and God to receive glory and honor and power."[94] In their dialogue of praise the Church below recognizes and sometimes entreats the prayers of their heavenly partners; and they both anxiously await the day of consummation when the victory of God will be finally and fully revealed to all. In addition to this mystical adoration, in its hymns, the church recalls and is encouraged by the memory Christian heroism and sanctity in every age.

In its calendar of feast days the Church below brings to memory particular saints who lives give witness to the power of the Holy Spirit and the truth of the gospel. These men and women, so configured to the image of Christ, inspire moral and religious energy that buoys the church struggling below in its ongoing, often stumbling, journey toward the great reign of God.

---

[94] Revelation 4:8, 11.

The saints are named in worship in a variety of ways, not the least of which is in the pronouncement of the scripture lessons, where the lector might say: "a reading from the holy gospel according to Mark . . ." or "a reading from Paul's letter to the Romans. . . ." Even if the apostle's name is not prefaced by his title of honor the Church recognizes the testimony of these who were "chosen by God to be his witnesses."[95] Likewise the Church recalls the special place of the Mother of God in the economy of salvation when it affirms in the Creed belief in Jesus Christ . . . born of the Virgin Mary. In less frequent contexts such as the Easter Vigil, ordinations, and All Saints Day a Litany of Saints is sometimes prayed as a prayer addressed to the Father, through the Son, in the Spirit, recalling to the communal consciousness the historical procession of the faith.

Inasmuch as persons participate in the public prayer and worship of the Church they are in some way participating in honoring the saints. As a component in the direct worship of God this public liturgical remembrance is the highest form of veneration. It seems inescapable for even the most puritan of Christians without wholly repudiating the public worship of the Church.

Private Devotion

Must one venerate the saints to be a Christian? No. According to the sixteenth century Counter Reformation Council of Trent, the veneration of the saints is not a must, not even for Roman Catholics. The conciliar claim is that such veneration is "good and useful."[96] The veneration of the saints is not necessary for salvation and is not even a duty of Christians. No official Church teaching or law demand that an individual believer must remember, honor, or venerate Mary, the apostle's, or the saints in ones own private prayer or practices of personal piety. Recommendation is not requirement; the matter is left to personal discretion.

As the reformers rightly realized, absolutely no biblical text mandates the practice of honoring or invoking the saints. Furthermore, none of the Creeds, concilar teachings, or theological writings of the first Christians makes such a requirement. In fact, it was not until the last session of the post-Reformation Council of Trent that the Church dealt directly and officially with the issue of "the Invocation, Veneration, and Relics of the Saints." In chapter three of its twenty-second session the council clarified

---

[95] Acts 10:41
[96] Council of Trent 25 (1563); see *Canons and Decrees of the Council of Trent,* trans. C. Trent (Rockford, Illinois: Tan Books & Publishers, 1978) 215.

that though "the Church has been accustomed at times to celebrate, certain masses in honor and memory of the saints; not therefore, however, doth she teach that sacrifice is offered unto them, but unto God alone."[97]

In its twenty-fifth session, the council tackled the complaints of the reformers, especially the popular practice of calling upon saints for special favors. The council maintained that "the saints who reign together with Christ, offer up their own prayers to God for [all believers and] that it is good and useful suppliantly to invoke them."[98] It went on to affirm that "their salutary examples, are set before the eyes of the faithful; that so they may give God thanks for those things; may order their own lives and manners in imitation of the saints; and may be excited to adore and love God, and to cultivate piety."[99] Lastly, it demanded from bishops and teachers that from the doctrine of the saints "every superstition shall be removed, all filthy lucre be abolished; [and] finally, all lasciviousness be avoided."[100]

While the council clearly defended the remembering, honoring, and invoking the saints it did not advance or declare any requirement so to do. The language of the council, that invoking the saints was "good and useful" ascribes value and implicitly encourages these prayers but in no way makes them essential or obligatory.[101] The 1933 revision of the *Code of Cannon Law* "commends . . . and promotes authentic veneration [to Mary and] the other saints who help the faithful by their example and their prayers."[102] In the same vein, the Second Vatican Council recognized the saints above as members of the whole people of God, through whom God reveals his voice and face, giving the Church struggling below an example to imitate and a witness of hope. To love the saints, thank God for them, imitate their discipleship, and request their prayers, *Lumen Gentium* states, is "supremely fitting."[103] These carefully chosen words certainly mean to persuade persons that honoring the saints is definitely appropriate behavior but they definitely do not mean obligation.

---

[97] *Canons and Decrees of the Council of Trent*, trans. H. J. Schroeder (St. Louis: Herder, 1941) 146.
[98] Ibid., 235.
[99] Ibid.
[100] Ibid., 235-236.
[101] See George Kretschmer and Rene Laurentin, "The Cult of the Saints," in *Confessing One Faith: A Joint Commentary on the Augsburg Confession by Lutheran and Catholic Theologians*, ed., George Forell and James McCue (Minneapolis: Augsburg, 1992) 273.
[102] *The Code of Canon Law*, trans. The Cannon Law Society of Great Britain and Ireland (Grand Rapids, Michigan: Eerdmans, 1983) cannon 1186.
[103] *Lumen Gentium*, no. 67.

So "for the Church the veneration of saints is entirely legitimate and important. For individual Christians however, it is neither a duty nor a necessity for salvation, but it is part of the freedom of individual piety."[104] *The Common Statement of the Lutheran Catholic Dialogue in the United States* came to a parallel conclusion:

> Precisely because the Church regards the invocation of the saints and Mary as "good and beneficial," the individual Catholic is strongly encouraged to make use of, and participate in, such prayers. Many Catholics continue to respond to this encouragement with enthusiasm. But there is no reason for thinking that a person who refrained from personally invoking the saints would forfeit full communion with the Catholic Church. This freedom now enjoyed by Catholics would certainly be enjoyed also by Lutherans should a greater degree of communion between the respective Churches be achieved.[105]

Venerating the saints is an element in the public liturgical witness of the Church in which individual believers share, in as much as they are shaped by and participate in the worship life of the Church. The Church encourages individual believers to honor, imitate, and request the prayers of the saints as they are led to do so in the Spirit. No one is ever required to venerate the saints as a necessary act of salvation.

The Succession of the Saints

The Holy Spirit makes persons holy. Believers really become what they are declared to be in Christ Jesus by the power of the Holy Spirit. The presence of the Holy Spirit is seen to the extent that holiness wells up in people. These holy people form a Spirit filled continuum of gospel witnesses, validating the Church's identity and the truth of its message. Without the succession of the saints, apostolic succession is but a sounding bell or a tinkling symbol, a tradition without meaning, and an office without substance. But ordinary people, in ordinary time, being made holy is the true and living witness that the Holy Spirit has not abandoned the Church and that grace continues to be given to the world in every age.

---

[104] Georg Kraus, "Saints, Holiness, Sanctification," in *Handbook of Catholic Theology*, ed. Wolfgang Beinert and Francis Schussler Fiorenza (New York: Crossroad, 1995) 638-639.
[105] Anderson, *The One Mediator, the Saints, and Mary*, no. 95, 57.

That the Church is a community of sinners is verifiable, but that it can nonetheless be characterized as holy is not only a hopeful prospect, directed toward the eschaton, but also a confession based upon the actual and realized experience of holiness by so many men and women in all periods of Church history. The creedal confession of the holy Church is no free-floating pronouncement, but is filled with the life stories of people who have been sanctified and graced by God through the ages.[106]

The doctrine of the Holy Spirit requires holy people. The community of simultaneously sinful yet redeemed people, on the way to glory, but always in need of reform, is the Church and testifies to the life transforming grace, as the Holy Spirit moves in its history and creates a river of holy lives.

Summary

The celebration of the saints, official, local, and otherwise, involves first the recognition that all members of the Body of Christ profess one and the same faith, preserved and passed on to them through the succession of the saints. All the saints, living and dead, share the same luminous ideal, the same effective rule, and the same fruitful sources of spiritual life. "By passing along the narrow road they widened it, and while they went along, trampling on the rough ways, they went ahead of us."[107] Following Jesus the pioneer of our faith, the saint's hope in the victory of mercy over sinfulness and the patterns of holiness they trace in history help make our life possible. Bearers of our past, they signal our future.

Second, the celebration of the saints involves imitation, that is recalling and being encouraged by Christian heroism and sanctity in every age. In this way, the saints are the links in the chain by which we are reminded of our spiritual origins in the Christ Event. The apostles entrusted the Gospel message to disciples commissioned and appointed by them to oversee the Christian community. From these disciples to the present day runs a continuous line of preachers fulfilling the apostolic commission. Stemming from the root of the historical Jesus, and blossoming along the vine of these historical preachers grew the fruit of their preaching the universal Church on earth. Over time the external structures of this

---

[106] Herman Wegman, "Successio Sanctorum," in *Time and Community*, ed., Alexander Neil (Washington, D.C.: Pastoral Press, 1990) 231.
[107] Augustine, Sermon 306c.1; in *Sermons* 9:37.

community became more fully organized and indeed larger and more visible. But it is the same Church and so in a true sense the Church as a whole, as one organism, has itself seen Jesus, stood beneath his cross, and experienced his resurrection. In this way it is the Church, comprised of saints living, yes, but mostly dead, that brings us into the closest historical relation to Jesus, by not only pointing out that his life, work, and message is recorded in cherished documents but experienced in the lives of generations past, many in whom the divinity of Christ blazes forth in external manifestation, and in thousands of millions in our own time who are the sons and daughters of God, brothers and joint heirs with Christ Jesus, filled with his Spirit of new and abundant life.

The faith of the one Church is affirmed in its Creeds, written in its scriptures, proclaimed by its preachers, and lived by its saints. It is the special task of the community of the Church to attest to the truth of its proclamation by living it. If the glory of God is the human being fully alive, then in the saints, God's glory shines through in radiant and attractive ways. Saints are a sign of God's presence, the image of Christ on earth, living parables. Through their testimony living evidence of God is revealed to all people and the meaning of faith, hope, and love are better understood. Every life that is lived in faith is a persuasive and inspiring incarnation of the Church's proclamation. "A demonstration of Spirit and of power,"[108] more effective than the "lofty words of wisdom"[109] the life of faith is the most convincing proof of Christianity. The saints attest the Gospel before the world and communicate their living faith to the weaker members of the Body of Christ. Saint's feasts proclaim the victory of Christ in them and set that example before us.

The more we recognize ourselves surrounded by saints and their witness,[110] the more we find ourselves inadvertently attracted to the idea of following their path. "To lead a moral life, [we need a] flesh and blood existent."[111] Saints are flesh and blood instances of life lived well before God. It is hard to read much about Blessed Teresa of Calcutta, for example, and not find ourselves being tempted, if only for a moment, to drop everything and serve God and neighbor as she did. While the vast majority of us will not, and one might argue should not, do this literally, her example may gently spur us to engage in volunteer work among the poor, support our local benevolent ministries, or affirm with her in the face of overwhelming need

---

[108] 1 Corinthians 2:4.
[109] 1 Corinthians 2:1.
[110] Hebrews 12:1.
[111] Edith Wyschogrod, *Saints and Postmodernism: Revisioning Moral Philosophy* (Chicago: The University of Chicago Press, 1990) 3.

"God does not call us to be successful only faithful."[112] Whether famous, like Teresa, or known only to us, in the face of our grandmother or godparent, saints change us simply by existing. "There's no getting round the saints."[113]

Third, the celebration of the saints may involve invocation. The practice of invoking the prayers of the saints is not commanded in scripture nor accompanied by its word of command or promise, but developed early in the church's history as an expression of the truth that in Christ all believers are connected to and significant for each other, even across the chasm of death. Its theological bases are the doctrines of forgiveness, resurrection and everlasting life and the fellowship which Christians have with one another in Christ.

Just as believers ask persons on earth to pray to God on their behalf, so believers may request saints above, alive in Christ, to remember them before God. In doing so, believers are drawn more closely to one another and join more intensely as a whole, thereby experiencing evermore fully the passion and love of Christ Jesus. In the context of private prayer, such piety expresses an awareness that others besides ourselves are in Christ and their living faithfulness is of benefit to us.

Since death does not end our mutual participation with one another but more likely deepens it, it is legitimate, good, and useful, although not necessary to ask brothers and sisters who are with Christ in the eternal mystery of God to pray for those still on pilgrimage. When understood primarily as a communion with Christ and a manifestation of the interrelatedness of the caring community it is not intrinsically opposed to the spirit of the New Testament. While superstition and excess can corrupt the dynamic of this practice it may be rightly ordered in the context of Protestant faith.

Fourth, the celebration of the saints occurs most appropriately during the celebration of Holy Communion. The Lord's Supper is a concrete and particular expression of the people of God as a holy community comprising members above and below, all joined together in Jesus Christ. The Risen Christ is bodily present to the saints above who feast at the marriage supper of the lamb and to the saints below who are granted a foretaste of the heavenly banquet. Gathered around the table the community gives thanks for the mighty acts of God in Jesus Christ and the continuous

---

[112] José Luis González-Baldo, *Mother Teresa, In Her Own Words* (New York: Gramercy Books, 1996) 56.
[113] Austin Farrer, *A Faith of Our Own* (New York: World, 1960) 14.

acts of the Holy Spirit; this includes the deliverance of all God's people and God's continued work to perfect his people in holiness.

It is good and right to name saints before God and before the community, to bring them to memory, be inspired by their witness, and join them in prayer and praise to Christ, the Savior of all. The right response of those below to those above is to love them, thank God for them, follow their example, and to join them in prayer. When we praise God in their company during the celebration of Holy Communion each of these actions occur in and through Christ Jesus, who is "glorified in his saints."[114]

Through the Communion of Saints, Christians above and below, are companions with one another and help one another on the way of salvation through, with, and in Christ. "Just as Christian communion among wayfarers brings us closer to Christ, so our companionship with the saints joins us to Christ, from whom, as from their fountain and head, issue every grace and the life of God's people itself."[115] We all participate in the same love of God and neighbor, we all sing the same hymn of glory to our God, we all belong to the same Christ, have the same Spirit, and form the same Church. All are companions along the way of salvation and sanctification, as Augustine preached on the feast day of Perpetua and Felicity "If we are not capable of following them in action, let us follow in affection; if not in glory, then certainly in joy and gladness; if not in merit, then in desire; if not in suffering, then in fellow feeling; if not in excellence, then in our close relationship with them."[116]

---

[114] 2 Thessalonians 1:10.

[115] *Lumen Gentium*, no. 50, in Walter Abbott, ed., *Documents of Vatican II* (New York: American Press, 1966) 78-85. This Dogmatic Constitution of the Church restores the companionship model over the patron-client model of the Communion of Saints by enfolding the saints in heaven within the whole community of God's holy people, living and dead, energized by the life-giving Spirit and equally called to discipleship. The Church below remembers the bright patterns of holiness of those who once struggled below but have now received their reward with in glory. Their hope is strengthened and their worship enriched when the Church below joins the their unending praise of the company of heaven.

[116] Augustine, Sermon 280.6; in *Sermons* 8:75.

Chapter Twelve

Conclusion

This book began with the premise that the corrective theology of the Reformation broke the historic union among all members of the kingdom of God, especially between the pilgrim saints below and those triumphant above. While the theology of the Church's true treasury was corrected, Protestant Christians were left bereft of a satisfactory explanation of their creedal claim: "we believe . . . in the Communion of Saints."

In the reclamation of this important doctrine this book attempted to critically present but sympathetically understand the historical and theological development of penance, Purgatory, and prayers to the saints, as well as the Reformers ultimate rejection of not just the abuses of those things but of the things themselves. It then sought to construct a biblically sound eschatological context through which one could envision, in part, the life beyond, affirming that the departed saints exist in God. With that framework to lean on, it then endeavored to described the essence of that life and explore the various interactions between believers below and those above. Concluding that the Communion of Saints is that spiritual bond which knits together the faithful below and the saints above in a mystical, organic, and historic unity within which there exists a mutuality of faith, prayer, and love that is best and most fully expressed in the Eucharistic feast of the Lord's Supper.

The great protestant hymn "For All the Saints," written in 1864 by Anglican Bishop William W. How (who was known as the "poor man's bishop") perhaps stands as the best musical icon presenting what has been so far claimed concerning the Communion of Saints. Its first verse sings:

For all the saints, who from their labors rest,
who thee by faith before the world confessed,
thy name, O Jesus, be forever blest. Alleluia, Alleluia! [1]

In such we are reminded that the saints are those persons on earth and in heaven, that is, in this life and in the life beyond, who have been chosen by God and set apart for God in, by, and through Jesus Christ, who continues his work in their lives through his Holy Spirit, and in the world through his

---

[1] William W. How, "For All the Saints." in *The United Methodist Hymnal*, 711.

Church, of which they are members. The resting saints above serve as our examples of faithful living and dying and we receive the benefits of their holiness in that we are the heirs of their legacy. The common faith that we confess calls all persons to be saints, not through their own power, but by the action of God in them.

Jesus Christ is all sufficient for salvation. Our entire hope of salvation rests on Jesus Christ and his gospel, the true treasury of the Church, whereby the good news of his saving work is made known. His person, life, and work, determine the content of the gospel and all Christian life. He is the one mediator between God and humanity who was crucified once and for all. He was resurrected and ascended into heaven where he is exalted to God's right hand and makes intercession for us, who are saved by grace through faith, and therefore can pray directly to God through Christ. Christ's grace is mediated to us in a variety of ways, primarily through the Holy Spirit, the Holy Gospel, Holy Baptism, and Holy Communion, in the Holy Church.

All justified believers are saints by the grace of God in Christ and through the continued action of God's grace in their lives grow into mature Christians and evermore fully participate in the life of God. Holiness is a gift from God, through Christ, by the Holy Spirit. It is conferred through baptism and confirmed, preserved, and deepened by Word and Sacrament, and the other means of grace. All persons who are sanctified in the One who sanctifies, Christ Jesus, constitute the Communion of Saints. This includes believers both living and dead. This communion is a product of the eternal life granted us in Christ who was resurrected from the dead for the forgiveness of our sins.

Hence, the second verse affirms that Christ is indeed the means of both justification and sanctification.

> Thou wast their rock, their fortress, and their might;
> thou Lord, their captain in the well-fought fight;
> thou in the darkness drear, their one true light. Alleluia, Alleluia! [2]

This message serves as a corrective to late medieval period popular piety which was marked by a great emphasis on the intercession of deceased patron saints who were invoked to grant favors, remedy specific needs, and cajole mercy from a stern God. The reformers rejection of the cult of the saints was based on their understanding that such customs, as practiced in popular piety, were commended nowhere in scripture and more disturbingly, detracted from trust in Christ alone.

---

[2] William W. How, "For All the Saints." in *The United Methodist Hymnal*, 711.

The practice of invoking the saints was thought to transform the kind and merciful Christ, the sole mediator between God and human beings, into a dreaded judge, who is placated by the prayers of the saints or by a multitude of ritual works. This ultimately resulted in the sacrilegious sale of indulgences, the overextended powers of the papacy, particularly over the souls in Purgatory, and other abuses. When Luther called for an academic debate on the use of Indulgences and their relationship to what had become the sacrament of penance, the cult of the saints became a related issue.

In their reaction, the reformers allowed that the departed saints could be remembered, but omitted invoking them from their liturgical celebrations, and frowned upon it in private practice. In reformed commemoration the saints were remembered for their bold faith on earth through their words and deeds. Chief among them were biblical figures, such as John the Baptist, the apostles, and the Virgin Mary, who was said to embody God's unmerited grace and typify the Church. Great teachers, such as Ambrose and Augustine were also revered. Honoring the saints meant giving thanks to God for the example of their lives, full of God's mercy and faithfulness, which then strengthens one's own faith, and helped one to imitate their faith, love, and other virtues. Of such we are reminded in verse three of the fine hymn:

> O may thy soldiers, faithful, true, and bold,
> fight as the saints who nobly fought of old,
> and win with them the victor's crown of gold. Alleluia, Alleluia! [3]

So, within the Communion of Saints believers suffer with Christ as a prelude to being glorified with him. They also participate in the joys and sufferings of their sisters and brothers to share their joy and relieve their suffering. This is done through solidarity in prayer and worship, remembering God's promises and preaching his gospel, sharing all things, and through correction and example. The saints are best honored when we thank God for them, are strengthened as a result of their grace filled testimony, and imitate their life of faith. This is the sacred communion of which we sing in verse four:

> O blest communion, fellowship divine!
> We feebly struggle, they in glory shine;
> yet all are one in thee, for all are thine. Alleluia, Alleluia! [4]

---

[3] William W. How, "For All the Saints." in *The United Methodist Hymnal,* 711.
[4] William W. How, "For All the Saints." in *The United Methodist Hymnal,* 711.

The saints of heaven and the saints upon the earth are the two modes of the one Church, the body of Christ, the fullness of him who fills all in all. Their unity is most fully expressed at the Lord's Table, often times called "Holy Communion." At the table the saints upon the earth mystically participate with the saints in heaven as the mighty acts of salvation are made present through Word and Sacrament. The saints below and the saints above both enjoy the same and real presence of Christ, and anticipate together the coming marriage supper of the Lamb.

Faith, then, does not mean mere individualistic decisionism but rather being born into the communion of saints, the one Church. As members of Christ's body, believers participate in a mystic union with the Triune God and with each other. Through the work of the Holy Spirit, in the Word, and in the Sacraments the life-giving presence and grace of Christ comes to those he has gathered. They in turn respond with worship, the fruits of the Holy Spirit, and good works.

As believers are sanctified in Christ in this world, the great cloud of witnesses that are the saints above, and within their number, some paradigmatic figures, witness to God's grace, inspire those below to greater faith and faithfulness, and encourage thanksgiving for one another. Verse five proclaims the saints inspiring testimony:

> And when the strife is fierce, the warfare long,
> steals on the ear the distant triumph song,
> and hearts are brave again, and arms are strong. Alleluia, Alleluia! [5]

Because the New Testament commends believers to pray for one another through Christ we can have confidence that our sisters and brothers in heaven pray for us, and even ask them so to do. How's outstanding hymn, however, makes no reference to invoking the saints beyond receiving their confession and looking to their example. In as much, we are reminded that no one is obliged to invoke the saints in private prayer, but that one can hardly have public worship without the saints, although one need not address them directly, as very few of even catholic prayers do.

The theological principles that should govern proper veneration and invocation of the saints stem from the creedal faith. There is one God, who is Father, Son, and Holy Spirit. There is one merciful Savior who is the sole mediator between God and humanity. All gifts of grace given to human beings are the work of the Holy Spirit. In the one Church all members are bonded together in one communion. Any devotional practice that

---

[5] Ibid.

overshadows the person or work of the Father, Son, or Holy Spirit is out of order.

Devotional practices should be scriptural and in line with the great biblical themes of salvation by the grace of God in Christ. They should harmonize with the Church calendar, seasons, fasts, and feasts, and above all, they should move those engaging in them on the way of sanctification in Christ and with all his saints. Within these guidelines, the Communion of Saints forms a great parade, led to the right hand God, by Jesus the pioneer and perfecter of all faith. Christ's victory is proclaimed as

> From earth's wide bounds, from ocean's farthest coast,
> through gates of pearl streams in the countless host,
> singing to Father, Son, and Holy Ghost: Alleluia, Alleluia! [6]

The saints on earth and in heaven share in a mystical life of mutual prayer and praise of God; which includes adoration of God, singing, and acts of love. The saints in heaven pray for those upon the earth and the saints upon the earth enjoin their heavenly partners to respond to and unite in their worship. Both the saints in heaven and upon the earth anxiously await that great and glorious day of consummation when the victory of God will be finally and fully revealed, when Christ Jesus will come in glory and power, with all his saints, and God will be all in all.

---

[6] William W. How, "For All the Saints." in *The United Methodist Hymnal,* 711.

Bibliography

Abbott, Walter. ed. *Documents of Vatican II*. New York: American Press, 1966.

Adam, Karl. *The Spirit of Catholicism*. New York: The Crossroad Publishing Company, 1997.

Alexander, Franz, and Selesnick, Sheldon. *The History of Psychiatry*. New York: Harper & Row, 1966.

Alighieri, Dante. *The Divine Comedy, Purgatory*, trans. Mark Musa. New York: The Penguin Group, 1984.

———. *Purgatory*, trans. Allen Mandelbaum. New York: Bantum, 1984.

Althaus, Paul. *The Theology of Martin Luther*, trans. Robert C. Shultz. Philadelphia, Fortress Press 1966.

Anderson, George, et al. *The One Mediator, the Saints, and Mary: Lutherans and Catholics in Dialogue VIII*. Minneapolis, MN: Augsburg Fortress Press, 1992.

Anselm. *Monologion and Proslogion*, trans. Thomas Williams. Cambridge: Hackett Publishing Co. 1995.

———. *Why God Became Man*, trans. Joseph M. Colleran. Albany, New York: Magi Books, 1969.

Appleton, George, ed. *The Oxford Book of Common Prayer*. Oxford: Oxford University Press, 1985.

Aquinas. *The Summa Theologica of St Thomas Aquinas*, Second and Revised Edition, 1920 trans. Fathers of the English Dominican Province. 2000 Online Edition by Kevin Knight, accessed 5/2/2006.

Ariès, Philippe. *The Hour of Our Death*. New York: Barnes & Noble Books, 2000.

Aristotle. *Nichomachean Ethics*, trans. David Ross. New York: Oxford, 1998.

Arnold, Eberhard. *Inner Words*. Rifton, New York: Plough, 1975.

Atwell, Robert. "From Augustine to Gregory the Great: An Evaluation of the Emergence of Purgatory," *Journal of Ecclesiastical History* 38 (1987): 173-86.

Aulen, Gustav. *Christus Victor*. New York: The Macmillan Co. 1931.

Augustine. *City of God*, trans. Henry Bettenson. Harmondsworth, Middlesex: Penguin Books, 1984.

———. *Confessions*, trans. John K, Ryan. New York: Doubleday, 1960.

———. *Expositions on the Psalms*, trans. J .H. Parker. Oxford: Oxford Press, 1847-1857.

———. *On Christian Doctrine*, trans R. P. H. Green. New York: Oxford University Press, 1997.

———. *Sermons*, 3 vols. edited by John E. Rotelle, O.S.A. New York: New City Press.

———. *The Trinity*, trans. Edmund Hill. New York: New City Press, 1991.

Ballie, John. *And The Life Everlasting*. New York: C. Scribner's Sons, 1934.

Balthazar, Hans Urs Von. *Creedo: Meditations on the Apostle's Creed*, trans. David Kipp. New York: Crossroads, 1990.

———. *Dare We Hope "That All Men Be Saved."* San Francisco: Ignatius Press, 1996.

———. *Theo-Drama: Theological Dramatic Theory*, 5 vols. San Francisco: Ignatius, 1983.

———. *The von Balthasar Reader*. New York: Crossroads Publishing Company, 1997.

Barclay, William. *The Apostle's Creed for Everyman*. New York: Harper and Row Publishers, 1967.

Barnes, John C. and Petrie, Jennifer, ed. *Dante and his Literary Precursors*. Dublin, Ireland: Four Courts Press, 2004.

Barth, Karl. *Church Dogmatics*, 13 vols. Edinburgh: T&T Clark Ltd, 2004.

———. *Creedo*, trans. Robert McAfee Brown. New York: Charles Scribner's Sons, 1962.

———. *Dogmatics in Outline*. New York: Harper & Row Publishers, 1959.

———. *The Epistle to the Romans*, 6th ed., trans. Edwyn C. Hoskyns. London: Oxford University Press, 1933.

———. *The Resurrection of the Dead*, trans. H. J. Stenning. New York: Fleming H. Revel Company, 1933.

Bede. *Ecclesiastical History of England* ed. A. M. Sellar. New York: Kessinger Publishing, 2004.

Bebb, Phillip N. and Sessions, Kyle C. *Pietas et Societas: New Trends in Reformation Social History. Essays in Memory of Harold J. Grimm*. Kirksville, MO: NP, 1985.

Beinert, Wolfgang and Fiorenza, Francis Schussler, ed. *Handbook of Catholic Theology*. New York: Crossroad, 1995.

Berkhof, Louis. *Systematic Theology*. Grand Rapids: Erdmann's, 1941, 1976.

Bettenson, Henry. *Documents of the Early Christian Church*. London: Oxford, 1963.

———. *The Early Christian Fathers*. Oxford: Oxford University Press, 1956.

Biel, Gabriel. *Exposition of the Cannon of the Mass*. Oberman: Courtenay, nd.

Black, James M. "When the Roll is Called Up Yonder." *The Baptist Hymnal*. Nashville, Tennessee: Conventional Press, 1977.

Bloesch, Donald G. *Essentials of Evangelical Theology*. San Francisco: Harper & Row, 1982.

———. *The Last Things: Resurrection, Judgment, Glory*. Downers Grove, Illinois: InterVarsity Press, 2004.

Boehmer, Heinrich. *Luther in the Light of Recent Research*. New York; Castle Press Philadelphia, 1916.

Boettner, Loraine. *Immortality*. Grand Rapids, Michigan: Eerdmans, 1956.

Boggis, R. J. Edmund. *Praying for the Dead: An Historical Review of the Practice*. (London, n.p. 1913).

Book of Common Prayer. The Seabury Press, 1979.

Book of Common Prayer. New York: Church Hymnal Corporation, 1979.

Boros, Ladislaus. *The Mystery of Death*, trans Gregory Bainbridge. New York: Seabury Press, 1973.

———. *We are Future*, tr. by W. J. O'Hare. New York: Search Press, 1971.

Braaten, Carl E. ed. *Mary: Mother of God*. Grand Rapids, MI: Eerdmans, 2004.

Braun, Jon E. *Whatever Happened to Hell?* Nashville: Nelson, 1979.

Bray, Gerald. *The Doctrine of God*. InterVarsity Press 1993.

Brown, David. "No Heaven without Purgatory." in *Religious Studies* 21.4 (1985).

Brown, Peter. *The Cult of the Saints; Its Rise and Function in Latin Christianity*. Chicago, IL: University of Chicago Press, 1981.

Brunner, Emil. *Eternal Hope*. London: Lutterworth, 1954.

Brunner, Francis. *The Early Liturgy to the Time of Gregory the Great*. Notre Dame: University of Notre Dame Press, 1959.

Buis, Harry. *The Doctrine of Eternal Punishment*. Grand Rapids, Michigan: Baker, 1957.

Bunyan, John. *The Pilgrims Progress*. New York: Dodd, Mead 1979.

Burn, A. E. *Niceta of Remesiana, His Life and Works.* Cambridge; Cambridge University Press, 1905.
Bussell, Frederick William. *Religious Thought and Heresy in the Middle Ages.* London; Robert Scott Roxburghe House, 1918.
Calvin, John. *The Institutes of the Christian Religion,* ed. John T. McNeill, trans. Ford Lewis Battles. Philadelphia: The Westminster Press, 1960.
———. *Psychopannychia.* Leipzig: Deichert, 1932.
Cannons and Decrees of the Council of Trent, trans. H. J. Schroeder. St. Louis, MO: Herder, 1941.
Canons and Decrees of the Council of Trent, trans. C. Trent. Rockford, Illinois: Tan Books & Publishers, 1978.
Carol, Juniper. ed. *Mariology,* 3 vols. Milwaukee: Bruce Pub. Co., 1960.
Cartwright, Colbert S. and Harrison, O. I. Cricket, eds. *Chalice Worship.* St. Louis, MO: Chalice Press, 1997.
Cassidy, Frank P. *Molders of the Medieval Mind.* St. Louis, Missouri: London, B. Herder Book Co., 1944.
Catechism of the Catholic Church. New York: Doubleday, 1995.
Catherine of Genoa. *Purgation and Purgatory, the Spiritual Dialogue,* trans. Serge Hughes. New York: Paulist Press, 1979.
Cha, K. Y., D. P. Wirth, and R. A. Lobo. "Does Prayer Influence the Success of in Vitro Fertilization–Embryo Transfer? Report of a Masked, Randomized Trial, 2001" *Journal of Reproductive Medicine* 46:781-787.
Chaucer, Geoffrey. *The Canterbury Tales,* trans. David Wright. Oxford: Oxford University Press, 1998.
Chrysostom, John. *Interpretatio Omnium Epistularum Paulinarum,* trans. F. Field. Oxford: Clarendon, 1849-1862.
Code of Cannon Law, The, trans. The Cannon Law Society of Great Britain and Ireland. Grand Rapids, Michigan: Eerdmans, 1983.
Cohn, Norman. *The Pursuit of the Millennium: Revolutionary Millenarians and Mystical Anarchists of the Middle Ages.* Temple Smith, 1970.
Collins, Adela Yarbro. "The Apocalypse." *The New Jerome Biblical Commentary.* Englewood Cliffs, New York: Prentice Hall, 1990.
Congar, Yves M. J. *A History of Theology,* trans. Hunter Guthrie. Garden City, N.Y., Doubleday, 1968.
Constitution of the Presbyterian Church, The (U.S.A.). (Louisville, KY: Geneva Press, 1996)

Cooper, John W. *Body, Soul, and Everlasting Life: Biblical Anthropology and the Monism-Dualism Debate.* Grand Rapids, MI: Eerdmans, 1989.

Corpus Christianorum Series Latina. (Turnhought, Belgium: Brepols, 1953).

Corpus Scriptorum Ecclesiasticorum Latinorum. (Vienna: Tempsky, 1866).

Crane, Frank. ed., "The Gospel of Nicodemus." *The Lost Books of the Bible.* Word Bible Publishers, 1926.

Creighton, Mandell. *A History of the Papacy.* New York; Logman's and Green, 1925.

Croix, G. E. M. de Ste. "Suffragium: From Vote to Patronage." *British Journal of Sociology* 5 (1954): 46.

Cullman, Oscar. *Immortality of the Soul or Resurrection of the Dead? The Witness of the New Testament.* New York: McMillan, 1958.

Cunningham, Lawrence. *The Catholic Heritage.* New York: Crossroad, 1983.

—————. *The Meaning of Saints.* New York: Harper & Row, 1980.

Dallen, J. *The Reconciling Community: The Sacrament of Penance.* New York, Pueblo, 1986.

Dalmais, Irénée Henri. *Eastern Liturgies,* trans. Donald Attwater. New York: Hawthorn Books, 1960.

Delehaye, H. *Les Origines du Culte des Martyrs.* Bruxelles: Bureaux de la Societe des Bollandistes, 1912.

Dermenghem, Émile. *La Vie Admirable et les Révélations de Marie des Vallées d'après des Textes Inédits.* Paris, Plon-Nourrit et Cie, 1926.

Dodd, C. H. *The Apostolic Preaching and Its Developments.* New York, Harper & Row Publishers, 1964.

Dostoevsky, Fyodor. *The Brothers Karamazov.* New York: Alfred A. Knoph, 1990.

Downing, John. "Jesus and Martyrdom," *Journal of Theological Studies* 14 (1963): 279-293.

Driscoll, James F. "Adam." *The Catholic Encyclopedia.* New York: The Robert Appleton Company, 1907.

Dubois, Jacques and Lemaitre, Jean-Loup. *Sources et Méthodes de L'hagiographie Médiévale* [Sources and Methods of Medieval Hagiography] (Paris, 1993).

Dyggve, Ejnar. "The Origin of the Urban Churchyard." *Classica et Mediaevalia* 8, 2 (1952): 147-158.

Edwards, Graham Robert. "Purgatory: 'Birth' or Evolution?" *Journal of Ecclesiastical History* 36, 4 (1985): 173-186.

Eire, Carlos M. N. *War Against the Idols: The Reformation of Worship from Erasmus to Calvin*. Cambridge: Cambridge University Press, 1986.
Emery, Pierre-Yves. *The Communion of Saints*. London: Faith, 1966.
Erickson, Millard J. *Christian Theology*. Grand Rapids, Michigan: Baker Book House, 1983.
Eusebius. *History of the Church*, trans G. A. Williamson. Penguin Publishers, 1975.
Every, G. "Toll Gates on the Air Way." *Eastern Churches Review* viii, 1976.
Farrer, Austin. *A Faith of Our Own*. New York: World, 1960.
Feuerbach, Ludwig. *The Essence of Christianity* (1841) ed. George Eliot. New York, 1957.
Fiorenza, Elisabeth Schuessler. "Feminist Theology as a Critical Theology of Liberation," *Theological Studies* (1975) reprinted in Gerald Anderson and Thomas Stransky, eds., *Mission Trends* No. 4. Grand Rapids: Eerdmans, 1979.
Forell, George and McCue, James. *Confessing One Faith: A Joint Commentary on the Augsburg Confession by Lutheran and Catholic Theologians*. Minneapolis: Augsburg, 1992.
Forsyth, P.T. *This Life and the Next*. London: MacMillan, 1964.
Freud, Sigmund. *Totem and Taboo*. New York: Norton, W. W. & Company, Inc. 1913.
———. *Moses and Monotheism*. New York: Knopf Publishing Group 1938.
Gallup Index of Leading Religious Indicators, The. Princeton, NJ: The Gallup Organization, 2005.
Gambero, Luigi, and Buffer, Thomas. *Mary and the Fathers of the Church: The Blessed Virgin Mary in Patristic Thought*. Ignatius Press, 1999.
Ganfort, Wessel. *Wessel Ganfort, Life and Writtings, Principal Works*, ed. Edward W. Miller, trans. Jarred W. Scudder, 2 vols. New York, 1917.
Genet, Harry. "Big Trouble at the World's Largest Church." *Christianity Today* (Jan. 22, 1982).
George, Timothy. *Theology of the Reformers*. Nashville, TN: Broadman Press, 1988.
González-Baldo, José Luis. *Mother Teresa, In Her Own Words*. New York: Gramercy Books, 1996.

Gordon, Bruce and Marshall, Peter, eds. *The Place of the Dead: Death and Remembrance in Late Medieval and Early Modern Europe*. New York: Cambridge University Press, 2000.

Great Britain. *Diplomatic Documents and Papal Bulls*. New York; Kraus, 1963.

Gregory the Great. *Dialogues*, trans. Odo Zimmerman. Washington: Catholic University of America Press, 1959.

Greshake, G. Starker. *Als der Tod, Zukunft – Tod – Auferstehung – Himmel – Holle – Fegefeuer*. (Mainz, 1976).

Hapgood, Isabel F. and Manly, Joanna. *The Bible and the Holy Fathers for Orthodox*. Menlo Park, California: Monastery Books, 1990.

Hardy, E. R. "The Blessed Dead in Anglican Piety," *Sobornost* 3, no 2 (1981): 173.

Harnack, Adolf von. *Outlines of the History of Dogma*, trans. Edwin Mitchell. 1893; reprint, Starr King Press, 1957.

Harris, W.S., Gowda, M., Kolb, J.W., Strychacz, C.P., Vacek, J.L., Jones, P.G., Forker, A., O'Keefe, J.H., and McCallister, B.D. "A Randomized, Controlled Trial of the Effects of Remote, Intercessory Prayer on Outcomes in Patients Admitted to the Coronary Care Unit, 1999" *Arch Intern Med.* 159:2273-2278.

Herte, Adolf. *Das Katholische Lutherbild im Bann der Lutherkommentare des Cochlaeus* 3 vols. Fakultäts-Schrift:Münster, 1943.

Hick, John. *Death and Eternal Life*. London: William Collins Sons & Co. Ltd., 1976.

Hill, Edmund. O.P. *The Works of Saint Augustine: A Translation for the 21st Century*, 19 vols. ed. John E. Rotelle, O.S.A. Hyde Park, New York: New City Press, 1990.

Hoekema, Anthony A. *The Bible and the Future*. Grand Rapids, Michigan: Erdmann's, 1979.

Hoffman, Bengt R. *Luther and the Mystics*. Minneapolis: Augsburg, 1976.

Howard, Thomas. *Evangelical Is Not Enough: Worship of God In Liturgy and Sacrament*. Ignatius, San Francisco, 1984.

Humphreys, Fisher. *The Death of Christ*. Nashville: Broadman, 1978.

Iserloh, Erwin. *History of the Church*. New York; Crossroads, 1986.

Isaac of Nineveh, *The Ascetical Homilies of Saint Isaac the Syrian*. Boston, MA: The Holy Transfiguration Monastery, 1984.

James, William. *The Varieties of Religious Experience.* New York: Longmans, Green, 1923.
John of the Cross. *The Dark Night of the Soul,* trans. Kurt Reinhardt. New York: Frederick Ungar Publishing Co., 1957.
John Paul II. *Enchiridion Indulgentiarum, Normae de Indulgentiis.* Libreria Editrice Vaticana, 1999.
——. (November 1998) *Incarnationis Mysterium,* or "The Mystery of the Incarnation," bearing the subtitle Bull of Indiction of the Great Jubilee of the Year 2000.
——. (September 29th, 1999) *The Gift of Indulgences.* L'Osservatore Romano Weekly Edition in English (6 October 1999): 15.
——. "Visit to Mauthausen," *Origins* 18, no. 8 (July 7, 1988): 124.
Johnson, Elizabeth A. *Friends of God and Prophets: A Feminist Theological Reading of the Communion of Saints.* New York: Lexington Publishing Company, 1998.
Johnson, Luke Timothy. *The Creed: What Christians Believe and Why It Matters.* New York: Double Day, 2003.
Kelly, J. N. D. *Early Christian Creeds,* 3rd ed. New York: Longman Publishing Group, 1972.
Kidd, B. J. *Documents Illustrative of the Continental Reformation.* Oxford, The Clarendon Press, 1911.
Kierkegaard, Søren. *The Gospel of Suffering.* New York: James Clark Co., 1892.
Killinger, John. *You Are What You Believe: The Apostle's Creed for Today.* Nashville: Abington Press, 1990.
——. *Jessie: a Novel.* San Francisco, McCracken Press, 1993.
Kirsch, J. P. *The Doctrine of the Communion of Saints in the Ancient Church,* trans. John R. M'Kee. Willits, CA: Eastern Orthodox Books, n.d.
Kittel, G. and Friedrich, G., ed. *Theological Dictionary of the New Testament,* 10 vols. Grand Rapids: Eerdmans, 1964-76.
Koslofsky, Craig M. *The Reformation of the Dead: Death and Ritual in Early Modern Germany, 1450—1700.* New York: St. Martin's Press Inc., 2000.
Köstlin, Julius. *Luthers Theologie.* Leipzig, LPS: 1901.
Kreeft, Peter J. *Everything You Ever Wanted to Know about Heaven but Never Dreamed of Asking.* San Francisco: Harper & Row Publishers, 1982.

Hans Küng. *Creedo: The Apostles Creed Explained for Today*. New York: Doubleday, 1992

———. *Does God Exist. An Answer for Today*, trans Edward Quinn. New York: Vintage Books, 1981.

———. *Eternal Life? Life After Death as a Medical, Philosophical, and Theological Problem*, trans. Edward Quinn. New York: Doubleday & Company Inc., 1984.

Lande, Carl. *Friends, Followers, and Factions*, ed. Stefen Schmidt, Laura Guasti, Carl Lande, and James C. Scott. Berkley: University of California Press, 1977.

Lea, H. C. *A History of Auricular Confession and Indulgences*. London; Ire and Spottiewood, 1963.

Le Goff, Jacques. *The Birth of Purgatory*, trans. Author Goldhammer. Chicago, 1984.

Lewis, C. S. *Letters to Malcolm: Chiefly on Prayer*. New York: Harcourt, Brace, Jovanovich, 1973.

———. *The Four Loves*. London: Collins, 1963.

———. *The Great Divorce*. New York, The Macmillan Company, 1946.

———. *Till We Have Faces: A Myth Retold*. New York: Harcourt Brace & Company, 1956.

Loades, D. M. *The End of Strife*. Edinburgh : T. & T. Clark, 1984.

Loofs, Frederich. "Descent to Hades" in *Encyclopedia of Religion and Ethics*, ed. James Hastings. Edinburgh: T. & T. Clark Publishers, 1995.

Lossky, Vladimir. *The Mystical Theology of the Eastern Church*. New York: St. Vladimir's Seminary Press, 1998.

Lubac, H. de. *Catholicism: Christ and the Common Destiny of Man*. San Francisco: Ignatius Press, 1988.

Lull, Timothy F. *Martin Luther's Basic Theological Writings*. Minneapolis, Minn: Fortress, 2005

Lunt, William Edward. *Papal Revenues in the Middle Ages*. New York; Octagon Books, 1965.

Luther, Martin. *Commentary on Galatians*. Grand Rapids: Fleming H. Revell, 1988.

———. *D. Martin Luther's Werke; Kritische Gesamtausgabe*. Weimar: H. Böhlau, 1883.

———. *Sermons of Martin Luther*, 8 vols. ed. J. N. Lenker. Grand Rapids: Baker, 1988.

Marimon, John P. "Purgatory Revisited." *The Downside Review* (1994): 121-141.

Markus, R. A. "How on Earth Could Places Become Holy? Origins of the Christian Idea of Holy Places," *Journal of Early Christian Studies* 2:3 (1993).

Martelet, Gustave, S. J. *L'au-delà Retrouvé: Christologie des fins Dernières*. Paris: Desclée, 1974.

Marthaler, Berard. *The Creed*. Mystic, Connecticut: Twenty-third Publishing, 1987.

Marx, Karl. Contribution to the Critique of Hegel's "Philosophy of Right." *Deutsch-Französische Jahrbücher* (February, 1844).

Matzko, Davis. "Postmodernism, Saints, and Scoundrels," *Modern Theology* 9 (1993): 35, n. 35

McBrien, Richard. *Encyclopedia of Catholicism*. San Francisco: HarperSanFrancisco, 1995.

McGinnis, Charles. *The Communion of Saints*. St. Louis, MO: B. Herder, 1912.

McGrath, Alister. *I Believe: Exploring the Apostles' Creed*. Downers Grove: IL, InterVarsity Press, 1997.

McNeill, John T. and Gamer, Helena M. T*he Medieval Handbooks of Penance: A Translation of the Principal Libri Poenitentiales and Selections from Related Documents*. New York: Columbia University Press, 1990.

Meyendorff, J. Byzantine *Theology: Historical and Doctrinal Themes*. London 1974.

Migne, Jacques Paul. *Patrologia Graeca*. 166 vols. Paris: Petit-Montrouge, 1857-1886.

———. *Patrologia Latina*. 221 vols. Paris: Minge, 1844-1864.

Moeller, Wilhelm. *History of the Christian Church*. Durham, NO; Labryinth Press, 1910.

Murphy, Gardner. *Historical Introduction to Modern Psychiatry*. New York: Harcourt & Brace, 1949.

Musurillo, Herbert. *The Acts of the Christian Martyrs*. Oxford: Clarendon Press 1972.

Myconious. *History of the Reformation*. Liepsburg; Liepsburg Press, 1718.

Neil, Alexander. *Time and Community*. Washington, D.C.: Pastoral Press, 1990.

Newman, Barbra. 'Hildegard of Bingen and the "Birth of Purgatory"' *Mystics Quarterly* 19 (1993) 90-97.

Ntedika, Joseph. *L'Evolution de la Doctrine du Purgatoiure chez Saint Augustine*. Paris, Nauwelearts, 1966.

O'Connor, Flannery. *The Violent Will Bear It Away*. New York: The Noonday Press, 1955.

Ombres, Robert, OP. "Images of Healing: The Making of the Theology of Purgatory." *Eastern Churches Review* VIII (1976): 22-86.

―――――. "Latins and Greeks in Debate over Purgatory, 1230-1439." *Journal of Ecclesiastical History*. 35 (1984): 1-14.

Origen. "Epistle to the Ephesians" in *The Journal of Theological Studies* 3:401.

Orsy, L. *The Evolving Church and the Sacrament of Penance*. Danville, New Jersey, Dimension Books, 1978.

Ozment, Steven E. *The Age of Reform (1250-1550): An Intellectual and Religious History of Late Medieval and Reformation Europe*. New Haven: Yale University Press, 1980.

―――――. *The Reformation in Medieval Perspective*. Chicago: Quadrangle Books, 1971.

Pannenberg, Wolfhart. *Revelation as History*. New York, NY: Macmillan, 1968.

―――――. *The Apostle's Creed*, trans. Margaret Kohl. Phildelphia: Westminster, 1972.

―――――. *What is Man?* trans. D. Priebe, Philadelphia: Fortress Press, 1970.

Paterson-Smyth. J. *The Gospel of the Hereafter*. Toronto: Musson, 1910.

Paul VI. *Sacramentum Paenitentiae*. Available from Libreria Editrice Vaticana http://www.vatican.va/holy_father/john_paul_ii/motu_proprio/documents/hf_jp-ii_motu-proprio_20020502_misericordia-dei_lt.html. Accessed 31 May, 2006.

Pauli, Johannes. *Schimpf und Ernst. Die alteste Ausgabe von 1522*, ed Johannes Bolte. Berlin, 1924.

Peake, A. S. ed. *The People and the Book: Essays on the Old Testament*. Oxford: Oxford University Press, 1995.

Pearsall, Arlene Epp. *Johannes Pauli (1450—1520) on the Church and the Clergy*. New York: Lewiston, 1994.

Pelikan, Jaroslav. *Luther's Works*, 55 vols. St. Louis: Concordia/Philadelphia: Fortress Press, 1955-1975.

―――――. *Mary Through the Centuries : Her Place in the History of Culture* (New Haven, CT: Yale University Press, 1998).

———. Pelikan, *The Emergence of the Catholic Tradition*. Chicago: University Chicago Press, 1971.

Pierozzi, Antoninus. *Confessional*. Rome: NP, 1490.

Pinsky, Robert. *The Inferno of Dante*. New York: The Noonday Press, 1994.

Pius X. *"Lamentabili Sane" (3 July, 1907) On the Doctrine of the Modernists: Pascendi Dominici: Syllabus Condemning the Errors of the Modernists: Lamentabili Sane*. Pauline Books & Media, 1973.

Plato. *Phaedo*, trans. David Gallop. Oxford: Clarendon Press, 1975.

Pomazansky, Michael. *Orthodox Dogmatic Theology*, trans. Hieromonk Seraphim Rose. St. Herman of Alaska Brotherhood, 1994.

Popovich, Justin. *Orthodox Faith and Life in Christ*. Belmont, MA: Institute for Byzantine and Modern Greek Studies, 1994.

Portalie, Eugene. *A Guide to the Thought of Saint Augustine*. Chicago: Regnery, 1960.

Purtill, Richard. *C.S. Lewis's Case for the Christian Faith*. San Francisco: Harper & Row, 1981.

Quasten, J., Puimpe, J. C., and Burghardt, W. *The Works of the Fathers in Translation*. 44 vols. New York: Paulist Press, 1946.

Rahner, Karl. ed. *Sacramentum Mundi*. New York: Herder & Herder, 1968.

———. "All Saints," *Theological Investigations* 8, trans. David Bourke. New York: Seabury Press, 1977.

———. "Why and How can we Venerate the Saints." *Theological Investigations* 8, trans. Davod Bourke. New York: Seabury, 1977.

Rahner, Karl and Metz, John Baptist. *The Courage to Pray*. New York: Crossroad, 1981.

Ramsey, Ian. ed. *Prayer and the Departed: A Report of the Archbishop's Commission on Christian Doctrine*. Grand Rapids: Eerdmans, 1971.

Ratszinger, Auer. *Dogmatic Theology 9: Eschatology*, trans. Michael Waldenstein. Washington D.C.; The Catholic University of America Press, 1988.

Ratzinger, Josef. *Introduction to Christianity*. San Francisco: Ignatius Press, 1975.

Reynolds, William J. and Price, Milburn. *A Survey of Christian Hymnody*. Carol Stream, IL: Hope Publishing Company, 1999.

Robinson, H. Wheeler. *The Christian Doctrine of Man*. Edinburgh: Clark, 1911.

Rotell, John. trans. ed. *The Works of St. Augustine: A Translation for the 21st Century*, 10 vols. with notes by Edmund Hill. Hyde Park, New York: New City Press, 1990-1995.

Schaff, Phillip. *A History of the Christian Church*, 8 vols. New York: Charles Scribner's Sons, 1910.

————. *A Select Library of the Nicene and Post-Nicene Fathers of the Christian Church*, 2nd series, 14 vols. Buffalo, New York: Christian Literature, 1887-1894, reprint Peabody, Mass: Hendrickson, 1994.

————. *The Creeds of Christendom*, 3 vols. Grand Rapids, Michigan: Baker Book House, 1931.

Schewring, William H. *The Passion of Perpetua and Felicity, together with Sermons of Saint Augustine upon these Saints*. London: Sheed and Ward, 1931.

Schmitt, Keith Randall. *Death and the After-Life in the theologies of Karl Barth and John Hick: A Comparative Study*. Amsterdam: Rodopi, 1985.

Scotus, Duns. *Oxford Commentary on the Sentences* (Wadding).

Shaw, Brent. "Body/Power/Identity: The Passions of the Martyrs" *Journal of Early Christian Studies* 4 (1996).

Shinners, John. *Medieval Popular Religion*. Ontario: Broadview Press, 1999.

Sophrony, Archimandrite. *The Undistorted Image*. London: NP, 1958.

Stephens, W. P. *The Theology of Huldrych Zwingli* (Oxford: Claredon Press, 1986).

Stone, Darwell. *A History of the Doctrine of the Holy Eucharist*, 14 vols. London: Longmans, 1909.

Stott, John. *Evangelical Essentials*. Downers Grove, Illinois: InterVarsity Press, 1988.

Sullivan, John F. *The Externals of the Catholic Church*. New York: P. J. Kennedy and Sons, 1959.

Swete, Henry Barclay. *The Holy Catholic Church, The Communion of Saints*. London: McMillan, 1915.

Tappert, Theodore. *Luther's Works*. Saint Louis, Concordia Publishing. House, 1955-1958.

————. *The Book of Concord*. Philadelphia: Fortress Press, 1959.

Tentler, Thomas N. *Sin and Confession on the Eve of the Reformation*. Princeton, W.J., Princeton University Press.

Teresa of Avila, *The Life of Saint Teresa of Avila by Herself*, trans. J. M. Cohen. London: Penguin Classics, 1988.

Tilley, Maureen. "The Acetic Body and the (Un)Making of the World of the Martyr." *Journal of the American Academy of Religion* 65 (1991): 470-497.
Tillich, Paul. *Systematic Theology*. 3 vols. Chicago: University of Chicago Press, 1963.
Tugwell, Simon. *Albert & Thomas: Selected Writings, 363-418*. New York: Paulist Press, 1988).
Turner, C. H. "Niceta and Ambrosiaster." in *Journal of Theological Studies*, 7 (1906): 203-19, 355-72.
Twain, Mark. *The Innocents Abroad*. New York: Penguin Group, 2002.
Tyndale, William. *An Answer to Sir Thomas More's Dialogue*. New York: Parker, 1850.
United Methodist Book of Worship, The. Nashville, Tennessee: The United Methodist Publishing House, 1992.
United Methodist Hymnal, The. Nashville, TN: The United Methodist Publishing House, 1989.
Valentin, Gröne von. *Tetzel und Luther*. Soest: Nasse, 1860.
Vassiliadis, Nikolaos P. *The Mystery of Death*, trans Fr. Peter A. Chamberas. Athens: The Orthodox Brotherhood of Theologians, 1997.
Volz, Carl. *The Medieval Church*. Nashville: Abington Press, 1997.
Voragine, Jacobus de. *The Golden Legend*, trans. William G. Ryan. Cambridge: Princeton University Press, 1993.
Wainwright, Geoffrey. "Wesley and the Communion of Saints." *One in Christ* 27 (1991).
Walls, Jerry L. *Hell, the Logic of Damnation*. Notre Dame, IN: University of Notre Dame Press, 1992.
———. "Purgatory for Everyone" in First Things 122 (April 2002): 26-30.
Walsh, Brian, and Middleton, Richard. *The Transforming Vision*. Downers Grove, IL: InterVarsity, 1984.
Ware, Timothy (Bishop Kallistos). *Eustratios Argenti: A Study of the Greek Church under Turkish Rule*. Oxford: Oxford University Press, 1964.
———. "'One Body in Christ': Death and The Communion of Saints." *Sobornost/Eastern Churches Review* 3:2 (1981): 179-191.
———. *The Orthodox Church*. Harmondsworth, England: Penguin Books, 1963.
———. "The Orthodox Experience of Repentance," *Sobornost/Eastern Churches Review* 2:1 (1980): 24-25.

Warfield, Benjamin. *The Plan of Salvation*. Grand Rapids, Michigan: Erdmann's, 1942.
Watson, Phillip S. ed. *The Message of the Wesleys*. New York: McMillan, 1964.
Weil, Louis. "The History of Christian Litanies." *Liturgy: Journal of the Liturgical Conference* 5, no. 2 (Fall, 1985): 33-37.
Wendel, François. *Calvin: The Origins and Development of His Religious Thought*, trans Philip Mairet. New York, Harper & Row, 1963.
Wesley, John. *The Works of John Wesley*, 13 vols. Peabody, Mass: Hendrickson Publishers, 1991.
──────. *Journals*, ed. Nehemiah Curnock. London: Epworth Press, 1938.
Wiedermann, Gotthelf. *"Cochlaeus as Polemicist," Seven-Headed Luther*, trans. Peter Newman Brooks. Oxford: Clarendon Press, 1983.
Wiener, Norbert. *The Human Use of Human Beings*. Boston: Houghton Mifflin, 1950.
Williams, George Huntston. *The Radical Reformation*. Kirksville, Mo: Sixteenth Century Journal Publishers, 1992.
Wilmore, Gayraud, and Cone, James. *Black Theology, A Documentary History, 1966-1979*. Maryknoll, NY: Orbis, 1986.
Wilson, Stephen, ed. *Saints and their Cults: Studies in Religious Sociology, Folklore, and History*. London: Cambridge University Press, 1993.
Witvliet, Theo. *A Place in the Sun*, trans. John Bowden. Maryknoll, NY: Orbis, 1985.
Woodward, Kenneth. *The Making of Saints: How the Catholic Church Determines Who Becomes a Saint, Who Doesn't and Why*. New York: Simon & Shuster, 1990.
Woznicki, Andrew. *A Christian Humanism: Karol Wojtyla's Existential Personalism*. New Britain, CT: Mariel, 1980.
Wyschogrod, Edith. *Saints and Postmodernism: Revisioning Moral Philosophy*. Chicago: The University of Chicago Press, 1990.
Zwingli, Huldrych. *The Latin Works of Huldrych Zwingli*, trans. ed. Samuel M. Jackson. Durham, N.C.: Labyrinth Press, 1983.
──────. *Samtliche Werke*, 8 vols. ed. Schuler and Schulthess. Zurich: NP, 1828-1842.

www.ingramcontent.com/pod-product-compliance
Lightning Source LLC
Chambersburg PA
CBHW071428070526
44578CB00001B/31